The
Pioneer Swedish Settlements
and
Swedish Lutheran Churches
in America
1845-1860

by Eric Norelius

Translation from the Swedish (1890) and Index by Conrad Bergendoff, Augustana Historical Society, Rock Island, Illinois, 1984

THE PIONEER SWEDISH
SETTLEMENTS AND
SWEDISH LUTHERAN CHURCHES
IN AMERICA
1845-1860.

Selected Chapters of Volume I of Eric Norelius'

DE SVENSKA LUTERSKA FÖRSAMLINGARNAS OCH

SVENSKARNES HISTORIA I AMERIKA (1890)

translated by Conrad Bergendoff

1984
Augustana Historical Society
Rock Island, Illinois

Augustana Historical Society
Rock Island, Illinois
1984

Augustana Historical Society
Publication No. 31

ISBN: 0-910184-31-3
Library of Congress Card Number: 84-71391

Printed by Wagners Printers, Davenport, Iowa

Contents

Introduction	IV
Acknowledgements	VI
Bibliography	VII
Swedish Title Page	VIII
Author's Preface	IX
Part I The Immigrant Groups	X
Part II The Swedish Lutheran Congregations	X
Illustrations	XI
Index	413

Introduction

It is soon a hundred years ago since Eric Norelius brought out the first volume of his history. It still remains an unparalleled source for the beginnings of Swedish immigration to America a century and a half ago. In his introduction the author clearly tells of his motives, his method, and his goal.

He says he lived through much of this decade of history himself. He came to this country in 1850 in one of the earliest waves of Swedish immigration. He came to the Middle West where the first settlements were being made. As a theological student he was along at the founding of some of the earliest congregations. He became a journalist and came into contact with all the centers of Swedish population. As a church leader his name became associated with the beginnings of the churches in Minnesota. He was as well acquainted with all the places and people of this period as any other individual person.

From the first he displayed a sense of history. As he mentions, he started gathering records, minutes, journals, letters. He became historian of the Augustana Synod largely because he had already distinguished himself for his interest in what had taken place. Since his time, almost every historian of Swedish immigration has had recourse to his work. But with the fading out of the language, his work has been unavailable to the English language reader. To make it accessible has been the motive of this translator.

Volume I is a massive book of 864 pages. I have selected for this translation those chapters which do bear most directly on the title of the work — the history of the early Swedish settlements and of the Swedish Lutheran congregations. Another considerable part is made up of biographies of the early leaders. While this is valuable, especially for the autobiographical sections included in the biographies, much of the material has to do with the spiritual experiences of these men while in Sweden — often in very great detail. I have omitted these sections, the more readily since there are now biographies in English of Hasselquist, Esbjörn, O.C.T. Andrén, Erland Carlsson.

Also omitted is the part devoted to Unonius and to the Janssonists at Bishop Hill. The Gustaf Unonius story is fully told in his *Memoirs* published by the University of Minnesota as a publication of the Swedish Pioneer Historical Society. Norelius' chapter on Jansson is, he admits, drawn from other sources in Sweden and the

U.S. — hence not his own work. The final section was devoted to the organization and polity of the Augustana congregations and is omitted here along with a listing of the Swedish press before 1860. None of these chapters add much to the account of the particular settlements.

This translation thus covers one chapter from Part I — the survey of the various waves of immigration before 1860 (chapter two in the original-chapter one in the translation). The other 19 chapters of Part II give us an account of the settlements and congregations in Iowa, Illinois, Indiana, Jamestown, N.Y., Minnesota, Wisconsin, Michigan, Kansas, New York, Massachusetts.

True, the larger immigration came after the Civil war. But by 1860 the streams had carved out the first channels into the Midwest and the foundations of the Swedish communities had been established. The author's personal participation gives a freshness and immediacy to his motives that makes of these pages almost an eye-witness account. No wonder that the work has been termed by later scholars as "unique", "classical", "monumental".

Years later Norelius published a vol. II (Rock Island, 1916). It is largely the story of the development of the Augustana Synod through its "Conferences" and constitution. This work has been superseded by scholarly treatments of George Stephenson (*The Religious Aspect of Swedish Immigration*, Minneapolis, 1932) and G. Everett Arden (*The Augustana Heritage*, Rock Island, 1963), and is not included in the present translation.

In time Norelius was esteemed as a patriarch of the Augustana Church. He was present at the organization of the Synod in 1860 and was its president at the 50th anniversary in 1910, having served as head both of the Minnesota Conference and the Synod many years. He died in 1916 at the age of 83. His biographer, Emeroy Johnson, wrote *Eric Norelius Pioneer Midwest Pastor and Churchman* (Rock Island, 1954) and Arden translated his *The Journals of Eric Norelius* (Fortress Press, 1967).

I have used the Swedish letters å ä ö for names and places in Sweden, but I have omitted the marks, as the immigrants usually did on their arrival in this country. å usually became o. I have retained the marks in the case of Esbjörn since he returned to Sweden. For the Swedish län I have used county. As far as possible I have retained the style and spelling of the original.

Conrad Bergendoff

V

Acknowledgements

I express my gratitude to the Augustana Historical Society which has sponsored my translation, to the secretary, Dean Betsey Brodahl, who gave invaluable assistance in the preparation of the typed manuscript, and to Joel Lundeen, former archivist of the Lutheran Church in America, who read the galley proofs and made helpful suggestions.

The printing of the work has been made possible through a grant from the Lutheran Brotherhood of Minneapolis, Minnesota, as a part of its philanthropic educational program. This grant is deeply appreciated.

I dedicate the translation to the memory of my father whose now almost century old copy of the Norelius volume has been used in the task.

Conrad Bergendoff

Bibliography — Beginnings of Swedish Immigration

Ander, Fritiof — T.N. Hasselquist. The Career and Influence of a Swedish-American Clergyman, Journalist, and Educator, Rock Island, 1932.

Arden, G. Everett — The Augustana Heritage, Rock Island, 1963.
The Journals of Eric Norelius, Fortress Press, 1967.
Translated by G. Everett Arden.

Carlsson, Esbjörn, Hasselquist, Norelius, Letters — Augustana Library, Rock Island.

Elmen, Paul — Wheat Flour Messiah: Eric Jansson of Bishop Hill, Carbondale, Ill., 1976.

Hemlandet, det gamla och det nya. Galesburg and Chicago, 1855-1914.

Johnson, Emeroy — Eric Norelius, Pioneer Midwest Pastor and Churchman, Rock Island, 1954.

Johnson, Eric and Peterson, C.F. — Svenskarne i Illinois, Chicago, 1880.

Korsbaneret-Kristlig Kalender. Chicago, Moline, Rock Island, 1880-1950.

Lindquist, Emory — Erland Carlsson, Shepherd of an Immigrant People, Rock Island, 1978.

Olson, Ernest W. — History of the Swedes in Illinois, Chicago, 1908.

Olson, Oscar N. — O.C.T. Andrén, Ambassador of Good Will, Rock Island, 1954.

Olsson, Nils William — Swedish Passenger Arrivals in New York, 1820-1850, Chicago, 1967.
Swedish Passenger Arrivals in U.S. Ports, 1820-1850 (except New York), Stockholm and St. Paul, Minn., 1979.

Rönnegard, Sam — Prairie Shepherd, Lars Paul Esbjörn and the Beginnings of the Augustana Lutheran Church, Rock Island, 1952.
Translated by G. Everett Arden.

Stephenson, George M. — The Religious Aspects of Swedish Immigration, Minneapolis, 1932.

Unonius, Gustaf S. — A Pioneer in Northwest America, 1841-1958.
The Memoirs of Gustaf Unonius. Translated from the Swedish by Jonas Oscar Backlund and edited by Nils William Olsson, Vol. I, Minneapolis, 1950, Vol. II 1960.

DE SVENSKA

LUTERSKA FÖRSAMLINGARNAS

OCH

SVENSKARNES HISTORIA

1

AMERIKA.

v. 1

ETT BIDRAG

AF

E. NORELIUS.

ROCK ISLAND, ILL.
LUTHERAN AUGUSTANA BOOK CONCERN.
1890.

Author's Preface

Ever since my youth a love for my church and my people has prompted me to gather and preserve whatever I could find that throws some light on their history in this land. I have confined my work to the present century and the more recent countrymen. The history of the older Swedes on the Delaware has been treated by others and most recently in a very worthy way by Prof. J.A. Enander in his *History of the United States*.

It is hardly fifty years since the newer immigration from Sweden turned to this country and one may question if it is not too early to begin to give an account of the history of the Swedes in America. In reply to such a question, I would remark that time is a destroyer, the earliest newcomers pass away, year after year the oldest historic spots disappear, the oral tradition becomes less trustworthy. I have long had the ambition, while still able, to preserve our memories in a more enduring way and to transmit them to a coming generation, hoping it would have interest in the activities and experiences of the fathers. But time and strength have not been sufficient until now. Now I have come so far that I can present a first part of the work. Whether I can go beyond this lies in the hand of the Lord.

This volume does not pretend to be more than a contribution to the history of the Swedish Lutheran congregations and of the Swedes in America. I had first intended only to publish the historical documents I had in my possession without any commentary. But on further thought I came to the conviction that it would be more satisfactory to place them in historical order and give such explanation as I could. Thus this is what I have sought to do without the least claim to historical skill. Still I think I can rightly assert that this work has the merit of being trustworthy. I have lived through much of what is here told and been so close to the events that I ought to be able to judge the authenticity of the historical records. Yet I will not allege to have been correct on every point. I have made every effort to present the sources and as much as possible use their own words, even at the risk of being criticized for giving the reader a miscellany. The intelligent reader, I am sure, will count my method an asset, not a liability. Water is clearest at its source.

To all who kindly helped me with contributions and information for this work I am deeply indebted.

Vasa, Minnesota, Oct. 26, 1890.

E. Norelius

Minnesota pg 401

Part I

Chapter 1   The Various Immigrant Groups and their
             Destinations 1844-54 (In the Swedish Original
             this is Chapter 2)   1-40

Part II
             The Swedish Lutheran Congregations,
             to 1860   41-412

Chapter 1   The Swedish Settlements and Congregations   45
             in Iowa

Chapter 2   The Settlements and Congregations in Illinois: 65
             Andover, Berlin, Illinois

Chapter 3   Galesburg, Knoxville, Illinois   117

Chapter 4   Moline, Rock Island, Geneseo, Illinois   129

Chapter 5   The Swedish Lutheran Immanuel Congrega-   147
             tion, Chicago, Illinois

Chapter 6   St. Charles, Geneva, DeKalb, Illinois   173

Chapter 7   Rockford, Pecatonica, Illinois   184

Chapter 8   Princeton, Illinois   199

Chapter 9   Indiana Settlements and Lutheran   208
             Congregations

Chapter 10   Jamestown, N.Y., Sugar Grove, Pa.   235

Chapter 11   Minnesota; the First Settlers and First   249
             Religious Activity

Chapter 12   Chisago Lake, Minnesota   255

Chapter 13   Marine, St. Paul, Taylors Falls, Rusheby,   295
             Minnesota

Chapter 14   Vasa, Red Wing, Minnesota; Stockholm,   313
             Wisconsin

Chapter 15   Spring Garden, Cannon River and Cannon   359
              Falls, Minnesota

Chapter 16   The Union Settlement, Carver County,   367
              Gotaholm Scandia, Minnesota

Chapter 17   St. Peter, Scandian Grove, Minnesota   383

Chapter 18   Vista, Waseca County, Minnesota   393

Chapter 19   Other Swedish Settlements where no Lutheran 399
              Congregation had been Organized by 1860:
              Wisconsin; Minnesota; Iowa; Michigan;
              Illinois; Indiana; Kansas; New York; Boston,
              Brocton, Mass.

Illustrations

Pastor Olof Gustaf Hedstrom   3

Professor L.P. Esbjörn   18

Colonel Hans Mattson   36

Pastor M.F. Hocanson   54

The Old Church in Andover   104

Pastor Jonas Swensson   115

Doctor T.N. Hasselquist   123

Pastor O.T.C. Andrén   142

The Old Immanuel Church   157

Pastor Erland Carlsson   163

The Immanuel School House   167
   First Home of Augustana College and Theological Seminary

Pastor A. Andrén   193

Pastor P.A. Cederstam   283

Pastor E. Norelius   326

The Old Church in Vasa   330

Pastor J.P.C. Boren   358

Pastor P. Beckman   365

Pastor P. Carlson   373

Part One
Chapter I

Survey of the Earlier Immigrant Stream, the Directions it took
and the Apparent Reasons that Caused these Divergent Courses.

The main reason for the emigration from Sweden was undoubtedly the hope for a better economic condition in America. Except for
the Erik Jansonists, few certainly left the homeland in order to find
here greater religious or civic freedom. Around 1840 much began to
be written in the popular newspapers about the United States in
North America, its rich resources, its rapid development, its desire to
have people come here, and the ease with which people here could
advance their condition, etc. This information awakened here and
there in individuals and smaller groups the desire and courage to set
out on the long journey, in order to see for oneself the distant land
and assure oneself of the truth of what had been heard. One must
admit that it required much greater courage to make the journey to
America in the beginning than after the course became old and well
travelled. These pioneers then wrote home to their relatives and
friends in Sweden, and through their letters, which often praised
America extravagantly while probably too often being silent about
the dark sides, kindled the wide spread emigration fever resulting in
a still greater emigration. The most compelling force in the movement from Sweden to America was the exchange of private letters.
    Characteristic of the emigration from Sweden in the earlier
period was the fact that the groups were made up of relatives and acquaintances, and usually of persons from the same locality, and that
they moved to the same destination and settled in the same place
when they came to America. This explains why in the oldest Swedish
settlements the people are generally from the same region in Sweden.
This ceased to be the case as communications gradually improved or
after the ocean was crossed by steam boat.
    Before we turn our attention to the various groups who came
here during the first years of Swedish immigration, we ought to mention a Swedish man who exercised not a little influence on the directions taken by the immigration stream when it reached the American
coast. I refer to the Methodist pastor O.G. Hedstrom in New York,
personally known to older folk and in general well-known. Through
the help of a friend and with the author's permission I am able to

quote a memorial sermon on this man.[1]

"Olof Gustaf Hedstrom, son of Corporal Johan Hedstrom and his wife Carin, was born in Trernshed parish, Kronoberg County, Sweden, May 11, 1803. The couple has seven children, five sons and two daughters. The son Olof Gustaf was put early to the tailor's trade, but when 21 he left his parental home and fatherland. In 1825 he signed on a warship bound for South America. During the voyage he served as private secretary to the commanding officer. The vessel arrived safely in New York harbor, where the crew was discharged and authorized to return to their native land. Because he was robbed of all his possessions Hedstrom was forced to remain in New York. He soon found employment in a clothing store, owned by a Mr. Townsend, a cousin of a woman who four years later became his life's companion. After a few years Hedstrom, who had good business sense, became a partner with Mr. Townsend, and a little later we find him as owner of his own clothing store in Pittesville, Pa. where he was a successful business man. January 11, 1829 he married Carolina Pinckney, an American, born June 21, 1804 in Mamaroneck, West Chester Co., N.Y. The marriage was blessed with ten children, of whom 9 are dead. The couple lived 48 happy years together, until death separated them. The aged widow is present today at the dedication of this monument. Hedstrom was not converted at the time of the wedding, but two weeks later he was converted to the living God through the ministry of Dr. Phebous in New York. The old was now gone, everything had become new. The love of God had totally filled his young heart, with the natural result that he had compassion for the unconverted and longed for their salvation. His heart was especially troubled for the conversion of his parents and sisters and brothers, and he could not feel satisfied until he could personally talk to them about his own conversion and direct them to the Lamb of God who had made him happy. Four years later, 1833, he undertook an adventurous voyage via sailing vessel to his fatherland with no other goal for his trip than to be a means in the hands of the Lord for his family's salvation. He was not unsuccessful in this venture. On his arrival he fell on his knees and gave God his heart's thanks for His great love. He embraced in tears his old beloved father and told how God in His love and grace had forgiven him all his sins and given his soul happiness. The parents were in a short while converted, as well

---

[1]A sermon at the grave of Olof Hedstrom, by Pastor H. Olson, Oct, 17, 1886, received by the author from J. Engberg, Chicago.

as Jonas, his brother, who accompanied him to America, where he became the father of Swedish Methodism in the West. Now they are all together in the heavenly Father's house.

OLOF GUSTAF HEDSTRÖM.

"Before long Hedstrom returned to America. Not long afterwards it became clear that the Lord had called him as a special instrument in His hand. His serious piety combined with his talents and zeal for the salvation of souls led to his being selected for the ministry. In 1835, six years after his conversion and two years after his visit in Sweden, he was received on probation in the New York Conference, to which he belonged until his death, 42 years later. During the first ten years (1835-45) Hedstrom preached among English speaking people. Wherever he worked God gave him marked success. He was strong in his faith, witnessing to his Saviour, wherever he went. In 1841 he was in Windsor circuit, Delaware district, and said to a 16 year youth who lived with his parents next door to the Hedstroms, 'Daniel, I expect to see you converted to God before I leave here.' His expectation was fulfilled, Daniel turned to God and joined the Methodist Church. He grew up and remained in the truth and fear of God. He is still living. His name is Daniel Steel.

Today he is professor of theology at Boston University, one of the saintliest and learned men in the Methodist Church. In 1844 a lively exchange of letters occurred between Hedstrom and some Christian friends in New York about beginning missionary work among the Swedish people in New York. Hedstrom was not eager to encourage such a mission — "it is as dark as a pocket," he used to reply. But the hand of the Lord can transform anything, as was shown also here. A young merchant in New York, George T. Cobb, was greatly interested in this matter. He gave $50 to start a subscription for a so-called Bethel Ship. Pledging went better than expected. Fully convinced that this venture was God-inspired, Mr. William G. Roggs and several other members of the Asbury M.E. Congregation in New York, bought the vessel "Henry Seeds," which lay in North River. This was later renamed "John Wesley."

"May 14, 1845 the New York Conference assembled in the Forsyth St. M.E. Church, New York. Hedstrom came to the meeting, but still unconvinced about the mission. The soul of the enterprise was Dr. Terry. He met Hedstrom at the church door and asked him to go along to brother Peter Bergner's home, which was near to the spot where the Bethel ship lay. It was just at dinner time that the two servants of the Lord entered the Bergner home. Time was short, important matters were to be decided. Hedstrom and Bergner (who was Swedish) exchanged a few words in Swedish, and cried together. All in the room fell to their knees, in tears and in prayer. When they arose from prayer, all of Hedstrom's doubts about this mission were gone, and he burst out, 'I believe it is of the Lord, and if the Conference appoints me I will come to the ship.' In that house was great rejoicing. Everybody enjoyed the simple meal, happy in their hearts that there was hope soon to have missionary activity among the Swedes in New York. The Conference neared the end. The last important business, when the bishop read the list of appointments, was due. Among the first of the appointments: 'North River Mission — Olof Gustaf Hedstrom.' Thus a Swedish Methodist preacher was named to work among Scandinavians. This was the first such appointment. Since then many have been made — a fruit of this first one. For example, the bishops of our church appointed not less than 254 preachers for service in the Scandinavian lands and among Scandinavians in this country. All of these are members of Annual Conferences. 'It is of the Lord and a wonder to our eyes.' May 25, 1845 Pastor Hedstrom preached for the first time on the Bethel Ship.

Since he had worked for so many years among Americans he had some difficulty in expressing himself fluently in Swedish, so the first two Sundays he wrote his sermons. But on the third Sunday and afterwards he needed no manuscript, but preached ex tempore. Any one who knew Hedstrom knows that he was not fashioned to stand in the pulpit and read a sermon. Hedstrom continued on this vessel until 1857 when it was replaced by another, but retaining the same name. On the new boat he was active until 1875 so that his missionary work in the Swedish mission spanned 30 years (with the exception of a short period when a Norwegian pastor, O.P. Peterson, took over, because of Hedstrom's ill health).

"Hedstrom's preaching extended over 40 years, and continued until two years before his death. In 1863 he paid a second visit to his native land. Among other places he visited the village Lyckeby, three quarters of a mile from Karlskrona. He preached wherever he came and in Karlskrona he held forth five straight nights in a rather large meeting place. The writer of these lines had the privilege of listening to the blessed truths he interpreted. Never shall I forget that week. I had then been converted four years and during that time had tried to nurture my spiritual life with a gospel that was at least two thirds 'antinomianism.' This food was meager and spiritual strength suffered. The seventh chapter of the Letter to the Romans was at that time the gauge by which most Christians measured their spiritual condition. Pastor Hedstrom was no "antinomian" — he was a biblical Christian. In faith, doctrine and life he was a genuine apostle. I remember Hedstrom's statement, 'Where is it written that you shall carry a load of sins with you on the road to heaven? This is a teaching of the devil. The Bible teaches that Jesus Christ, the Son of God, by His blood cleanses from all sin, and it is the will of God and your great privilege to be cleansed from all your sin — today is the acceptable time, today the blessed day.' The blessed seed which Hedstrom spread did not grow immediately but it did not lose its vitality.

"Three years later several godfearing sailors visited Karlskrona. They has been won for the Lord by Hedstrom's ministry on the Bethel ship, and now they raised Methodism's banner in Karlskrona. Hedstrom was received with respect and confidence by both high and low, rich and poor. Even the pastors of the State Church showed him much friendliness, some opened their churches to him. His biblical teaching and clear exposition of full, free and present salvation from sin may indeed have been novel to their ears, but his entire life and conduct was a living and powerful exhibition of his teaching. His whole life breathed saintliness, seriousness and true humility. His influence was great. This story among others was told: A dean had opened his church for Hedstrom and invited him to lead the full service. But Hedstrom firmly refused to read the customary fixed prayers and the usual many announcements. So it was agreed that after the sermon the dean himself would ascend the pulpit and read the remaining prayers and announcements. But the dean who was seated near the altar was so absorbed in Hedstrom's earnest sermon and prayer that he forget altogether to perform his part of the service. On the same trip he visited the German Conference in Bremen, and spoke there. Also he baptized a daughter of Professor Warren, who received the name Christina. This Professor Warren is now President of Boston University. In a letter to me, September 25 last year, Professor Warren wrote, 'Among the German brethren, whose conference he visited that year he made a most favorable impression. The geniality of his conversation, the unction of his prayers, the sweetness of his apostolic spirit charmed all with whom he came in contact.'

"On the Bethel ship Hedstrom was a father for the Scandinavians who came to New York. He was a messenger of divine comfort to the sorrowing and defenseless. He dispensed temporal and spiritual gifts to those in need regardless of persons. Thousands of Bibles and New Testaments were distributed on board the *John Wesley*, along with other religious material. He came on board vessels as soon as they had anchored in the port, inviting crew and passengers to come to the Bethel ship, and speaking the Word of God to them. What he thought of the value of the Bible in connection with citizenship in this great Republic, can best be grasped in the words he often addressed to the immigrants when he came on board their vessels or when they came aboard the Bethel ship: 'Dear fellow countrymen! You have come here to become citizens of the great American Republic. This land, the greatest in the world is grounded on the Bible, and you cannot become worthy citizens here unless you read the Bible and carry out in practice in your life what it prescribes. If therefore you will promise to read this book and follow its instruction I will give each family a Bible, in the name of the American Bible Society.'

"Few have the gifts that Hedstrom had in public speaking. The sermons were serious and stirring. He awakened those who were

Christians to seek eagerly for holiness, 'without which no one may see the Lord.' The unconverted he roused from their spiritual slumber. He himself believed in and experienced biblical holiness. He delighted in class meetings, prayer meetings, and camp meetings. His ability in judgment was keen, not least in sizing up a candidate for preaching. His manner was friendly and courteous, in conversations he was humble and condescending. Never too eminent to shake hands with any one, his hand was always outstretched in Jesus' name, to extend help to one in need. In visiting he paid attention to the children in the home as well as to the adults. He was self-denying, self-sacrificing, and helpful, a tender husband and a good father. Wherever one met him, in church, on the street, at home, one received the impression that he was a man who lived to be a blessing to others. In truth, few this side of heaven enjoyed as he did the experience of the grace of God and cleansing by the blood of Jesus.

"Even his death bed was a powerful sermon on full salvation, on cleansing from all sin through faith in the blood of Jesus. It was not given him to die in his own home, which at that time was in Cape May, New York. During a conference meeting he was visiting in the home of Mr. Albert Chellberg, 299 Third Avenue, New York when he was taken ill March 13, 1877 and here his eyes closed in final sleep. He suffered great pain the last two weeks but heaven was present in his room, and not a word of murmur or of complaint came from his lips. He died as he had lived. Christ was his life, death a gain. He entered triumphantly into the joy of his Lord May 5, 1877. The funeral took place the 8th of the same month. The sermon was preached in St. Paul's M.E. Church by Dr. Lucius King, after which the body was brought to this place. Dr. King and Hedstrom had been close friends from early days and had an understanding among themselves that the one surviving should preach the funeral sermon for the other. Of this our departed brother, Olof Gustaf Hedstrom, it can be truly said, though dead he still speaks.' Inasmuch as he is the father of Scandinavian Methodism, it is proper that we — even belatedly — honor his memory by raising this monument at his grave. But his monument is not only this attractive granite stone, here — there is a better. It consists of the 30,000 Scandinavian Methodists now living, together with the thousands who with him have joined the triumphant Church in heaven. May his mantle fall upon us all who are his children, and upon all our beloved Churchı Peace to his memory."

The Bethel ship was known by almost all early immigrants and for many years was the only public place where Swedish immigrants could gather and receive spiritual and physical help. Here many Swedes were converted to Methodism, receptive as they were for spiritual impressions after the long worrisome sea voyage and on landing in a new world where at the start everything must have seemed strange. Hedstrom's mission on the Bethel boat became a mighty propaganda for Methodism among our people not only here but in Sweden to which its influence extended. The plan was remarkable and the mission could doubtless have achieved much more if greater means had been available. I remember vividly my first meeting with O.G. Hedstrom, the Fall of 1850. As soon as our vessel landed one of his assistants came aboard, the aforementioned Bergner, an older man, if I remember aright, from Jämtland. He spoke kindly to us, distributed tracts and invited us to the service that evening aboard the Bethel ship, not far from where our boat lay. A little later Hedstrom himself came. He gave us good advice about our trip inland, was ready to help us orient ourselves, led in prayer on the deck and invited us to the Bethel ship. We did go there. The boat was made into a chapel with benches and pulpit, and well lit. We sang from the Swedish Psalmbok, Hedstrom spoke, and some arose and offered prayer. We stayed in New York over Sunday and heard him preach several times. The order of service was not exactly the Swedish one, but followed it in general. His sermon we felt was warm hearted, but content and orderliness were rather mixed, without distinction between law and gospel. The line of thought was not very clear, and his language was a broken Swedish, yet tolerably intelligible. In personal conversation we found him spiritual and devout yet not fanatical. If we engaged in speaking about doctrine and Confessions he seemed confused, but he assured us that he wanted to be Lutheran in a genuine and sincere way. He was then 47 years old, well built, a little above average height, had a devout, honest and friendly face and an amiable manner, was well dressed in black coat and white necktie. I visited him in his home, which for those days seemed well-to-do. His wife seemed to be a gentle and cultured lady, an old fashioned American. Through his position and encounter with immigration into New York and his relationship with his brother Jonas in Illinois Hedstrom for many years exerted a strong influence on the immigrant stream and the direction it took inland.

Concerning Jonas Hedstrom I can give some information, partly drawn from *Svenskarne i Illinois*,[1] partly from my own memory.

[1]Eric Johnson and C.F. Peterson, Chicago 1880, pp. 286, 287, 289

When O.G. Hedstrom visited Sweden 1833 and probably returned the same year he brought with him his younger brother, Jonas. "The latter supported himself the first years working as a blacksmith in New York and Pennsylvania. Up to this time he had lived a rather careless life and by no means as a saint. But an important change took place when he heard two older Methodist women tell of their religious experiences. He is lost from view for a few years but in 1838, he appears in Illinois, working for a short while in Farmington. He had made the acquaintance of a family in New York by the name of Sonberger, and when the family moved West and settled in Victoria, the young Hedstrom was also drawn there. Here he began to preach, in 1839, and for this purpose used the Salem school house in the Town of Victoria. He settled in this Township about this time and remained until his death, a few years before 1880.

"Hedstrom did not give up his trade to become a preacher, but alternately preached and employed his sledge hammer. Possibly his zeal for Methodism more frequently drew him to the pulpit. At least this happened when the Swedes started making their way toward Victoria. They offered him a welcome mission field and nothing pleased him more than to lead them into the realm of his religious faith. And he was successful. Wherever he appeared with his forceful if not always eloquent sermons he won one or more of his fellow countrymen to his opinions." "He organized the first Swedish Methodist Congregation west of the city of New York on Dec. 15, 1846, in Victoria, with 5 members. Gradually several other congregations developed in the region, and J. Hedstrom became presiding elder over them in 1845, serving two years in this capacity."

I met J. Hedstrom several times during the Fall-Winter 1850-51. He was altogether Americanized yet spoke Swedish better than his brother. Of average height, with well formed head and face he seemed to be intelligent, even almost shrewd. He was somewhat forbidding towards strangers, but very free among friends and acquaintances. His dress and behavior were those of the ordinary American farmer of that period. I remember well his light blue, broad shouldered, somewhat well-worn overcoat, his plush cap pulled down on his head, his pants legs stuffed into his boots — a customary caution in Illinois mud. He was most bitter against Esbjörn, and had no scruples of conscience against invading in his sphere wherever he could. I came into conflict with him once in Moline when I tried to defend the Lutheran doctrine of the Lord's Supper which he ridiculed. He appeared offended and called me a "whippersnapper." One easily provoked him. On the same occasion I heard him preach at the home of Olavus Bengtson, the first Swedish Methodist in Moline. He used Romans 7 as text, and interpreted the latter half of the chapter to mean that Paul was subject to the Law when he speaks of his spiritual condition but that later he became free of all sin. He insisted on Christian perfection. In preaching he shouted and carried on to stir the emotions. He seemed to have an unusual gift to polemicize, especially against Lutheran teaching. He was fanatically devoted to the Methodist Church, exalting its progress and victory over everything else, and seeing it alone as affording salvation.

Naturally J. Hedstrom informed his brother in New York about the land in the West, its extent, its fertility, its cheapness. Consequently he undoubtedly recommended to the scattered Swedes who came to New York seeking suitable dwelling places for themselves and awaited friends and acquaintances to strike out westward to Victoria, Illinois. This explains why the earliest immigrant groups from Sweden trekked so far into the interior though land was available much closer.

The Immigrant Groups in Chronological Order

I want now to write about the various immigrant groups in the order in which they came prior to 1854 and as far as I have been able to learn about them follow them in their course:

1. *Daniel Larson from Haurida parish, Småland and his company, 1844.* Daniel Larson, born in Haurida parish, Småland, 1821 and now living in the town of Goodhue, Goodhue County, Minnesota has given me this information. Reading the letters of Unonius in the newspapers he and up to 50 persons in his neighborhood decided to go to America. The journey took place the Fall of 1844, on the Swedish vessel *Superior*, each person paying 60 riksdalar. After a ten week voyage they landed in Boston around Christmas time. Larson's father, Lars Landberg and all the others, except Larson, continued on to Sheboygan, Wisconsin, where the father died in 1846. Larson does not know what happened to the others. Larson himself stopped in Brocton (N. Bridgewater and Campello) near Boston and worked there as a shoemaker for seven years. He returned to Sweden in 1851 and when he came back here he was accompanied by 60 persons. Some went in various directions, but a part remained with Larson in Broc-

ton. This was the beginning of the Swedish settlement in Campello or Brocton. They were joined by a growing number of newcomers, who found work in the shoe factories. Daniel Larson left Brocton in 1868 and moved to a farm he had bought in the Town of Goodhue, Minnesota. He is still living and without doubt is the earliest of the immigrants still living.

2. *Peter Kassel and his company, 1845.* In Kisa Östergötland the desire to emigrate awakened early. It seems to have originated when Captain P. von Schneidau moved to America 1842 and lived one while in the Unonius' settlement, Pine Lake, Wisconsin. He wrote home to his father Major Schneidau, who lived in Kisa, and the contents of his letters became known in the region. The thinking and talking about America led some of the bolder men to a decision to emigrate. Peter Kassel became the leader. He was at the time about 50, had been a miller, and before that a foreman on a farm. He was considered skillful, had constructed a kind of threshing machine driven by hand, could figure and write and was known to be temperate and religious. The company included Kassel, his brother-in-law Peter Anderson, a Johan Danielson, etc., in all 5 families, 4 from Östergötland, 1 from Stockholm. They sailed on the brig *Superb* from Gothenburg to America 1846, and landed in New York. Their intention had been to go to Wisconsin, presumably Pine Lake, but when they were told in New York that there was better land in Iowa they decided to go there. Their route took them from New York to Philadelphia, to Pittsburg, down the Ohio River and up the Mississippi to Burlington, Iowa. From there they trekked inland 42 miles and established the settlement New Sweden in Jefferson County. The pioneer group was constantly strengthened the following years by additional parties from the same region of Sweden.

3. *The Erik Jansonists arrival from southern Helsingland, Gestrikland, Dalarne, etc. 1845-54.* Immigration began to take on new dimensions with the coming of the Erik Janson party. They left Sweden because of religious reasons, not finding there the freedom they demanded for the exercise of their faith. They were a peculiar sect that could not find peace on any terms within the Church of Sweden, and at that time dissenters had no legal standing. If they were to adhere to Jansonism there was no other choice than to emigrate. The person who seems to have been the first to turn their thoughts to America was Gustaf Flack, from Alfta, Helsingland. He was in America in the 1840's, and had spent some time in Victoria and

in Chicago. In 1843 he wrote home to his friends and told them about the great country in the West and its possibilities. In any case it is certain that the Jansonists in 1845 sent Olof Olsson of Söderala, with wife and two children, to America as a scout to find an appropriate place where the sect could make its home. The Olsson family reached New York safely where it immediately met pastor O.G. Hedstrom. "He set about to convert the Olssons to Methodism and succeeded, requiring no great change in faith since Jansonism really had much in common with the teaching of John Wesley. With Hedstrom's blessing and prayers the Olssons proceeded to Victoria, Knox County, Illinois where Jonas Hedstrom, the brother of O.G. lived. Here they stayed until the following year, when the first of the Janson parties arrived."[1]

Later the same year a larger group left Gefle, but as to their arrival or destination *Svenskarne i Illinois* gives no information. It does say that "Erik Janson came in July 1846 with a small party to Victoria. Before he left his native land he developed in detail the plan for the emigration and as leaders had chosen Jonas Olson, Olof Johnson, Olof Stenberg and Anders Berglund." The same work explains what the obstacles were for departure in large numbers. "At that time it was extremely difficult to procure suitable vessels for emigration to America. The few Swedish ships that sailed for America carried mostly iron ore and lacked facilities for passengers. However, whatever arrangements were possible were made for the Jansonists. But there were no regulations against overcrowding and the ships were small, so that quarters became very limited and uncomfortable. Some of the vessels were old and rotten and could hardly withstand the seas. One in fact disappeared without trace either of crew or passengers. One went down near Newfoundland, though the people were saved. One took five months to cross, those on board suffering many hardships including sickness and hunger."[2]

At the same time as Erik Janson reached Victoria in July 1846 he was joined by "the first of the boat loads to arrive — the group under the leadership of L.G. Larson. This Larson was the richest of those who had become members of the sect — he had contributed 24,000 riksdaler to the common treasury."

Jonas Olsson and his party came in October. By the start of winter there had now come together over 300 people. They called

[1]Svenskarne i Illinois, p. 27.
[2]Ibid. p. 29.

the place Bishop Hill, and erected two log houses, four large tents, and one tent for a church.

On one day in June 1847 not less than 400 young men and women arrived, not counting the children. A large part of the company had walked by foot from Chicago to Bishop Hill. The leaders were John Bjork, A. Anderson and a certain Hammarback.

No large company seems to have arrived in 1848, but 1849 brought another host, under the leadership of a certain Nylund, this group made up mostly of people from Norrland. When they came they carried with them cholera, and within a short time no less than 143 died. The Norrlanders left the place and sought fortune elsewhere. They may be the company that later settled at Mission Point on the Fox River — a part of these later became Mormons.

The last large group of Jansonist emigrants was very likely the party that came in 1850, led by Olof Johnson and Stenberg. These two had been back in Sweden to gather the remaining Jansonists. They got together 160 persons and with them sailed from Sundsvall. Between 50 and 60 of them died in the port of Milwaukee. The leaders became involved with the authorities of that city, who forced them to remunerate the city for expenses incurred by the sick of the party.

Later, in the Fall, Jons Anderson brought 80 colonists who had left Gefle on the *Condor*. Finally, in 1854, a party of 70 arrived. This was the end of the Jansonist emigration which had stretched over 9 years. One can only guess at the total number, but probably it did not exceed 1500. The emigration did reveal that it was possible for a massive number to migrate.

4. *The first Swedes who came to Chicago.* According to *Svenskarne i Illinois* Gustaf Flack was the first Swede to live in Chicago, where in 1843 he had a small store near the Clark Street bridge. About the same time a man named Ostrom was there, then a Swedberg. In 1845 Captain P. von Schneidau arrived from Pine Lake. First in 1846 a large group of Swedes came direct from Sweden and settled in Chicago., The earlier band that year consisted of 15 families, but it is not known where they came from in Sweden. They were very poor and suffered great need. Captain von Schneidau is praised for being both "interpreter and comforter" of these pitiable people. He helped them find work with B.W. Ogden and A. Smith, who set them clearing a piece of land just north of the present Division Street. The wage was 50 cents a day, the worker provided his own

food. The women did laundry work for 10-25 cents a day.

October 3, 1846 a large party of Swedish immigrants came under the leadership of Jonas Olson. They were all from Vestmanland, and on leaving Sweden had the intention of joining the colony at Bishop Hill, but changed their mind on reaching Chicago and remained there. Among them were Anders Larson, Jan Janson — a brother of "the prophet," Erik, John P. Kallman, Pehr Ersson, Peter Hessling, A. Thorsell, and a certain Kallstrom. To begin with they all lived in one house on Illinois Street between Dearborn and State. This group seems to have been the core of the congregation which G. Unonius organzied in 1849.

From then on the great immigration stream flowed through Chicago. Many persons spent a longer or shorter period there, many stayed there for the rest of their lives. In the source already quoted, we read, "The number of Swedes grew in 1847 with 40 new families from Sweden, another 100 came in 1849. The times were now somewhat better. The daily wage was 75 cents, though the cost of living was, if anything, higher than at present. A barrel of flour was worth 6 or 7 dollars, meat 6 to 8 cents a pound. Rent was very high, $20 a month for 5 or 6 meager rooms. With the 400 Swedes in 1849 came cholera, which raged more or less every year up to 1854, the worst year. 500 came in 1850 and 1,000 in each of the following years. In the 1852 group were some from Vestergötland, whom the Norwegian pastor Paul Andersen found sick and helpless — these became the core of the Swedish Lutheran congregation. Through this period of sickness, destitution, poverty and sorrow Pastor Unonius proved to be of great comfort and aid for his needy fellow-countrymen, and deserves grateful acknowledgement. Special mention should be made of Mrs. Unonius for her laudable spirit of self-sacrifice and unselfish and loving service to these poor people — a service not soon forgotten."

5. *New immigrant groups from Östergötland and Kalmar provinces 1846-48.* A party of 75 left Kisa and environs in 1846, sailing on the ship *Virginia*, under Captain Johnson, intending to join P. Kassel in Iowa. They were robbed of their money in Albany, New York, and could not go on beyond Buffalo. Between these two points they had "to nourish themselves on wild plums, which they found along the canal bank, and anything else they could come across." They remained in Buffalo two years before they had earned enough to continue. Meanwhile their plans were altered by the following

events: in 1847 another group from the same parts of Sweden had come to New York, also hoping to reach P. Kassel in Iowa. In New York Pastor O.G. Hedstrom persuaded them to go to Illinois and the region where his brother lived. Thus they came first to Victoria and were there directed by Jonas Hedstrom to Andover as a place suitable for a Swedish settlement. In this way they became the pioneers in this place. Among them were N.J. Johnson and wife from Jerda, Kalmar County, Anders Johanson and family, Friberg and family, Nils Nilson, Hurtig, etc.

Meanwhile they had learned about their friends who were in Buffalo. They wrote to them, advising them to come to Andover, and some of them did this, Among those who came in 1848 to Andover were Samuel Johnson and family from Södra Wi., the Holland Elm family from Gammalskil, Östergötland, the Erik Peter Anderson family from Kisa, Samuel Samuelson and family from Kisa, and the widow of Mons Johnson (who died in Buffalo) and a son, also from Kisa.

The other part of the group which came to Buffalo in 1846 went to Sugar Grove, Warren County, Pennsylvania and became the first Swedish settlers in the Jamestown area. They were led to this destination thus: One of the Swedes, Germund Johnson from Kisa had two young daughters who were placed in the Orphans Home in Buffalo because of the parents' poverty. They were taken from there by two ladies who lived in Sugar Grove, Pennsylvania. When the father learned this he visited his children and found them in favorable conditions, whereupon he decided to move there with the rest of his family. Gradually the others in Buffalo followed. These included Carl M. Johnson, from Hessleby Jönköping County and his brother Fredrick with family, an old soldier from Horn, Östergötland named Norman, Carl Johnson and family from Sund, Samuel Dahl and his sister Karolina.

Before the removal of the group from Buffalo to Sugar Grove their number was increased by new arrivals from Sweden, such as Anders Pet. Johnson, brother of Carl and Fredrik Johnson, and sister Johanna; Helena Louisa Peterson; the sisters Lisa and Lena Anderson — the latter three from Lönneberga, Kalmar County, etc. These first settlers around Sugar Grove and Jamestown received additional numbers the following years.[1] One of the above group, Samuel

[1]Ibid. pp. 74, 366, 367.

Johnson from Södra Wi. died in 1887 in Orion, Illinois where he had lived many years. He was God-fearing and experienced person, a Lutheran by faith.

Germund Johnson and family moved to Vasa, Minnesota and farmed there for several years. Then he moved to Red Wing, where he lived the later years but spent much of his time with children in Alexandria, Douglas County and Stevens County until his death August 1888 in Hancock. His wife "Kara" died a few years before him — both are buried in Vasa. They were Methodists, rather outspoken, not mincing their words.

Carl M. Johnson moved to Paxton, Illinois 1863, served a few months in the Union army, moved 1866 to Farmersville, near Paxton, and now lives there on his farm.

Fredrik Johnson has resided many years in Hessle Valley, Pennsylvania, near where the old Lutheran Church stood, and as far as known, is still there. One of his sons, L.A. Johnston,[1] is pastor of the First Swedish Lutheran Church in Rockford, Illinois.

Anders Pet. Johnson, the third brother, moved to Vasa, Minnesota 1859, with his family, bought a farm there and became prosperous. He was a Lutheran, died in Vasa 1879 at the age of 58.

These three brothers were from the Hessleby parish, and gave the valley where they settled in Pennsylvania the name Hessle Valley. Helena Louisa Peterson married Erik M. Anderson around 1851. In 1855 they moved to Vasa, Minnesota, where they homesteaded and still live on the same farm. They were along when the Vasa Swedish Lutheran congregation was organized and have ever since been among the most faithful members.

6. *The immigration parties, 1849.* We know of several of these this year. A new load came from the old center of emigration, Kisa and environs, and from Grenna and neighborhood. I have this information from Nels Magnus Kilberg, in Swedona, Mercer County, Illinois, who was born in Kisa February 6, 1821. Together with 300 persons he left from Gothenburg, the Spring of 1849, on the vessel *Charles Tottie*, Captain Bäckman, and landed in New York after 7 weeks and 4 days. From New York the company travelled to Buffalo, packed in 3 small boats. Before they reached Buffalo cholera broke out on one of the boats. By steamer they crossed the lakes to Chicago. "Chicago wasn't much to see," Kilberg remarks, "the area was thinly

---

[1]Johnston became the first American-born president of the Augustana Synod.

populated, and everywhere on the marshy streets one saw dead dogs and cats." From Chicago the party went on canal boat to Peru. In Peru they hired 9 horse and wagons at $18 a load to Andover. In Chicago they had met Captain Vistrom (various spellings), who guided them to Andover, where they arrived at the end of July.

Originally the party had planned to reach P. Kassel in Iowa, but because of cholera and other sickness they had to stay in the Andover area. Still they intended to go on in the Fall when there would be cooler weather. Late in the Fall Kilberg attempted to journey to New Sweden, but in Rock Island he waited in vain for a place on the steamboat to Burlington. He returned to Andover and settled in Swedona where he remained and still resides. In this party were Johannes and Carl J. Samuelson, from Tjäderstad, Östergötland, who established themselves in Hickory Grove, now Ophiem, where they with the years accumulated wealth.

This company included the first emigrants from the Grenna area. Among them was Johan Svanstrom, a tailor, and wife, born Nordquist, who lived in Brooklyn four years, moved 1853 to Campello, Massachusetts, and in 1861 to Red Wing, Minnesota where they now reside and are members of the Swedish Lutheran congregation. Johannes Peterson, from Örserum, Grenna, after a period in New York moved to Indiana and now lives in Beaver, Illinois. Svanström relates that the group from Grenna comprised about 30 persons.

One party after another from Östergötland and Kalmar County arrived year after year and settled in Andover, Swedona, and neighboring localities.

In 1849, too, another party, from Gestrikland and southern Helsingland emigrated to America under the leadership of Pastor L.P. Esbjörn. In those districts from which the Jansonists had come others than Jansonists were thinking of moving to America. Many were committed Christians who did not want to set out without a Christian minister. They found such a one in L.P. Esbjörn, pastor in a factory town Oslättfors, Hille, who decided to accompany them to America. The question of how he would support himself at first in the new land troubled him. Esbjörn had become acquainted with Methodism through the Englishman George Scott, and been impressed by his generous spirit. He seems to have entertained the hope that the American Methodists might be equally unselfish and that from them he might receive some help in his ministry as a Swedish Lutheran minister. There was even some correspondence about this with the Methodist

PROFESSOR L.P. ESBJÖRN.

Jonas Hedstrom in Victoria of whom Esbjörn had heard through persons who had migrated before 1849. The Swedish Church Mission Board meanwhile granted a small subsidy. June 29, 1849 he sailed from Gefle on the Swedish vessel *Cobden* along with 140 others and they landed in New York at the end of August or early in September. The destination was Victoria, Knox County, Illinois, but something happened to alter this plan. When Esbjörn met with pastor O.G. Hedstrom in New York he discoverd that the Methodist Church neither would nor could support him as a Lutheran pastor. If he wanted their help he must without qualification transfer to the Methodist Church. But this Esbjörn refused to do — a decision his wife firmly seconded. Esbjörn then turned to the American Home Missionary Society, with headquarters in New York, asking if it would be willing for a time to support him as a Lutheran minister. From one of their agents he seems to have received an encouraging reply.[1] This, together with what is stated in *Svenskarne i Illinois* undoubtedly contributed to the decision to change destination. On pages 75 and 76 we read, "On landing in New York Pastor Esbjörn and his party were met by a Captain Viderstrom[2], who was to be their guide westward. He had belonged to the Bishop Hill Colony, which had arrived three years earlier, but had left and now resided in Andover. In New York a "Land Association" had bought a large tract of land in Henry County and laid out [on paper] the Town of Andover. Pastor Esbjörn and his group had planned to go to Knox County, but when the land company promised ten acres of land for a Swedish Lutheran church, it was decided to head for Andover instead. The journey was made by canal boat to Buffalo and by steamboat to Chicago. After passing Detroit another of the Esbjörn children died (one had died shortly after the start of the trip) and was buried in a very primitive coffin in a sandbank along the shore of Lake St. Clair. Pastor Esbjörn became a victim of cholera, and with his family had to remain in Chicago while Captain Viderstrom guided the rest of the party to Andover. Three weeks later Esbjörn followed to Andover only to find to his dismay that the greater part of his company had been persuaded by the Methodist pastor, Jonas Hedstrom, to leave Andover for Victoria".[3]

Before this the same J. Hedstrom had recommended Andover as a fine place for Swedes, but when he learned that Esbjörn would not become Methodist, he belittled the place and did all he could to entice Swedes from it.

Among the Swedes who came with Esbjörn was John Anderson from Hille. He was somewhat prominent, known for his straightforwardness, good humor, cheerfulness, and what passed then for a warm piety. I remember how when he found himself in difficulty he would with loud voice burst into an old hymn and so sing his worries away. Only a year after his arrival in America he and another man from Hillebo, Matts Erson, who came in the same party, set off for California to dig gold (the gold fever had just broken out). They came back 1851, if not richer, at least somewhat wiser. About 1859 he and his sons moved to Colorado, where he probably still lives, while the rest of the family stayed in Andover. Another of this group was Olof Nordin who resided in Andover a few years.

[1] Letter of Rev. Wm. Kirby, Jan. 9, 1950 in archives of Am. Home Miss. Society.
[2] Probably same as Vistrom.
[3] *Svenskarne i Illinois*, 75-76.

Esbjörn was still weak when he preached his first Sunday in Andover, in the Francis School. He sat in a chair and appeared deeply moved. His introducctory theme was, "When I am weak I am strong." Through the winter he lived in the well-known "Mix place." He bought a small place south of the woods, down toward the Edwards river. It was 10 acres, with very primitive buildings, and he moved there in the Spring of 1850.

The same year 1849 witnessed the beginning of Swedish immigration to Texas.[1] S.M. Swenson from Lettarp, Barkeryd parish, Småland was the first to guide Swedes to Texas. He had worked in a store in Eksjö before going to America in 1836. He worked wherever he could for a while in New York and then attended a school in Sing Sing, New York. He found employment on a railroad in Baltimore and rose to the position of bookkeeper. Through his chief he came to Texas 1838 and started a business in Brazoria (now Houston) together with Dr. Long. Some time after the latter's death he married the widow, who died in 1850. Swenson visited Sweden around 1849 and brought back with him around 50 Swedish farm hands. Almost all of them earned their passage by working for Swenson, some say up to two years, after which each received also a piece of land. Apparently Swenson was already then a wealthy man. These who came in this way are now scattered in various directions, many, most likely, now dead.

At the outbreak of the Civil War Swenson had to leave Texas because of his political views. He as well as his intimate friend, Governor Sam Houston, were too clear-sighted to join the Secessionists. Only a few Southerners realized the strength of the North.

Swenson, a perceptive merchant, sold in good time an article soon to become without value, namely his negro slaves, for he had been a slaveholder. The hostility towards Swenson caused him to flee to Mexico. It is said that under the fire-place in his house he had buried a large sum, reputedly $25,000. Swenson was twice married. A man who brought a message from Mexico to his wife was murdered. Swenson never returned to Texas, but went on to New York where he engaged in the banking business and probably still lives there. His mother in Lettarp died a few years ago. She had visited her son in Texas before the War. She was widely known and praised in Sweden for her excellent art-weaving.

[1]Information from Pastor M. Noyd, Round Rock, Texas, and D. Larson, P.G. Veber, Goodhue, Minn. et. al.

Vice consul Swante Palm came to Texas around 1844. During the war he meant much for the Swedes, placing them under the protection of the Swedish flag. In many ways he earned their gratitude. In early issues of *Hemlandet* there were several letters from Mr. Palm indicating that he was then a good friend of the political system in the South. He was a literary person and is known to have a large and valuable library. The larger numbers of Swedish immigrants came in a later period, between 1867-75. Pastor Noyd claims that "nine-tenths of the Swedes there have come under contract to work for their passage. Some of the older settlers made a real business of bringing in Swedes. On leaving Sweden they signed a contract to work for two years in exchange for passage. When they arrived they were hired out at a fixed wage on various farms. They were often ill-treated and some ran away. But the minority endured the agreed terms and many are now in better circumstances than those who had traded in them. In later years those who have come to Texas have usually paid for their passage by one year's work, sometimes even by serving 100 days."

Most of the Swedes in Texas have come from the eastern part of Jönköping County — Tveta district, and now reside in and around Austin, the capital. The oldest and largest rural settlement in Texas is at Round Rock, Williamson County.

7. *The Immigrant Groups of 1850.* Beside the already mentioned Jansonists of this year with Olof Stenberg and Jons Anderson as leaders, there were some other parties from the northern districts. In fact this year marked the beginning of emigration from North Helsingland and southern Medelpad. What occasioned the migration fever here were letters from particular persons or families who had gone to America the previous year, for instance Erik Sannman and A.G. Svedberg from Hudiksvall, Eric Sund from Tuna and And. Snygg[1] from Bergsjö. The latter wrote from Victoria, where he stayed a while, and gave the folks at home a rosy colored picture. His letter was copied and read in wide circles, kindling a flaming emigration fever. Toward the end of July there gathered in Gefle over one hundred persons from Hassela, Bergsjö, Gnarp and Hudiksvall in Helsingland and from Altmar and Stöde in Medelpad, as well as some others from other parishes. By August 17 they left on the Swedish sailing vessel *Oden*, Captain Norberg, for New York.

In the group were many so-called "Lutheran Readers" or

[1]According to *Svenskarne i Illinois*, the first to settle in Altona, Ill.

"Hedbergians" as they were also called, who were unhappy in the Church of Sweden. They purposed to establish in America a *genuine* Lutheran communion where they could use the "old books" without being censored. To succeed they wanted before they left to assure themselves of a minister who would follow them to America as soon as possible. While in Gefle awaiting passage they sent a deputation to Stockholm to call Pastor Viberg, who as yet had not become a Methodist. While he was not available he recommended Gustaf Palmquist, a school teacher, and they called him. Palmquist promised to accept and come to America the following year or sooner, if possible.

After a sea voyage of 11 weeks the party landed in New York October 31. A few stopped there, but the greater number followed the usual immigrant course inland, with the usual difficulties, heading for Knox or Henry County, Illinois. Some reached Andover in the middle of November, others remained in Chicago, Princeton, Galesburg, Rock Island, Moline, etc. Remnants of this group continued on in the spring of 1851 to Minnesota where they founded the oldest Swedish settlement in that state, at Chisago Lake.

Since I was a member of this party in 1850 I am in better position to describe its experiences in migrating than of any other, and I do so, not because ours were so extraordinary. On the contrary they were the ordinary conditions immigrants then endured, and I desire only to portray the troubles and hardships encountered by the pioneers as a picture of those days.

In this period one crossed the ocean on a sailing vessel. Usually the immigrants had their own provisions and prepared their meals on facilities on deck. Many a time a great wave swept you off your feet and the contents of pots and pans washed into the ocean. The comforts on board were few. To cross in 7 or 8 weeks was considered a speedy voyage. It took us 11 weeks from Gefle to New York. For many it took much longer, and distress was acute when water and food gave out. Needless to say, the time became depressively long, but one could bear it if in good health. Many became sick, many found their grave in the ocean. Nine of our party died on the sea, two sailors died accidentally.

In New York we disposed of the rest of our provisions, thinking that we could easily obtain what we might need on the way. This was a mistake, for often it was very hard to get necessities. We left New York November 4th and paid $8 for the trip to Chicago. We were stowed away with our baggage on the deck of the steamer *Isak*

Newton, like animals, and spent the night without sleep or rest. Five o'clock next morning, while it was still dark, foggy, and rather cold, we landed at Albany, where we and our belongings were dumped on to the ground. We did have an interpreter along from New York, a "fine gentleman," Mr. Paulson, but he did us more harm than good and left us when we needed him most. We went by train from Albany to Buffalo, an advantage over earlier immigrants who had to traverse this stretch by canal boat. At noon on the 5th of November we boarded one of those new immigrant trains, which in little or no degree differed from ordinary cattle cars. For us who never before had seen a train or had any idea how one was to ride on one the event was nevertheless remarkable. Again a sleepless night on the road. Two o'clock in the afternoon of November 6th we reached Buffalo. We did not know where to turn to find the steamer that was to take us across the lakes. No one paid any attention to us, none of us spoke English. There we stood in a cold and drenching rain on a dirty street, like a flock of sheep. It was especially hard for the children and poor women, yet they kept up their courage. Finally I ran into a couple of Germans with whom I could make myself understood, and through them we found our way to the steamship office. Off we went with our bundles. While on our way through the city Anders Ersson from Gnarp got separated from his wife, and there was a frightful running hither and thither before she could be found.

We had to wait until the 8th for the departure of our boat. Where should we stay until then? The boat company made no provision. After a good deal of running and searching we finally found a Norwegian by the name of Larson, who had a small place where some could stay. Others found room at a German Jew's place. I remember that when we had paid our bill and were on the street starting off he came out with another bill and forced us to pay a shilling (12 1/2 cents) per person because we had left behind us some creeping creatures. Naturally we paid, for we could not really prove our innocence, but we were impressed by his business ingenuity.

In the evening of November 8 we boarded the *Sultana*, a poor old hull which was to bring us over the lakes to Chicago. The rooms meant for the immigrants were already taken by Irishmen and so crowded and unclean that we had neither the possibility nor the desire to force our way down into them. There was no other recourse than to stay on deck, but this was forbidding in view of the length of the journey and the seasonal cold weather. Those who were too weak to endure being on deck and had the means rented two ordinary passenger rooms for 40 dollars and as many as could stowed themselves in these. We witnessed many beautiful examples of Christian compassion those days on the part of the more affluent in our party toward the poverty stricken and sick who lacked both food and a dry place to lie down. It was our good fortune to be safe from heavy storms on the voyage, for the ship was in poor condition and heavily loaded. We ran aground on Lake St. Clair and lost almost a day in getting it afloat again. Most of the passengers were set ashore on the Canada side, suffering both hunger and cold. After the transfer of some of the cargo to another boat the vessel came loose and amid much confusion we were able to continue during the night.

Late at night the 14th of November we arrived in Chicago. The city then had a population of 28,260. It looked like a vertiable swamp with small frame houses scattered about, yet something about the place made one surmise that in time a great city would grow here. I was prompted to write in my diary, "Chicago promises to be the greatest city in the West," a prophecy that has been fulfilled. We spent the 15th in Chicago preparing for the journey westward. At that time there was no railroad west of Chicago. We were somewhat uncertain of our goal. In Sweden we had heard most about Victoria. We also knew that pastor Esbjörn had left for America the year before to go somewhere in Illinois, but where he and his party had settled we did not know before we got to Chicago. There we learned that he lived in Andover, and we decided to go there because we believed that it would be helpful if we could talk to him and get his advice as to where we should settle. We met Pastor G. Unonius, pastor of the newly organized Episcopal Church in Chicago. We sensed that he was not friendly towards Pastor Esbjörn, but he gave us much helpful counsel and helped us in arranging a contract with the agent of the canal company for our passage to La Salle or Peru. He procured an interpreter for us, one of his members, Per Ersson from Westmanland and brother in law of the adventurer Ruth, who shot and killed Erik Janson. He was a kind and honest person who gave us great help. We paid him 10 dollars to accompany us to Peru, about 100 miles from Chicago. The cost for each passenger on the canal boat was then 11 shillings.

As we went aboard the boat the morning of November 16th it began to snow and feel like winter. It took us until the evening of the 19th to reach Peru. We completely filled the hold and when all were in we were like packed sardines. Per Anderson from Hassela, the richest one in the party who acted as a sort of leader, had bought a cook-stove in Chicago. He set this up in the hold to give us a bit of heat. He and others had provided themselves with some flour and proceeded to bake pancakes on the stove lids when there was no other food. The worst was that one could get no rest. It was so crowded that one could not find a place on the floor to lie down. We made a rule that place should be reserved for two persons to lie down for ten minutes, and make way for others when the time expired. The rule was put into effect and thus one could get a longed-for nap. If the sleepers did not arise when called they were helped up by strong arms.

From Peru we had about 60 miles to Andover, which one could cover by carriage if one had the means, or by foot. Those who hired horse and wagon — at $18 per load — remained in Peru to Nov. 21. I and 14 others left our baggage in Peru and started off on foot the afternoon of the 20th. The weather was quite mild, and we walked at an easy pace. After the hardships we had experienced we did not feel able to move rapidly, besides women and children were in our party. It was not easy to find the way since we could not speak to anyone. About all we could say was "road to Andover," but east of Princeton and quite a way beyond no one seemed to know anything about Andover. It began to get dark and we wondered about where or how we would spend the night. We thought about making a fire along the road and camping around it, but the ground was wet and low, and there was no firewood, so this idea was rejected. It got darker, we were tired and hungry. Finally we came upon some woods, and there on a sandy, dry spot stood an old dilapidated school house, made of oak logs, long since deserted. Nearby were two farm houses, where we tried by sign language to ask for quarters. So we resorted to the school house. One of its two windows was gone and the door broken down, but inside was a stove with some pipes yet not long enough to lead the smoke through the roof. Gathering up some corn stalks, bark and twigs we soon had a fire. Olof Nilson from Långskog in Attmars parish, an agile and clever person who could meet any emergency, had a long Swedish copper bottle and a bag of flour — the only edible stuff in the whole party. In the bottle he cooked a porridge while I went to one of the farm houses nearby and succeeded by many gesticulations to procure some milk. That was our meal for that day. After eating while we were sitting on the floor around the stove to warm us a dark-bearded man carrying a gun and followed by two dogs stuck his head in the empty window and looked at us, we thought, with astonishment. No doubt he wondered what kind of gypsy folk we were, but said nothing. We wondered if he was about to drive us out, so we tried to talk to him and have him understand that we were decent folk. He just shook his head and went on. We gathered fallen leaves and made a bed around the stove. During the night my brother tried to keep warm by nestling up to the stove, with the result that he burned away the whole back of his coat.

We had breakfast the 21st in the same way we had eaten the night before, then continued on our journey. That afternoon, after we had gone quite a distance, the other group who had hired wagons caught up with us. They had gotten irresponsible drivers who carried on as if it were a joke. Women and children were placed on top of the load and boxes. The men ran breathlessly along the side to hold up the wagon if it threatened to tip, and were fearful that this wild ride would end in a crash. And so it did. A short distance from Princeton there was a bridge over a small stream. Two of the drivers were racing to see who could cross first. They came on it about the same time, but one wagon was forced off the bridge, throwing the passengers from a considerable height into the stream. When we reached the spot we discovered that it was Anders Westerlund, the elder, from Bergsjö and his family that had suffered this blow. The wife and daughter had been hurt, but the worst injury was to Westerlund himself. When the load tipped he had attempted to jump off, but in doing so he hit his head against the bridge so hard that his skull was cracked. At first he didn't think it was so bad, in fact he walked into Princeton. When toward evening we got there he was sitting on a stone by the "tavern" and complaining about his head. Again it was difficult to find a place to spend the night. There were very few houses then in Princeton, beside the one small, unattractive inn, which was rapidly filled. Erik Wester, the well-known adventurer was already in Princeton, its first Swede. He had a small barber-shop but could do nothing for us. Some of the drivers went on beyond Princeton and found places to stop wherever they could. We who had no places were in sore quandary. Some of those walking had fallen behind. We were afraid that they might miss the way to Princeton, so I went back to look for them. After walking a couple of miles I found them to our mutual delight. When we got to Princeton it was getting late. We found all the homeless ones in and around Wester's shop, among them the sick Westerlund and his family. The old man was getting worse and weaker. What should we do? We could not stay in the barber shop. By good fortune we met a Swedish farm hand from Östergötland, who worked for a minister 1 1/2 miles from the town. He thought the owner would allow us to stay in his barn over night. We had no other choice so we gratefully accepted his suggestion. All of us proceded there, with A. Westerlund and his family. The latter were taken into the kitchen, where the old man died during the night. The rest of us, including some small children, crawled up in the hayloft and bedded down in the hay as best we could. It was a very cold night, and in the morning we could not straighten ourselves. We had to leave the corpse with the minister, who for $10 offered to take care of the burial. On his return the careless driver was arrested and put on trial, but with what result I could never ascertain.

Some of those who walked, as well as some who had been riding, remained in Princeton and became the first Swedish inhabitants in this place. Of them I remember Hans Smitt, Olof Nilson, Anders Larson, Anders Nord, Olof Janson, Stefan Berglof, Hans Kamel, and their families. Afterwards some of them moved away, but others lived there many years. The rest of us continued our journey, after we had each bought some bread in Princeton, but we were stiff from the cold and our feet were sore. It was November 25th. We now learned that the wife of Anders Ersson from Gnarp had given birth to a girl baby at the place where they stayed that night outside of Princeton. The child lived, and next morning the mother took her place on top of the load and continued on the frozen and bumpy road to Andover!

We were on the way all that day, until darkness fell. We were able to find place in a farm house, where for a small price we were allowed to sleep on the bare kitchen floor. Compared to the previous night we thought the accommodations were excellent. By now we had come close enough to Andover so that people we asked knew about it, but we were still 20 miles away. On November 23rd we had a real snowstorm and it was quite cold. In the afternoon we finally reached Andover. We had imagined it at least a good sized village, but to our astonishment discovered it was a wide prairie with a house here and there. Those who had been riding were of course considerably before us and fortunately had right away met Esbjörn, who helped them get rid of their troublesome drivers.

The journey was so far completed, but now came the serious question, "Where shall we live?" "What shall we live on?" Winter was upon us, and we found ourselves in a poor and new settlement. Many of us had not a cent of our own and besides were in debt for at least a part of our travel. The only possibility was for each one to scatter in a different direction and seek to support himself as best he could.

As mentioned I have described this journey in more detail than necessary. But I have done so to show what the immigrant trains were like in those early years of Swedish immigration. Still many others faced even worse than we had done.

Other immigrant groups 1850. Somewhat earlier that year a party had come on the vessel *Sofia*, Captain Lind, from Gefle. It consisted of only 48 persons, the majority of whom settled in Andover and Galesburg, at least to start with. Among them was foreman Vaerner and family from Strömbacka in Bjuråker; Magnus Englund and Envall from Enånger; Akerberg, who resided for a long time in Moline; Erik Swenson from Högs parish and Jan Hakanson from Bollnäs; Daniel Nilson and family from Norrbo. The latter family came to Marine, Minnesota 1851 and became the pioneers for the Swedish settlement there. Daniel Nilson moved after many years to Green Lake in Kandiyohi County where he died some years ago.

Yet another group the same year from the Northern districts. Early in the summer, 1850, the brig *Marie*, Captain M. Åsander, sailed from Gefle with 111 emigrants on board and landed in New York after a sea voyage of 10 weeks. The party followed the usual route to Buffalo, across the lakes to Chicago, thence by canal to Peru and then by carriage to their destination, namely Andover. One contingent seems to have stayed in Manitowoc, Wisconsin and then continued to Waupaca, Wisconsin. The others scattered, but mostly they either spent a short time or decided to locate in Henderson and Wataga, Knox County, Illinois. The greater part of this group were persons from Jerfsö, Ljusdahl, and other parishes in Helsingland and a few from Dalarne. Individual letters from former emigrants of their acquaintance and prospects of better economic conditions seem to have prompted this company's emigration.

In the party we might name the following: Lars Olson and family from Ramsjö, annex to Ljusdahl. He took the name here of Williams, and lived first in Henderson, then Wataga, and latest in Vasa, Minnesota, where he still resides — his wife died in Vasa. This Williams was a cousin of Pastor Esbjörn. Per Olson from Jerfsö took the name Williamson. He located in Wataga, died in 1855, leaving a large and respected family known for their considerable wealth. Mons Olson from the same parish in Sweden settled in Victoria. The Rehnstrom family, also from that parish, made their home around Galesburg, the old man Grells from Ljusdahl, stayed in Andover.

The party that went to Waupaca, Wisconsin and stayed several years included the Thompson family, Erik Person, Per Larson, Erik Olson. All were from Jerfsö. Around 1861 they moved to Nest Lake in the neighborhood of New London, Kandiyohi County, Minnesota. They scattered during the Indian rebellion in 1862 but most returned. The older people are now mostly gone, but their descendants are here and doing well. The well-known Peter Thompson, banker in Worthington, Minnesota and candidate for lieut. governor 1888 on the Temperance ticket, is a son of the above mentioned Thompson.

The "old fellow of Stenbo" also came to America this year (1850). The village of Stenbo in Forsa parish in Northern Helsingland was beautifully situated on Lake Forsa. It was the headquarters of the Jansonists during Erik Janson's last years in Sweden, and there he had acquired property. Here it was that the Jansonists put to the flames the many piles of Lutheran devotional books they had brought together, and sang their "let us thank and praise the Lord" as these so-called "idols" and "black magic books" went up in fire and smoke. I have myself seen and admired the beautiful site of the place. It was here that the rich and mighty Stenbo "old fellow" Jon Olsson lived as a minor king on his lovely well-tended and well-built homestead. He early sided with Erik Janson and sheltered his assemblies. His sons, especially Olof, were counted among "the prophets" and were among the first to migrate to America. During the winter of 1849-50 Olof (called Stenberg) returned to Sweden to gather the remaining members of the sect and bring them to America. It was decided that the old man too should come, but he would not accompany the son but travel on his own. He was a widower. After selling his place he leased a schooner in Hudiksvall, loaded it with iron and took along all his property, even the wooden bowls. Everything went well on the ocean. There were a few with him, at least some of whom were not Jansonists. In New York he sold his cargo of iron, but it must have cost him a pretty penny to cart the heap of scrap he carried along inland. It seems that at his introduction to Bishop Hill, where he finally landed, he was not inclined to stay. It may be that he hesitated to turn over his considerable wealth to the common treasury. There may have been some other reason. In any case I found him at the beginning of January 1851 in Moline, where he had bought two houses, one of frame, one of brick, with large lots. Rumor had it that in addition he had $20,000 in gold in a Rock Island bank, and he was looked on as a very rich man. The old fellow was peculiar, and retained his old home customs. He went around in an old fashioned coat which almost touched the ground, and the genuine leather apron was almost as long. Thus apparelled he ran around the streets — he was nimble in his movements — and if he found a piece of coal, an old shoe, a broken dish or a stick of wood, he picked it up and brought it home and placed on a pile in the middle of his ante-room. In the cellar under the house he had set up the forge he brought with him from Sweden — he didn't seem bothered by the smoke that filled the house. Also in the cellar he had built a Swedish oven and I witnessed the baking of large, thin, round, Helsing bread loaves. He was hospitable in an old fashioned way, and more than once I ate his genuine cabbage-soup with a wooden spoon out of a wooden bowl. When he had broken the thin loaf into the soup bowl he shook the flour from his hands into it. He did not want any of God's gifts to be missed unnecessarily, or that food should be wasted. One night I had the honor of lying with him under the same sheepskin, but that night we didn't sleep much for we got into a dispute as to whether the earth goes around the sun or the sun around the earth. He held the latter and knew all the Bible passages that were relevant. Each held to his own opinion, but we remained none the less just as good friends.

Finally they lured him to Bishop Hill. Though advanced in years the old fellow was interested in getting married. In that way they got him there, for there they had found a suitable bride for him. She met his fancy, and he moved to Bishop Hill with all his possessions which presumably had the same fate as all the other sums deposited there. He did not live long after this.

I know of only one family who were in the old Stenbo man's company, namely Per Berg from Högs parish, who became one of the pioneers at Chisago Lake. In time he moved to Fish Lake and is probably still alive.

The emigration from Helsingland and Medelpad continued for some years, though reduced in numbers. It cannot be considered very large after the Jansonists left. Yet there were some good-sized groups in 1853 and 1856.

8. *The immigrants of 1851.* This is the year that large numbers began to emigrate from northern Skåne, otherwise migration was not great from Sweden that year. The pioneer of this movement from northern Skåne with a destination in Knox County was Christen Jonsson from Åkarp. He travelled to America in 1848 in company with one of his sons. He knew of only one Swede in America, pastor

O.G. Hedstrom in New York, who advised him to go to Knox County, Illinois, which he did. He stopped 3 weeks in Bishop Hill, then went to Galesburg. What enticed him to America were the many glowing accounts in the papers about the free and fertile country in the West, and he wanted personally to see if one could fare better here than in old Sweden. After a year and a half he returned to Sweden, satisfied with America.

Meanwhile a small party, composed mainly of young farm workers from the area of Kristianstad, made the journey to America. It is not known whether or not they had been influenced by the letters of Ch. Jonsson. In Gothenburg they chanced to meet another group of emigrants, from Östergötland. Together they were about 100, who came over on the vessel *Ambrosius*, Captain Beckman, and landed in Boston. In this company was a devout family from Önnestad, Ola Nilson, which found its way to Andover. Others were Hans Mattson, later Col. Mattson, from the same parish, who stayed a while in Boston, T.G. Pearson from Stoby, now in Vasa, Minnesota; John Johnson, a nephew of Pastor T.N. Hasselquist; Johannes Jonson, later Pastor Johnson. Those from Östergötland left the party in Buffalo and proceeded to Sugar Grove, Pennsylvania. Most of those from Skåne went on to Illinois, ending up in Galesburg and Knoxville, where they knew a carpenter Lofgren who had emigrated to America the year before.[1]

9. *Immigrants in 1852.* The immigration this year was considerable and from different sources. From northern Skåne a multitude came to Knox County, Illinois. From the northeastern Jönköping County (Viste) they came to Indiana, and from Kronoberg County, to Chisago County, Minnesota. The great migration from Vestergötland began to move this year, while immigrants still came from the older sources in Östergötland and Norrland. It now becomes difficult to trace the paths of the various groups, but I call attention to some of them.

1) *The immigrants from northern Skåne. How Pastor T.N. Hasselquist came to America.* The aforementioned Ola Nilson and family from Önnestad, now in Andover, was well acquainted with Hasselquist from the time that he served as pastor in Önnestad. As Esbjörn's field widened and an associate became all the more necessary, especially for Galesburg and its neighborhood, Ola Nilson spoke

---

[1]Around 1849 an American lady had visited a well-to-do family in Ignaberga, accompanied by a Swedish maid from America. The latter had told some of the young men about the new land and they decided to emigrate. Among them were this Lofgren and wife and Nils Jacobson, sons of Per Jacobson in Ignaberga.)

to Esbjörn about Hasselquist and the possibility of bringing him here. Esbjörn consulted with the small congregation in Galesburg and succeeded in getting it to issue a call to Hasselquist to come over and be its pastor. This call he must have received early in 1852. He accepted, was married in May to Eva Cervin from Kristianstad, and at the end of August left in company with 60 emigrants from northern Skåne for America. At the time he left Sweden he was assistant pastor in Åkarp and Vittsjö. The voyage took the group to Hamburg — a route usual for emigrants from southern Sweden — then by sailing vessel, and to New York, by September 28th. Then the well worn route to Chicago. Because of the cholera epidemic, again raging in Chicago, the train stopped outside Chicago and discharged the passengers onto the open prairie. At first the immigrants did not know where to turn. Immigrant agents appeared, but the newcomers did not trust them. They hoped Pastor Esbjörn would meet them in Chicago, but where would they find him? Finally it was decided that Mrs. Hasselquist, who could speak English, should go with Nils Randau, an able and dependable member of the party, and look for Esbjörn. When they got into the city they met a driver who they guessed was Swedish. They spoke to him and sure enough they were right. His name was Lind. They learned from him that Esbjörn had not yet arrived in the city, but was expected, since the Synod of Northern Illinois was to have its second annual meeting there in the Norwegian Lutheran Church. He directed them to the Norwegian Lutheran pastor, Paul Andersen. Esbjörn did not come as soon as expected, for the death of his wife occurred in those days. He had also lost his horse, yet he did get to the meeting in Chicago. Meanwhile Hasselquist was invited to stay with the hospitable Norwegian pastor. He had a mild attack of cholera, but was given good care. The remainder of the party continued on their way by canal boat to Peru and then by carriage to Galesburg and Knoxville. At the Synod meeting in Chicago Hasselquist was received as a member. He remained a few days with Pastor Andersen, then continued via canal to La Salle, where he was met in La Salle by carriage which Esbjörn had arranged after his return home. It was at the end of October when Hasselquist came to Andover. He stayed over a Sunday and preached there. The church then had as yet neither windows, floor, or ceiling; services were held in the basement. His introductory words were based on 2 Cor. 11:2, "I betrothed you to Christ to present you as a pure bride to her one husband."

Afterward Esbjörn guided them to Galesburg and Knoxville to introduce the new pastor to the congregations there. They came to Galesburg in a driving rain. They met a Swede, and Esbjörn hoped to cheer him by telling him the new pastor had now come. The man responded, "What is he doing here?" The young couple found this less than encouraging.

That Fall the aforementioned Christen Jonsson came back from Sweden to Galesburg with a party of some 30 persons, among them his family of wife and 8 children, his old mother, and Nils Eliason, now in Chicago, Per Bodelson, now in Moline — all from northern Skåne. Christen Jonsson did not live long.

Some other groups came the same year. Sven Peterson was with a company from Gammalstorp in Blekinge. Nils Hokanson from Hjersås in Skåne had come back from California to Sweden and then returned in August of the same year with 50 who were all from Skåne except 5 from Gammalstorp and 1 from Jemshög. Most of these settled in Knoxville and Galesburg. One of them was the brother of Nils, P.L. Hokanson who later became Swedish vice-consul in Chicago.

Still another band left Jemshög, Blekinge, under the leadership of Peter Swenson. One of them, Hokan Olson, later became a minister. The following years brought large crowds from northern Skåne and Blekinge to the Galesburg region. It is hardly now possible to follow their paths.

2) *The Indiana immigrants from Viste and elsewhere.* The tanner apprentice Carl Peter Moberg from Grenna along with other young men from Jönköping had visited America early and lived here a few years. According to statements of Daniel Larson from Haurida, Moberg had come back to Sweden in 1844, settled in Grenna and there became a city council member. He and others spread abroad information about America in that region, giving rise to the desire to emigrate. Johannes Peterson, a peasant's son from Örserum, Grenna parish, was in America 1849, spending one or two years in Orange, Green County, New York. For some unknown reason he moved to Lafayette, Indiana in 1851. The above mentioned Moberg came back to America again in 1850, this time with his family and brother-in-law, tavern keeper Erikson from Jönköping, and others. They too took the road to Indiana and stopped at Yorktown, 14 miles from LaFayette. These were the first Swedes in this part of Indiana and they drew others there.

Thus, Johannes Peterson wrote to his brother Peter Peterson in

Örserum, urging him to bring his family to America. He followed the advice and a considerable number in Grenna went with him. They left in the summer of 1852, sailing from Gothenburg on the ,ship *Tanaro* to Boston. From there they moved westward to Albany, Buffalo, Toledo and LaFayette. They endured many hardships but were upheld by the hope of a better future in America. Another group from the same region soon followed. In 1853 and 1854 still other parties from Grenna, Vireda, Ölmstad, Skärstad, Adelöf, and neighboring parishes. They found their way to Indiana and settled in LaFayette, West Point, Attica, Millford, and Yorktown.

One of the parties in 1853 deserved special mention. Nils Hokanson, a wealthy peasant from Grantjärn, Vireda parish, with his family and a few others whose passage he had paid, travelled to New Orleans and then up the Mississippi and Ohio Rivers to Evansville in Indiana. From there they did not know where to turn. None of them could speak a word of English, and no one in the town understood what kind of people these were and where they wanted to go. Then an old devout woman, Mrs. Bjorklund, exclaimed, "There is nothing else we can do than to pray to God, if we pray He will surely help us." And they did pray, as many as were so minded. On the second day of their predicament there appeared unexpectedly a Swede, the only one in the place, who had lived there a long time, married to a German lady, and almost altogether divorced from his native tongue. The preceding night he had experienced a peculiar restlessness and in the morning had a feeling that he should go down to the boat landing. When he got here he found a whole flock of his countrymen, to his great astonishment. He gladly served as an interpreter and assisted them to go on to LaFayette, to their acquaintances and friends.

The immigration to this part of Indiana from the aforementioned places continued for a few years, so that by 1855 the number of Swedes was around 500. But cholers took many of them, especially in 1854. In 1856 some began to move to other parts of America.

3) *The coming of the Kronobergers.* Emigration from Kronoberg County seems not to have begun in any large number before 1852. In that year not a few left for America. Some took the route to Chisago Lake, Minnesota, becoming forerunners of the mass from this district that in following years settled on this frontier. Of those who arrived this year Magnus Johnson from Koppramåla in Linneryds parish was the leader.

4) *In Vestergötland there was the beginning of movement.* From

this large province there were indeed individual emigrants before 1852, but a mass of farm people did not come earlier than this year. The pioneer from here seems to have been a wagon-maker from Timmelhed, And. Anderson. He came in 1851, lived a while in St. Charles, then moved to Taylors Falls, Minnesota, where he died. One of his daughters was married in 1855 to Pastor Erland Carlsson.

One company from Vestergötland made St. Charles its goal in 1852, but lost many of its members there though through cholera and dysentery. After a while many scattered here and there, only a small number remaining. In this group were three brothers and their families, namely Thim, Lars Fran, and Anders Larson from Vings parish. Later one moved to Red Wing, on to Vasa, Minnesota. All are now dead, but the children are alive and prospering.

The same year another group came, and as previously mentioned, finally landed in Chicago after much hardship, only to suffer attacks of cholera. Some of these formed the core of the Immanuel Lutheran Congregation.

10. *Some of the immigrant groups of 1853.* Since the immigrant stream was now beginning to swell only a few particular groups can be described here.

1) *How Pastor Erland Carlsson came to America.* Pastor T.N. Hasselquist had organized a Swedish Evangelical Lutheran congregation in Chicago January 16, 1853, probably at the urging of the Norwegian pastor, Paul Andersen. The congregation chose as pastor J.P. Dahlstedt of Vexiö diocese. The call was forwarded to Dr. P. Fjellstedt in Lund. In case Pastor Dahlstedt could not accept, Fjellstedt was authorized to transmit it to any minister he deemed best and most promising. Because of ill health and other reasons Dahlstedt was out of consideration. The call, by the special providence of God, was turned over to Erland Carlsson who then had been serving for nearly four years in the Vexiö diocese as an assistant pastor and chaplain in a mill town. Confident that this was God's will and with royal permission Carlsson set out in company with 176 emigrants on Friday, June 3 from Kalmar. Travelling via Lubeck, Hamburg, Hull and Liverpool, the party landed in New York August 13th after a long and uncomfortable voyage. On arrival in Chicago, August 22nd Pastor Carlsson was welcomed at the railroad station by members of his new congregation.

A large part of this group, which came from Kronoberg County and Blekinge, continued on to Chisago Lake, Minnesota. From the very beginning Carlsson had his hands full to counsel, help, and be concerned about the thousands of immigrants who streamed through Chicago. But he was cut out for just that. The work meant overexertion, and he was often exhausted, yet he endured for many years.

COL. HANS MATTSON.

2) *Hans Mattson and the trek of people from northern Skåne to Vasa, Minnesota.* As we have already noted, H. Mattson arrived in Boston, 1851, where he stayed for a while. When his father and brother came in 1852 from Sweden, he travelled with them to the West, and lived in and around Moline until the following year when he returned to Boston to meet his mother, other relatives, and a rather large group which he guided to Minnesota via Moline. With some of these be began the Swedish settlement in Vasa, Goodhue County, Minnesota in the Fall of 1853. From this date to 1860 there followed an influx direct from northeastern Skåne to this settlement, so that it became one of the larger ones in America.

3) *A company from Helsingland and southern Medelpad* came late in the Fall of 1853 from Gefle via New York and Chicago. In Chicago some remained for some time. Some went on to Rock Island and Moline, and then the following year to Minnesota, where to begin with they stayed in Chisago Lake. Members of this group became the founders of the Swedish pioneer settlement in Cambridge, Isanti County, Minnesota.

11. *1854, the Cholera Year.* A large emigration from various parts of Sweden took place this year, but a huge number was swept away by cholera which raged more violently than in any previous year. The misery which was apparent along the highways of immigrant travel, Chicago, Rock Island, Moline and elsewhere, defies description.

This year witnessed an increase in the migration from Värmland. Erik Peterson was one of several brothers in Karlskoga that belonged to a wealthy and eminent family. One of the brothers had gone to Australia, Erik to California. He had looked around in America for a suitable spot for a settlement. He thought he had discovered such on the Wisconsin side of Lake Pepin. He went back to Värmland and returned here in 1854 with a host of relatives, friends and acquaintances from his home region. Many succumbed to cholera in Chicago and later Moline. There was deep distress. For some reason Erik Peterson, who was treasurer for most of the group, had left the party in Chicago and gone ahead to Moline. In all probability he did intend to proceed to Lake Pepin, for he had written to his fellow travellers that when they met in Lake Pepin they would receive their money. This caused anxiety among those interested, and they brought charges against him before the Swedish consul in Chicago. The result was that Peterson received a telegram to come back to Chicago and was required to pay what he had obtained from others. When he reached Lake Pepin with what remained of the party they established themselves on the eastern shore and called the place Stockholm. Thus began the large Swedish population in Pepin County, Wisconsin, which increased each year by new groups mainly from Värmland. Erik Peterson was sometimes called "the king in Stockholm," and admittedly he liked the role of ruler. He might have been of great good here, but he was too selfish and capricious and religiously altogether without principles, harming both himself and others. An accident led to his death in 1887.

In Rockford Swedes had begun to make their home 1852-53. A large increase occurred in 1854. Though various provinces of Sweden were represented, Västergötland and Småland furnished the largest numbers.

Many from Habo and nearby parishes in Västergötland and from several parishes in Småland came to Geneva and St. Charles for a while. Sooner or later many moved to various places in Minnesota, especially Goodhue County. The congregation in Cambridge is more than half made up of members of this group or their descendants.

Among others in this party were Carl Johan Fors and family, now in Goodhue; Johannes Holm with his large family, whose son Anders had come to America a couple of years earlier and been in St. Charles or Geneva; Johan and Ludwig Miller, J.P. Gustafson, who were from Habo and Bankeryd and now live in Spring Garden, Goodhue County, Minnesota; J. Rystrom and Jon Pehrson from Jemshög, who later became a pastor in the Augustana Synod. This group numbered around 450, many from Skåne and Blekinge, and had left Liverpool on the sailing vessel *Esmeralda*. Emigrant agent Jonson of Gothenburg was along as interpreter. In Liverpool they had played the role of Charles XII grenadiers. A contract had been made to carry the baggage from the railroad station to the docks. One driver had piled a double load on his large wagon and then demanded double the price. When the Swedes would not pay more than the price agreed on per load, the driver refused to unload. The Swedes paid no attention to his demands and began to take their things off themselves. A boy driver on top the load used his whip on the Swedes while the old man himself stood on the ground, yelling and upbraiding them loudly. The Swedes got angry. One climbed up and threw the boy to the ground. A couple from Habo held the old fellow while the rest unloaded the wagon. That was it. A whole row of policemen stood looking on, laughing at the whole affair, and remarking, "those Swedes aren't too easy to take on."

In another party that came to Geneva that year was Peter Carlson, later a pastor in the Augustana Synod, with his relatives and others from Småland, in all about 30. They had come over after 10-11 weeks at sea, and on their arrival cholera cut down half their number within a short time.

Immigrants from Vestergötland founded the East and West Union settlements in Carver County, Minnesota. In 1853 Johannes Hult and family from Bitterna, Jonas Carlson and family from Ryda, together with several others from the same region, came to America on the *Minona* and landed in Boston. In Gothenburg they had joined with other emigrants from Skåne, Halland, and Blekinge, so that in all they were 84 on the voyage. The party separated in Buffalo, when the majority went on to Illinois, and Hult and a few with him went to Dunkirk. Here he met his brother Anders who with a third brother Peter, had come to America the year before. Peter was now in southern Illinois, working on the Illinois Central railroad.

In Dunkirk they worked for a farmer in harvesting for 75 cents a day. "Since we got our meals and tools we thought it was an unusually high wage," they reported. Then they decided to look up Peter. They went by train to Cincinnati, by boat to Shawneetown in Illinois, and by horse and wagon 60 miles to the railroad construction site. They stayed until the following March, working occasionally for $1.25 per day, feeding themselves. They suffered much from illness. One married couple died.

In March 1854 they set out by horse and carriage to St. Louis, Missouri 60 miles away. Their intention now was to buy land. They happened to meet a Swede who advised them to go to Minnesota. They followed his advice, took boat up the Mississippi arriving in St. Paul April 12th. By May they had established themselves in E. Union, 4 miles from the Minnesota River. Nils Alexanderson from Kronoberg County was already there before Hult's coming and right afterward Sven Gudmundson from Elfsborgs County's Hössna appeared. "After we had found a home for ourselves," J. Hult narrated, "I wrote to Jonas Carlson who had been in our company across the ocean and then was in Princeton, Illinois, and in a few months he came with his family. Then I wrote to Anders Stomberg who had come in 1852 and dwelt in Indiana. He came with his family and others in the Fall of 1854 — they were from Herrljunga, Elfsborg County. Then they wrote their relatives, and so a large settlement developed here."[1]

The settlement at Scandian Grove, Nicollet County, Minnesota also arose out of an immigration direct from Sweden. A party came in 1856 from northern Skåne with A. Thorson, who with his brother-in-law Andrew Nilson, has rendered great service in the starting and development of this community.

These are some of the well-known, probably the outstanding, immigrant groups who up to 1854 came from Sweden, and constitute the pioneer settlements in America. Prior to 1860 not many immigrants came by steamship. After that date it became more usual and finally the common means, and then began the mass immigration of thousands

[1]Information from J. Hult, East Union, Carver Co., Minnesota

annually. Since this change occurred it is no longer possible to follow the groups to certain destinations. No longer are the migrants from one province, and when they reach these shores they disperse into the older settlements and from there to new communities.

PART II

The Origin and Development of Settlements and Lutheran
Congregations in America before 1860.

Foreword

The rich opportunities for fruitful and easily acquired land, as
well as favorable laws, which welcomed and encouraged the influx
and settlement of people from other countries, enticed persons to forsake their ancestral homes in order to seek here their fortune. Everywhere the land stood open, awaiting the diligent and honest worker;
the rapid development in all directions of every kind of industry
needed all forces that could be recruited; for newcomers as well as
for natives the gates stood open for livelihood, prosperity and honor.
In such circumstances there undoubtedly lay a powerful impulse to
fuse all these nationalities coming together in this land into a unity
and thus prevent the rise and establishment of colonies of foreign
groups. But such a fusion cannot happen all at once, and on the other
hand there are important reasons for the origin and maintenance of
such colonies and settlements for an extended time. These reasons
are: language, nationality and religion. How precious is not one's
native tongue in a strange land, at least as long as one is ignorant of
the language there! As a rule the immigrant seeks his fellow-countrymen with whom he can communicate. He knows the pleasure of living together with people whose national view of life, whose ways of
thinking, being, and acting harmonize with his own views and
customs. Yet slowly these ties loosen, and the second generation
among the Swedish immigrants is usually far advanced in change of
language and in American ideas. The rate of this change depends
naturally quite a bit on situation and circumstances. In cities
Americanization in language, customs and sentiments takes place
rather rapidly, more slowly in the large Swedish rural settlements,
though even there the children and young people prefer the English
language and have absorbed the American spirit and thoughtpattern.
What has delayed a complete Americanization, and may yet do so
for a long time, is the recourse to a rich supply of Swedish literature,
especially Swedish newspapers with a very considerable circulation,
and the presence of Swedish schools and colleges, but above all, of
the Swedish form of worship.

Religion has been and is the strongest force in creating and
maintaining the Swedish pioneer communities in America. Our
Swedish Lutheran people have gathered around the church and it is
around the church that the largest settlements have arisen. The congregation has been a far more influential factor than the local com-

munity, and congregational life has affected our people much more than the American civic organization. True, this has sometimes been criticized as showing a lack of interest in citizenship, but on the other hand it is acknowledged that our people in general and our church people in particular are among the most law-abiding of this country's citizens. Such criticism is therefore unwarranted. From the Christian point of view it must be admitted that the highest obligation for Christians is to set religion and its duties in the foremost place, in accordance with the words of Christ, "Seek first the kingdom of God and His righteousness and all these things will be yours as well."

Chapter One

The Swedish Settlements and Congregations in Iowa.

In 1845 a small group left Östergötland for America and established itself at New Sweden, on the Skunk River, Jefferson County, Iowa. This place, originally called Brush Creek, was 42 miles west of the thriving city of Burlington, on the Mississippi River.

The small party consisted of 5 families, 4 from Kisa in Östergötland, and 1 from Stockholm, as well as a few unmarried persons. We know the names of P. Kassel, the leader; Peter Anderson, his brother-in-law; one Danielson; Berg and family from Stockholm; a shipmaster from Stockholm, Dahlberg, who had been in America a couple of years before Kassel and whose family came with Kassel. It seems that Dahlberg met the party in New York, that he knew about Iowa, advised it to go there, and himself went along. He later left New Sweden but it is not known for what destination. Another member of the party was an Okerman, who had been in America before and served as a soldier for three years. He went back to Sweden, but was now here again with Kassel. He served as interpreter for the party on the way to Iowa. The next year he left for Fort Des Moines, re-enlisted in the U.S. Army, and met his death in the Mexican War. These are the names of some of the pioneers who settled in New Sweden.

After they had acquired land and begun to feel at home in the new country P. Kassel and others wrote home to Sweden and told what they had learned, praising everything. This enticed a whole mass from Östergötland. Several families came to New Sweden in 1846. Another large group left the same year to come here but, as mentioned elsewhere, got no farther than Buffalo because of lack of means. Two families and two single men from Stockholm arrived in 1847. There was now a small number of renters in the place. There was much sickness among those who came first, and they had difficulty in becoming accustomed to the climate and food of the country; grief, lack of proper care, poverty and need all contributed to ill health and death. The more affluent in the party did what they could to help those in need, and in this were aided by Americans in the neighborhood, when they learned of conditions. At that time the area was sparsely settled, homes being far from each other.

Soon the hardships were overcome. The newcomers began to adjust to the climate and the habits and customs of the land. They won general confidence, by industry and the blessing of God they were soon in better circumstances. Now they began to realize their spiritual needs — the preaching of the Word and the use of the sacraments. Among the Americans a preacher would now and then make a visit. But the Swedes, especially the older ones, would not understand him. A man named Hokanson (later Pastor M.F. Hokanson who had come to America in 1847) from Stockholm was asked to lead in their devotional gatherings. He had sought to conceal his spiritual life, partly fearing he might be called on to serve as minister, partly for other reasons, but when he realized the dire spiritual conditions in which many found themselves, he could not remain silent. He began to proclaim the Gospel simply and to praise the love of Christ who so graciously receives sinners. The result was that in 1848 the people did call him as their religious leader. He did not immediately agree, for it was not his intention to remain in this place. But after some thought and reflection on God's wonderful dealing with him he yielded to the insistent prayers of the people and accepted the call as from God. He did not intend to devote himself to the task indefinitely, for he was conscious of his weakness and incompetence. In view of the great need and emergency he hoped to keep the people in the Lutheran faith and confession until the numbers increased and conditions improved to the point where they could call a pastor from Sweden. Then he would withdraw.

Hokanson began his work as pastor here in 1848. The settlement grew each year, and the congregation increased. No formal organization took place, but the members looked on themselves as members of a Lutheran congregation as was the custom in Sweden. The Word of God began to bear fruit, many were awakened to spiritual life, the youth were confirmed, the sacraments administered, the liturgy of the Swedish Church was followed. The religious life was ordered as in Sweden, and with few exceptions everybody was happy and content.

In the summer of 1849 a Swedish Episcopal minister came on a visit. He strongly disapproved of their church arrangements, and tried to show them that it was impossible to have a congregation without a duly ordained minister. He claimed that a Christian community did not in any circumstance have the right to call a pastor who has not been consecrated to the office by a bishop. He criticized especially Hokanson for his presumptuous and inconsiderate behavior. Yet he was courteous and conducted himself in a worthy manner. In his *Memoirs* [Minnen] Unonius says nothing of this encounter except that he visited New Sweden. Had he followed the constitution of the Church of Sweden in regard to bishops, he could have helped rather than harmed these people, who were not breaking away from the Church, rather were loyal to it. But his blind devotion to the Anglican doctrine of apostolic succession prevented him from acting here and in other Swedish settlements with a real understanding of conditions. Hokanson could fall back on the words of Luther that in emergency a congregation could select one of its own, and since Word and Sacrament belong to the congregation it was necessary to have a leader who provides them. So he was clear in his conscience as to his own part, but he feared for confusion among the people. They had imagined that America was a land of freedom in regard to such matters, and not subject to criticism of religious arrangements, least of all by someone not invited to meddle in their religious practices.

Hokanson was troubled, too, by the fear that he might in this situation become known as a factionist, whereas he had always hated partisanship. He was an heir of the older pietism, and though he had become more evangelical through the reading of Luther and acquaintance with evangelical friends, he had remained firm in his adherence to the Church of Sweden even it relation to the State, and he was opposed to all forms of separatism. He had thought that so far away in the West he could be altogether unknown and unnoticed. Disappointed he was entertaining ideas of resigning his position and leaving the settlement. But how would it then go with the religious life of the people and with the souls that has been awakened and were touched by the grace of God? It was impossible under present circumstances for them to call a pastor from Sweden. His conscience would not let him leave this people, but he became deeply perplexed in this troublesome situation.

At this juncture Hokanson received letters, greetings, and encouragement from a Swedish Methodist minister, Jonas Hedstrom in Victoria, Ill., who promised to visit the settlement. The entire congregation was happy, and Hokanson who judged Methodism in America according to his acquaintance with the Wesleyan Methodist George Scott in Stockholm, had complete confidence in that Church's unselfish endeavor for the extension of the Kingdom of God everywhere. So a letter was sent welcoming Hedstrom. He came in 1850 to New Sweden, but imagine Hokanson's dismay when he found his visitor was an enemy of the Lutheran Church! All liturgical practices were fanatically denounced, from baptism to burial, not least clerical bands and coat. The sinless perfection of the converted was proclaimed not only as possible but necessary.

The people were both confused and embittered. Hokanson sought the counsel of the leaders, P. Kassel and Danielson, but found to his amazement that they seemed to favor the new teaching. The former confidence was gone, they were now silent and reserved. What was now to be done?

After Hedstrom's departure Hokanson began to explain the difference between Methodist and Lutheran doctrines, showing how the latter agreed with the Word of God and the experience of all the faithful. External forms he said were not of the same importance as the doctrine — one could have one or another form if not offensive, just so the doctrine was pure. He proposed that the congregation should decide if present practices should continue or changes be made. He would be agreeable in any case, since he was not bound to forms, but he would not preach any other than the old Lutheran doctrine, indeed would defend it against all attacks. No one seemed to object to the latter, but Kassel and Danielson requested several changes. Not realizing the peril of making changes under the present circumstances, even if they be in indifferent things, only in order to satisfy sect spirit, it was resolved not to have sponsors at baptisms, omit the prayers for churching of mothers unless requested, and in place of the usual confession of sins there be an extempore prayer by the preacher. Calm was restored for the present.

After a couple of months Hedstrom returned. Kassel, Danielson and a Mr. Jocknick who had come to the settlement in 1847 from the Mexican War, received him with open arms. For a week he preached every day and went into the homes preaching the doctrine of perfection, condemning indiscriminately the whole Swedish clergy, calling the Lutheran Church the Babylonian whore. As best he could Hokanson opposed him. The people became frightened and exclaimed "What shall we believe. The preachers contradict each other." They were in doubt, cried and complained — they left all work and followed Hedstrom about. All the while Hedstrom was seeking by hook and crook to persuade Hokanson to become a Methodist. Hokanson refused, became troubled and depressed and in this mood made the mistake of resigning his position as leader in the presence of Hedstrom, Kassel and Danielson.

This increased the agitation. The people did not want to lose Hokanson as leader, but wanted him to become Methodist. Not successful in this, Hedstrom began in Hokanson's absence to cast reflection on him and undermine confidence in him.

Finally a Lord's Supper was arranged to which the true church members were invited and over half went over to Methodism. Most of them were good souls who earlier had experienced in some measure the grace of God in their hearts.

Thus this little planting of the Lord, which had just begun to grow, seemed doomed to destruction. Hokanson stood there with only a few of his former friends. The former peace was gone. Partisanship and hatred, before unknown, came in. Spiritual poverty and humility disappeared, instead arose a bold spiritual pride. The situation was deplorable. Yet Hedstrom thought he had done a great deed.

How was it possible for the people to be so led astray? The reason was that as immature Christians they had neglected to study for themselves the Word of God and the writings of old reliable teachers. They believed everything their beloved teacher told them, relying altogether on him. Now when he and his teaching were rejected they had no ground on which to stand, no treasured knowledge of their own, nothing by which to test. So they fell for this new charming teaching, which promised them sinless perfection in this life and liberated them from the distress of conflict with the flesh.

When the remnant regrouped Hokanson was again asked to be the leader. He considered himself relieved of this responsible position, and wanted to recommend another older, experienced Christian named P. whom he believed would not be averse to a call. On voting Hokanson was again elected. In his anxiety and fear that the choice depended more on the loyalty of the people than on the will of God, he proposed that the matter be settled by lot. The members fell on their knees and silently prayed that the Lord would in this way indicate which of the two should serve as teacher. The lot was cast, it fell on Hokanson. Now he saw that he must accept the call as of the Lord, but he did it with trepidation. Gradually calm was restored in the community, some of the Methodists returning. Many accepted the Word of God as a living force and it now appeared that the deplorable uproar had awakened many from spiritual slumber. Others began themselves to search the Scriptures, became established in the Truth and assured in their minds.

Brighter Prospects for the Lutheran Congregation

Shortly afterwards, the Lutherans received a letter from a Swedish pastor named L.P. Esbjörn, urging them to remain loyal to their faith and avoid all association with the Methodists, who had acted in like manner in Illinois. He exhorted Hokanson to continue as he had started and not be frightened by anyone, and promised to pay a visit soon. Esbjörn came in May 1851. He preached for them, exhorting and strengthening them in faith, told them of the situation of the Lutheran Church in America, promised to care for them and see that they became members of a Lutheran Synod. Thus he brought them encouragement and happiness.

During the summer Esbjörn arranged for Hokanson to receive license, or authorization, from the Joint Synod of Ohio, to serve as minister, as well as $70 as a subsidy for him from the same body. He also gave some assistance toward their church building.

New immigrant groups soon increased the population and the most of them joined the Lutheran congregation. Aided by the $300 gift from pastor Esbjörn the congregation built a small church out of rough-hewn logs. The worship forms of the Church of Sweden were again adopted, honesty and orderliness prevailed and the congregation had peace. Several Methodist preachers did come and tried to break in, but now the people knew them and their tactics, were not afraid of them, nor opening their church to them. Among these Methodists were the preachers A. Erikson, Peter Kallman, P. Nyberg, Smith, Jocknick and Kassel.

Early in April 1853 the congregation rejoiced in a visit by Pastor Hasselquist. He was helpful in developing their organization, and while he was there a sort of constitution was adopted by the congregation. In letters of Esbjörn to Hasselquist of March 24 and April 2, 1853, we learn that it had been proposed that Esbjörn and Valentin also should be in New Sweden on this occasion. But Esbjörn was prevented by sickness and Valentin couldn't afford the trip. Evidently Hasselquist traveled by horse and buggy from Galesburg, and the journey took four days each way.

New Disturbances. The Baptist Intrusion

Afterwards came the Swedish Baptist preachers, G. Palmquist, Fr. O. Nilson, A. Norelius and Rundquist, in that order. Through the first two the settlement was torn in conflict on the question of [infant] baptism. The Methodists quieted down and slowly withdrew. But the Lutherans, who had gained confidence in Palmquist by his evangelical sermons before he turned Baptist, were more vulnerable. Palmquist and Nilson were fanatical in their presentation of the Baptist doctrines, and everyone became involved. Hokanson was deeply disturbed. Palmquist and he were close friends from Sweden. Some of the deacons of the congregation were secretly inclined toward the Baptists, betraying the congregation, and hostile toward Hokanson. Yet Hokanson was sure in his own mind and thought no one could change him. The danger seems almost to have passed when some of his closest friends who lived a life of faith began to waver and soon allowed themselves to be re-baptized. Again a defeat and ruin, he thought. He was overwhelmed by fear and confusion and—fell. But he delayed a little time before being rebaptized.

A letter to Hasselquist from John Johnson, his nephew, then residing in Burlington, casts light on conditions in New Sweden and Burlington and Hokanson's plight at that time. The letter bears the date of February 26, 1854, and I quote the following from it:

I write at the request of many, and ask that Uncle may come here soon. The Lutherans are now without a pastor. Hokanson was here today and preached, then resigned from the Lutheran congregation. He is now Baptist, not yet baptized, but very likely will be as soon as possible. The Baptist Nilson has been up there with Hokanson preaching a whole week. As soon as Hokanson came to Burlington he was asked to baptize a child, but replied, 'I cannot do it, for I find no ground in Scripture for infant baptism.' This was last night. In his sermon he explained how he had come to think as he now does—Hoping to meet pastor Hasselquist in Burlington he had not fully decided what to do, but he claimed that Lutherans lack basis for infant baptism. He gave his farewell sermon this afternoon, taking as text Acts, ch. 20—There was quite a commotion in church, two divisions—one Baptist, one Lutheran, the one happy, the latter sorrowful. There are 11 here in Burlington who have become Baptists since Christmas, and it is possible there will be many more if a Lutheran pastor does not come here occasionally.

The congregation earnestly desires that Uncle would come as soon as he can, next Sunday if possible, otherwise on Palm Sunday, when we would celebrate the Lord's Supper.

I met Hokanson and had but a brief word with him. He said he wanted to meet Pastor Hasselquist, and that he also intended to write him soon and let Uncle know about his present condition. He has not yet preached his farewell sermon where he lives (New Sweden), but will probably do so next Sunday.—The congregation here is in a great deal of distress as to who is right, the Baptist or the Lutheran doctrine.—I write on behalf of the whole congregation.—

As soon as he could Pastor Hasselquist drove to Burlington and New Sweden. As he approached Hokanson's home, he met Hokanson, his wife, and a few others, bearing a basket of clothes, and walking down to the river. Hasselquist greeted him in a friendly manner and asked, "Where are you going today?" to which came the reply, "to receive the right baptism." "Then go in the name of the Lord!" said Hasselquist and continued on his way to the home in company with Mrs. Hokanson who had no desire to be a Baptist.

One can be sure that later there was an important conversation between them. God was gracious to Hokanson and led him to see what was right. With reasonableness and wisdom Hasselquist restored order again. Hokanson received back his office and worked among this people until November, 1856.

Since I believe it will tend to the glory of God and give a truer picture of the times, and especially reveal the sincerity and honesty of Hokanson in this sad distrubance, I want to quote from a letter, written by Hokanson to Esbjörn March 29, 1854, shortly after his restitution. I happened to be in Andover when it arrived and it was shared with me. It moved us, who had grieved deeply over Hokanson's defection, to indescribable joy and humble thanksgiving to God. This is the letter:

Dear Brother in Christ!

Since last I wrote you I have received two letters for which I heartily thank you! Thanks especially for the last one. In a fraternal spirit I have accepted all the serious, but brotherly, reproofs and truths you have given me. But what shall I now say, my heart is troubled. Behold, the devil has sifted me, but the Lord Jesus has prayed for me (I believe this) that my faith may not fail. Yes, my faith has been tested, hard tested. May it lead to improvement and establishment in the right faith and truth! Truly I had anxiety, conflict and strife before I could leave the Lutheran doctrine, not because I wanted to accept another, but because I loved the Lutheran and was unwilling to leave it. As you correctly observe, Brother, my mistake was in not seeking light and comfort in God's own Word but in reaching for Wiberg's book—the result was that I was deceived.

If I had misery before I joined the Anabaptists, I had no less afterwards. Remorse, anguish, despair and terror overwhelmed me, so that I was on the point of leaving wife and property. I became so disgusted with my new brethern that I hardly wanted to see them. One single day I was in their company, then I separated myself wholly from them. I regret, bemoan and deplore the unfortunate day that I disavowed the baptism I received as a child. May God for Jesus' sake forgive me my sin and comfort me in my wretchedness, so that I might come back to my former, peaceful, and blessed condition! May my fall be a warning to others! I will even confess that I never was fully convinced, but in a state of fear and agitation I went as a criminal to the place of execution. Brother Hasselquist was here last week. He has taught, restored and comforted me.

I now begin to see the difference between the baptism of John and the New Testament or Christ's baptism by the Spirit. The Anabaptists confuse these. I now have battle and strife with myself. My honor is discredited by my instability. I am ashamed in confessing my precipitation. Should a pastor behave in such a manner? My better self says, if you took such a step let it be therewith, otherwise you will be disgraced and demeaned all over the world. Yes, Brother, the old man in me suffers. Well, let it be so, let my reputation be whatever, just so God's will be done and I receive peace of conscience. Thanks that you, Brother, did not hastily write to the Synod President and demand my dismissal. My congregation has again called me and sympathetically begged me to still be their leader. Their love and confidence in me as well as their present need forbid me to say no. Though weak I nevertheless preached for them last Sunday.

With respect and friendliness,
M.F. Hokanson

New Sweden — March 29, 1854

This turbulence, too, like the earlier one had both good and bad consequences. The Lutheran Church lost some devout members, but others were awakened to a new life in God, and a small believing group of sincere souls gathered around Word and Sacrament and were happy in the Lutheran mother's bosom.

One while Swedish and Danish Mormon preachers were active in the settlement and tried to gain proselytes, but without success.

PASTOR M.F. HOCANSON.

Hokanson moved to Bergholm in Wappello County in November 1856, and the congregation was without a pastor until October 1858. During part of this time a school teacher by the name of Sandblom led in worship services. In January 1857 he was recommended to obtain a license from the Synod of Northern Illinois, to serve as pastor in New Sweden. For some reason he withdrew his application. Later he became a Methodist and settled in New Sweden as a farmer. During the vacancy Pastor Hasselquist visited New Sweden and Burlington as often as his time allowed, but this was not often. Also the two men who were studying theology under Hasselquist, Hokan Olson and John Johnson, came to the congregation and preached for the people.

At a meeting of the Mississippi Conference in Galesburg, April 1858, Sven Nilson appeared as a delegate from New Sweden and presented an urgent appeal from the congregation that it be provided with a pastor. The members promised a salary of $200, free residence and fire-wood, and held out the hope that other neighboring places would join them in securing added remuneration. The Conference resolved to issue a call to a pastor's assistant in Blekinge to serve New Sweden, but the attempt was fruitless.

Conditions in the Community and Congregation, the Spring of 1858.

An article in *Hemlandet*, No. 7, 1858 affords us a description of conditions in the settlement at this time. We read:

"The settlement lies in a wooded tract some 40-50 miles west of Burlington. A stream flows through the southern part— in rainy periods it becomes rather restless and violent. The land is, or rather was, marked by some trees and brushwood, with occasional larger trees, such as oak and others. In places it is quite hilly. As one enters the woods from the open prairies the scenery is unattractive, except for a farm now and then along the road. But as one approaches the Swedish settlement it begins to look more friendly and pleasant. The Swedes live near each other, the houses surrounded by open, cultivated fields. These together with smaller or larger groves of trees left standing and the few larger trees, combine to give the impression of a Swedish landscape. The soil is excellent, and is said to be firmer and more dependable than the deeper prairie land. So far there has not been a single year of crop failure. Not only have land values risen considerably recently and conveniences increased by the growth of the settlement and the cultivation of the land, but the coming of a railroad has increased the prospect of prosperity. (The reference is to the Burlington and Missouri Railroad, which then had reached Rome on the Skunk River, 4 or 5 miles from New Sweden, with the hope of a station only 2 miles from the Lutheran Church[1]).

"At this time (1858) there were not less than around 500 of our countrymen in the area, of which number 100 were families. The majority hail from Linköping County, but others are from various parts of the fatherland. The first to come were in 1845, thereafter the population has grown every year, but especially in the Fall of 1857, when the numbers increased by one-sixth. One can easily imagine the obstacles and trials encountered by the first

[1] *Hemlandet*, 1858:10

settlers. 86 families now own no less than a total of 5065 acres, 1788 of which are already cultivated. Only 360 acres were purchased as "government land" at $1.25 per acre. The rest has been bought by others at a price of $2 to $24 per acre. The 86 families own individually as follows: 1-200 acres, 10 between 100-200 acres, 12 between 80-100 acres, 9 between 60-80 acres, 36 between 40-60 acres, 13 between 20-40 acres, 5 under 20 acres.

"In regard to the church the largest number have been loyal to the doctrine and creed of the Church of the motherland. Pastor F. M. Hokanson has been a faithful servant of the Lutheran congregation, until a year or so ago he accepted a call from a smaller Swedish community further west in Iowa. Hitherto no one has described his toils, troubles and suffering, but we hope the story may soon be told. We would not claim that Brother Hokanson has had only difficulties in his first place in America, for he has there experienced wonderful proof of the 'steadfast Shepherd's' concern and the efficacy of His precious grace. New Sweden will undoubtedly remain for him a beloved home on earth.

"The congregation has a building of oak timbers, and holds quite a large number, though it would soon prove to be too small if the church had a leader around whom they could confidently gather. They are eagerly and seriously seeking such. At present a Baptist (?!) has volunteered to lead the public devotional hours.

"The Methodists have a congregation in the community and a building of about the same kind and size as the Lutherans. They have the advantage of a resident pastor, who, according to Methodist custom, remains 2 to 3 years. The present one is a Mr. Nyberg.

"Also there is a small Baptist congregation, started some over one year ago by the Baptist minister (F.O.) Nilson, with 13 members but it has neither church building nor pastor."

The Congregation during H. Olson's Pastorate 1858-68

On the call of the congregation and with the advice and cooperation of the Conference, H. Olson came to New Sweden in October 1858. There were then about 100 communicant members. The small log church, 32 ft. long, 24 ft. wide, was adequate, except at festive occasions. The congregation owned 2 acres on a corner, across from the church, with a log cabin, 16 ft. square, as residence — in 1859 two rooms were added. At this time there was talk of building a new church. A special meeting was held January 21, 1860. It was decided to remove the log structure and in its place erect a frame church, 50 ft.

long, 30 ft. wide, 16 ft. high side walls, with balcony and tower. Work started in March 1860. The members, blessed with very favorable weather, worked with great zeal and progress. While the building was going up the question arose about obtaining a bell in the tower. J.P. Anderson loaned the congregation $150 and at his own expense made a trip to St. Louis, to order the bell. When the tower was ready there was a small well-sounding bell ready to be hung there. In calm weather its tone could be heard 6-7 miles away.

The church was hardly finished when a new proposal was made. Mr. J. Lovendahl expressed the wish to be allowed to build a small organ, four octaves, for the balcony. J.P. Anderson agreed to contribute the necessary material. The church was completed by August 10, 1861, when it was dedicated. Pastor Hasselquist was present and gave the dedicatory address, based on St. John 5:2,3. It was a rare festival for the congregation, which now had a new and large enough edifice, almost entirely paid for. The organ was finished the next year, costing the congregation about $200.

The Spring of 1862, in the Lenten season, it seemed that the angel of the Lord in a spiritual sense descended and stirred the waters of this Bethesda. A spiritual movement and awakening was apparent throughout the congregation. Many anxiously inquired, "What shall I do to be saved?" It would be possible to describe several remarkable awakenings and conversions from this period, but it is sufficient to say that the movement was general and that the leader was fully occupied in instructing, guiding, and caring for the troubled souls. True, many promising blossoms fell away, but many ripened and bore fruit. Afterwards many recalled thankfully the spiritual Spring time they had witnessed. Then they were prepared, as Israel at the foot at Sinai, to promise "All that the Lord commands us that we will hear and do." After the glorious Spring and time of blossoms came Fall and Winter, but every thing will serve for the best to those who fear the Lord. The season of heat was not wanting, with vexations and trials.

By 1868 the communicant membership had grown to over 200 communicants. Immigration direct from Sweden still continued, but moving away had also begun, especially to the new settlement in Freeport, or Swedesburg, to which also Pastor H. Olson removed in 1869. A larger parsonage, meanwhile, with six rooms, had been built [in New Sweden] in 1867.

To the East and the West of the Lutheran Church two other Swedish churches were built, one a Baptist, one a Methodist. Neither one of these grew much after the original attempts. At the end of this period the Methodist congregation counted 50 communicants, the Baptist, 21.

Pastor Olson describes the development of the settlement in secular matters thus: "When I came here our countrymen had not been able to cultivate much around their homes. Most of the land was covered by low woods. Many were in debt for more than their small holdings were worth. Some left and moved to Illinois. But the Lord soon gave us better times. Our neighbors talk about and admire the industriousness and diligence of our countrymen. For instance I read recently in the *Burlington Hawk Eye* an article in which our settlement was given as an example of what can be achieved by diligence, industry and orderliness. Anyone who saw our place 10 years ago would now hardly recognize it. Here are now large cultivated fields, where formerly were bushes and thickets. Instead of small log houses one now finds impressive frame houses. Some have large and splended orchards and vineyards, and what is of most importance — the majority have paid their debts."

2. Burlington

As far as the church is concerned the Swedes in Burlington were an annex to the congregation in New Sweden. Therefore I treat of them here though there were older settlements in Iowa. Not long after the establishment of New Sweden there were Swedes who came here and made their homes, but I have not been able to discover who were the first. By 1850 they had reached the number of a couple hundred in and around the town. Pastor F.M. Hokanson reported in 1857 that "there are not many property owners. Mostly they are families who stay here awhile, and then go farther inland, but others come in their place. There are a number of young people who work in the town. The majority are from Östergötland. In the Spring of 1851 pastor Esbjörn and I were guests in the home of a Swedish man, Brydolph by name, who was married to an American woman. He seemed prosperous. He was the son of a pastor in Nerike and had served in the Mexican War. He later lost an arm in the Civil War but attained the rank of colonel. He was an educated and intelligent person, very tolerant, but without religious interest and Swedish sentiments."

Hokanson worked among the Swedes in Burlington as early as 1850, seeking to hold them in the Lutheran Church. The Methodists attempted to win some for their faith, though without much success prior to 1860. On the other hand the Baptists made great inroads among the Lutherans in 1854. As in New Sweden there was no formal organization of the Lutheran congregation before 1859. There was some talk of it in May 1851 when Esbjörn visited the place, preached and administered sacraments, but he did not seem to be in a hurry to form a congregation. Nor did I hear of any urging that Hokanson, who was with us a few days in Burlington, should undertake an organization. Yet the Swedes considered themselves already as a Lutheran congregation, and many were devout and concerned about churchly order. Hokanson came once a month. Many attended services both in the morning and the afternoon, were attentive to the Word. Many began to inquire about the way to life, and some attained a life of true faith. These latter exercised a great influence on all the others. The greater part of the young people were open for the Word of God. On the Sundays when Hokanson was not present, they still came together both in the morning and afternoon. Then one of the older persons with spiritual experience would read the Word, there would be singing of hymns and spiritual songs, and some one would lead in prayer.

When Palmquist and Nilson came in 1854 they came under false colors. At first they preached the Gospel without mention of baptism and not letting any one in any way understand that they were Baptists. When they had gained the confidence of people they would broach the question of baptism with individual believers and lead them astray. They then proceeded to preach openly and almost exclusively on baptism. The unity of the congregation and mutual trust was now destroyed. The most devout and mature submitted to re-baptism. Others withdrew, no gatherings were held on Sundays, some became bitter. The Baptists assembled by themselves, partly because they were ashamed to meet the others, partly because they now considered themselves a pure congregation of God which did not want to associate with the unbaptized. Later most of them moved to Minnesota, where they founded a settlement they named Scandia, by Clear Lake in the vicinity of Waconia in Carver County. Hokanson's joining with the Baptist naturally made matters worse, but since no one doubted his sincerity or honesty, he was able after his reinstitution to continue without hindrance his ministry, as he had begun. Afterwards the people held to the Lutheran faith, but spiritual revivals did not occur except in a few individual cases. For many years they had no church building, but they had the privilege of assembling without cost in a large and attractive school house in the town. After Hokanson's move from the area in 1856 a Mr. Sandblom served for some time.

When H. Olson in the Fall of 1858 received license from the Synod of Northern Illinois to serve as a pastor he was stationed in New Sweden with the provision that he should visit Burlington as often as his time permitted. A formal organization of the congregation took place in 1859. It was entered in the Synod's statistics in 1861, when S.G. Larson became the first resident pastor of the congregation.

3. Swede Point, Boone County, Iowa

In 1846 a widow by the name Dalander with her 4 sons and 2 daughters joined a party from Östergötland, presumably from the Kisa area, leaving for America. They intended to reach Racoon Fork, in Iowa (near Des Moines) expecting to meet with P. Kassel. In this they failed. One part then got to Jefferson County (New Sweden) where they did find Kassel, and stayed there. Others in their search had seen the areas to the northwest and found attractive prairies with woods, not yet on the market. They thought it would be better to take claims there, since they had already spent so much of their money in travelling about. So each laid claim to several hundred acres in Boone County, at a place later called Swede Point. It was 25 miles north of Des Moines, now the capitol of Iowa, but then called Fort Des Moines, a small dirty place consisting of a few log houses.

Northward were hardly any habitations. Here they were almost by themselves, without any tools. They built small log houses and supported themselves as best they could, not always without need and distress. Gradually they acquired farm animals and began to till the soil and soon had enough for their support. But it was 80 miles to the nearest mill, where they could have their grain ground, and 25 miles to the nearest town, Ft. Des Moines. One can easily imagine the plight and privation of these few families during these days. But they were patient and waited for better days.

Meanwhile two of the widow Dalander's sons found work to the south and had some income, while two remained at home and cultivated the land, thus each contributing to the welfare of the family, so that when it became possible to purchase their claims they were able to buy most of what they had claimed. Not many others were in a position to meet the terms of purchase, and had to leave the claim, losing all the effort they had expended on it. These then moved 25 miles further north and settled in Webster County near the Des Moines River. Here they took claims on both sides of the River, began again to build and cultivate, and succeeded eventually to retain at least the area they had worked.

Little by little circumstances improved in Swede Point. Around 1857 the Dalander family was rich and respected. On their own land they had platted a town, called Swede Point, which grew annually in population and activity. Most of the settlers were Americans, but in 1855 there were 10 Swedish families. Before 1860 the land in the vicinity cost from 10 to 25 dollars an acre. There were not then many Swedes, but they were known for their honesty and proper behavior, their hospitality and friendliness. Some were seriously God-fearing.

From the beginning there was an older, devout person who led in the religious gathering and held the group to the Lutheran profession. His name was Jacob Nilson. When the old man was unable to continue his place was taken by one of the Dalanders. In this way they encouraged the members by the reading of Scripture and prayer, and the old man would give serious talks, which were not without blessing, especially for the youth. Swedish Methodists did try to intrude on them and convert them, but without success. The Swedes were more cautious here than they have been in many other places, and they didn't want to hear other than Lutheran preachers. When any preacher came and offered to preach for them they first inquired as to his church connection, and if he were not Lutheran they would neither listen nor open their houses to him. It was not that they were fearful, but they wanted to live in peace in the faith in which they had been nourished. Only a couple of individuals joined the Methodists before 1857. Pastor M.F. Hokanson visited the place a few times before 1855. Afterwards a Norwegian was there a short time. His name was O. Anfinson, licensed by the Synod of Northern Illinois to serve as minister among the Norwegians in Story County, Iowa, but never ordained. A Swedish Evangelical Lutheran congregation was organized in 1859, with a membership of 36 communicants. It was cared for by Pastor F.M. Hokanson up to 1867, when the communicants had grown in number to 108.

4. The Swedish Settlement in Webster County — Swede Bend

The first Swedes who settled here were those who had been unable to secure their claims in Boone County. Others have come since, either directly from Sweden or from other settlements, drawn by the cheap lands prior to 1860. To begin with they acquired only government land, but when this was exhausted they bought from speculators at 2 1/2 to 4 dollars an acre. After 1857 the price of land began to rise.

Originally the land was not very attractive. It was somewhat low-lying flat land with some trees along the water courses. The soil is good for corn, not so favorable for wheat but rye thrives well. Soon there was no lack of rye bread and pork in the homes. Even up to 1860 the Swedes, with few exceptions, lived in their primitive log houses. Within the homes everything, customs and costumes, remained Swedish for a long time, especially among the older folk. One was received with hospitality and friendliness. Now the people are well-off. Some are from Östergötland, some from Kalmar County, Småland, and a few from northern Sweden.

Ungodliness characterized the community at first, not only unmindful of religion but behaving ill also in civic matters. For some years they were left to themselves, and no minister of any denomination came to preach to them. The first one who did come was a Swedish Protestant Methodist by the name of Smith. He had been dropped by his own denomination and wanted to try his luck here. He thundered away at the commandments, and the people condemned in their consciences, repented and confessed their sins. Yearning for the forgiveness of sins they now fell eagerly for the Methodist doctrine of righteousness, which not content with a sinner being accounted righteous declares that he is made righteous, that is intrinsically holy and without sin in all his life. Yet some began to discover that sin was not altogether gone, the old nature still persisted. People became anxious, confused, and were not sure what they should think about this new doctrine.

They sent for Pastor Hokanson (1854?) and asked him to show them the difference between the Lutheran and Methodist doctrine, especially in regard to justification. The result was that almost all came back to the Lutheran faith, and this so decisively that he had to let each one subscribe his own name, else they were not sure that they had departed from Methodism. Those who did not return became bitter and reviled the others. There were those who never went over to the Methodists but remained Lutheran.

News of the situation spread, and soon the Episcopal-Methodist preachers P. Kassel and And. Erikson appeared, to denounce the Lutheran doctrines as they are now proclaimed. We Methodists, they said, are those who teach what Luther taught — the so-called

Lutherans only oppose all living Christianity. So the people believed them and went over to the Episcopal Methodists. Then Smith returned, and the Protestant Methodists were locked in conflict with the Episcopal Methodists. The latter won. But then the Baptist preachers came, and converted many to the Baptist faith, who allowed themselves to be rebaptized. P. Nyberg and And. Erikson were soon on the scene, bringing them back to Methodism. And. Erikson remained here and upheld the Methodist banner. He hailed from Bollnäs in Helsingland, came to America in 1849, settled first in Victoria, Illinois, where he owned 10 acres of land. This he sold in 1854 and bought an 80 acre farm in Swede Bend, where he remained until his death, sometime between 1870-80. He was probably in the Esbjörn party from Sweden, 1849.

On this battle-field, where the population did not go much over 100 even in 1860, a Lutheran congregation was organized in 1859 by Pastor M.F. Hokanson, with a communicant membership of 40. The congregation built a frame structure in 1865, and remained under Hokanson's care until 1866 — it then counted 130 communicants. The first resident Lutheran pastor was C.J. Malmberg who came in 1867.

5. The Swedish Settlement Bergholm in Wapello County, Iowa

In 1847 the aforementioned Peter Anderson from New Sweden together with C. Kilberg (from Halland and who in 1885 lived with many relatives in Seattle, Washington Territory) and some others moved to Wapello County and settled down in the place now called Bergholm. Each acquired several hundred acres, consisting both of forest and open land. The area is attractive, the climate fresh and healthful. The tract developed significantly even in the first ten years. Several towns grew up on all sides, Blakesburg 4-5 miles away, Cuba 3 miles, Eddyville 9 miles, Ottumwa 10-12 miles. The last named soon became an important town. Almost an excessive number of sawmills and flour mills were built. Just before 1860 cultivated land sold for 10-12 dollars, untilled was cheaper, but property was steadily rising in value.

Swedes came into the region during several years. Around 1853-54 many families and single persons came direct from Sweden. By 1857 there were 22 Lutheran families. For a time they lived without any contact with or knowledge of other Swedes in America. They conducted themselves properly in civic matters, were sociable, hospitable and amiable. In time some became wealthy, all were in good circumstances. Their holdings varied, from 40 to 400 acres each. Most had come from Halland district, some from Östergötland.

After a while they began to long for the preaching of the Word and the use of the sacraments. They were not in a position to engage a resident pastor, even if such had been available. But the older persons called an American Lutheran pastor, named Schaeffer, to come every third Sunday to preach and care for their religious needs. The more recent members were not satisfied, for they did not understand the minister and they wanted someone who could preach in Swedish. Pastor Schaeffer served only one year. Then Pastor Hokanson was called to visit them, and he came as often as it was possible for him.

Finally in the spring of 1856 an Evangelical Lutheran congregation was organized, called Bergholm and numbering 50 communicant members. Pastor Hokanson was called to be resident pastor and in November he moved there. A healthy spiritual movement was soon evident also here. As usual Methodists and Baptists appeared and tried to divide the congregation and win the unstable, but they were unsuccessful, thanks to the pastor's activity, and next to the grace of God to Peter Anderson. He defended the Lutheran position and in every possible way tried to hold the Lutherans together in their faith. He strove to effect the organization of a congregation and the securing of a resident pastor, himself contributing quite large sums for this purpose.

Hokanson moved in 1859 to Swede Point, and Pastor H. Olson was in charge of the congregation through 1861. There was a vacancy for a year until in 1862 Pastor Hokanson was again called. The congregation does not appear in the statistical table of Synod in 1860, but in 1861 reported 59 communicants. The church building dates from 1863. 113 communicants were listed in 1868. The number was due to the fact that the settlement was small at the beginning and never received any increase from outside.

These are the first congregations in Iowa, 5 in number, which antedate the formation of the Augustana Synod in 1860.[1]

[1]Sources: Information from Pastors M.F. Hokanson and H. Olson, from Pastor T.N. Hasselquist in *Det Gamla och Nya Hemlandet*, Pastor L.P. Esbjörn, author's own notes and observations.

Chapter Two

Andover, Henry County

Andover is situated about 20 miles southeast of Rock Island and Moline and 25 miles north of Galesburg. We quote from *Svenskarne i of Illinois:* "The northern part of the Andover Township has as fertile land as can be found anywhere, while the southern half is more stony and hilly and in some places consists of 'bottomland.' The northern branch of the Edwards river enters the township in section 24, the southern in section 35, then join in the southwestern corner of section 22 and flow through the district in a western direction. A wooded area, Oak Grove, begins in section 13 and stretches westward through the entire township, varying in width from one half to three fourths of a mile."

From the same source we learn that the first white man to settle here was a Dr. Baker, who arrived May 6, 1835. In June of the same year the first steps in establishing a settlement occurred when a minister, Pillsbury, a Mr. Slaughter and a Mr. Pike, came as a committee to seek a site for a colony already organized in New York State. They selected a large piece of land and laid out a part for a town. Streets, alleys, market place, etc. were measured and charted, and a name adopted, Andover, presumably from Andover in Massachusetts, the location of a renowned Congregational theological seminary.

The land colony in New York very likely had the pious purpose of establishing here on the prairies a Christian community while at the same time making money on the land. But such a speculation was never realized, for in place of a strong society of native Puritans there developed in time a large settlement of Swedish Lutherans.

In the first years the population was small and faced with many difficulties and privations. The closest post office was in Knoxville, over 30 miles distant. To mail a letter cost 25 cents.

The first white child born in Andover was Mary E. Woolsey, who later married Edmund Bucks.

The First Swedes in Andover

As far as is known the first Swede to settle in Andover was Sven Nilson, a former sailor who came in 1840. Ten years later I found that he had married a woman from my home town, Hassela, where she had been known as "Stigs Lena." She had been — or pretended to be — converted by the Jansonists and went with them to America in 1849. The Nilsons lived on the prairie, south of the Edwards river. He died before 1880.

Captain P.W. Virström and Wife

Svenskarne i Illinois relates thus of his history: "It is true that Captain Virstrom was one of the pioneers in Andover, but second after Sven Nilson, the first Swede in Andover, was Johanna Sofia Lundquist, who later married Virström. This lady was born in Nyköping January 15, 1824. Her father, J.E. Lundquist, was a factory inspector, who later moved to Forsa in Helsingland, became an ardent Jansonist and in 1846 emigrated with the party.

"In the fall of 1846, when large groups started for the Bishop Hill Colony, a Swedish sailor working on the Great Lakes learned that a band of his fellow countrymen had arrived in Buffalo. He made his way there and found the immigrants under the leadership of Nils Hedin and on their way to Bishop Hill. This Swedish sailor was P.W. Virstrom, born in Vaxholm 1816, and now a sea captain. The immigrants persuaded him to accompany them to their destination as an interpreter. In Bishop Hill he was as indispensable as a physician (he had some experience in this field) as he had been on the way as their interpreter. He stayed until July 1847. Then he moved to Andover where he found the above mentioned Johanna Sofia Lundquist, whom he married shortly afterward. They were the first Swedish married couple in Andover. In the fall 1847 they travelled to New Orleans, came back in the spring 1848, left again for New Orleans in the fall, returning in the spring 1849. In 1850 they travelled by land over the great wilderness to California, and came back in 1854. February 25 Virstrom died in Bishop Hill. The widow remarried in 1856, to an American, M.B. Ogden, and lives in Victoria, Knox Co."

In the same year that Virstrom came to Andover (1847) several families arrived who seem originally to have planned to join Peter Kassel's settlement in Iowa but were directed by the Hedstroms to Illinois and Andover. Among these were N.J. Johnson and family from Jerda, and Anders Johanson from Lönneberga, Kalmar County. At the same time or a little later came a Friberg family, a Nils Nilson, a Hurtig family, and in 1848 John A. Larson, from Oppeby, Östergötland. The last named was then a young man but later came to play on important part in the civic life of Andover and the region.

N.J. Johnson and Nils Nilson were the first to own land in Andover. Each one bought a 10 acre lot in 1848 for which they paid $1.25 per acre. Johnson's primitive hut has stood all these years and probably still stands.

Anders Johanson died in 1849. His widow remarried, to Samuel Johnson, of Orion. In her younger days she was an energetic and strong woman who if necessary could take a man by the scruff of the neck.

N.J. Johnson and wife probably yet live in their old place. Nils Nilson still lived in Andover a few years ago. Friberg moved to Colfax, Iowa. Hurtig, who lived south of 'deacon Bucks place,' died 1849, but his wife lived a few years ago in Polk County, Nebraska. John A. Larson did not remain in Andover — he moved to Galesburg and learned the wagon-maker trade. In 1850 he went to California, endured as did all California travellers those days all kinds of difficulties without much in return. He came back in 1851, stayed in Galesburg till 1853, then returned to Andover, bought Rev. Pillsbury's place, where he has remained. For his country-men he has been a great help in civic affairs in Andover and he deserves their gratitude.

Among those who came in 1848 were Gabriel Johnson and Gustaf Johnson; the Samuel Johnson family from Södra Wi.; Holland Elm and family from Gammalkil; the Erik Peter Anderson family; the Samuel Samuelson family; the widow and children of Mons Johnson (who died in Buffalo), all from Kisa. These five last-named families had left Sweden on the ship *Virginia* 1846, had been robbed of their money in Albany, and been in dire straits on the canal ship to Buffalo. They intended to reach Kassel's settlement [in Iowa]. Instead they were forced to remain in Buffalo two years to earn means to continue their journey. One part stayed in Sugar Grove, Pennsylvania,[1] one part went on to Illinois, including the aforementioned five families.

A larger increase in the settlement at Andover came in 1849. In the summer a group arrived from Östergötland and the Kalmar county. The people from Östergötland came on the vessel *Charles Tottie*, with the intention of reaching New Sweden, Iowa. On account of sickness some were forced to remain in Andover and vicinity, — among them

---

[1] In Buffalo one family had to place 2 daughters in public care. Thence they were brought into the home of a woman who lived in Sugar Grove. Later the parents moved there — this was the beginning of the large Swedish community in Jamestown, N.Y.

Nils Magnus Kilberg and family, from Kisa, who settled in Swedona, where they still live, and Carl John Samuelson and brother Johannes, with families, who established themselves in Hickory Grove, Lynn Township, south of Andover Township. These brothers were born in western Eneby, Östergötland, then (at least John) moved to Opphem in Tjäderstads parish and thence to America. When a railroad was built through Hickory Grove, a station was erected bearing the name Ophiem, to remind the settlers of the old Opphem — Americans pronounced it "Ofim." The brothers became very prosperous and in time had large wealth. In 1880 their farms were appraised at $130,000. They have contributed large sums to churches, to the school in Rock Island, and other charitable causes.

Also that year Nils P. Peterson came from Lönneberga, Kalmar County, who more recently has lived in section 33 of western township and is in good circumstances; Anders Peter Larson, A.P. Peterson, the Pehr Swenson family from Djursdala, Kalmar County, etc.

In the Fall, 1849, the Esbjörn company came to Andover. Esbjörn himself was left in Chicago, suffering from cholera, and did not get to Andover before October. When he arrived he found that the majority had been induced by pastor J. Hedstrom in Victoria to locate there. Among those who stayed in Andover were Jonas Anderson and family from Hille in Gestrikland, Matts Ersson and family from the same parish and the Olof Nordin family. Jonas Anderson and Matts Ersson were drawn to California by the gold fever in 1850, but came back 1851 without any great riches. Anderson then entered business in company with G.E. Peterson but went bankrupt in the crisis of 1857. Together with his sons he moved to Colorado in 1859 and may still be living there. His wife remained in Andover, with the daughter who married Erik Westerlund in Osco township. Jonas Anderson was by nature honorable, forthright and friendly, possessing an old fashioned piety, but given too much to adventure.

Newcomers in 1849 also include S.P. Strid, a soldier from Östergötland, and Öke Olson from Ofvansjö in Gestrikland, who came to New York with the Jansonists in 1846 and then to Andover.

These are some of the pioneers in the Andover settlement. *Svenskarne i Illinois* tells us about their economic situation:

"Lack of housing is always one of the great difficulties which is encountered by the newcomer when he moves beyond the boundaries of civilized society to establish new communities — this the Andover Swedes had to endure.

"An even more serious affliction is illness, which results from the change of climate and food confronting these persons. A variety of diseases attacked them and year after year took their toll until they became acclimated. Cholera annually haunted them from 1849 to 1854 and often left devastation among them. John Elm tells us that in 1849 he worked with two threshing crews of 18 men each and only he and two others survived the cholera attack.

"It was not always possible to find paying jobs. Wages were always low. The current rate was 35 to 50 cents a day, and usually payable in kind — meat, animals, etc. On the other hand necessities were cheap. A cow could be bought for $8.00. Horses which now bring $100 were then $40. Pork could be obtained for 1 1/2 cents a pound, wheat for 35 cents a bushel, corn for 12 1/2 cents a bushel, and potatoes by digging them up. For the friends of spirits it was a golden age — a gallon of whiskey cost 12 1/2 to 15 cents. The situation changed in 1853 when railroads began to be built. The circulation of money increased, there was a greater demand for labor, prices of farm products rose. In 1857, however, the panic turned things upside down, so likewise in 1873, though in a lesser degree. Still these crises brought some good, for they upset and destroyed the unreasonable and destructive banking system which was then in vogue and over-whelmed the nation with a completely valueless paper currency."

The First Religious Activities in Andover
before the Coming of Esbjörn

It is not possible to determine how early Jonas Hedstrom, the Methodist pastor in Victoria, visited the Swedes in Andover, but very likely he paid them a visit now and then even the first year that they were settled there. There is no doubt that he was the first Swedish pastor to preach in Andover.

Early in the summer of 1849 pastor G. Unonius[1] visited there and conducted services. In his *Reminiscences [Minnen]* (pp. 374 and 397 of latter part) he gives this account: "During my first year in Chicago, after the cholera epidemic seemed to have subsided, I undertook a journey inland in order to learn more of the conditions in the Swedish settlements which were becoming increasingly numerous in Illinois and Iowa." He had planned to visit Bishop Hill, among other places,

---

[1]The Swedish Episcopal minister from Chicago.

but did not venture there out of fear of somehow being murdered there. However such a fear was unnecessary, foolish and unjust. He continues: "In Andover, a small place where pastor Esbjörn located the following year[2], together with a rather large number who had emigrated with him and there gradually built up one of the more populous Swedish settlements in Illinois, there were already many Swedish families. On their urging I had announced a service where I was now expected. Several of the immigrants there had experienced deeply-felt losses, for also among them cholera had broken out, snatching parents from children, children from parents. The epidemic was now not so violent, but my first errand when I arrived on Saturday evening was to visit a number of sick or dying.

"A large number of the people here had become Methodists, and much dissension and confusion reigned in religious matters. Many families were divided among themselves, and as often is the case along with religious fanaticism appeared indifference and apathy, giving opportunity for ridicule and mockery, in the beginning directed toward secondary things often ending with a turning away from a true and sensible Christianity. However those emigrants who had arrived during the summer — probably the majority of the residents — declared that they still wanted to adhere to the tenets of the Swedish Church, and it was really on their request that I had come.

"The Sunday morning sun rose clear and glorious across the wide prairie; not a breath of air bent the flowers on their stems. One group after another, displaying a motley array of Swedish peasant holiday attire, gathered for the coming service; the women with their checkered and rosy kerchiefs on their heads, and a psalmbok clasped between their hands, a small bouquet intertwined within the white handerchief, the men with their long hanging watch chains and homespun coats. Everything reminded me keenly of a Sunday morning in rural Sweden, when the church people silently and devotionally approached the house of God. I seemed to be transported back there and almost expected to hear the church bells calling us to enter the opened temple. But here there was nothing of that sort built by human hands. Nor were any of the local houses large enough to hold the oncoming closely packed groups of men, women and children, of whom the majority were uniting in a Swedish högmessa (liturgical Sunday service) for the first time in this strange land. I had never been privileged to proclaim

[2]Norelius makes a correction — Esbjörn came that same year, 1849, in October.

the Word of God to so large a Swedish congregation.

"In a near-by locust grove as many benches and chairs as were available were placed. In the shadow of the leafy branches of a great three there was a table, covered with a white linen cloth, this was to serve as altar. The girls had ringed it with a garland of the meadow's loveliest flowers. Thus the church was soon in order. Seldom does it fall to the lot of a pastor nowadays to officiate in one so large and festive. Dressed in the simple Anglican liturgical garb I went before its altar. The blue sky above was the temple vault. Around us a winged chorus joined in a "jubilant hymn to the Highest." And then was heard the choir of devoted voices, "Hosanna, Holy is God, Almighty God, All merciful and all-wise God"[1] After the sermon the holy sacrament was distributed to the kneeling people on the grass before the altar. Assuredly He was present, who is not bound to place or time and who once in a desert region satisfied a hungering people that had followed Him and listened to His Word — assuredly He was here even in this wilderness among us, multiplying His blessing, so that even now it may be said, "They all ate and were satisfied."

Yet this same Unonius, who experienced such poetic exaltation on this Arcadian occasion, both earlier and later held strictly to the prosaic doctrine of the Anglican episcopate.

There may have been other services between this service and the first one conducted by Esbjörn after his arrival, but I have not been able to verify such.

The Organization of the Swedish Lutheran Congretation and its History until 1860

Since this congregation has justly been considered the mother congregation of the Swedish Lutheran Church in America it is appropriate to present in as great detail as possible the documents, memories and notes that relate to its history.

In Esbjörn's "Narrative concerning the origin of the Swedish Lutheran congregations in North America and their present condition, given at a meeting of the clergy of the Uppsala Archdiocese (Sweden) June 14, 1865," we read:

"After the emigration of Erik Janson and his followers in 1846 many Swedes left for the new world, but no pastor went with them. So I felt impelled to emigrate in order to minister to them, lest they

---

[1]From a Swedish hymn, written by S. Hedborn.

and their children lapse into heathendom or, deprived of care by their own church, they might be caught up in one of the numberless more or less erroneous sects found in this land. I was urged to take this step by fellow-countrymen who had emigrated and who complained bitterly of their spiritual need. After receiving government permission, and a commission with travel expenses from the Mission Society of the Swedish Church, I undertook the important voyage in 1849 in company with 140 emigrants from Helsingland and Gestrikland. This is not the place to describe the perils and difficulties of the journey, the cholera and other diseases, suffered on the way and after arrival. In short, after many troubles we found ourselves in the distant west, 218 (Swedish) miles inland. Here we encountered a significant number of Swedes from Östergötland and Småland, some of whom had come the previous year, others the same year, and had settled in Andover, Galesburg, Rock Island and Moline, in the state of Illinois. As soon as I regained strength after sickness I began to hold services, in a schoolhouse or private dwelling, according to the teaching and liturgy of the Swedish Church.

"Now at once there broke out a storm which under present circumstances could not be avoided by a missionary. Lacking any instructions from the church authorities at Upsala or the Swedish Missionary Society I had to determine for myself what guide lines to follow. Two principles became normative for me, 1) to seek to keep my countrymen faithful to the doctrines of the Evangelical Lutheran Church, and 2) to seek to make this doctrine living in them, or rather to keep them living in God. Now there was present here a Swedish Methodist preacher,[1] who was supported by the Methodist Episcopal Church for the express purpose of winning the Swedes to that body. Before our arrival he had worked with some success among the deluded followers of Erik Janson. Now he sought by all possible means to fulfil his purpose among the Swedes who had followed me and those who had already come to these places. He travelled among them, preaching and going from house to house. Beyond his sermons the burden of his presentation was that the Lutheran Church was dead, is the Babylonian whore from whom every one who wishes to be saved must depart, that in Sweden there is no true Christianity, the Swedish minister has come to place the freedom seekers under the "bonds and fetters of the State Church," in America there are no Lutheran congregations, that the Methodists are

[1]Jonas Hedstrom in Victoria

the true living Lutherans, under another name, that they preach sanctified lives, while the Lutheran preachers allow sins of weakness and thereby permit their people a certain degree of sinfulness, that he himself was not teaching more than he had learned from his mother at her spinning wheel, and other things of this kind. Furthermore he pictured Andover, where we were settling, as a poor and sickly place, whereas every advantage lay in the place he lived (Victoria). There he could procure excellent land at low cost and on good terms, etc. Many were influenced by him, moved there and became Methodists, especially since they were told to enter on a 6 months trial period. Several of the more talented lay men were commissioned as preachers, with subsidy from missionary treasuries of the Methodist Church. The poverty stricken Lutheran pastor, weakened by cholera and persistent fever, could do no more than patiently travel around, preach the Word of God, and by it seek as best he could to refute every false teaching. There could be no thought of starting at once a congregation. One needed time to consider what should be done. There was no Lutheran pastor, congregation, or synod in all this region of the United States to which one could turn for counsel or support. Help for support of the minister could not come from the newcomers, who were mostly poor. The sectarian preachers often proclaimed that they had no salaries and if one joined them churches and preachers would be without cost.

"I therefore had to look for help from some missionary society. Fortunately I was recommended by a noble American clergyman to the American Home Missionary Society, whose headquarters were in New York. This Society could not, of course, support preachers who were strangers, distant, and unknown, without any supervision on the site. It was arranged, therefore, that I should be received as a missionary of the Society under the supervision of the Congregational Church's association or synod of Illinois, though with the express provision written into the *Minutes* of the Association that I should preach the Gospel, administer the sacraments, follow the order of worship and exercise discipline as an evangelical Lutheran minister of Jesus Christ. These *Minutes* were printed in the *Northwestern Gazeteer*, published in Galesburg. Whoever wishes can there see that whereas I was under the "supervision" of another denomination, I was and remained a Lutheran missionary with completely free hands. To the credit of the Congregational Illinois Association it should be added that though at their meeting I fully and freely presented the teaching and faith of my church and myself on the sacraments, election, fall from grace, etc. no attempt was ever made to persuade me or any of my people to leave the Lutheran Church. They were persuaded on the other hand by my sincere and forthright presentation of my own personal spiritual experience that it was my intention to work for a true and living Christianity among my countrymen.

"In the Spring of 1850 an evangelical Lutheran congregation was organized in Andover, and later one in Princeton, in Moline, in Galesburg. The one in Andover consisted of 10 members, to begin with, and though I had a bound Church Records book with me from Sweden, trouble makers had made so much of the fear of the "State Church bonds and fetters" that I did not dare to bring it out and there enter the names, but for some time had to be satisfied with a list. Under such circumstances it was natural occasionally to venture here and there a variation in the words of the Swedish liturgy. In the prayer after the sermon, "Holy Spirit" was substituted for "Good Spirit," some change was made in the exhortation to the sponsors at holy baptism, free prayer might be used instead of some of the prescribed ones. This seemed necessary in a region where none of the many religious groups had any liturgy, to show that we did not seek to bind the people to the "bonds and fetters" of the State Church."

Thus far, from Esbjörn's narrative.

As a commentary on and complementary to the above statement I wish to include various letters and documents which throw light on Esbjörn's relationships and standing with the Congregationalists, at the same time as they bear on the earliest history of the first Lutheran congregations in Illinois. The documents are preserved in the archives of the American Home Missionary Society, in the Bible House, New York City. They have been copied by Professor C.M. Esbjorn[1] who has kindly supplied them to me. We encounter here a "sour apple" in our history. One might wish it would be otherwise, but the facts speak and truth must take its course. I translate all that affords us information.

> "Galesburg, Knox county
> Illinois, December 10, 1849

Doctors Badger and Hall[2]

Dear Brothers!

The undersigned, the Home Mission Committee of the Central Association, (of Illinois) have been instructed by the

[1]A son of Pastor L.P. Esbjörn
[2]Secretaries for the American Home Missionary Society

Association, at an extra meeting December 5, to forward to you the following presentation and request:

Pastor Lars Paul Esbjörn, an evangelical minister from Sweden, came to the Association with the request that he might be taken under its care and be recommended by its mission committee to the American Home Missionary Society for receiving support while he works among the Swedish people who have moved here.

After having heard Mr. Esbjörn's credentials and after conversing with him freely regarding his doctrinal stand and personal experiences in religious matters, a committee was appointed, consisting of J. Blanchard, Vail and Hawley, to make a report on his case. Following the committee's report the Association voted to approve Mr. Esbjörns' request on the following conditions:

1. That he has the responsibility of a member to the Association.

2. He shall preach and administer the ordinances (sacraments), ceremonies (rites) and church discipline as an evangelical Lutheran servant of Christ.

3. He shall work in Andover and Galesburg. In Andover there are already 180 Swedes and in Galesburg 100. In Knoxville and Henderson, each five miles from here in opposite directions, there are also Swedes living. These have no shepherd.

A Methodist brother[1] has sought to do something for them, and a very few have been helped spiritually. But in this whole region (and Swedes are continuing to settle all over this region) there is not to our knowledge a single congregation, or even a Methodist class, exclusively for the benefit of the Swedes, except the Prophet Janson community which combines the worst traits of the Papacy and Mormonism.

The intention was to organize congregations in Andover and in this place, but since both the moral and immoral consider themselves church members indifferently, it was thought best first to build a church here and then organize a congregation. But he needs support immediately.

Pastor Paul Andersen in Chicago was promised to come down and help organize a congregation on an evangelical foundation. Mr. Esbjörn has a wife and four children. He has preached here on two Sabbaths with much satisfaction to the Swedes.

[1] J. Hedstrom

The people in Andover are now engaged in circulating a sub-scription list for his support. But since almost all our Swedes have been deprived of all their possessions by the prophet Janson, even the best they can do will be insignificant.

We have thought that a subsidy of $300 is the minimum sum by which he can support himself on this field for the present, and since it is your custom to commission clergymen to develop congregations on field where there are none, and since his needs are pressing, we hope that you may send him a commission and at this time a subsidy.

The Swedes appointed a building committee here yesterday, and we hope that a building may soon be erected, but it will be necessary for the Americans to supply the means, except for the labor.

On behalf of the Association

L.H. Parker   J. Blanchard   Eli Farnham

Committee for Home Mission of the Central Association, Illinois."

The following excerpt from a letter of Rev. Wm. Kirby, who seems to have been a sort of superintendent for American Home Missionary Society's missions in the West, is obviously intended to endorse the above request. I include it for the information it affords about Esbjörn and the Swedes in Andover and Galesburg.

"Jacksonville, Illinois, January 9, 1850.

Rev. Mr. Badger. Dear Brother

— While I was in Knoxville, the Rev. Mr. Esbjörn came to speak with me regarding his work among the Swedes in Henry County and Galesburg. He said that he had visited you in New York and informed you about his position and the purpose of his moving to the United States and Henry County; that he had been encouraged about receiving help on condition that a field opened up for his activity. I consulted with brethren in the area. All thought well of him both in regard to talent and piety. Och Mr. Blanchard writes me that the committee of the Central Association with which he had united has sent a request for help in his support and that they had asked for $300 — little enough.

"The Swedes for the present can do little or nothing to help in his support. They cannot properly support themselves. No congregation has at present been organized nor would it be prudent to organize any until one has learned what is the character of the members, whether they are evangelical or rationalistic. With the help of Galesburg citizens they intend to erect a church building during the winter, and Esbjörn has already begun his work.

"The Methodists have a missionary among the Swedes in Victoria and he preaches for those who come together to hear him. He is an intelligent person, but without education. He worked a few years as a blacksmith in Victoria, but for a few years now has devoted himself to the welfare of his countrymen. He serves them in both temporal and spiritual matters. He has taken or drawn away several hunderd from Janson in Bishop Hill, who is a second Joseph Smith, and has obtained medical help for their sick. He speaks English well, has an American wife, seems in truth to be a follower of Christ, has organized a class of 20 members, and tries to be what he wants to be — useful in the Master's service. But he is Methodist, and for the newcomers there is a charm in the Lutheran name. Esbjörn believes that he has a more immediate approach to them as a Lutheran than any one else of some other confessional color. I do not doubt that this is true. I asked about the number of families, etc. but suppose that the committee has given all necessary information on this point. The Methodists allocate $300 for their mission, less an amount for the presiding elder. I hope that the A.H.M. Society will rejoice over an opportunity to support evangelical influences through a competent clergyman among these strangers in our midst. —."

Esbjörn Receives his Commission reading thus:

"American Home Missionary Society Office,
No. 150 Nassau Street,
January 14, 1850

"To Pastor L.P. Esbjörn!
Inasmuch as the Executive Committee of the American Home Missionary Society has been assured of your regular standing and prospect of competent labor as a servant of the Lord, and wishing to support and encourage people in needy areas to receive and maintain the constant administration of the Christian ordinances, it has appointed you as its missionary to proclaim the gospel for the distressed Swedish people in Galesburg, Andover, and vicinity in Illinois, under the supervision of the Mission Committee of the Central Association for a period of 12 months from the inception of the work under this commission; to receive from this committee $300, if this amount proves necessary, as a supplement

to your support from the people among whom you work, so that the total salary will be $400.

"The conditions of this commission are 1) that you be required to have credentials showing that you are in regular standing as an evangelical minister, or licensed preacher, approved by the Presbytery, Association, or Classes, within whose borders you are appointed to work. 2) It is required that you do not receive subsidy from any other Mission Society during the period you are receiving help from this Society, except in the case of help from an auxiliary of this Society or of permission from this Committee, in which case that amount shall be substracted from the subsidy here granted. 3) You are required at the end of each quarter, from the day you began your work under this commission, to give a summary report on your work, describing the success you have had or the obstacles you have met, as well as anything of interest you may wish to tell, that falls in the categories mentioned in *General Instruction*. Statistical items are to be sent in March 1."

Items 3 and 4 touch on the matter of collections and sending in of money.

"On behalf of the Committee,

A. Fisher, chairman. Milton Badger, Charles Hall,
Corresponding Secretaries"

The document contains also: General Instructions, Suggestions, Instructions on making reports, and the following handwritten letter from Milton Badger:

"American Home Missionary Society's Office,
150 Nassau Street, New York,
January 14, 1850

Pastor L.P. Esbjörn! Dear Brother!

"In accordance with a recommendation of the Mission Committee of the Central Association in Illinois I send you the enclosed commission. You should turn to the Association's Committee with which you already are acquainted, to receive special instructions concerning those places where you are to do most of your work, and the division of time between them as well as concerning the best means for building up congregations and churches among your countrymen. We desire that you particularly pay attention to promote an evangelical teaching, the necessity of a new birth through God's Spirit, and not to receive as members in the congregations or admit to the Lord's Supper, any who are not able to give evidence of a new birth. Some of our German and Lutheran churches are quite loose on this point in that they follow their method of receiving members into a congregation through confirmation. Those who support this Society are quite determined in this matter, and it would trouble me if we were to give help to pastors and congregations who receive into membership such as give no evidence of having been born anew. You are at liberty to do what you can to obtain some part of your support from those whom you serve, and in each report indicate such sums. We support poorer congregations only on condition that they do what they can to support themselves.

Yours, in Christian fellowship, Milton Badger."

I wish to include some of Esbjörn's letters and reports to the American Home Missionary Society during the first year of his commission. These writings are of historic value for the period in question.

"Andover, Henry County, Illinois February 28, 1850

To Dr. Badger,

"I feel unable to express my gratitude for the commission and for the subsidy which enables me to do good among the Swedes. — I ask further to explain my intentions and my position here. From the day I left my native land I began to preach on board the boat two times each Sabbath and to hold morning and evening prayers with Bible expositions each day, etc. and continued such until we reached Chicago, last September 30th. These spiritual exercises were not fruitless — On my arrival in Chicago I fell sick with cholera and fever and had to stay there while the rest of my party went on to Andover, where we had been invited to settle and had received promise of help for a Swedish church.[1]

"When I arrived afterwards I found that the immigrant party had scattered. A Swedish preacher of the Methodist Society had been there and persuaded many of them, particularly the religious-minded to move to his area. I don't care to say much about it, but God knows what means and methods have been and still are being used to undermine my efforts. Yet I began at once and continue now to work among the Swedes in Andover and surrounding areas (namely, Berlin 8 miles, and Rock Island, 22 miles distant) hoping in God's help.

"I began to work in Galesburg in November (1849), so that I can count my present work in the Lord from the beginning of last December, and I pray that your Committee will kindly count my

[1]from the Andover Land Co.

commission from that date, though it is dated January 14, 1850.[1] I venture the more to make this humble request, since I have no hope to receive from my countrymen more than 40 dollars, which they have voluntarily promised without any request from me.

"My time is spent as follows: I preach every other Sabbath in Andover and Galesburg (25 miles apart), usually twice, and conduct evening prayer and Bible exposition in homes; visit the families and the sick; and occasionally I preach on week-days in Berlin and Rock Island; hold monthly meetings for missions and temperance causes; spread religious tracts.

"We have now begun to build a Swedish Lutheran "meeting house" in Galesburg, for which about $550 have already been pledged, and we have the bright hope of also getting one in Andover. I hope that these endeavors may through God's blessings become a means of promoting the spiritual welfare of the Swedish people around here and of gathering my poor countrymen in God's kingdom.

"I regret that many temporal and churchly obstacles have arisen, which I want to explain, in order that the true Christians of your Society might earnestly pray for me and my people and cooperate with me.

"1. The first obstacle is the general poverty of the Swedes, which compels them to be so concerned about their temporal livelihood that their minds are but little open to the truths of religion.

"2. Many of them are now traveling to California to find gold. This has given rise to a universal agitation among them and is a source of confusion and a temptation to greed. Many have no time to think of their souls, since their thoughts, their talk, their deeds and their plans, are centered on California. For 3 or 4 weeks they have been leaving and in all probability this will go on for several weeks. — (He says he has warned against and tried to persuade them with the Word of God, but nothing seems to help.)

"3. There are a few Swedes here who had gone over to the Methodist Episcopal Church before I came. Their preacher declares openly that it is his purpose to get all of the Swedes into his church. While I am preaching in one place, he comes to my people in another (he preaches, and invites any one at all who wishes, to come to the Lord's Supper where he lives). Such controversy is deplorable, and much faith, humility, patience and prayer are necessary to combat it.

"4. The Swedes have been members of a State Church, and the greater number of them have lived in places where the true

[1]Evidently the Committee did not do so.

religion, conversion, and new birth and santification are unknown or mentioned with contempt and disdain.[1] Ignorant of the
language and customs of this land they do not know the spiritual
endeavors and biblical attitudes of the Christian people here, and
when, as I have often done, I have told them of this, both on the
sea voyage and here, they think they themselves understand,
especially if they get to hear of any faults and scandals among the
Christians.

"5. My own intention and my conscience as well as the regulations of the American Home Missionary Society impose on me
the duty not to accept any one into membership in the congregation or admit to the Lord's Supper, unless he is born again. But
just here is the strait gate on the narrow path for a Swedish missionary. The Swedes consider it infamy for any one at all to be
denied the Lord's Supper. They will subject themselves to anything else but this. Consequently if one held strictly to this principle they would seek membership with the Methodists, who in this
matter are more loose, especially the Swedish Methodists. Among
them it is sufficient to have experienced some action of the Holy
Spirit's calling grace to be received, at least on probation, so it is
just those who are spiritually moved that go over to their fellowship, as we have seen already. On this matter I have consulted
with Pastor P. Andersen in Chicago, a Norwegian pastor belonging to the Frankean Ev. Lutheran Synod, before I received your
commission. He said that occasionally he felt compelled to admit
Scandinavians to the Holy Supper, though they were not
members of any American church, when they expressed a sincere
desire for it, promised to use the Word of God and to pray for
their conversion, and on the basis of their having been members
of the State church at home were not to be compared with those
in this country who stand outside the church.

"Last December 2 (1849) I held a communion service in
Andover in accordance with this principle, first speaking privately
with each of the communicants and exhorting all who I deemed
unconverted to repent and pray for conversion. I received their
promise so to do. I persuaded some to wait with communion,
which they did. It was necessary to hold the Lord's Supper for the
true children of God and to do with the others as I mentioned.

"Since I have not yet received your Instructions, and material enough is present to organize a society (congregation), I shall
follow this plan ad interim and provisionally under present circumstances.

[1]This would pertain to those opposed to the State Church and its Lutheran doctrines.
(Translator)

6. Futhermore we have among us, especially in Galesburg, a large number of those who earlier had been Jansonists then left Bishop Hill though they still are Jansonists in heart, still perfectionists (in the spirit of Joseph Smith). They are still proud and selfish, still favoring the preachers who preach perfectionism above a minister who in his prayers will from time to time pray for the forgiveness of sins. All these circumstances lead me to say that seldom is a minister put in such a quandary, especially if probably his friends, and the missionary society that supports him, hardly comprehend what is the combined effects of all this, yet want to see fruits of his ministry.

"I do not mention this in self-pity. I know the difficulties in the ministry. But I name them to show that I have no reason to expect much fruit among the Swedes for the present. If it pleases God to let me work, pray, and wait for progress as Egede and the Brethren Church did in Greenland, I will be satisfied, knowing that He has promised that His Word will not return to Him void.

"So I will do all I can, and though I do not like to speak about my own endeavors — a fault that also attaches to missionaries — I yet would say that I am ready to offer all my powers of body and soul to bring my countrymen to a living faith in Jesus Christ and to be a helper to their salvation. By the grace of God I will do whatever the commission and the Word of God obligate me to do, insofar as time, the size of the field and circumstances permit. I pray and believe that everything will redound to the glory of the blessed Saviour and to the salvation of the souls of at least some of the Swedes. May God grant this for His own sake. Amen. Since I spend almost all my time among the Swedes, I cannot learn the English language very quickly, and therefore find some difficulty to express myself and avoid mistakes, but I hope you will pardon me. Asking for your prayers, I am respectfully, yours in Christ Jesus.

L.P. Esbjörn"

Further: "Annual Statistical Report (1 March 1850)

1. Name: The Swedish settlements in Andover and Berlin (Henry County), Galesburg (Knox County) and Rock Island (Rock Island County). State of Illinois. Address, Andover, Henry County, Illinois.

"2. No congregation is yet organized. Several persons of the Central Association in Illinois believe that it best to wait with an organization until a meeting house has been built or until time and circumstances are more suitable than now. After careful consideration of all phases I, too, think so, but I hope the time is not far off when we can build a living house of God on the principal corner-stone, Jesus Christ.

"3. The average number of those attending the Swedish services of worship — in Andover, about 70, in Galesburg 80, in Rock Island 30, in Berlin 12.

"4. _____ From 12 to 15 of the total number may be considered converted. The Spirit of God often works through the preaching of the Gospels, most in Andover. _____

"7. 8. Sabbath schools for the Swedish children can hardly be organized in the winter months, but I am anxious to do so in Spring and Summer.

"9. A temperance society has been organized in Andover with 43 members, but I am sure the number will rapidly increase, for in general the people are temperate in regard to liquor. As soon as time permits I plan to organize additional societies. ____

"12. A church building for the Swedes has been started in Galesburg, as stated above.

Yours in Christ Jesus,
L.P. Esbjörn"

In the next quarterly report, Andover, Henry County, Illinois, May 27, 1850, he mentions among others these items:

"On March 18 (1850) 10 persons united in an Evangelical Lutheran congregation here in Andover, following a blessed service of preaching and prayer. Since that date one person after another has come, acknowledging and confessing themselves as helpless sinners, hungering and thirsting for the righteousness of Christ, and joined our congregation through a public declaration, so that we now have 28 members. — The most promising place is Andover, where the Swedes have come direct from Sweden, the least promising is Galesburg, where the majority of Swedes are former Jansonists and where we encounter other hostile forces.

"The meeting house in Galesburg is naturally delayed, though a large part of the American population have evidenced a deep and friendly interest for the promotion of the Lord's cause through me. We have a great need of a meeting house in Andover, where we meet in my house until we can build a place.

"We now have promising Sabbath schools in Andover and Galesburg.

"The Swedes hereabouts are more than ever lacking in money on account of the unusually high prices of provisions here in the West. Still during this quarter they have made a collection of $2 to the American Home Missionary Society. _____

"For the reason mentioned our people have not been able to support me, nor will they be able to do so until the Fall. I am therefore in great need of temporal support. I ask that you might send me my quarterly salary, on receiving this, for I have had no income for four months and am in debt to a number of people fornecessities. _____

L.P. Esbjörn"

The First Members of the Swedish Lutheran Congregation in Andover

The list is copied very carefully from the original by Prof. C.M. Esbjörn, who has kindly lent me the transcript. He says of it, "The following seems to be the origin of the Church Records in Andover. Undoubtedly it is "the list" which Esbjörn refers to in his published account of the beginning of the Swedish Lutheran Congregations in North America, as the form he "had to be satisfied with for some time."

Many names are crossed out, and before some there are abbreviated notes, for example 'Prof' or 'Prop,' which seems to mean either that the person was received on confession (proof), or had been proposed for membership, probably the former. I give only the names, thus:

"On March 18, 1850 the Swedish Ev. Luth. Congregation in Andover was organized.

L.P. Esbjörn	And. Pet Larsson
Jon Andersson	Mrs. Esbjörn
Mats Ersson	Mrs. Jansson
O. Nordin	Christina, with Knapp
Sam. Jansson	Stina Hellgren

March 23

Johannes Samuelsson	Sw. P. Strid
Wife Marie Charl. Persd:r	wife Anna Sofia Nilsd:r
G. Soderbergs wife	Stina Lena Andersd:r
Per Samuelsson	Samuel Samuelsson
wife Sara Jons dotter	(Kihlbergs wife
	(Fredrika Samuelsd:r
Greta Stina Ols dotter	Jon Peter Johansson
And. P. Persson	wife

Carl Johans wife
And Sundgren
Virstrom and wife (crossed over)
Carl Johan Brown
Carl Johan Samuelsson
Nils Magn. Kihlberg
Carl Johansson[1]
O. Dahlberg
Mats Erssons wife
Christina Alm

Greta Stina Olsd:r exclud.
Erik Ulric Norberg[2]
Johanssons wife Maja Stina Anders d:r
Olaus Bengtsson[3]
not   (wife
public   (Swen Johan
received (wife
        (Olaus Peterson
Carl Pet. Johansson
wife Carolina Persd:r

In reports to the Am. Home Miss. Society Esbjörn mentioned the organization of a Temperance Society in Andover. Among Prof. C.M. Esbjorn's transcripts of old documents we find these names of this original

"Temperance Society in Andover:

L.P. Esbjörn
P.W. Virstrom
Jon Anderson
Carl Joh. Samuelsson
Johannes Samuelsson
O. Dahlberg
Sven Strid
Samuel Jansson
Per Samuelsson
Samuel Samuelson, V. Eneby
Carl Johansson
N.M. Kihlberg
Matts Ersson

Anders Hellgren
Olaus Olsson
Joh. Fredr. Olsson
Gustaf Hellgren
Oke Olsson
A. Per Larsson
Nils P. Petersson
Jonas Jacobson
Olof Nordin
Olaus Petersson
Samuel Samuelsson from Hessleby
19 women"

[1] the one who moved to Moline and became a Baptist?
[2] also in Bishop Hill and Chisago Lake
[3] Probably the same one who lived in Moline and in whose home the Methodists met.

From the same source we have

"Swedes in Galesburg
who probably in some degree welcomed Esbjörn's activity, but are not indicated as members of the congregation. The list may antedate the founding of the Galesburg Church. The names:

Renstedt	Erik Olsson
Linde	Nils Hansson
Thorsell	Nils Hedstrom
Youngberg	Swen Larsson (in same
Modin	house)

Dahlgrens — next house
Samuel — Fuller's shop
Mrs. Hammar — ditto
Klintberg — Mr. Dele
one more ditto
Kellmans
Grip at Kellmans
wife of Berglund
wife of Hellstrom
Nybergs wife at Thorsell"

Continuation of Esbjörn's reports to the Am. Home Miss. Society.

Andover, Henry Co., Ill.
Sept. 2, 1850

I have continued preaching the Gospel for the Swedish people in Andover, Galesburg, and surrounding places, visiting the families as far as circumstances permit, teaching in the Andover Sunday School and conducting the one in Galesburg, which has some fine teachers in students from Knox College — The congregation in Andover now has 40 communicants.

A married couple has been under discipline.

We have not organized a congregation in Galesburg thus far because of opposition and other difficulties. I mentioned in my previous report the plans for a Lutheran "meeting house," and progress has been made to the point where we have a neat frame building, 30 by 40 by 18 feet, erected on a good thick foundation, with tower. Funds were raised by a subscription in the city. We hope soon to organize a small band of true believers. I hope that it may be a good leaven among our people there. In Andover, too, where the Swedes have been unable to do something similar, the prospects are brighter for building a meeting house since we have begun to receive friendly help from Christians in this land. May God in His bountiful mercy reward them and all who help us in our spiritual need! Especially may He bless the Am. H.M.S. to whom, next to God, we are in debt for all our progress, and whom we regard as our first helper in this land to secure for us and our children Christian institutions and ordinances.

Though Rock Island is not really a part of my parish I have felt constrained to heed their pleas for me to come and preach for the Swedes there. God has blessed the work through His Holy Spirit and some of the Swedish people there now belong to the Andover congregation.

Early last June I attended a conference meeting (in Sharon, Walworth County, Wis.) held by pastors of the Frankean Lutheran Synod. I had there the opportunity of learning to know these pastors and the local Lutheran congregation, and of preaching at two Norwegian settlements on the way. I hope I may have contributed some spiritual gift, by God's grace, whereas I personally was encouraged in our common faith.

On account of this meeting and a spell of sickness I have had to miss some Sabbaths in Galesburg. But in my absence another Swedish person has led in the reading and exhortation of the Word of God.

Both my clothes and my strength have become worn by these travels. I had hoped that my clothes from Sweden would last two years but already after one year they are of little use. At present almost my whole family (a weak wife and 3 children) are sick with fever, as are myself and many of the Swedes. Our people have suffered much loss through the heavy and continuous rain. Wheat and hay have been greatly damaged. Therefore I cannot expect that they will be able to support me as they did last winter. Together with them I exclaim, the Lord gives, the Lord takes, blessed be the name of the Lord. Yet I cannot but explain our situation and humbly ask that I might receive my third quarterly salary as generously and promptly as you sent the second quarter's, for which I use this opportunity to express my sincere gratitude as well as the thanks of my family and congregation.

Respectfully

L.P. Esbjörn

Following is a petition in Swedish from the congregation in Andover to the AM. H.M.S. for support to Pastor Esbjörn for the following year [1851], signed by Johan Samuelsson, Samuel Jonson, Peter Larson, "deacons and trustees," dated December 3, 1850.

It says in part,

"that Pastor L.P. Esbjörn has proclaimed the saving Word with zeal of the Spirit and untiringly, touching the heart of the sinners, and with the help of God's Spirit, has awakened their consciences to bring them to true repentance and faith, while nurturing the faithful with the saving Word of life. We wish greatly to keep him. But the members of the congregation are widely scattered, for the most part are poor and unable to support themselves, and all have come here within a year and still seeking to make a living, [therefore we seek the help of the Society].

We do have a Methodist Congregation attempting organization, also a "Prespetering" (sic) Church, but with God's help we want to retain the pure Lutheran faith.

Here are many hindrances and obstacles but we hope that God will help us to overcome them. Since Swedes are continuing to come here to live it is very necessary that we have a minister of our native country's faith and confession, who can work among them in our language, for the building up of the Kingdom of God. Our congregation now has 46 communicant members, living at various distances around here. Or an average 50 to 60 attend the worship services.—"

The petition was accompanied by a recommendation from the Mission Committee of the Central Association, consisting of L.H. Parker, J. Blanchard, Eli Farnham. It testifies that

Pastor L.P. Esbjörn has worked faithfully and successfully among the Swedes in Andover and Galesburg during the past year. Rock Island and Berlin now have large settlements of Swedes who need a part of his attention and activity this coming year. We endorse the accompanying petition and recommend the same amount as last year's, 300, with permission to extend his ministry to the places mentioned as he deems best.

(There follows 3 pages of "Reflexions" by Norelius, wherein he reproaches Esbjörn for the arrangements made with the American Home Missionary Society. While achnowledging Esbjörn's need to secure some income Norelius questions the moral right of a Lutheran pastor to become a missionary of a Presbyterian — Congregational Church, without compromising his calling. In the light of later history

Norelius' charge is unfair. He does not grant the American friends a tolerance that enabled them to support work which brought no advantage to their own denomination, and left Esbjörn with "free hands." He suspects Esbjörn of "unionism" — a word he himself shied away from. But Norelius knew nothing of ecumenicity and gave a cool reply when his Synod much later was invited to join the Faith and Order movement. Galesburg was the scene of controversy between Congregationalists and Presbyterians in Esbjörn's time, and Norelius could hardly be expected to understand the divisions. Nor did he understand the generosity of Christian pastors willing to help a strange people in their own midst, and his "Reflections" casts more light on himself than on Esbjörn.)

Continuing Esbjörn's "Narrative," Norelius quotes:

"The small congregation in Andover grew steadily, despite all opposition, as well the congregations in Moline, Galesburg and Princeton. Church buildings were necessary — the newcomers could not afford them. The leader, as was customary in this land, had to go out and solicit help. During the summer of 1851 he undertook a journey of 3600 English miles, visiting chiefly German and American Lutheran Synods and congregations and their members (also members of other bodies) in the distant, more populous and well-to-do, states of Ohio, Pennsylvania, New York and Massachusetts. As a result all 11 arduous weeks of travel about 2200 dollars was raised for church buildings among the Swedes. $1500 of this sum was a donation of the widely acclaimed Jenny Lind. This enabled Andover to build a brick church 45 feet long, 30 feet wide, with a basement for school room and sacristy. In Moline a "frame house" was erected as church. Two or three hundred dollars were alloted for a church in New Sweden, Iowa. A beginning was made in Galesburg, mostly through generous pledges by American citizens. But the zealous Methodist (Jonas Hedstrom) spread false reports about the small number of Swedish Lutherans and their "similarities to Roman Catholicism," etc. This caused the donors to cancel their pledges. The church building fell into the hands of a Wesleyan Methodist group, from whom the Swedish Lutherans bought it some years later.

Addenda and Commentary on the Above

When the writer came to Andover in November 1850 and met Esbjörn services were being held either in Esbjörn's own home south of the woods, where there was plenty of room on the few chairs and benches in two or three small rooms, or in the Frances school not far from where the new church now is. On some occasions Bible study and prayer meetings were held at the Mix place. Everywhere were signs of poverty. People were animated by a certain kind of religious interest, a kind of attempt to compete with Methodism. There was something unnatural, if I may thus describe it. Services followed in general the order of the Swedish Church, Esbjörn clad in clerical coat with bands. At prayer meetings Methodists were often in attendance and no one prevented their speaking and prayer, though Esbjörn apparently suffered, especially when things became violent.

Esbjörn, I am afraid, did not feel unmixed joy when I and my company arrived. Many of us were decided "Luther Readers" and shared the views of pastor Hedberg in Finland. We abhorred all work-righteousness, were prejudiced against the new Church hymnals and all interpretations of the Word of God that did not accord with Luther's writings. We laid great stress on the instrinsic value of Word and Sacrament, and we advocated the unconditional absolution.[1] From the start we were naturally opposed to Methodism, but neither were we altogether satisfied with Esbjörn. It seemed to us that he emphasized too much the work of grace in the heart and not enough stress on Christ and His work for us, that he favored sanctification above justification by faith. Yet in conversation and discussion with him we could not charge him with any false or un-Lutheran teaching. He agreed with us on some points, and on those where we had some differences he sought wisely and reasonably to put us right. That our Lutheranism was not superior to his became clear enough not long afterwards in the controversy with Baptists, when many of the strictest "Lutheran Readers" went over to them.

Because of poor roads and sickness Esbjörn was not able to visit often in Galesburg, Moline and Rock Island, yet he did occasionally. On these journeys under these circumstances he was really pitiable. I cannot forget the time he once came back from Galesburg. Weather and roads were of the worst. At the Edwards river the frail horse and the rickety wagon had gotten stuck in the mud, so that he had to get off, get down in the water, unhitch the horse and lead the mudstained animal home. At home the whole family was sick with malaria. Though he himself shook with the fever he had to go out in the slush to the cow-barn and milk his cow (I had, unfortunately not learned the art). Such travels and experiences were not uncommon for him at that time.

[1]direct absolution by the pastor in confessional, as against conditional "if confession is sincere"

Concerning his journey to raise funds I can add the following: I accompanied him from Moline to Columbus (Ohio) because it had been decided that I should enter the Lutheran "Capital University" in Columbus. We left Moline the morning of April 24th, 1851, by steamer and reached Burlington the same evening. We stayed there until May 4th. The day after our arrival I looked up a German pastor by the name of Dressel and got his permission to hold a Swedish service in the evening. About 200 of our fellow countrymen were present. On April 26 Esbjörn went by stagecoach to New Sweden and remained there over Sunday, while I stayed in Burlington and conducted a service in a school house outside the town. On the 29th Esbjörn returned in company with M.F. Hokanson, who struck me as being rather young. In the evening we had a service with Holy Communion in the same school house. On May 4th we continued our journey to St. Louis. There we stayed briefly and got acquainted with only one Swede, a Dr. Jacoby if I remember right. In Louisville, Ky. we had an experience that could have been tragic. Esbjörn was acquainted with a couple of merchants there, Ahlmark and Collini, whom we wished to meet. The Ohio River has rapids just outside the city and boats avoid them by using a 4 mile canal around them. It was already evening and since it took the boat two or three hours to get through, we decided to walk into the city to look up our countrymen. We finally located them. It was now after midnight, all the stores were closed. We thoughtlessly pounded hard on the door of Ahlmark and Collini store, forgetting we were in Kentucky. After a while a window was slowly opened above us and hand with a pistol appeared. Had not Esbjörn immediately mentioned their and his names, we had certainly been shot, for our countrymen took us for robbers. Now we were admitted and warmly welcomed.

May 10th we arrived in Columbus via Cincinnati. Here we were well received. Esbjörn stayed a few days, giving a number of speeches in his broken English and receiving some contributions from the various Lutheran congregations. Then he continued on his way and I stayed in Columbus.

A couple of excerpts from his letters to me that same year (1851) serve to cast light on his thinking and activities as well as on conditions in Andover and its surroundings.

"Andover, Henry Co. Ill. Aug. 21, 1851

My Dear Brother in the Lord!
Grace and peace be with you now and forever!
"Hearty thanks for your dear letter! As usual I have been so

occupied with a variety of errands and my time has been so taken up with travels that I have not been able to answer it before this. For the same reason there are many things here that wait to be done. Furthermore I get depressed and exhausted when so much depends on me. I am sorry to hear that you have again been sick, but the Lord be praised that you are well again. I hope that you continue to enjoy the grace of God in this respect, but especially I hope and pray that in humility and sincerity you will keep close to the Lord Jesus Christ, so that He may be your life, and you may have Him not only for justification but also for sanctification. Often it is difficult to have and experience both, truly and in right order. There are many who are strictly correct in doctrine and zealously strive for true Lutheranism, confess and believe true justification by faith, but forget sanctification — they cry Lord, Lord and are not anxious about the will of the Father who is in heaven. Others are so concerned about sanctification, that they forget its true foundation, which is faith — they shout "Christian duty, Christian efforts, Christian life" from morning to night. The former is as dangerous as the latter. Both lead to perdition — both unbelieving love and loveless belief. Those most zealous for purity of doctrine are most often in peril of falling in the former trap. I see from your letter that you have come across some of that kind where Christianity is worn on their sleeves. During the twelve years I have experienced the unmerited grace of God I have seen many such both here and in Sweden and in many cases found that not all that glitters is gold. As you grow in service and experience you will doubtless observe the same. Let everything make for your own humility and increase of sincerity and faithfulness in grace. Let your heart be concerned not only about faith, but with the object of faith, Jesus Christ the crucified.[1] No one becomes faithful or continues in faith if he tries to force himself or others force him, saying, 'You must believe, you must believe in spite of everything.' This word "must" is a command which does no good. No, if a person is to come to the "mystery" of faith, so that he not only talks about it, but experiences it, then he must[2] look on Christ in His Atonement and love as if He were painted before our eyes, as He was for the Galatians. Look therefore upon Christ, who is the beginning and fulfillment of faith, then you will grow in faith and love and be prepared sometime to break the bread of life to your fellow country men with blessing.

[1] Norelius says in a note that he abhors this fine pietistic distinction.
[2] Norelius puts "sic" here.

"Thanks for the news. I don't have many, except that I came home on July 7th with over $2100 for our church building. We hope to get also a building in Moline and one at Skunk River (= New Sweden, Iowa). In Andover we are in full speed making brick. We have been hindered by terribly wet weather, but now things are improving. Many Swedes have come from Östergötland and Småland, but nothing has been heard of those from Helsingland. It is reported that there are 300 Swedes in Peru. The second Sunday I was home the Andover congregation was increased by 18 persons. Methodism here is on the way out. While I was gone the Methodist preacher paid no attention to his people here. This has opened the eyes of many as to their partisan spirit and indifference to things spiritual. Here in the West the Spring and Summer have been miserable, with rain and flooding. In Andover the mills and saws have been more or less destroyed. In Moline a part of the dam is gone, likewise in Camden [Milan] and elsewhere.__

Your friend in Christ,
L.P. Esbjörn"

"Andover, Henry Co. Ill. Nov. 27, 1851
Dear Brother in the Lord Christ!
Grace and peace!
However busy I am, I must hasten to thank you for your dear letter which was most welcome for me. I learn from it that the Lord protects and guides you, to the praise of His name. May He protect and continue to help you! But I also note that you are in economic distress, wherefore I have taken up a few collections among our people to help you with what is most necessary. I am sending herewith $10, to begin with. Please send by return mail a receipt so that I can inform the donors. This is not much, but it helps a bit on the way, and I hope God will provide more.

I am sorry that you don't have much opportunity to speak Swedish. You are to be commended for at least reading the mother tongue daily.

Brother, you are a little mistaken about what I said concerning faith, justification and good works. I did not say that they have and believe the true righteousness, but that they "*confess* and *believe*" the true righteousness. I was speaking of just those *confessing* and dead heroes of faith. Even if they could talk eloquently and *previously have had* much experience but now do not bear the fruits of faith, they are still with all their boasting withered branches. I do not judge too severely a person's deeds but I want to see a poverty of spirit and repentence in those who say they believe. A person can be deficient in deeds, but he doesn't excuse his deficiency, as I sadly have found in my many years of experience to be the case among various kinds of Christians. I have many times found true what you yourself say, that they "bear their faith on their sleeves," and often most among those who talk big and judge haughtily.

"Thanks for your detailed story about happenings in Columbus. I read with pleasure what you tell, though I am terribly pressed for time to reply. Now I scribble these lines in the midst of cares and trouble with Johanssons in Moline.[1] The church there has been roofed and covered on three sides. It is 24 × 30 feet and will look rather attractive. In Andover we hope to have the basement ready so that it can be used at Christmas. That church will be 30 × 45 feet, a good brick and stone building. The trustees have given us 10 acres of land in the village._____

"Methodism here loses more and more. The Swedes are beginning to be disappointed in its hocus pocus. Palmquist is now in Galesburg, at least for the present, working among the Swedes as a Lutheran preacher. So far he has no license [from a Synod]. If we had 3 or 4 hundred dollars we could buy back the building we have together with the Wesleyans, and have our own Lutheran congregation.

Your brother in the Lord.

L.P. Esbjörn"

Palmquist's Name Reminds Us that We Are now at the Beginning of The Baptist Controversy

The account given in *Svenskarne i Illinois* p. 293, about "the Swedish Baptists in Illinois" is not altogether accurate. A.T. Mankie and P. Soderstrom were certainly not among the eight who are said to have come from Sweden with Fr. Nilson. I never heard of more than one Mankie, whom I knew and who accompanied Esbjörn as a lay delegate, when the Evang. Luth. Synod of Northern Illinois was organized in Cedarville [Wisconsin]. P. Soderstrom was in the same group as I in leaving Sweden and surely was not a Baptist. Both these persons became Baptists after Palmquist had joined the sect and began his activity. I very much doubt that Fredrik Nilson and those who came with him from Sweden had anything to do with the start of the Baptist congregation in Rock Island. Palmquist was really the one who began the Baptist [Swedish] movement in Illinois. To throw light on the movement I have to refer back to Sweden and my travel companions.

[1]Johansson later became a Baptist.

As already mentioned it was our plan when we emigrated to found in America a colony and establish an authentic Lutheran congregation. While in Gefle waiting for our ship the faithful had a meeting and elected a committee to go to Stockholm and ask pastor A. Viberg to be our minister. We knew and acknowledged him as a true Lutheran, who was in sympathy with our views. We hoped that already next year he might follow us to America. When Viberg did not feel he could accept our call he referred the committee to a school teacher, Gustaf Palmquist, a brother of the book publisher P. Palmquist. He proved willing to accept the call and to come to Illinois the following year. We had this answer when we emigrated. But when we got to Illinois the group scattered in different directions. One part stayed in Princeton, the first Swedes in that city. Another part remained in Andover, a part in Rock Island and Moline, and finally, a little later, a part in McGregor, Iowa. New ideas and experiences crowded on us, we were no longer as unanimous as we had been in Sweden. One went here, another there — no colony or congregation was now possible. Still there was one man who clung to the original plan, though it was realized in another way than had been contemplated. This man was Per Anderson (Joris Pelle) from Hassela. In the Spring of 1851 he journeyed to Minnesota and founded the settlement that later became the large and well-known Chisago Lake.

Palmquist came as planned to America in August, 1851 and later, towards autumn, to Illinois. The following letter to me reveal his news and purposes.

"Andover, Oct. 2, 1851

Dear Brother in Christ!

"The grace and peace of God increase in rich measure in your heart now and evermore! Amen.

"For your letter, dated Moline and Rock Island Feb. 3 (1851) thanks! In Sweden I several times intended to write you. But pressing duties and the decision to come to America resulted in my neglect. I need not tell you about my journey, for now I am here — here to proclaim His virtue who has called me to His wonderful light. So far I have not met any of those who wanted me to come. But from what I have learned these Swedes live in various places, so it won't be possible to meet them. But shortly I intend to travel to Rock Island and Iowa, hoping to find some of them, at least, whose names I know, including Sandman.[1] May the Lord guide for the best!

[1] E. Sandman from Hudiksvall, who emigrated 1849 — now residing near McGregor, Iowa.

"At present I am living with Jonas Anderson in Andover, so my address will be here until further change, in which case Jonas Anderson will forward mail to me. Insofar as I have heard and can find, the Swedes who called me to come here will be in no position for a long time to form a congregation and support any leader. Meanwhile since I am here I truly believe there will be opportunity for me to witness to the truth. If God gives me work I believe He will also give me food and clothes, for 'the laborer is worthy of his hire.'

"I have much to tell about the progress of God's kingdom in Sweden, but I hope to have better opportunity if possibly in the near future we can get together. Viberg is still in Stockholm. His health is poor, it is a question if he will ever be well again. He was anxious that I bring you his greetings. The Hudiksvall people and others have now left the Church, and therefore been fined 20 riksdaler per person by the magistrates' court. The verdict was set aside by the Appeals Court, but it is feared that the highest court will sustain it. Now as before there is no religious freedom in our land, and I doubt we will have it in our life time. Coercion in bodily and in spiritual matters leads many to emigrate to America. Many of the faithful in Christ send their greetings to you here. —

"I don't have time for more. May He who out of pure love separated us from the evil of the present world keep us without reproach until the end. In Christ we are free, joyful, saved, pure and perfect. We are nothing, He is all. May He remain so in our hearts to the end. Then shall we experience the goal of faith, namely our soul's salvation. This is my heart's wish for the friend and brother in Christ.

G. Palmquist"

Galesburg
January 9, 1852

"Brother Norelius!

"The grace and peace of God be with you and dwell in your heart now and forever! Amen.

"I thank you for your letters which have reached me though long on the way. On account of a number of trips and other business I have not had a chance to write until now. As you see I am now in Galesburg, and this on Esbjörn's insistent urging, staying here during the first part of winter, or probably to the end of February. Then I plan to move to Rock Island, and will stay there until in the Spring. I might undertake a journey up into Wisconsin and Minnesota. Then I would decide whether to remain there or some other place. On this account I have not joined any church and most likely will not do so before I make this trip. I stand on Lutheran ground in everything except baptism, on which I have some scruples. Not over its efficacy and power, but about the time and form in which it takes place, and this because of the difference I find between the first Christian Church and the present practices of the Lutheran Church. I find in the Scriptures no commandment to baptize children or example of such baptism. Our church fathers claim that child baptism was unknown before the end of the second century and not common until the time of Constantine. In the Bible passages where baptism is mentioned the act took place by immersion. I mention this so that you may gain assurance in this matter while you are at the school.

"This subject had aroused much attention the last few years in Sweden, especically in Stockholm and southern Sweden. Viberg had in this matter gone over almost wholly to Baptist principles. He had investigated and read more than most of us on the subject, desiring to find sufficient grounds for his former belief, but had not done so when I left Sweden. Yet there are differences among believers in Sweden as elsewhere. But we are one in Christ. By faith in Him we are made righteous and even holy in His sight; though we cannot often see or feel this, we are thus, and this gives me great joy and confidence.

"You ask what I think about Esbjörn and Hedstrom. I believe that we agree in the matter, indeed in everything. I remember well what you said in a letter to me while I was still in Sweden, and to that I say, Yea and Amen. If the former were clear in the fundamental matters, it would help him, for he wants to do right and he does his best. But the latter, he purposefully does wrong. At least I cannot conclude otherwise, for falsehood and deceit are not rare either in his preaching or conduct. And as far as holiness is concerned I see no difference between him and Erik Jansson. Wherever I have come I have encountered the doctrine of perfection and this weed has been planted by Erik Jansson and Hedstrom. If it is not death and ignorance that prevail then it is self-righteousness, which is even worse, — these are rich and so need nothing! I have found few of my fellow countrymen with whom I am in harmony. Many who were faithful in Sweden have since they came here been drawn into Methodism, or rather into the perfection teaching of Erik Jansson, for Wesley, the founder of Methodism, did not teach like Hedstrom here. Lately he has begun to oppose me indirectly, and to demean me and my preaching, carrying on frightfully. The people — the pitiable people — are so ignorant that they mostly believe him because he storms and makes such a racket. Alas, how miserable!!! The main subject of all my preaching has been Jesus Christ and him curcified, and I want no other main theme. The Lord have mercy on His people! O that light might come from heaven, so that errors would be revealed and souls be saved!

"Anders Ersson and Swedberg,[1] also Methodist preachers, have not carried on like Hedstrom, but they have been pretty well smitten by the holiness doctrine, which is most evident in every sermon, though in a refined form.—

G. Palmquist"

This letter was the first information I had that Palmquist was inclined toward the Baptists. I wrote him a warning letter immediately. He waited to reply until July. I give it here because of the light it casts on the beginning and development of the Swedish Baptists both in this country and Sweden.

Rock Island
July 9, 1852

"Dear Brother in Christ Jesus!

"The grace of our Lord Jesus Christ be with and over us now and forever! Amen.

"I thank you for the letter of 26th January. Partly negligence, partly other things have kept me hitherto from an answer. First, God be praised. I can inform you that I have had and still have physical health, though I have been mostly on the road and had to experience quite severe hardships in many forms. Spiritually, too, I am well in my faith in Jesus, my Lord and Savior, though I cannot grasp Him as I would or rejoice as I should. Still I am ransomed as I am, and always am redeemed, through His blood, that is, the forgiveness of sins . Therefore I would always be eager to do His will, and live acceptably to Him who for me is dead and arisen.

"Now a few words about baptism, not for proving anything about the Baptists, but only to tell when and how I came to think more deeply on this subject. It was while I was reading the Book of Acts, in 1845-1846. I read and reread my New Testament, but did not find anything to satisfy me sufficiently about child baptism. Not long afterwards I had a conversation with Johansson, a Baptist from Hull, England, and with Nilsson in Gothenberg, who had turned Baptist. This led me to search even more the Scriptures, Church History, the writings of Luther and others, such as the great and learned Martensen's work against the Bap-

---

[1]Ersson remained a Methodist until his death. Swedberg soon became a Baptist, serving as preacher around Lansing, Iowa.

tists, *The Scripture Guide to Baptism* by R. Pengilly, and *History of Baptism* by Hinton, and a German book of similar content. All this made me more certain that the Baptist doctrine was correct. I talked with many learned men to get clarity on the subject, but usually my scruples remained. When Viberg came to Stockholm about a year before I left I spoke often about it with him. Then he stood fully on Luther's foundation but lacked sufficient proof to demolish my scruples. Still my conscience did not prevent me from going on as before. Five weeks before I left Stockholm Viberg made a trip to Hamburg, where he learned to know a Baptist congregation which consisted mostly of faithful Christians. He found himself in full agreement with them as to faith and experience except on the question of baptism, for in this he held firmly to the Lutheran interpretation. When he left he was given a small book on the subject. He read it on the way home and became convinced thus that the Baptist was the correct teaching. He came to Stockholm, where many of the best Christians had already entertained Baptist notions. Now they were the more confirmed. They held these ideas when I left. When I came here I thought much on the situation, but for fear of offense did not publicly raise the issue. Still I did discuss the question in private conversation, though infrequently, because of the current controversies about the Methodist's holiness doctrine and the Lutheran's work-righteousness. These questions became more important in my thinking. My purpose lately, however, was to join the Lutherans. But I could not do this in these settlements without yielding to the authority of Esbjörn, who here was the leader, but who was no less oppressive than the State Church of Sweden. I made a trip northward to Sandman, 200 miles beyond Rock Island, (Lansing, Iowa), as well as to Minnesota — St. Paul and Stillwater, 500 miles away, to see if there would soon be a Swedish settlement and a place where I could work and find support. I did find Swedes there, but widely scattered, 4 or 5 families in a spot but 30 to 100 miles away from another, all in indigent circumstances. So I came back to await Viberg from Stockholm, who I believe is now on his way here, to join the Baptists. I had thoughts of doing the same, for the above mentioned reasons. On my return I heard of a strong Baptist movement in Galesburg (among the Americans), which led me to visit there to see what conditions were. I found them rather remarkable. A Baptist preacher by the name of Barry had come there for a few weeks and preached the Gospel in spirit and power. This had resulted in great blessing. On 6 Sundays he had baptized 106 persons, received

10 by letter of transfer, so had increased the congregation by 116. But that which gave me most wonder and joy was the healthy life of faith which the majority, as far as I could judge, evidenced.

"Several times I was urged to join them, but was not then so inclined. Though I did not object to their main theme I wanted to know the situation better. After a few days I understood better, and could not find anything that was not in accordance with Scripture. Furthermore no preacher was subject to bishops, rules or regulations — such do not exist. Each one was altogether free. I was satisfied and decided to join, this happened the 27th of last June. I imagine that I will soon go out as a preacher of this church. It doesn't make much difference what name we bear, only that we are children of God, striving for the glory of God's name and the promotion of the salvation of man. Each one for himself needs be sure that he lives the life of faith in the Son of God, and then holds to the Truth in every part, not because our forefathers so thought but because I myself have found that the Lord so teaches in His word. If henceforth He holds us to the Truth, the Truth will always make us free. I have greetings from Viberg. I recently had a letter from him. He hopes to come to America early in June, partly for his health's sake, partly to receive a right Christian baptism. He says he is altogether convinced of the truth of baptism. He proposes to stay here over winter, then return next summer to Sweden as a Baptist missionary, if he here can receive support for such a purpose. I haven't time for more. May God bless you with his grace and peace through faith in our Lord Jesus. This is the wish of your friend and brother in Christ.

G. Palmquist"

Palmquist was a likeable person, not ill-endowed as a preacher, and an unusually congenial individual. He knew how to accommodate himself and to attract young people through evening schools and singing sessions. It was evident that those who hitherto had had confidence in him would be won for his new teaching. Rock Island became the headquarters of his activities. On August 8, 1852 the first Swedes were baptized — Peter Soderstrom and two others. On the 13th of the same month a Swedish Baptist congregation was organized there which gradually attracted Swedes in Rock Island and Moline. From there the movement spread in other directions among the Swedish settlements. It led to hot disputes, and serious strife arose in many places about the question of baptism. For my part it meant deep distress to see the majority of my old friends and zealous "Luther Readers" who formerly had laid great stress on the objective nature of baptism, now became ensnared in the Baptist rationalism, then sliding deeper, and many finally rejecting all Christian faith and ending as outright free thinkers. Esbjörn was deeply anxious. In fear that I had been or might be contaminated by this error he wrote me an enlightening and warning letter, containing these words:

"Since many of your friends (among them even Viberg) have fallen into this error I lay it, before God, on your conscience to consider all I have said so that you are forewarned when very likely they will come and try to draw you into the same delusion. If you are already taken in or become so, pray the *Lord* to enlighten you — in such an important matter let not personal considerations sway you. If unfortunately you do embrace the error, let not your conscience permit you to accept favors from a Lutheran school and then become a servant of a strange and erroneous communion. Do not wonder and take it ill that I speak so in love to you. I have seen so many waver and fall who in this issue have not understood the foundation, the firm foundation, of our confessions. When Viberg and Palmquist can be misled there is danger also for their friends. Old Smith and Soderstrom could not remain in the Lutheran Church because children would have to be baptized, though they could have no children. It has come so far."

In a later letter, August 14, 1852, he wrote:

"I thank you heartily for your letter, which gave me great joy, first for your Christian sympathy and friendly comfort in my sorrow,[1] and further as I find that you are not affected by the Baptist error and one-sidedness to which some of your friends have fallen victim. I cannot express how much joy this has given me. My joy is the greater when I find how you are able in reading Calvinistic authors to take the good and sift out the valueless and groundless. They go on page after page and in whole books just because they cannot accept John 3:3,5 and 1 Peter 3:21, etc. in the simple and childlike way that the Lord has ordained, without making a great ado about reason. Their rationalism shows most clearly in their cry, "How can children *believe* when they cannot *understand?*" The Lord says otherwise in Matt. 18:6 and Luke 1:15, latter half.

"Now I would ask and urge you to write in a Christian, serious and affectionate manner to your Christian friends, especially

[1] Esbjörn's wife had recently died.

Per Anderson, Anders Ersson, Per Soderstrom and Smidt in
Moline, to others, to Sweden, to any you may know in Galesburg.
This error has taken root especially in Galesburg, somewhat in
Rock Island and Moline, but not here in Andover where I have
been in a better position to guard against it.—"

In the same letter he adds:

"For a long time I have not been able to get out because of
sorrow, sickness, death, and lack of a horse. A frightful attack of
cholera has afflicted newcomers from Småland and Västergötland. We have buried around 30 — many more have been sick.
— I have taken into the house 3 families — almost all their
members sick, some gravely, 2 have died.
    "The basement of the church has been covered and provided
with windows and floor. A place for the steeple is open. In the
upper story the roof is not completed, nor windows, though here,
not in place. We lack plastering, benches, pulpit and altar, and
our means are exhausted. Help, any one who can help."

In these controversies a change is apparent in Esbjörn's doctrinal
position, less clear to himself, maybe, than to others. Yet he himself
acknowledged such a change, in his own words. In a letter of May 12,
1853 to me he wrote:

"For some time I have found it necessary once again to read
the symbolic books,[1] in connection with the many opinions and
strifes here. This re-reading has not only made the Gospel more
clear and living for me, but also deepened by conviction concerning the purity of our Church's teaching and its agreement with
the Scriptures. Especially the Formula of Concord has shown me
that the inclination towards anti-nomism of some of those who
claim to be the most strict Lutherans is *not* the doctrine of the
Lutheran Church. Also one finds that in the private writings of
Luther, especially of his earlier life, there are expressions and
ideas which the Church never accepted. For example what Luther
says about contrition in the beginning of his sermon on repentance
in 1518 is repudiated in the Apology of the Augsburg Confession,
art. 5, written 12-13 years later with the consent of the beloved
father. But enough of this. In general I have so much enjoyed
reading again the symbolic books of our Church, and received such
value and increase of faith and life, that I wanted to advise you, in

[1]The doctrinal statements of the Lutheran Church.

case you have not recently gone through them, to do as I did, begin with the Augsburg Confession and proceed to the end of the Formula of Concord."

Certain it is that from this date on there was a soundness in Esbjörn's Lutheranism, and it was a joy to hear the fresh and courageous witness with which he proclaimed and defended the Gospel. The baptismal controversy continued and increased in strength for a few years, until it finally became exhausted and lost its influence on the majority of our Swedish people, mainly because of an awakened clarity regarding the Lutheran teaching and the inner weakness of the Baptist position.

Gustaf Palmquist was the leader for the Baptist movement among the Swedes in Illinois and Iowa until 1854. Pastor Viberg was a visitor also in America during 1853. That year Fr. O. Nilson came, after his banishment from Sweden. Besides these a number of preachers arose among the new converts in this country.

The Andover Congregation

Until the Fall of 1852 pastor Esbjörn was the only Lutheran pastor in Henry, Knox, and Rock Island counties and his parish extended almost 50 miles from one end to the other. He visited and cared for Galesburg, Knoxville, Henderson, Andover, Rock Island and Moline. Much of his time was spent on carriage between these places. At that time roads and bridges were in bad shape, and the difficulties he suffered in bad weather caused deterioration in his strength and health. But that Fall he received help when pastor T.N. Hasselquist arrived from Sweden and took over Galesburg and the region around it. A licensed candidate for the ministry, C.J. Valentin, was assigned to Moline and Rock Island. Thus Esbjörn's field was limited mainly to Andover and its surroundings. But the Andover congregation was itself quite extensive. It included, first of all, Berlin — now called Swedona, La Grange (or Elägran as the Swedes pronounced it) — now under the name Orion, Hickory Grove, now Ophiem. In a word all the newly settled Lutherans in the Andover region were considered part of the Andover congregation. Berlin and La Grange early became separate centers for services and in time were organized as congregations. The Fall of 1853 the Andover congregation had 210 communicant members, the amount contributed to the pastor's salary that year was $80. An appeal, dated Andover June 17, 1853, directed 'to all

Ministers and Members of the Lutheran Church in the U.S.' was signed by L.P. Esbjörn, Erik Westerlund, Nels Petterson, Samuel Janson, N.M. Kilberg, contains the following concerning the church building:

> "On the advice of our leading benefactors we began to build at once. — But in 1851 the weather was unusually rainy and we met with great difficulties. Brick was spoiled, mills and dams were carried away in floods, what we bought was very expensive and had to be hauled 30 miles. Winter cut short our work, but we continued it last year despite many obstacles, such as poor harvest, low wages, and a frightful attack of cholera with its consequences. Among other things we were forced to use not a small part of the lumber which we had bought and hauled in for the church, as coffins for the poor, deceased immigrants. — During the winter we have held our services in the basement, which is not plastered, and is partly open to the sky, since there is no floor in the upper story and a 10 foot square hole appears in the roof where a tower is supposed to be erected."

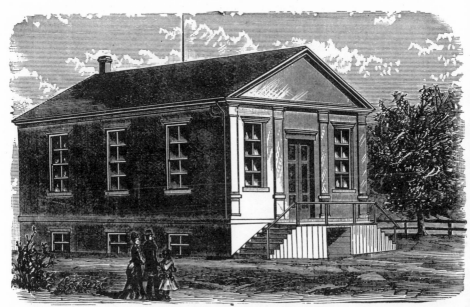

THE OLD CHURCH IN ANDOVER.

By the First Sunday in Advent, Dec. 3, 1854 the church was sufficiently finished so that it could be dedicated. This event was part of a

Conference meeting then being held in Andover, and in the Conference *Minutes* we read:

> "Advent Sunday, Dec. 3, was a holiday of special grace. The Word of God was proclaimed for an unusually large congregation, with power and Spirit, and a significant number received the Lord's Supper. The high point and feature of the day took place in the dedication of the church. The members who had worked and striven for more than 3 years raised with joy their voices in hymns of thanksgiving to the throne of God. One could easily observe that they were highly edified and strengthened to go on without wavering in the battle for the Lord. At 3 o'clock an English sermon was delivered by Rev. Doing (a Presbyterian), who had been invited by decision of the Conference."

The church which had been erected, accommodating 300 or more persons, if really packed, was at that time considered something remarkable, but would now be deemed too small and insignificant even for an ordinary barn. It is not at all built in churchly style — one can hardly imagine a more prosaic and unattractive form, either outside or inside. Building and windows are rectangular. The ground floor was a dark hole, but had to serve as living space for newcoming immigrants, many of whom ended their days there. The pulpit, surrounded by a half circle altar rail, right in the middle of one end reminded one of a kitchen cupboard formerly found in rural Sweden. The pulpit's upper part where the pastor stood, was not much larger than a split salt barrel, and set right against the wall.

The old church still stands and the Andover people have given it a new roof, largely in response to the pleas and efforts of older women who were along at the beginning. It is an eloquent memorial from the early period. It still serves as a school house. The Synod ought to have enough interest to preserve this monument, which has become more remarkable with the years. In front lies the old cemetery where so many of Andover's first Swedes rest.

Dissension in the Congregation — Esbjörn's Leaving

Following the heated strife with Methodists and Baptists, from which both pastor and congregation seemed to have emerged with a fuller consciousness of what they possessed in the Evangelical Lutheran Confessional books, the congregation grew both inwardly and externally, in stability and numbers. The liturgy of the Church of Sweden and its practices were more closely observed, while at the same time emphasis was placed on a healthy spiritual life. Granted that the latter was less obvious than the churchly rites, yet one cannot complain about a congregation which in a sensible and orderly spirit cares for the preaching of God's pure Word and the administration of the sacraments within its walls. On the contrary one has reason greatly to thank God for such a condition after one has seen the destructive results of the sects' attacks, sweeping like a prairie fire over the fields and leaving in its wake a black, burned, desolate terrain, making people altogether unfit for faith.

The calm which had settled over the congregation in Andover unfortunately was disturbed by candidate B.G.P. Bergenlund, who appeared there in the Spring or Summer of 1855. We learn something of this individual from two letters written to pastor Hasselquist, the first from Jamestown, N.Y., undated but undoubtedly from early 1853, the second from Sugar Grove, Pa., May 15th. He seems to have come from Ignaberga or thereabouts, in Kristianstad County, and he had met Hasselquist in Sweden. He set foot, supposedly in New York, January 10, 1853, had been robbed of all his money — 200 crowns, lost some of his clothes, but somehow got to Jamestown. Now he wrote to Hasselquist, and asked to be informed "on conditions among the Swedes in the West, if perchance there was any place where a preacher of the Lutheran religion was desired, for here I find certain Swedes trying to draw them to other sects." Also he says, "I would be thankful if I can get any information on what education is required to become a Lutheran pastor in America, on how a person is chosen by a congregation to be its pastor, to what body or person one should apply for ordination or for help to support oneself or find a church, etc. Here in the Jamestown region are several hundred Swedes. Several want me to stay here, but they are very poor. A few belong to the Methodist Church." Then he asks for advice, "how one should act when one is requested by some to administer the sacraments, since here one can turn only to American ministers." The immigrants "desire services in Swedish and according to the Swedish Handbook. In the American churches they lack especially the confession of sins and the Creed. I have now been here 3 weeks, and the people, at least some of them, hunger for the Word of Life."

From his second letter we learn that Hasselquist had replied and asked answers to three questions: "1) Have you really been converted to the Lord, and though poor in spirit, are under the discipline of the Spirit and in faith's blessed union with your Saviour?" "2) Have you thought through the differences between us Lutherans and especially Methodists and Baptists, who are most zealous in gaining adherents and have won over a number of persons including even ministers?" "3) Are you in your heart loyal to the teaching of our Church, so that after a while you aren't attracted to another Church and thereby create offense?" To the first two he answered rather well, though somewhat vaguely and jumbled. To the third he replied, "Yes, I am now more than before completely convinced of its superiority over others, so that with God's help I will if necessary give my life for it." He adds that the Swedes in the place have "drawn up a document, wherein I am accepted for a year." Finally he asks some peculiar questions: "How about Esbjörn, some say he is not a Lutheran pastor but has gone over to the Presbyterian doctrine or Church? Does Hedstrom in New York have a fund he can use as he sees fit or according to some regulations? Can pastor Hasselquist obtain a license for me at once or later? Must one be able to preach in English to be ordained?" He signed both letters "Berglund," not "Bergenlund."

In the summer of 1853 Hasselquist visited Jamestown and Sugar Grove and met with Berglund. He got the impression that in view of the dire need of pastors Berglund might possibly be used in the service of the church. In any case he advised him to be present at the annual meeting of the Synod of Northern Illinois, in October 1853 at Galesburg, to submit to examination. B. did appear and underwent the examination for license. According to the report on the examination, "we have examined B.G.P. Bergenlund in dogmatic theology, church history, biblical exegesis, Latin, Greek and German, and found that he posseses considerable knowledge in these branches, and we recommend that he be given license for one year." Consequently he was authorized to serve as a minister until the next annual meeting, whereupon he returned to Jamestown and Sugar Grove and began his work.

Before long various complaints were raised against the man, both in Jamestown and Sugar Grove, though particulars were hard to get at. At the Synod meeting in La Salle, in September 1854, the question of his license came up, and it was decided that it be continued until the difficulties in his congregations be investigated. Depending on the report that pastor Hasselquist would make after he made the authorized investigation, the Synod president would either recall or continue the license.

Late that Fall, when Hasselquist was in Jamestown and Sugar Grove, he tried in the brief time available to track down the complaints against Bergenlund, but was unable to discover anything that might lead to a decision. The disaffection with Bergenlund was probably not due to any real falsehood in his preaching, but rather to his peculiar, selfish, and negligent manner of life and of ministry.

In the Spring of 1855 he left his congregations without notice and in May appeared in Moline, Illinois. Esbjörn wrote to me in a letter of May 16, "Bergenlund has now unexpectedly come here, and proceeded to announce and hold services in the Moline congregation without seeing or informing me or securing the permission of the church Council." One notes that the Moline congregation was again under the care of Esbjörn after the removal of Valentin.

On June 14th Esbjörn wrote again: "Bergenlund has now obtained license and is here trying to find a position in Moline, in my congregation or anywhere. Probably arrangements can be made to have him as my assistant. I hope it turns out well."

What happened was that Bergenlund did not find acceptance in Moline, came to Andover and started going from house to house, gaining friends and their confidence. It was suggested that he become an assistant to Esbjörn and a teacher in the congregation's school. No doubt this proposal was well meant on the part of the people, for Esbjörn indeed needed assistance, but he was not happy to have Bergenlund as such. Interest in Bergenlund grew, and to prevent his going on without renewed license Esbjörn wrote to the synodical president and secured a renewal for him.

Midsummer day the congregation elected a committee to consider carefully "the question of providing an assistant pastor and school teacher and to bring to the congregation its advice and a proposal in this matter." Later the committee rendered the following report:

> "By more than a 2/3 majority the committee decided to recommend strongly to the congregation not to make any arrangement with B.G.P. Bergenlund, the minister who had been proposed for these duties, and this because of reasons the committee considered valid. If nevertheless the congregation should decide to accept him the committee hereby recommends that he be accepted on probation until the following October (when the Synod would meet) and on these conditions: 1) that he pledges both in public and private teaching faithfully to follow the confessions of the Lutheran Church in its symbolical books, and in

the conduct of the public worship services not to deviate unnecessarily from the order and customs of the Lutheran Church, 2) that in brotherly consultation with the pastor of the congregation he agrees to a schedule by which there be services every Sunday in Andover's church, two services a month in Berlin and one service a month in La Grange, unless there be important reasons which would necessitate exceptions, 3) that he hold school 5 days a week for children of the congregation — 1 month in Andover, 1 month in Berlin, 1/2 month in La Grange and 1/2 month south of the [Edwards] river, 4) that as salary the congregation pay him 10 cents per communicant and 3 cents a day for each of the school children, but 2 cents a day for each one if there are 3 or more children in the family, also board during school terms, 5) that the pastor's salary remain as before unchanged.

On behalf of the committee:

L.P. Esbjörn   J.E. Stenholm
Samuel Johnsson   N.M. Kilberg
Jonas Anderson   Peter Magnus Magnusson"

Despite the objection of the majority of the committee the congregation called Bergenlund to be assistant to the pastor and school teacher, which shows that he had many friends in the church. But the more secure he became the more he displayed his pecularities. If it was his natural bent or if he sought notoriety is uncertain, but in his individual behavior or in public performance he was different from other people and at least from other ministers. For example, he could appear in unsuitable clothes when he led in the worship service even with gloves on his hands; when at the altar he might sometimes stand at the corner and assume a comical posture; when he sang the liturgy and pronounced the benediction he sometimes ascended the pulpit. Once in teaching the confirmation children, he took the boys and the girls separately up in the balcony and explained the 6th Commandment, while the other group sat in the church. I leave out many other oddities.

At the synod meeting in Waverly, October 1855, when the question of Bergenlund's license was taken up by the Ministerium, the committee (O. Anderson and Erl. Carlsson) to whom the relevant documents had been referred, reported: "that it had found these documents contained favorable testimonials regarding Mr. B's character and conduct together with an appeal to Synod's Ministeries that his license be renewed so that he might continue as a pastor's assistant in Andover." One of these letters was signed by 55 persons in Andover, one by 5 from Sugar Grove, Pa. The committee mentioned that there were difficulties in his case, which has been brought up at the Ministerium a year ago, and therefore recommended that Ministerium investigate them thoroughly.

The report on the investigation reads, "The matter was explored and discussed as far as the presented testimony permitted, but since none of the charges against Bergenlund could be proved, the following resolution was adopted: Inasmuch as brother Bergenlund has moved into brother Esbjörn's parish and intends to be his assistant, therefore be it resolved that his license be renewed for one year, on the express provision that while he is in this relationship he unqualifiedly submits to the arrangements and directions of pastor L.P. Esbjörn."

This highly imprudent act of the Ministerium, by which Esbjörn was forced to accept an assistant entirely against his will could only have ill effects. Esbjörn tried to accommodate himself as best he could. He drew up an "Instruction for vice-pastor B.P.G. Bergenlund" which is given here in full especially because it affords a picture of the congregational life at the time. It reads:

"Since the respected Synod of Northern Illinois at its latest meeting in Waverly resolved that as long as he is in Andover the Rev. Bergenlund shall perform his public and personal ministerial duties under my directions, the following instructions shall guide him in my absence:

1) In public and personal acts he is to show diligence and love in proclaiming the Word of God according to Holy Scripture and the symbolical books of the Lutheran Church.

2) At the worship service he is to follow the use and manner of our Church and in the customary formulas and prayers not to make more or other changes than those the Conference and I have made.

3) Receive members into the congregation according to the formula adopted by Synod.

4) Diligently instruct and confirm the congregation's confirmation class according to the ancient Christian usage of the Lutheran Church.

5) Hold examination in the homes of the congregation's districts (rotar), therewith carefully examining especially the youth in Catechism and Bible, and hold communion service the first Sunday of every other even month. He may, where conven-

ient, also hold study periods in preparation for communion or preaching.

6) Hold Sunday School for the youth as often as possible.

7) Officiate at weddings, baptism (of children), churching (of mothers), and funerals, according to the accepted usage.

8) In all matters physical and spiritual advance the well-being of the congregation, and show himself by teaching and living to be a worker without reproach.

9) In no way to allow, but rather strongly hinder, division in the congregation or the growth of parties, nor permit the introduction of alien religious elements, but avert all measures that could cause future divisions.

10) Keep church records in good order, as determined at the latest Conference meeting, hold congregational business meetings with a prior 8 day announcement, and as far as possible announce at regular services any other gatherings.

11) Not to permit unauthorized persons to preach or hold group meetings.

12) In regard to preaching by preachers of other denominations to follow closely the congregation's decision of June 27, 1852.

13) To preach in Berlin every third Sunday, and on all other Sundays and major holidays in Andover.

14) In general to observe the regulations of Synod for licentiates, such as that of not meddling in the affairs of other congregations without consent of the pastor.

15) To be concerned about the quality of church music and its improvement according to the authorized Haeffner Choral Book.

16) To seek in writing the advice of myself or the president of the Mississippi Conference if difficult or important matters arise which are not covered in these instructions.

If any of these directions are violated it shall be the duty of the trustees to inform me immediately, or if they fail or are unable to do it other members of the congregation, especially the Church Council shall do so.

L.P. Esbjörn
Andover, Jan. 13, 1856"

At New Year's Esbjörn started his work as agent for the Scandinavian professor's fund, first in Andover, then in Moline, Galesburg, etc. The plan was to spend some time in this country and then travel to Sweden — the latter was never realized. Meanwhile Bergenlund gained increasing foothold in Andover and began to act all the more independently without much attention to the instructions he had received. As a result Esbjörn resigned. In the beginning of March he had some thought of moving to the present Stockholm near Lake Pepin, Wisconsin. March 3, 1856 he wrote me in these words, "A brief notice in *Hemlandet*, No. 5, concerning the Swedish settlement east of Lake Pepin has kindled the idea of coming there, if God so wills. Now I would like to hear more from you, especially if it should mean an encroachment on you or affect your prospects if I settled in the proposed Swedenburg." But later that Spring he received a call from Princeton (Ill). This he accepted before Midsummer and with his family he moved there a little later.

Bergenlund remained in Andover, but seems to have held his position only by virtue of the arrangement which made him an assistant to the pastor. In the Fall before the meeting of Synod, 1856, the congregation, or a part of it had resolved to petition the Synod at its meeting in Dixon either to ordain Bergenlund or give him an honorable dismissal. But the Synod's Ministerium did neither, because of the "difficulties" some people had with him. It was decided, therefore to offer him a renewal of license for one more year."

A characteristic letter of Bergenlund to Pastor E. Carlsson at about this time is included here, since it helps us to understand the man better and because it throws some light on the history of the congregation.

"Andover, Henry Co., Ill.
September 4, 1856

"My dear trusted Brother!

"Again rumors are afoot in the camp, for through Brother Esbjörn's doings and trickery 27 members against 17 in a congregational meeting have demanded that Hokanson in Iowa be called here as pastor. But the majority did not realize that calling a pastor was to take place on a week day, so the greater part of the congregation decided to do what they could to retain me, either as pastor or layman, if Esbjörn could unfairly in Synod deprive me of the call which the Lord has given me to proclaim Jesus' Gospel to my poor fellow country men.

"Esbjörn repeated the old gossip, despite the fact that the records of Synod state that no charge could be proved, added other lies and said at the congregational meeting that he would do what he could to prevent my licensing. May God convert the poor brother! Now I would say to you as a friend that if Synod should be so unjust as to reject me, this would give joy to all enemies and to those in other denominations, who know that by the grace of God I am a competent teacher. Then I shall be forced to reveal much in both American papers and Swedish papers in Sweden and here about conditions, to the discredit of pastors and members of Swedish congregations. I do not ask of people to whom I have done no ill, but good, for grace and right to preach, for the Lord has sent me and ordained me, but I am unhappy and sorrowful in heart that my fellow pastors should be so hostile to me and the good that the Lord can perform through me. Were I to go to other sects I would surely find a place and better salary, but I should not do this, but serve in the Church in which I myself found life.

"I understand this much, that the American Lutheran preachers do not agree in all points with what the Swedish ones say. You know that here are 'Old and New School Lutherans.' Were all those who now are new school Lutherans to be cut off, how many would there be left? Were those who are friends of 'The Lutheran Observer' to be foiled, what kind of Lutheranism would that be? We know in part, we prophesy in part. For my part I will rather proclaim the Word of God freely, without license, everywhere, than be the object of so many flaming arrows as hitherto—

B.G.P. Bergenlund"

Andover's confidence in him seems thereafter to have increasingly diminished; it became clear that a great mistake had been made. In May 1857 he wrote to the synodical president that an arrangement had been made whereby his relationship to the Swedish Evangelical Lutheran congregation would be dissolved as soon as a pastor could be secured from Sweden. He asked for permission to visit vacant churches and new settlements, a request the president readily granted. I do not know when he left Andover, but his relationship to the Synod was determined at its meeting in the Fall of 1857. A committee (S.W. Harkey, O.C.T. Andren and J. Swensson) to whom his case had been referred, recommended his ordination, but after a long discussion the Ministerium resolved not to renew his license and that his name be removed from the clerical roll. This step was taken not because of any false doctrine, but because of his peculiar and un-ministerial behavior which made it impossible for him to be in charge of a congregation with any success. He roamed around the country a few years, especially in Minnesota, then in 1860 after the Scandinavians had withdrawn he rejoined the Northern Illinois Synod which ordained him. He preached mightily against the Augustana Synod, especially Esbjörn whom he assailed bitterly. Later he took off for Sweden, sought and obtained entrance into the Gothenburg diocese as a pastor in the Church of Sweden. But his oddities followed him and the old Bishop Björk during his lifetime had no little trouble with him.

When the Andover congregation realized its disappointment with Bergenlund, it called Pastor P. Peterson of the Vexiö diocese to be its pastor. He had, according to a letter to Pastor Erl. Carlsson, July 4, 1857, promised to come. This hope miscarried. The same man was called to several other congregations but never came to America.

During the vacancy Pastor O.C.T. Andrén of Moline visited the church, but he already had his hands full and could not come more than once a month. The congregation was in sore need of a pastor, but who could it call?

Pastor Jonas Swensson called to Andover

On the advice of Pastor E. Carlsson a call was extended in the Spring of 1858 to J. Swensson in Sugar Grove, Pennsylvania, who had come from Sweden two years earlier. Swensson was a conscientious person who was not prepared to move from a congregation on any kind of excuse. Therefore he found it difficult to decide what to answer. After much deliberation, many prayers and inner strife he finally decided to accept the call. It caused him much pain to leave these congregations in the East, as his diary attests. "I told the congregation of my decision about leaving," he wrote, "but I felt so deeply for the poor people as sheep without a shepherd, that I wavered much in my resolve."

The 6th of September 1858 he left Jamestown after a tender farewell, and on the 19th September he was installed with ceremony in his ministry. This was the first festive installation to take place in the Swedish Lutheran churches. We quote from his diary: "On September 18th brothers Carlsson and Norelius accompanied me (from the Synod meeting in Mendota) to Andover, where I was solemnly installed in my office the following day. The church was overflowing with worshipers, and the day was a festive one. First Carlsson gave the installation sermon, on Hebrews 13:17, and with deep seriousness impressed upon us the reciprocal duties of myself and the congregation. Then followed the installation, and my sermon. In the afternoon Norelius and Carlsson preached."

At his accession the congregation consisted of 496 communicants — the largest in the Synod. Despite the financial crisis 1857-58 the economic situation of the people in the parish was in general favorable. The most severe trials of pioneer life were now back of them, and they could view the future with hopes brighter than they had previously had.

PASTOR JONAS SWENSSON.

Here Swensson remained uninterruptedly at his post for 15 years until the Fall of 1873, when he was called from the militant Church on earth to the eternal rest of the triumphant Church. Here he was to perform his real life's work in America. During his time the first parsonage was built and the present stately church, in which he had to experience both joy and sorrow. But the greater part of his ministry lay after 1860 wherefore it is not treated in this volume.

In connection with Andover brief mention can here be made of Berlin, the present Swedona.

Berlin was the first congregation which grew out of the old Andover one. The place lies about 8 miles west of Andover and has a rather pleasant site in Mercer County, along the Edwards River.

Nils Kilberg was among the first Swedes here, since 1849. In 1850 Gustaf Larson and Anders Samuelson came from Sunds parish in Östergötland. Peter Magnus Magnuson, L.P. Esbjörn's father-in-law, came from the same parish quite early, but most came in 1855.

Already in Esbjörn's time Berlin began to be an independent preaching place, and a frame church was built 1858. The congregation was organized 1859 by Pastor Swensson. In 1860 there were 227 communicant members and the budget of $805 almost equalled that of Andover.

Chapter 3

Galesburg and Knoxville, etc.

Galesburg lies in the middle of the western part of Knox Co., 164 miles west of Chicago, 43 miles from Burlington, 50 from Rock Island. It was founded in 1836 by a colony from Oneida Co., New York, led by Pastor G.W. Gale, from whom it is named. The colonists were a God-fearing people and determined first of all to establish both churches and schools. Already in 1837 they began Knox College. A Ladies Seminary was built in 1841. The village was incorporated February 14, 1857 and in 1873 it became the county seat. The first locomotive steamed into the city December 7, 1854 on the nearly completed Chicago, Burlington and Quincy R.R. The first newspaper, the "Knox Intelligencer" appeared January 1, 1849.

The First Swedes in Galesburg and Knoxville

In 1848 Galesburg had only the following Swedes: John Youngberg and family, one of the first of the Bishop Hill colonists, who later moved to Galva but then returned to Galesburg after some time, and then moved to California in 1860; Nils Hedstrom, a tailor, now living near Victoria; Anders Thorsell from Djurby in Westmanland, a member of the original party that settled in Bishop Hill; a family by the name of Modine; a widow Kristina Muhr, and a shoemaker named Olof Nilson.[1] People disappointed in Bishop Hill thus became the first Swedes in Galesburg.

In the story of the congregation in Andover we have already seen the list on which Esbjörn had written the names of some, probably of most, of the Swedes who were in Galesburg 1850. I learned to know some of them when I made a visit there late that year. To describe Galesburg and Knoxville at that time and my experiences there I quote from my diary: On the 19th of December, 1850 my brother and I walked from Andover over the prairie to Galesburg, a distance of some 25 miles, in an area thinly populated. We were tired when we reached Galesburg by evening, and found quarters with a certain Renstedt. Galesburg is a small town with small frame houses and, at least this time of the year, dirty streets. There are a few Swedish families here mostly Methodists, or so inclined. There is no work for

[1]From *Svenskarne i Illinois*, 133.

newcomers. On the 20th Renstedt went with me and we tried in every way to find a place where I could support myself for the winter, but in vain. On the 21st I met A.G. Svedberg (later a Baptist minister in Rock Island and in Lansing, Iowa) and Erik Sund who had come to this region the year before and whom I knew somewhat from home. They were now ardent Methodists and willing to help me find a place. Svedberg accompanied me to Knoxville, 5 or 6 miles from Galesburg, but the little village yielded neither advice nor help. I stayed over night with a kind shoemaker, Adolf Anderson, maybe the only Swede in the place.

On my return the following day, the 22nd, to Galesburg, I found room with a Swedish tailor, named Hedstrom, until Monday the 24th. While there I had the opportunity of being along one evening at a Swedish-Methodist class meeting, the first I had attended in America, and I thought it very peculiar. A young man from Dalarne was leader, very stern in manner. He thundered at the people that they should stand up and say something or pray, a command not all could comply with. One young farmhand newly arrived became frightened, stood up and read a few verses from the Swedish hymnbook, his teeth chattering and his knees trembling. The performance gave me a painful impression. On Christmas Eve I became acquainted with a Norwegian student at Knox College, a brother to the Norwegian pastor in Chicago, Paul Andersen, a friendly young man who showed me much kindness. Right on Christmas Eve he found a place for me to work a week for an American farmer by the name of Hitchcock who lived at the border of the town. Here I spent my first Christmas in America, but, oh, what a Christmas! My hosts were Presbyterians or Congregationalists, and on principle celebrated no Christmas. Dogs had killed 7 or 8 of his sheep one night, my work on Christmas day was to help skin these sheep. Oh God, I thought, if this is the way they celebrate Christmas in America then it is no fun here. Then I visited a few days with the aforementioned Captain Ljungberg[1] and at the end of the month returned to Andover.

So my memories of Galesburg aren't so pleasant, but I have recounted them to enable my readers to judge how Galesburg looked at the close of 1850.

We have seen from Esbjörn's reports why there was delay in the organization of a congregation in Galesburg. According to an article in *Korsbaneret*[2], 1888, this took place August 24, 1851, with a membership of 40 — their names are not recorded. A Sunday School

[1]Youngberg?
[2]by Norelius

had been started as early as the Spring of 1850, but it was conducted in English and by students of Knox College, so did not serve the needs of a Lutheran congregation.

As a rule Esbjörn visited the congregation every other Sunday until Hasselquist's arrival. Services were held in an unfinished building which was claimed by the Wesleyan Methodists but originally was meant for the Lutherans. We learned something about this building in Esbjörn's reports to the American Home Missionary Society. "After Hasselquist came this building, 40 × 28 feet, was bought for a sum of $600." In the Fall of 1851 Pastor Esbjörn came to Galesburg with a preacher, G. Palmquist from Stockholm, arranging that he should conduct services. We have already seen what were the results. Also we have already told of the coming of Hasselquist and the people from North Skåne. Hasselquist arrived October 28, 1852 and a new day dawned for the Swedish Lutheran congregation there.

The Development of the Congregation during the Hasselquist Period 1852-1863

Here I ask to use a part of the above mentioned article in *Korsbaneret*. "No work but has its own trials and worries, and least of all is this the case with the work of an evangelical minister. The pastors of Lutheran congregations, especially pioneers, who in the deepest sense are preparers of the way, can relate various incidents in the strict school of trials and difficulties. So also here. Other denominations did everything they could to undermine confidence in the newly arrived pastor among the Americans in the city. Especially they held forth that one should not support a minister who 'preached for money.' Yet the pastor was received with unusual graciousness by the American Colton and others. A large dinner was held, attended by the American pastors as well as by teachers at Knox College, in order to make the acquaintance of Pastor Hasselquist.

"We want to mention some things from Pastor Hasselquist's earliest years. At first he lived in a couple of small rooms in a house where the other half was occupied by an intoxicated former Erik Jansonist, who despite his drinking was decent enough, but whose wife quarreled from morning to night. The larger room served all purposes — study, kitchen, parlor, etc. Conveniences and furniture were accordingly. At first there was no bed in the house, the floor had to serve. The table consisted of the box in which the pastor had brought his books. For its uniqueness we mention that some of the other religious groups called Pastor H's books his "idols," for studies were considered as pernicious for a minister! The house was so loosely constructed that when it rained the floor was covered with water. But was this important, when it was a question of doing the Lord's work?"

"Pastor Hasselquist chose the first three verses of 1 Corinthians, chapter 2, as text for his initial sermon. It made a deep and lasting impression on those present. 'When I came to you, brethren, I did not come proclaiming to you the testimony of God in lofty words or wisdom.' That this text served as a keynote for the great and ever the same, yet infinitely varying theme, which was to occupy this preacher throughout a successful career in the Lord's vineyard, that we know who are so well acquainted with both the man and his activities. Those in attendance brought candles and chairs with them to the service, and the preacher could hardly make out the objects in the church. 'It was a wonderful worship hour and still stands there clearly in my memory. Poverty and its attendant inconveniences were lightly and gladly endured when one did not expect anything else'."

"As mentioned the congregation bought the building which stood in the same spot as the present one occupies, and enlarged it on either side at the rear." — "The membership increased significantly before the end of the year". Inasmuch as the annual meeting was held early in October, before Hasselquist's arrival, the number of members was not reported to Synod that Fall. But in 1853 when the Synod met in Galesburg in his church, Hasselquist reported that his pastorate included four congregations and 191 communicants, most of whom presumably belonged to the one in Galesburg. Not less than 165 had been received during the year, evidently by letter from Sweden.

"The Sunday School was reorganized in August 1853, with 5 teachers and 27 pupils. English remained the language in 2 classes but gradually decreased in use and Swedish became the language of the members of the congregation."

1854 a Year of Cholera and of Grace

Galesburg and the surrounding region had been spared from cholera, until this year, when the feared plague appeared. Not so many of the Swedes in Galesburg died, probably 10 or 12, but in Knoxville there were 40, and in the small settlement usually called Spoon Timber, later Wataga, 5 or 6 succumbed. The malady reached Galesburg through the workers on the railroad who continued to work despite the torrid heat. In Galesburg and Knoxville the sickness proved to lead to an awakening and be of spiritual blessing to our countrymen.

The awakening was apparent even during the summer, and the pastor decided to hold evening meetings daily for a whole week in order to serve the seeking souls with instruction from the Word of God. Confirmation of 14 children, older and younger, who had been instructed for about half a year, took place on Sunday, August 17th, and this was the start of the evening gatherings. Pastor Hokanson from New Sweden, Iowa, had promised long before to be present and help, which he did, and on the same trip attended the Synod sessions in Peru. On the day before confirmation a large group had just arrived from Sweden. The week before the first cholera death occurred, altogether unexpected. It was as if in this death the Lord called, "He that hath ears, let him hear!" The evening meetings brought overflow crowds. Several deaths occured, but there seemed to be no fear of contagion. The spiritual interest dominated. By the end of the week about 100 persons asked to become members in Galesburg and Knoxville. In the interviews "many tears flowed and many confessions came from hearts one had least expected." Many touching events took place among the sick and the dying, revealing the importance of Christian instruction in childhood even if it had long been lying as uninvested capital. "In conversation with two others," said the pastor, "I became ashamed of my folly, for when I could not immediately get the response I sought, I began to speak seriously about their perilous condition. Then tears came into the eyes of one, and I discovered an humble, poor and hungry heart, giving me reason for rejoicing instead of anxiety." He continues, "at the beds of the sick and dying there could be gripping moments. Four small children had been carried out from one house. While two small corpses were still in a home an American neighbor came in and looking at the two small travellers in grief wanted to share the bereavement of those who had to part from them. Instead one of those in the house responded with a happy face, "Isn't God good who ordains so well with His and our children." To which the American replied in tears, "Oh, to be as you are!" This poor well-meaning woman and her husband did not belong to any church. She could not read the Bible, to which she was directed in order to find the Savior who had made these Swedes so contented with their God's will. She complained bitterly and asked if someone would read for her, but no one could read English. "So general was the activity of grace," we hear further, "among both the sick and the well, that one of the deacons who had mingled among them, burst out with tears when I asked how things were going, 'God be praised!' Now I can enjoy going around among my countrymen; now it is not a matter of buying land and building houses, but about being saved."[1]

It is certain that because of this revival the congregation as a whole was aroused to clearer spiritual and Christian consciousness, and that many good fruits resulted. As so often happens, though, some misconceptions could emerge, of which I want to speak further on.

A Restless Activity

From this time on Pastor Hasselquist was engaged in restless activity. The Galesburg congregation grew continuously and made for ever more work. Unfortunately I have not been able to discover any dependable statistics on the congregation from the date of organization to 1860. Nor can I find any help in the way statistical tables were kept in the Synod of Northern Illinois. According to these records Pastor Hasselquist in the Fall of 1854 was in charge of 3 congregations and 4 preaching places, with a combined total of 270 communicants, baptisms numbering 18, confirmed 15, new members received 11. This was before the revival. The three congregations were Galesburg, Knoxville, Princeton. I take the preaching places to be Wataga, Monmouth, Henderson, and Oqwaka, which later developed into congregations.

In addition he made shorter or longer trips in various directions. In the winter he attended a Conference meeting in Chicago. Early in the Spring he was in Burlington and New Sweden, Iowa. Late in the Fall he visited Chisago Lake and St. Paul, Minn. From there he journeyed to Chicago and on to Jamestown and Sugar Grove. The Synod had commissioned him to investigate the difficulties the congregations were having with Bergenlund. He continued on to New York and Boston, where he obtained type for the paper he had started in 1855. Wherever he went he preached for his countrymen. In the Fall he received an assistant, P.A. Cederstam, who had come from Chicago to Galesburg. In March of the following year Cederstam, on the recommendation of the Conference was granted an ad interim license from the Synod president. But so great was the need for pastors in other places, as in Minnesota, that already in May 1855 Cederstam

[1]CF *Hemlandet* 1, 1.

was transferred there. To gain help in the spiritual program Hasselquist began to give private instruction and prepare several seriously Christian and talented laymen, of whom two were later ordained and worked with much success in the Lord's vineyard. All of this together with the demanding duties of publishing a paper added up to as much as could be laid on the shoulders of one man, but through the grace of God he was able to maintain his health and strength, so that his activities could redound to great good both for his own congregations and the whole Synod.

In May 1856 Hasselquist received a welcome and real help when his brother-in-law A.R. Cervin, M.A. (later Ph.D.) came from Sweden, stayed in Galesburg over a year, assisting in the editing of the paper and in preaching in Hasselquist's place. We will return later to him.

DOCTOR T.N. HASSELQUIST.

The congregations during the early years were in no position to pay the pastor a salary anywhere near what he needed, even though he lived as simply and self-denying as any minister could do. On Prof. Esbjörn's recommendation they also turned to the American Home Missionary Society and received some help toward the pastor's salary for two years. The economic conditions of the region and of the Swedes in Galesburg toward the end of 1856 are described in the November issue of *Hemlandet* that year under the caption "Swedetown in Galesburg:" 'Swedetown' is the name the Americans in Galesburg have dubbed that part of town where most of the Swedes live. It lies in the northeast quarter of town. Here is the Swedish Lutheran church and the majority of Swedish houses that are near each other. Otherwise, especially the last two years, lots have been purchased and houses built by Swedes in almost every part of town. Just why they settled here first is uncertain, probably it was because there was work available here. Certain it is that the number of our countrymen has steadily increased and at present exceeds 1000. It is probably impossible to give the precise number. But American census takers claim that with the exception of Chicago (and possibly Boston and New York) there is no place in America where so large a number of Swedes have made their home and as a rule have it so well as in Galesburg." There were then 73 Swedish owned houses, valued at least at $73,000. Two Swedes owned their own farm, and over a couple of hundred acres of woodland, 4 to 6 miles from town, had been bought by Swedes. Carpenters and mechanics who knew English and work-habits could earn $2 a day. Wainwrights, blacksmiths, cabinet makers, painters made from $35-$50 per month. Wages and positions had increased faster than living costs. One could get board in a Swedish home from $2-$2.50 a week.

While the Swedes were thus becoming better off they had also bought a church building which including site and furnishings cost at least $1500, now fully paid. But they had also gathered significant sums for other purposes, such as $400 for the newly established Scandinavian professorship.

As to church connections the Swedes belonged to one of four denominations. The Lutheran was the largest congregation, counting over 200 communicant members and an attendance on Sundays larger than could be cared for in the building, wherefore it has been decided to build a new and larger edifice within the next two years. The Swedish Methodists numbered 30-40 communicants. A few were Baptists or Presbyterians.

We read further, "a large number thus belong to no church. Yet most of them listen to the Word of God and many observe Christian ordinances as if they were members.

"In matters of morals we have to give the Swedes credit for being, in general, industrious, law abiding, and better liked by the native Americans above other immigrants. They are few who have secretly tried to avoid paying their debts or other obligations. And if there are a few who have not succeeded in forsaking their loyalty to the old Swedish idol, intoxicating drink, they are not able to disgrace here the Swedish name."[1]

Gradually more and more Swedes began to go into business for themselves and have succeeded well. During the summer of 1850 they began to discuss the establishment of a Scandinavian Fire Insurance Company, which was realized with assets of $20,000.

These facts reveal that by 1860 the Swedes in Galesburg had in general achieved a high level of economic and civic success. Naturally this was of importance for the Lutheran congregation, to whose internal workings and purposes we now return.

Church Discipline and Inner Ferment

That church discipline was considered serious one can learn from surviving minutes of the church council, the first dated February 2, 1856. Quoting from the historical article in *Korsbaneret*: "The worst enemies of the congregation seem to have been intoxication, unchastity and dancing." The old devil, swearing, raged then too and the church council did not forget to warn and exhort against it. Several persons were dropped from membership in 1858 for participation in dancing." "Serious condemnation was visited on those absent from, or showing disrespect, for the regular worship services, both inside and outside the church." "The strict discipline that was exercised indicate serious breaches; but not only obvious wickedness troubled pastor and council, for another dangerous ferment, at first very minor and harmless, still little by little leavened a part of the flour in the bushel-basket. Taking liberty with ceremonies increased, augmented by an alleged fear of a 'state-church'." "One while we had trouble in the church-council," the article recounts, "because of complaint by members regarding the order of worship. They did not think it right to stand up

[1] Cf *Hemlandet* 2: nos. 22, 23.

when the Word of God (Gospel and Epistle) was read, so they remained seated when the congregation stood." They demanded that the preacher not stand, but sit, at the altar, that he should not wear the clerical bands (prästkrage). They went so far that when, after his ordination, H. Olson wore the bands at a service one of the deacons went up to him and pretended to rip it off. "This seemingly insignificant leaven developed to the point that even before Pastor Hasselquist moved from Galesburg lists were circulated to gain members for a 'free church.' These lists contained a manifesto against the order of service, the clerical collar, and our Synod's state-churchism. These critics were joined by avowed separatists from Sweden, who propagated the idea of a pure congregation, and the doctrine of universal salvation (of all who believed) on the ground that Christ had accomplished all, repentance, amendment, etc. When seeds of this kind are sown with the total zeal of a partisan spirit they cannot but bear fruit."

This agitation culminated in the division of the congregation and the formation of the so-called "Second Lutheran Congregation in Galesburg." The source lay in a timid and thoughtless yielding to the American Reformed-Puritan sects by which the newcomers were surrounded and influenced. We have already seen how Esbjörn reacted under this influence in his first years. He showed that he could be just as free as the Reformed churches in regard to ceremonies — though theirs was not a true freedom, for they were as bound to their ways as any one else. But he did not avail himself of his freedom, for he feared that the result would be that the Swedish people would have been lost to the Lutheran Church. He saw that giving in was unnecessary and very ill considered, so he soon changed course. Galesburg was the very center of Congregationalism in northern Illinois and was strong in its influence. The Reformed attitude towards the order of worship and church ceremonies had already found a place in the Swedish congregation when Hasselquist began his ministry there. He was not one to set himself against it, but took things as they were. In my view he aided and developed this freedom even further during his early years. I leave unanswered whether it was due to Christian wisdom or a conviction of the correctness of such freedom that for some time he went with the stream. But I am sure that before long his clear vision discerned the unhealthy aspects of the tendency and its danger to Lutheranism and that he therefore called a halt.

But matters had gone too far and a separation ensued. Yet it was best for the congregation that it occurred, for the Lutheran character of the church gained thereby.

When Esbjörn returned to Sweden Pastor Hasselquist was elected as his successor as professor and president of Augustana's institution of learning. The school was relocated in Paxton and Hasselquist moved there the Fall of 1863, after an 11 year ministry in and around Galesburg. In 1860 the congregation reported 255 communicants, and expenses of only $422 — the pastor's salary evidently not included.

Knoxville

In the March 1857 *Hemlandet* J. Johnson wrote about this place and the Swedes and their condition there. When he came there it was an insignificant village with hardly 1,000 inhabitants. For two or three years thereafter there was hardly any growth and the building of a house here and there caused wonder. Then it became more lively but could not be compared with Galesburg. A good deal of rivalry existed between the two until Galesburg went far ahead. The building of the Peoria and Oqwaka road gave rise to brighter hopes in Knoxville, but the results were not as great as expected.

Proportionately the size of the Swedish population grew faster than that of the town. When Johnson (later Pastor Johnson) came there were only a few countrymen, and only one house was owned in town by a Swede. Just beyond the town were 24 Swedish homes with more or less acreage around them. Still farther out one could find farmers — 16 in number — who owned from 40 up to 160 acres. In 1857 the value of Swedish property in and around Knoxville was valued at $51,000. This compares with an earlier figure of $10,532 five or six years before — hence a gain of over $40,000. 432 Swedes were in Knoxville 1857 — the majority from Skåne, 236, followed by 163 from Blekinge, and only 33 from other parts of Sweden.

The Lutheran Congregation

The Swedish Evangelical Lutheran congregation here was organized by Pastor T.N. Hasselquist in 1853. I have not been able to find the names nor the number. Hasselquist served the congregation as long as he was in Galesburg, until 1863.

A small wooden church was built in 1854, and dedicated with festive services on Sunday, December 2, 1855. It was not quite finished, lacking painting and other items, but there was great rejoicing in having come so far after much anxiety and difficulty. Some help had been received from the local Americans, the rest had been raised in the congregation by various methods, finally by each member paying 1 dollar for each $100 he possessed, by his own evaluation. This small building, then described as "high and well-lit" cost around $1700, of which $800 had been paid. It had been planned to hold a Conference meeting in Galesburg in connection with the dedication in Knoxville. The date had been set for November 29, but only Pastor Erland Carlsson came. A letter explains that the others were prevented by heavy rains, and that Carlsson preached at the worship service on the morning of the first Sunday in Advent and at this service dedicated the Knoxville church.

During the first decade the congregation carried on with no unusual happenings, beyond what has been told concerning the Galesburg congregation to which Knoxville was considered an annex. In 1860 John Johnson, one of the deacons, was ordained, after having received private instruction from Hasselquist. That year the congregation had 173 communicant members, with expenditures of $249.11 for the year.

Three other small congregations grew up around Galesburg during this period, and were under Hasselquist's care. Wataga, organized 1856 had 32 communicants in 1860. Monmouth, organized 1853 had only 13 communicants in 1860. Altona, formerly called Walnut Grove, organized 1859 had 28 communicants in 1860. Their history belongs in a later period.

Chapter 4

Moline, Rock Island, Geneseo

The First Known Swedes in Moline and Rock Island

When I visited these places early in 1851 there were a few Swedes. Among them I recall Olaus Bengtson and family; the tailor Carl Johanson and wife, Maja Stina, from Kämpestad in Östergötland. These were the oldest here. As far as I recall the item in *Svenskarne i Illinois*, p. 116, is correct. O. Bengtsons came in 1847, walking by foot from Chicago and carrying their children and other belongings. Carl Johanson came in 1848 after a short stay in Andover. The names of both these families appear on the list of the first members of the Andover congregation, March 23, 1850. The explanation is that they were entered on the Andover list before there was a congregation in Moline. When I was in Moline, 1851, O.B. had already joined the Methodists and Jonas Hedstrom had his headquarters and meetings in this home when he visited Moline. Carl Johanson was at that time a Lutheran, but without any deep conviction. He received Pastor Esbjörn and acted as host both for him and the (later) congregation. In a small room 14 × 16 ft., which he rented in a brick house belonging to an American, Mrs. Bell, all could assemble who came to the Lutheran service. Johnson was helpful, and since he managed a broken English the newcomers depended on him early and late for assistance in their affairs. A few years later he became a zealous Baptist and a bitter opponent of the Lutherans.

I recall too Abram Anderson from Gnarp in Helsingland, an older day laborer, quiet and kind. He acquired some property, and before his death a few years later, bequeathed to the Lutheran congregation a lot and small house as a home for the future pastor. I have already mentioned, in a previous chapter, Jon Olson, the "old man from Stenbo." Per Anderson from Hassela and Per Berg from Hög, Helsingland, lived with Olson until the Spring of 1851 when they travelled to Minnesota and founded the Chisago Lake settlement. Peter Viklund from Ångermanland also was in Moline when he joined them and settled near Taylors Falls, Minn. where he died. The same year Daniel Nilson, from Norrbo, Helsingland, also went off to Minnesota, where he established the Marine settlement near Marine Mills.

Others included: Sven Jacobsson, a carpenter, I believe, from Värmland, who later moved to Vasa, Minn. but after a few years returned to Moline. M.P. Peterson, who moved to Walnut Grove (Altona) and then to Iowa. Hans Smith and family came in the summer of 1851 from Princeton — later he became a Baptist, and moved to Chisago Lake.

I recall in Rock Island J. Beck and Peter Soderstrom, both sons-in-law of Pastor J. Rolin in Hassela; Jonas Strand, Jonas Norell, Erik Thomasson, all three single men from Northern Sweden; E.M. Manke, later a Baptist, who is supposed to have died in the burning of the steamer *Austria* Sept. 13, 1858.

These are some of the Swedes whom I learned to know the winter of 1851. Most of them used to attend the Lutheran services in the home of Carl Johanson or other houses. Undoubtedly there were others,[1] but they seldom came to services. The following years brought many new parties of Swedes, some of whom stayed here when they found employment in the thriving plow factories or paper-mills. Some spent the winter here or longer before going on to other localities. Many died here in the severe cholera epidemic 1854, and there was much destitution and suffering. A brighter season followed. Moline and Rock Island have retained a good-sized Swedish population, which in general has done well, and some have worked themselves up to prosperity and affluence.

Among the early Swedes in Moline who have played an important part in the growth of the city and its industries, and become wealthy, Anders Friberg is noteworthy. According to *The Swedes in Illinois*, he was born April 8, 1828 in Skräflinge parish, Malmöhus county, but grew up in Gothenburg where he learned the blacksmith trade. He emigrated in 1850. He spent the first 9 months in Chicago, then spent a short time in Minnesota. Then he came to Rock Island and later moved to Moline, where he has had great success as a manufacturer. He has been and still is the moving spirit in the large Moline Plow Company, in whose shops many hundreds of Swedes have found employment. He is also the inventor of the renowned "Western Cultivator."

In the earlier years health conditions were not the best in Moline, probably because of drainage problems — ague was widespread. Rock Island claimed to be better because of the outcropping limestone on which the town was built.

---

[1] In a letter from Esbjörn, 1852, printed in Dr. Fjellstedt's paper, *Bibel vännen*, 5:9, the number of Swedes in Rock Island and Moline is given as "surely 100."

The Organization of the Swedish Lutheran Congregation
and its History until 1860

As we have seen Pastor Esbjörn early extended his activity to
Rock Island and Moline, followed closely by the Methodist minister J.
Hedstrom. A couple of weeks after my coming to Andover, in the Fall
of 1850, Esbjörn visited these places and organized a Swedish Lutheran
congregation, which though very weak in its first years has endured.
The Minutes of the meeting are complete and read as follows:[1]
"Minutes of a legally announced congregational meeting in
Moline, Rock Island County, Illinois, Dec. 1, 1850

Organization of the Swedish Evangelical Lutheran Congregation
in Moline

Resolved, 1) that for our own spiritual welfare and for the promotion of the true evangelical doctrine and the extension of the kingdom
of Jesus among our countrymen and our descendants, we unanimously
write and constitute ourselves as an evangelical congregation, to be
called the Swedish Ev. Lutheran Congregation in Moline, Rock Island
County, Illinois.

Resolved, 2) that only those can become members who give satisfactory assurance of a true change of heart, strive to live according to
the Word of God, and desire to become members of this congregation.

Resolved 3) that we accept the principle that the Holy Scriptures
of the Old and New Testament are the inspired Word of God; that this
Word has the ultimate authority and contains a sufficient and infallible
rule for man's faith and practice, so that what is not contained therein
and cannot be proved by it, is not required to be believed or performed
for salvation; that the Holy Scriptures are the only standard by which
one can test or judge all arguments, judgements and experiences in
spiritual things; that no law, tradition or custom is adopted or maintained which is opposed to Scripture; that symbols, decisions of councils
and human opinions are supported only insofar as they agree with the
Word of God, and finally that the symbolical books of the Lutheran
Church contain a correct interpretation and presentation of the Word
of God, wherefore we declare and accept them as the basis of our faith

[1]Printed in "Tempeltjenaren," a paper published by Pastor H.O. Lindeblad, Moline,
Dec. 1, 1887.

and teaching next to the Holy Scriptures.

Moline, December 1, 1850
I attest this is a correct copy of the original. O.C.T. Andrén"
I have not been able to discover who were the charter members, but among those I remember were Carl Johanson and his wife, Abram Anderson, M.P. Peterson and wife, Olaus Bengtson and family, P. Berg and family, Daniel Nilson and family, Olof Hinderson and wife from Hassela, Karolina Soderberg and Karin Soderberg from Svinhult, Linköping county.

Members from following years included, 1851 — Per Larson from Skurup; Carl Lindman and his brother-in-law Erikson and their families, the former from a place called "Kingdom" in Jersnäs parish. 1852 brought Per Bodelson; 1853, the widow Johanna Hallgren from Karlskoga, a wife Elna Mattson from Önnestad; 1854, Per Hanson from Trolle Ljungby, his wife Kerna (1857). In addition: A. Sjolin, and wife Anna, from Breared; Carl August Billington from Karlskoga and wife Anna; Charles Soderberg from Svinhult, Linköping county; Joh. Erik Johanson and Kristina Greta Peterson from Skede, Jönköping county; a wife Charl. Anderson from Säglora, Elfsborgs county, the widow Anna Kohler from Bjurkärn; the widow Inga Jansdotter from Asarum; the widow Maria Johanson from Karlskoga; Per Bengston from Skåne and wife Sofia (1856); Nils Anderson and wife Brita from Hösna, Elfsborgs county; the widow Anna Johanson from Berghem, the same county. 1855: Johan Janson from Karlskoga; 1856: Jorgen Lindahl from Ribe, Denmark, and wife, Eva; Per W. Nilson from Trolle Ljungby, Nils Ostergren from ditto and wife Ingred Bergstrom from Bergsjö in Helsingland; Carl F. Gard from Sjögestad and Anna Elisabeth from Åtvida, Linköping county; Peter Lind from Gnarp in Helsingland and his wife Emma Charlotta Uddvall from Christdala, Kalmar county; E. Lind and Anna Norberg, Anders E. Lind, Erik Olson, all from Gnarp; the widow Johanna Erikson from Berghem; Gustaf Gustafson and Sofia Peterson from Horn; 1857: Elna Hanson from Trolle Ljungby; Nils Peterson and wife Bengta, from the same place.

These were some of the earliest members of the congregation, of whom many are still living.

As already noted a church building was begun in the summer of 1851 with some of the money Esbjorn had collected on his trip to the Eastern states that year. The church was very small, built of wood, and stood on a site near the edge of the village where the new church now stands. It took a long time before it was finished, but even though it was only roughly enclosed it was used for the worship services. It was January 1857 before it could be dedicated. Pastor Hasselquist wrote about it in *Hemlandet*: "Again we have had the joy of taking part in a church dedication, namely of the Swedish church in Moline, Sunday, January 11 this year (1857). True, the church is one of the oldest of those erected by the Swedes of the present immigration, but there was a long delay before its completion, and the congregation has had no pastor for many years, probably on that account not feeling the need for this occasion. Now the building is nearing completion, the congregation has a resident pastor, and since the Mississippi Conference had planned to convene here the wish was expressed to have the dedication. On the appointed day a large gathering was present, hardly able to find room in the building. The congregation has an asset not possessed by any other Swedish church in America in that it has a church bell. Work on the belfry was just being completed and it was possible on Saturday afternoon to hang it in its place, so that henceforth its clear sound could call the people together. It is indeed not large but serves the same purpose as a larger one. May it never call in vain to the Lord's House! It may be the first church bell in a Swedish church in this land but I am sure it will not long be the only one."[1] Members of the Conference who were present were, L.P. Esbjörn (who had to go home on Saturday), T.N. Hasselquist, O.C.T. Andrén, B.G.P. Bergenlund, lay delegates Carl Lindman from Moline, N.P. Peterson from Andover, and Pehr Ingmanson from Knoxville. The building was later enlarged, then moved across the street when sold to an individual owner.

The Care of the Congregation

Pastor Esbjörn was the first Lutheran pastor to care for the spiritual needs of the Swedes in Moline and Rock Island, and as often as he could he continued to visit them. Since his other fields and his strength limited what he could do it is obvious that these places suffered. During the winter of 1851 there was not much evidence of a serious Christian spirit, but the people were willing to listen to the Word of God when there was opportunity, and they did show a certain interest in retaining their Lutheran faith. Through the visit of Jonas Hedstrom some

[1]*Hemlandet*, 1857, no. 2

had become attracted to Methodism, and this resulted in a lively, I may even say fleshly, controversy about spiritual things. This strife did however have the consequence that many began to value more highly what they possessed in the Lutheran Church and paid more attention to the preaching of the Word. In the Spring a more serious hunger for the Word was noticeable. I remember well April 22 when Esbjörn preached in Carl Johanson's home. The room was crowded and it became very warm. Esbjörn preached and sweated, then suddenly took off his coat and preached in shirt-sleeves, in a matter of fact manner. No one seemed disturbed, all listened attentively. Finally he felt altogether exhausted, sat down and said to me, "now you continue." Though taken aback by the order, I tried for the first time to say something in public. I do not remember what I said, but probably my youth and my gestures led to audible weeping and emotion in the small assembly.

Had there been a pastor here at that time probably fewer than was the case would have been affected by the Baptist movement which started a year later.

During the summer of 1852 Esbjörn became acquainted with C.J. Valentin, a young man from Stockholm. He had been in some kind of merchandizing, had not had much schooling but had a certain religiosity and zeal for the Lutheran Church. Whether Esbjörn turned to him or he to Esbjörn I do not know. In any case Valentin was present at the meeting in Chicago of the Synod of Northern Illinois, in October 1852, was given an examination and received license or authorization to serve as minister in Rock Island and Moline. In a letter of May 1853 Esbjörn wrote, " The critical lack of pastors led us to give a license to Valentin to care for Moline. Had he not been there Palmquist would have led astray every Swede in Rock Island and Moline." The latter is problematic, but one can assert that Valentin's ministry gave the Swedish Lutherans a gathering point, that the Lutheran services were maintained so that the people did not have to go to other denominations to attend a Swedish worship service.

It soon became clear that the Baptists considered Valentin an obstacle in their activity. With excessive bitterness they called him, "a dead ox, a most unworthy individual," etc. The controversy heightened at the beginning of 1853. Esbjörn came here to investigate the situation, and I will let him describe what he found. May 12 he wrote, "On a trip there recently I found great strife between Valentin and the Anabaptists, with faults on both sides, as often happens. On some points he has been too violent. His preaching has been too legalistic, (a matter that should not concern them as members of another congregation). The others, deplorably, are very bitter and critical. — If their faith is better than his it need not be proved by bellowing. — No wonder there is controversy when they are captivated by the Baptists, and when one part inclines towards a legalistic Christianity and another towards antinomism. But it is deplorable when they depart from a Christian spirit and forget the clear words of Scripture: Allow no charge against a pastor without two or three witnesses — words not spoken about good, pious and faithful pastors but about erroneous and guilty ones. — It boiled down to three points: 1) when he baptized the first child he forgot to give its name, 2) moved the "meetings" from Wednesday to Tuesday evenings, when the Baptists did the same, 3) at one "meeting" when he accepted a pinch of snuff he exclaimed, 'that was damned good snuff.' When I met with the deacons to examine Valentin, it was found 1) that at his first baptism in confusion and inexperience he really had committed this pardonable mistake, 2) that this change (which he and the congregation had right to make) simply meant a change of choir rehearsal to Tuesday evenings, so that an English class could take place on Wednesday evenings, a school both Lutherans and Baptists wanted to attend, but which the Baptists could not attend if held on Tuesday evenings when Palmquist had his 'meetings.' So this charge was a perversion of the truth. 3) this was a falsehood . . Two deacons[1] had on this occasion stood between Valentin and 'the old fellow' who offered the snuff, saw him take it, but testified that he had not said those words, or any other offensive ones. The 'old fellow' who spread the story furthermore was said to be *deaf.* — I admonished Valentin to exercise more patience and humility in his dealings with erring ones and to pray to the Lord for grace to receive more insight and experience in the Gospel and for a more evangelical style of preaching. On my return home I received an excited letter, whereupon I wrote him even more sternly. Then he wrote thanking me that I had warned him in a fatherly spirit, and later another letter in the same spirit. If he is sincere (so it seems) it appears that his rigid nature has been bent under the hand of the Almighty — may the Lord so grant for the sake of Jesus."

It appears that Valentin moved from Moline during the summer of 1853, for he was in Princeton in the Fall serving the Swedes for

---

[1]Carl Lindman and Nordin, according to another letter to Hasselquist

some time. He was absent when the Synod met in Galesburg that same Fall, but seemingly his license was nevertheless renewed. Again next year at the meeting in Peru his license was continued with the provision that he study under Esbjörn. Instead of doing this he left without permission for Sweden and stayed there several years. The Synod of 1855 suspended his license until he came to Synod, but it would be renewed if he proved himself worthy. For a few years no one heard from him, until he emerged again and "as a volunteer joined Company D, Illinois 52nd infantry regiment." But "he proved to be as poor a champion for the Union as he was for the cause of Christ, for just as he left his weak flock in Princeton, so he forsook his regiment. He deserted and fled back to Sweden. From there he wrote a letter explaining he could not with good conscience serve in the Union Army since his sympathy was with the South!"[1] He is reputed to have come back once again to this land after the war.

Esbjörn had to assume charge again after Valentin left Moline. When he could not come, a deacon, Carl Lindman, conducted services. This Lindman came from "the Kingdom" in Jersnäs parish Jönköping county, was a mason by occupation, and was richly endowed both in head and heart. He had a keen mind, was well-read, especially in religious literature, and was well able to express himself both in speech and writing. He was incorruptibly loyal to what he considered right and true, at times probably even to an extreme. He had rich spiritual experience, having started as a disciple of Murbäck but gradually coming to a more evangelical conception of the way of salvation, and holding firmly to Lutheran churchliness. As a deacon he undoubtedly used his talents during this period to the benefit of the congregation. Meanwhile Pastor P. Ahlberg in Sweden had been called as pastor and the congregation had received, in 1854, an affirmative reply. Rejoicing, however, was brief, for Ahlberg encountered hindrances, had to recall his answer, and remained in Sweden. Several other congregations also had tried to call a pastor from Sweden, but without results. When the Conference met in the Fall in Andover, it was decided that henceforth calls to Sweden should go through the Conference which would send them first to Dr. Fjellstedt, who was asked to direct them to suitable pastors. In this manner Pastor O.C.T. Andrén was called to Moline in the Fall of 1855. He accepted and arrived in Moline July 31, 1856.

[1]*Svenskarne i Illinois*, p. 188

Before treating of Pastor Andrén's ministry we wish to mention some items from the records which characterize the congregation's history. At the congregational meeting Sept. 12, 1852 this resolution was adopted: "In case the question should arise about the preaching or holding of services in our church or congregation by persons belonging to other denominations, this may not be permitted without the consent of the pastor and deacons, and such consent may not be given to others than properly ordained or licensed ministers of orthodox, Protestant, Christian denominations, who do not speak and have not spoken against our congregation's doctrine, constitution and worship, and have not either publicly or individually sought to or seek to demean and undermine our congregation, draw members away from it and cause them to break their vows to the congregation. Subscribed by Charles John Valentin, temporary vice pastor; Sven Jacobson, Trustee."[1] There is no record of any other congregational meeting until April 29, 1855, when the question of a church treasury was discussed. The resolution was quite comprehensive and its gist was that at each communion every member should pay 25 cents to the treasury. On confirmation each member of the class should make a gift, according to ability and circumstances. Also it was expected that gifts should be made at the churching of women, by the bride and groom at weddings, and by persons who had been saved from some imminent danger, as a thank offering to the Lord. Such gifts to the treasury should be publicly acknowledged at a service. Detailed instructions were given how the trustees should administer this fund, namely, for current expenses. Further it was resolved that "as hitherto offerings be received at each communion and on such occasions as the church council deems fitting — such as for the salary of the cantor, as decided last January, as well as for those purposes which are considered highly necessary and contribute to the honor of God's holy name, the extension of his kingdom and to the benefit of the neighbor. A majority of votes would determine the use of a collection." The Minutes are signed on behalf of the congregation by L.P. Esbjörn, Charles Lindman, C.M. Carlsson, N.P. Samuelson, N.J. Erikson, L.M. Johnson, Johannes Jacobson, G.A. Erikson, C.G. Gustafson.

In the following years it seems the fee was raised to 1 dollar at communion services. The custom provoked malicious remarks, but trying to defend it the congregational meeting of Feb. 22, 1857 resolved

[1]First Record book, p.3.

tageous, and this coupled with the quiet and moral tone that distinguishes the town from others, especially the sister cities, makes it a pleasant residential place. About half of the inhabitants belong to no church, the other half consists of Lutherans, Congregationalists, Episcopalians, Baptists, Catholics, Methodists, a Universalist society and a few Spiritualists. Moline's public school is renowned. It has an average attendance of 300 pupils, divided among 4 teachers. Ever since its founding Moline has been a 'temperance town,' and though it may not always have guarded sufficiently its purity, the covert saloons have not been happy and the drinker has not been respected. It is to be hoped that our countrymen, who in general enjoy a reputation as an industrious, honorable and progressive people, when they come to participate in municipal affairs will join the ranks of those who, with insight into what most truly contributes to the welfare of the community, seriously, forcefully and incorruptibly work and fight for these virtues.

"The first Swedes in this region came in 1848 and settled in Rock Island. In 1849 Swedes came to Moline, and soon outnumbered those in Rock Island, so that when Pastor Esbjörn organized a congregation in December 1850 it was decided to build a church in Moline, where an attractive corner lot was purchased for $60. Of the funds that Pastor Esbjörn collected on his Eastern trip 1851 Moline received $330. A subscription among Americans and Swedes netted $215 toward the building fund. A small bell was bought for $50 in 1856, and installed in the little belfry in 1857 it called to worship for the first time the evening of the meeting of the Mississippi Conference in Moline 1857. The cost for the building (36 1/2 × 24 1/2 ft.) not counting volunteer labor amounted to $646.83. The congregation grew in numbers and before long the entire membership could not be accommodated in the crowded building, so toward the end of last year it was resolved to build an extension of 13-14 feet. The male members were joined by friendly countrymen, even Norwegians, and with great willingness and rivalry bent to the work without compensation. In less than 11 working days the building was ready for plastering, and though the cold was bitter on several of those days we saw our countrymen untiringly at work on completing this building which the Lord gave us in a strange land as a gathering place where He would teach us the way to the true homeland. We hope soon to have the building furnished. Several of the young women in the congregation have contributed to the adornment of the temple by a gift of three beautiful lamps, two for the pulpit. Without any other burden than that assumed by a free will, and without burdening anyone in the future on account of this addition, we now possess a beautiful, spacious temple — a precious New Year's gift from our heavenly Father.

"About 300 yards from the church, on the same street, the congregation owns a house and lot, a legacy to the church in 1854 by Abraham Anderson, from Gnarp parish, Helsingland, to be used as a parsonage. The house was enlarged in 1856, so that it is now a comfortable and pleasant residence, which in summer stands in the shade of trees planted by the donor in the evenings after a hard day's work.

"Since its start until August 1, 1856, when the undersigned took charge the congregation has been served by Pastor Esbjörn and licentiate C.J. Valentin (1852-3). In the period of vacancies the Sunday services have usually been conducted by C. Lindman, a deacon.

"The number of communicant members exceeds 200. Children number 145, 75 of whom are over 6 years old. 66 can read Swedish well. Here, as undoubtedly also elsewhere in Swedish settlements, attempts have been made to persuade parents that it is not necessary to teach children Swedish. Very few have heeded the witless arguments of adversaries of our mother tongue who often are adversaries also of our church. The majority manifest a laudable diligence both in themselves teaching the children and in sending them to school. In order not to conflict with the child's need to learn English — a need we cannot at present meet in our school — we have one school on Saturday mornings. Both the Saturday and the Sunday School are well attended, on an average by 50 pupils. In prayer to the Lord we expect much blessing from the seed we are planting in the soil of childish hearts not yet trampled on or hardened.

"Our countrymen in Moline and vicinity have borne to a considerable degree their portion of the hard times which the Lord at times sends among men. The years 1850, 1852, 1854 are not soon forgotten by those who lived through them. Widowers, widows, orphans testify to us about those misfortunes which befell especially immigrants those years, when in a strange land they found themselves penniless, and surrounded by destitution, sickness and death. Yet, however, many and long the days of difficulty seemed and were to the afflicted they did pass. Little by little better times came. Through the industriousness for which in general our people were known they soon earned, in the good years of work and money, what was needed for debts and a frugal existence. Through the sweat of brow the older immigrants acquired house and lot. For a couple of years it was real lively in Moline. New houses were built, employment grew in the growing factories, and some thought they already saw the dawn of the day when their savings would make possible a house and untroubled life in city, or a farm broken up in the forests of Minnesota or on the prairies of Illinois, Iowa, Kansas. Then came August, 1857, and the storm which indeed cleared the atmosphere of the business world but also swept away many temporal possessions and many factories, leaving the workers without chance of earning daily bread. Though industry did not entirely cease it became so weak that our countrymen had to retrench in every way and put off to a hoped-for better future the realization of their longing for own home and hearth. In few places where Swedes are living have there been such hardships, yet the actions of our countrymen to each other in these years provides a heartening picture.

"There is a growing interest in the Scandinavian professorship, in the periodicals, in the 'Publication Society.' The more the high-minded, freed from the sycophants and slanderers, can depend on their own sight and consideration, they will love, care for and support these ventures which are designed for the best interests of both the Scandinavian generation now passing away and the rising one, and which are now considered as stumbling stones only by foes of our Church. We are convinced that the attitude which this poor congregation in these days of unemployment has shown these institutions will continue and grow stronger in the future, and will win friends among those who, because of prejudice, ignorance or maybe greed, if not opposing them yet are with those who do. (There follows a description of what children are doing for Passavant's Orphan Home).

Moline, March, 1854   O.C.T. Andrén"

From surviving *Minutes* of congregational meetings, notations in Church Records and elsewhere we learn how seriously Pastor Andrén took his work. He wanted order and system in everything and sought to foster a Christian congregation. As soon as possible he began to introduce more serious discipline. At a congregational meeting February 27, 1857 a proposal for church discipline was adopted "almost unanimously 'to be in effect' until the expected constitution for the Swedish Evangelical Lutheran Church in the West is ready and accepted." The proposal is in spirit and almost in form identical with what we now have in regard to discipline in the model congregational constitution which the united Chicago and Mississippi Conference prepared and which the Moline congregation adopted in its entirety October 18, 1857. At the time of this adoption an election of officers took place. Before 1853 there seem to have been only 2 deacons, and after January 1853 there were three. Since the new constitution now called for 6 in the future, this number was elected.

Those elected were Charles Lindman and N.J. Erikson for three years, John Jakobson and John Holmquist for 2 years, Per Bodelson and Nils Swenson (now in Vasa) for 1 year. As trustees for Moline — Pastor O.C.T. Andrén, N.J. Erikson, Per Larson, Joh. Jakobson, and for Rock Island, John Holmquist. There is no mention in the early *Minutes* of any incorporation of the congregation.

PASTOR O.C.T. ANDRÉN.

With the adoption of the constitution pastor and officers concerned themselves with implementing it. Several cases of discipline involved doctrine and conduct. It is significant that though the constitution authorized pastor and council to take action in cases of excommunication those charged had their case laid before the whole congregation which rendered judgment. We read of such an event in 1858: "After the pastor and congregation joined in prayer to the Lord of the Church for grace to act aright in this matter, the congregation was asked if any one wished to speak in defence or acquital of L.L. When no one in the well-attended meeting had anything to add, voting took place, in which all were in favor of his exclusion, no one for his retention. As a result L.L. was declared excluded from the fellowship of the congregation, with those consequences which are denoted in the constitution as to the loss of membership (Art V, 5, 4.)" At the same time the congregation declared it would joyfully receive the person again as soon as he repented. Such a solemn and Christian procedure could not but have a healthful influence.

Also the congregation was encouraged in its interest and participation in synodical fellowship. When the question arose of asking each congregation to contribute $25 annually to the salary of a professor for Scandinavian students in Springfield, Illinois, if such proved possible, Andrén presented the matter and the congregation agreed, on Sept. 18, 1857, to raise the sum through collections. On April 15, 1860 a large attendance was present when the congregation was to elect a delegate to the important Conference meeting in Chicago and to express its opinion about the separation from the Synod of Northern Illinois. The pastor explained the situation, stressing the significance of loyalty to the pure doctrine of the Church, for ourselves and our children. Sufficient time was allowed for discussion of all sides, whereupon the proposal was read: The Swedish Evangelical Lutheran congregation in Moline, Rock Island County, Illinois which hitherto has been a part of the Evangelical Lutheran Synod of Northern Illinois hereby peacefully withdraws from its churchly union with said Synod." The pastor led in prayer, imploring the presence of our church's chief Shepherd, the Lord Jesus Christ and the guidance of the Holy Spirit." Then he called on the members to stand if they wished to approve the proposal. "Not a single member remained seated. All men and women stood up, because, we want to believe, of their love for the pure doctrine of our church, realizing the great importance and consequences of this act for them and their descendants." The *Minutes* close with this prayer: "Lord, give us grace, that as we now have stood to confess our faith, we may stand up for Thee and Thy service, and may Thy pure Word be a lamp for our feet and the light on our way! Holy Father, sanctify us in Thy Truth, Thy Word is Truth!"

We have already noted that the church building was sufficiently completed to be dedicated in 1857. On January 17, 1858 a congregational meeting was held to consider insuring both church and parsonage in the Scandinavian Fire Insurance Co. which had been organized in Galesburg and started its business January 1 of this year. A committee was appointed to appraise the church property and its report gives us interesting information as to its size and value. It reads: 1. the church, a frame house, is 36 1/2 feet long, 24 1/4 ft. wide, 15 ft. high above the stone foundation, which is 1 1/2 ft. above earth. The nearest dwelling is 98 feet away. The value of building with belfry, bell, and inventory — pulpit, altar, 14 benches, 1 melodion, 1 wall-clock, 2 stoves and pipes, 2 large and 4 small lamps, etc. is placed at $1400. 2. The parsonage: A. The dwelling place 24 1/4 feet long, 18 1/4 wide, 10 2/3 ft. high, divided into 3 rooms, cellar under half the house. 2 chimneys. Distance to nearest house 45 feet. Valued at $600. B. Addition to dwelling, 24 1/4 long, 10 ft. wide, 7 1/2 ft. high, divided into two rooms. Valued at $100. C. Stable valued at $100. Compare these with present property of the Moline congregation!

At the congregational meeting May 16, 1852 it was decided to appoint a sexton — whose duties hitherto had been carried out on a voluntary basis by the deacons. The salary was fixed at $26 per year, to be met by a fee of 25 cents per member, and to be collected by the pastor. "If at the close of the year" the *Minutes* state naively, "the collected amount should exceed $26, the surplus shall be applied on the next year's salary." Experience proved that the balance was always in the opposite direction. C. Lindman and N.J. Erikson were appointed as a committee to make up the rules for the position. They are 21 in number. He shall open the church on time when service or school are held; heat and ventilate and put in order, scrub the floor at least 3 or 4 times a year; wind the wall clock 2 times a week; ring the bell 3 times with certain minutes between, for services and Christmas morning (julotta); keep the lamps in order, carry the melodion carefully before each service from the parsonage to the church and back again after the service; prepare for baptisms, wash the Communion vessels, arrange the window shades, carry the church key from and to the parsonage, use no substitute without permission, pay for anything he broke or damaged. Rule 20 read: "The most important duty of the sexton is at all times to display respect and reverence for the Lord God and His holy Word, His sanctuary and His servant, and with utmost care watch the fire." If he failed in this, the committee recommended, he should be quickly separated from his position. The proposal was adopted, and on June 17 N. Swenson was elected as the congregation's first sexton. It was hardly an enviable job.

Expenses were indeed not large at that time, but the resources were meager, so it was often difficult enough to raise what was needed. At the annual meeting in May 1858 income was reported at $114.14 and expenditures $124.75, the pastor's salary not included. In 1859 the income was $284.49 and expenses $277.70. An addition had been built onto the church — 14 ft. on the south end — at a cost of $101.30, plus many days of volunteer labor. In 1860 income had been $109.29 — half of it a loan — and expenses $129.43, and a debt of $70.15 rested on the congregation. Those in charge of finances complained at this meeting about the economic situation of the congregation, and this led to another meeting May 31, 1860, "to regulate the financial affairs of the church." A committee was appointed which worked out a plan and reported to yet a congregational meeting June 28, 1860 — the last under Pastor Andrén's leadership. The report was adopted, providing principally that the salary of the pastor should be paid through voluntary gifts, and that the annual fee for the church fund remain at 75 cents and be paid to the treasurer in quarterly installments.

Pastor Andrén's period was brief. He had been in Moline only 4 years, but how significant these years had been for the congregation. He laid a good foundation, and though the years were few, he managed to build also on the foundation in a way that has been a blessing ever since. The Synod selected him as an emissary to Sweden and Norway to raise funds for the development of its institution of learning. He and his family left in the beginning of September 1860, taking farewell of a congregation he loved but which he would not see again on this earth. The intention had been he would return after he had completed his mission. The Lord decided otherwise. He resigned as pastor of the congregation August 11, 1861. Pastor G. Peters had been called, on August 11, 1860, as vice pastor during Pastor Andrén's absence. On August 25, 1861 he was called as successor to Pastor Andrén, remaining in Moline until December 29, 1863 when he moved to Rockford. In 1860 the membership stood at 210 communicants.

Geneseo, Henry County, Illinois

In Geneseo, which had hitherto been counted as a preaching station of Moline, a Swedish Evangelical Lutheran congregation was organized in 1859 and a small frame church was built the same year. In 1860 the number of communicants was only 40. Pastor O.C.T. Andrén wrote in *Hemlandet*, 1859 the following about Geneseo: "On April 15 this year a Swedish Evangelical Lutheran Congregation was organized in Geneseo, Henry County. Mr. John Gustus from Åtvida parish, Linköping county, was the first Swedish settler in Geneseo. He came from Sweden in 1851. Most of our countrymen here came in 1854. Some are mechanics or farmers, working either in town or on nearby farms. Several have achieved a prosperous condition. All are doing well and have not been as affected by the hard times as those in other areas. Since the first Sunday after Easter 1855 they have gathered Sundays for worship in a rented hall under the leadership of John Gustus. In 1856 they purchased an attractively situated lot for $100. At the beginning of this year a small, pleasant frame church was erected, 32 feet long, 24 ft. wide, and 15 ft. high, which when enclosed and fitted with pulpit cost $350. Towards this Americans in the town have subscribed $141.50 and the Swedes $123.50. Sunday collections brought in $38.

There are 32 members in the congregation. Since they already have borne heavy expenses and soon must pay the builder and the lumber company, as well as care for plastering and painting, they would be thankful for any contribution, however, small, from individuals or churches."

From Pastor C.A. Hultkrans I have the information that the first deacons were John Gustus, Lewis Johnson, Gustaf Nilson and Lars Johnson. The first trustees were John Gustus, Peter Nymas, A.P. Swensson and Adel Savstrom.

Chapter 5

The Swedish Lutheran Immanuel Congregation in Chicago[1]

The First Scandinavian Congregation in Chicago

The first Norwegians and Swedes in Chicago were without any spiritual leader the earliest years. In the Fall of 1847 a certain Gustaf Smith appeared among them, claiming to be a Lutheran minister, but evidently a Swedish adventurer and impostor. Nevertheless he won their confidence, and a Scandinavian Lutheran congregation was organized in which both Swedes and Norwegians were to be united. A frame church building was started on Superior Street, between Wells and La Salle Streets, where the old Swedish church stood and Dr. Passavant's *Emergency Hospital* now stands. Smith and one of the church council members made a trip to the German Lutherans in St. Louis to appeal for funds for the building. They succeeded so well among the kind and generous Germans that a sum of $600 was realized. But Smith soon disappeared with most of the money. A violent storm tore the half-built church building off its foundation and left it almost wrecked. Dissension arose among the members, everything seemed hopeless.

Some of the Norwegians gathered around a Norwegian student by the name of Paul Andersen, who had studied at a Presbyterian college. They elected him pastor, whereupon he obtained ordination by a kind of Lutheran synod in New York called the Frankean Synod. This first Norwegian Lutheran congregation in Chicago bought the ruined property and erected the church again. This was in 1848.

Through the Swedish-Norwegian vice-consul, Captain von Schneidau, the Swedish Episcopal minister G. Unonius was brought from Manitowoc, Wisconsin. Some of the Swedes, as well as a few Norwegians, had united to call him as pastor of the congregation organized 1849 as "The Scandinavian Church Association in Chicago." It was to be an "Evangelical Lutheran Congregation with the name of St. Ansgarius," but in "affiliation with the Protestant Episcopal Church in the United States of America, the diocese of Illinois." Thus it was in reality an Episcopal congregation, but called "Lutheran" since, in the opinion of Unonius, the Episcopal Church was the same

---

[1]Cf. *History of Swedish Ev. Lutheran Immanuel Congregation, Chicago, Ill.* in *Korsbaneret* 1881 — unsigned but probably by Erland Carlsson

as the State Church of Sweden. In 1850-51 Unonius visited Episcopal churches in the East and collected between $4,000-$5,000 for a church building — Jenny Lind contributing the largest single gift, $1500. A church was built on the corner of Franklin Street and Indiana Avenue, as well as a parsonage.[1]

The Swedish Evangelical Lutheran Immanuel Congregation —

Organization, First Pastor and First Members

I quote from the "History" of this congregation in *Korsbaneret*, 1881.

> "The Swedish Lutheran Immanuel Congregation arose out of very unusual circumstances. A small party of immigrants from Vesterdgötland arrived in Chicago in the summer of 1851. They were transported by steamboat to Sheboygan, Wisconsin, and left there on the pier. There they lay with their baggage a couple of days, the women and children as well as the men under the heavens, unable to find anyone they could talk to or who would help them in any way. They became discouraged almost to the point of despair. When the steamboat returned from Chicago, they all went back with it. They were fortunate in renting rooms in the city from some Norwegian families who belonged to the Norwegian Lutheran congregation. Cholera was raging in the city, especially among newly arrived immigrants. One night when several of this party were victims of the plague, one of them expressed the desire to speak with a Lutheran pastor. Word was sent to Pastor Paul Andersen, who immediately in the middle of the night hastened to the sick and dying, and offered the cup of comfort which gives consolation and peace both in life and death. He declared to them the free, unmerited grace in Christ, prayed with and for them. In loving kindness and compassion he assumed the care of both the sick and the well and provided them with counsel and help. The confidence and love which bound these strangers to a concerned minister led them also to his church. Most of them soon joined his congregation, among them some very serious-minded Christians. Pastor Andersen already had a large membership and more than enough work

[1]Norelius had a long note explaining how, when Jenny Lind was in St. Louis, creditors of the Bishop Hill Colony (the Colony had large debts in St. Louis) sought to win sympathy for the colony and obtain a gift, but to no avail.

among his own countrymen, so was not seeking to draw Swedes into his congregation. But it hurt him to see how Pastor Unonius and his people tricked the Swedes into the Episcopal Church. He looked on them as sheep without a shepherd, and eagerly wished to see a Swedish Lutheran congregation come into being in Chicago. The first to realize it would be those who had joined the Norwegian Lutheran Church.

"When Pastor T.N. Hasselquist came to Chicago from Sweden the first part of October 1852 he stayed several days in the home of Pastor Andersen. When he left Paul Andersen made him promise to come back to Chicago at the earliest opportunity to preach for his countrymen and organize a congregation among them. Pastor Hasselquist attended a Conference meeting in Moline early in January 1853, and then boarded a small, packed, and uncomfortable stage coach for a tiring, long and expensive ride from Moline to Chicago.

"Dr. Hasselquist has described this visit and preparations for the organization of a congregation in a letter to Dr. P. Fjellstedt in Sweden, dated Chicago, Monday, January 17, 1853. "After attending the Mississippi Conference meeting in Moline I continued on to Chicago. Since Thursday of last week I have preached here five times. Yesterday morning I preached for the Norwegian congregation, and in the afternoon for the Swedes. At the latter I preached on 'Christian caution with regard to unfamiliar religious bodies.' After I had spoken a few words based on Jeremiah 6:16, Pastor Paul Andersen with a view to the important matters before us, offered a gripping prayer which brought tears to the eyes of most. Then both of us went within the altar rail and submitted to the Swedes three resolutions concerning organization, the basis of acceptance into membership, and the Lutheran character of the congregation. Members subscribed their names, a resolution was made to call a pastor, whereupon the service was closed with prayer, benediction, and the singing of Psalm (Hymn) 412:6 in the Swedish *Psalmbok.*"

For the moment I interrupt the *Korsbaneret* story, in order to quote from some of Dr. Hasselquist's letters, which throw light on the early history of the Swedish congregations in Chicago and St. Charles.

On Tuesday, January 18 Hasselquist wrote his wife from Chicago:

"I have now been in Chicago since about 9 o'clock Wednes-

day evening last week, when I left the station in the western part
of the city and started off, clad in heavy clothes with a bundle
under one arm and the bag in the other. I did not find Andersens
(Pastor Andersen) and went up and down unfamiliar streets, but
finally arrived, tired and perspiring—I have now preached
Thursday, Friday and Saturday evenings last week and both
morning and afternoon on Sunday. After the afternoon sermon I
spoke on Jer. 6:16, asked for the intercessory prayers of the
Norwegian congregation for our intended action, and pastor
Andersen led in a touching prayer. Then followed the organization of the Swedish Lutheran congregation, in which 64 communicants enrolled; with children the number is 100. This
number will increase during my stay here. Yesterday I was busy
writing a long letter to Fjellstedt asking that he send Dahlholm
(?) here or some other suitable pastor. Last night, tonight, and
tomorrow evening—sermons. On Thursday Andersen and I will
travel to St. Charles 50 miles by rail from here (?), where there
is a large Swedish settlement with a church building about
which Unonius and the Methodists have been contending. It is
said that a Methodist pastor is there. This notwithstanding we
will attempt to organize a Lutheran congregation there and if
possible obtain the church. I probably will not be back in
Chicago before next Monday. I have promised to remain over
the following Sunday and then celebrate the Lord's Supper. You
will have to inform the members there and they will have to put
up with it. I have not been lazy. I like Andersen more and more
and he is ever more candid and trustworthy. The Norwegian
congregation is very friendly—I have had several very interesting conversations with anxious Swedes—the most enjoyable experiences in a long time. God be praised! Hedstrom and others
had been here a long time and organized a Methodist congregation—I don't know how large it is. The Swedish Lutheran will
be in a very difficult position without a pastor. But in our
prayers we will place it under the care of the True Shepherd."

On January 22 he wrote again, concerning the visit to St.
Charles:

"Last Thursday Andersen and I travelled to St. Charles,
where for two days we held services, and a few hours ago we
returned to Chicago. Last evening a Scandinavian Evangelical
Lutheran Church was organized in St. Charles, with 34
members. The Methodists had already been there trying to gain

the building for their congregation of 13 members, but did not succeed. The church is and will remain Lutheran. A week from Monday, God willing, Andersen and I will again visit St. Charles, to hold a service that evening and on the following morning dedicate the new church, install the deacons, and celebrate the Lord's Supper at a service. The next day I will start homeward."

Again in Chicago Hasselquist wrote his wife on May 25, 1853:

"Though I haven't received any letters from you and assume that 'no news is good news,' I will send a few more lines as to the plans for the next few days. I also want to say something about last Sunday. I came to St. Charles at noon on Saturday and had a meeting that night at church. On Sunday morning, a little after 9 o'clock, the service began. Baptisms took place, then communion service with 70 communicants, and the regular service, ending a little after 1 o'clock. After dinner I rode by carriage 10 miles to another town, Elgin. There I gave communion to a sick widow, married a couple, gave communion to 15 persons, and explained the parable of the Prodigal Son. I was through by 9:30 that night. Next morning at 9:30 I took the train to Chicago, arrived at 1 o'clock, instructed a confirmation class at 2 o'clock and conducted a service in the evening. On the same day I had a letter from Bergenlund, wherein he answered my questions quite satisfactorily. He wants me to come there at once, before Hedstrom comes, who is expected from New York. Consequently I have decided, unless the Lord changes it, and I do not receive word from you that would necessitate my coming home, to set out for Jamestown next Monday. I should be there at least by late Tuesday evening. I would be there Wednesday and Thursday, and in Sugar Grove Friday, Saturday and Sunday. On Monday I would return to Chicago, and by Thursday leave there for my dear home.—Next Sunday I will have a busy day here. The Norwegian congregation will have its usual service, and receive an offering for me. Then (for the Swedish congregation) there will be confirmation, the Lord's Supper, the morning service. May the Lord Jesus grant me strength and grace! Again I have met some very fine Christians, including a servant girl in St. Charles who was acquainted with and loved *Pietisten*.[1] One night in church when I sang one of Ahnfelt's songs, several joined in. I was dumbfounded, for I had expected to spring something new and unfamiliar on them—"

[1]A religious journal from Sweden

I continue now from the *Korsbaneret* article:

"80 persons subscribed their names to become members of
the new congregation. Pastor J.P. Dahlstedt, in Hoffmantorp,
Vexiö diocese, had been nominated as pastor. The call was sent
to Dr. P. Fjellstedt in Lund, with authority, in case Pastor
Dahlstedt could not accept, to transmit it to some other minister
whom he deemed best and most suitable. Pastor Dahlstedt was
not in good health and when the letter came from America he
was out of the country for his health's sake.

"Through a special Lord's guidance the call was instead
turned over to Erland Carlsson who had been serving almost
four years in the Vexiö diocese. Assured that it was the will of
God and after permission of the government had been received,
he embarked, with 176 emigrants, on the steamer *Gautjod*, and
on June 3, 1853 sailed from Kalmar to Lübeck. The voyage from
Lubeck to Hamburg, Hull, and Liverpool to New York, was long
and uncomfortable. On Saturday August 13 the ship anchored in
New York's harbor. When on Monday, August 22 Pastor Carlsson
arrived in Chicago, he was met at the railroad station by members of his future congregation, who joyfully welcomed him.

"Between the sending of the call and the arrival of the
pastor the congregation had met on Sunday afternoons in the
Norwegian church for the worship service, at which a sermon
from one of our good postils was read. In the Spring Pastor
Esbjörn of Andover paid a visit to the congregation, preaching
and holding a communion service.

"On Sunday, August 28 (14 Sunday after Trinity) Pastor
Carlsson preached his first sermon for his countrymen here.

"Though there was great joy over the pastor's coming, prospects were anything but bright either for him or the congregation. Of the 80 persons who had signed as members at the organization in January there were now no more than 8 families and 20
single persons. The others had either moved away from the city or
been attracted to other denominations. Those still remaining
were all newcomers and poor. Not one family among the members was in a position to entertain the pastor. All of them lived
either in dilapidated shanties or in small and crowded rented
rooms. Consequently he had, to begin with, to rent from a
Norwegian family, and pay $10 a month for two rooms, board
and laundry. The small, poverty stricken congregation could pay
little or nothing toward his support. The newly arrived pastor felt
himself very much alone, a stranger in a strange land, but he

entered upon his work with assurance and confidence, certain as he was that if the Lord had called him to this difficult but important mission field the Lord who called would also provide both strength and progress for that work. On the first page of the *Records* book of the congregation he inscribed his motto, thus, "Relying upon divine assistance I am determined to declare the truth openly and faithfully, whatever difficulties may be thrown in my way." Both in his public and individual life he sought to realize and verify this motto. Among all these strangers he found to his joy and encouragement friends who were not 'strangers to the testament of promise' but who belonged to the 'citizenship of Israel and the household of God.' They readily shared both good and bad fortune with their pastor, and often they prayed, wept, and rejoiced with each other."

The First Members

The 8 families who still remained on Pastor Carlsson's arrival were:

1. Göran Swenson, a shoemaker, with his wife Maria Jonsdotter and children, from Timmelhed, Vestergötland. They moved to Geneva in 1855, then to DeKalb and finally to Rockford.

2. Carl Joh. Anderson, a shoemaker, and wife Kajsa Zachrisdotter, from Gullered. The wife died in Chicago, the husband remarried and moved to DeKalb and then, in 1877, to Nebraska, where he died. He became a "Mission Friend," and an opponent of pastor Carlsson and the Lutheran Church. He had passed the teacher's examination in Sweden.

3. Josef Carlson, a tailor, and wife Gustava Hokansdotter and children from Böne in Elfsborg County. He died early. The family continued to reside in Chicago.

4. Johannes Anderson, a shoemaker, and his wife Maria Petersdotter and children, from Esperöd, Elfsborg County. The family moved to Rockford in 1854, where the husband was for many years a leader in the Lutheran congregation.

5. Gustaf Johnson and his wife Rebecka from Böne.

6. Nils Sjodin and wife Ingrid Kajsa Isaksdotter from Säbrå in Ångermanland. They and their 4 children live on the South Side in Chicago.

7. Isak Peterson and his wife Johanna Swensdotter from Wimmerby; they moved to Rockford 1854 and belong to the Swedish Luth-

eran Zion church there. Their son, Carl J. Petri, is the present pastor of the Augustana Swedish Lutheran congregation in Minneapolis.

8. Jonas Johnson, a blacksmith, and wife Fredrika Andersdotter from Slöta in Vestergötland. They moved to Geneva 1854 where Johnson died that fall. The widow remarried, to J.P. Lundin, and they moved to Neoga, Illinois.

The 20 single persons were:

1. John Nilson, a mechanic, from Kjäråkra in Elfsborg County; he moved to Rockford 1854, invented a machine to knit stockings and founded a stocking factory. He died in 1883. In early 1854 I had him as a pupil in my school in Chicago, and I learned to know him as a likeable youth with unusual talent. In his later years he did not belong to any church.

2. Johanna Anderson from Rångedala; dropped 1854 from the congregation.

3. Jonas P. Johanson, a widower, from Stenberga; Jönköping County; later remarried and removed to St. Charles.

4. Karl Anderson, a tailor, born in Unnaryd, later from Habo.

5. Gustaf Swenson, from Linderås; moved to Lisbon 1854— there he met death while cutting down a tree.

6. Karl Fredrik Forsberg, a blacksmith from Sandhem, Skaraborg County; a member of the congregation until his death in 1880.

7. John Swedman from Näsby, Jönköping County. He had a wife, in Sweden, who came here later. They live in Lake View and belong the the Gethsemane congregation.

8. Eva Charlotta Anderson from Timmelhed—married Pastor Erl. Carlsson in 1855.

9. Johanna Swenson from Hössna, later moved to Minnesota.

10. Elsa M. Rosenquist from Ousby in Skåne, moved to Knoxville 1854, then to Abingdon.

11. Kajsa Lisa Svensdotter, a widow, from Böne.

12. and 13. Charlotta Gustafa Peterson and her brother Per Josua Peterson, from Näfvelsjö, Jönköping County. Both moved to Kansas.

14. and 15. Johan Aug. Rolf and his sister Lena Katharina Rolf from Åsheda in Småland. The parents died of cholera in 1852. The sister married a Swede, Karl Weise, in La Porte, Indiana.

16. Johanna Anderson, from Böne.

17. Gottfrid Carlson, from Böne, a son of Josef Carlson, aforementioned.

18. Johan P. Johnson from Svanhals.

19. C.J. Osterberg, from Böne.

20. Lars Johan Anderson, from Hellestad in Vestergötland.

All these 36 persons can rightly be considered charter members of the congregation. With the exception of Eva C. Anderson, who came to America in 1851, all came in 1852. Pastor Carlsson held the first communion service in the congregation on Sunday, October 9, 1853. The Northern Illinois Synod met on the following Thursday, October 13th, in Galesburg, when it received a request from the congregation to become a member of the Synod. This request had been voted on at an extraordinary meeting at the Sunday service, October 9th, when C.J. Anderson was elected a delegate to the Synod. At the same time the congregation voted to pay the travel expenses of pastor and delegate.

The first annual meeting was held January 27, 1854. At the time of organization there had been no election of council members, no adoption of a constitution, no record of *Minutes*. The only written statement from that meeting is a list of names of those who wished to become members of the congregation, recorded by C.J. Anderson. Thus it was necessary now almost to start anew.

A proposed constitution which had been prepared by Pastor Erl. Carlsson was adopted. I wish to give it in its entirety when I treat of the "Swedish Lutheran Church in Indiana." For the document presented in Chicago on this occasion was in part the same as that which the United Chicago and Mississippi Conferences in 1857 drew up as a model constitution for all of the Swedish Lutheran congregations.

The sums of the first year were not large. The income, consisting only of the collections received at services, amounted to $21.90. Expenses were limited to the lighting and heating of the church— $11.93, leaving a balance of $9.97. From the time of his arrival to the end of the year the pastor had received only one offering, taken on Christmas day and amounting to $18.75. No salary for the pastor for the coming year was specified; it was to be made up of voluntary gifts and contributions.

The meeting elected the first council members: deacons—C.J. Anderson, John Nilson and Isak Peterson; trustees—John Bjorkholm, Goran Swenson, and Gisel Trulson. The election was properly notarized and recorded and the congregation legally incorporated.

The Growth of the Congregation

From the time of Pastor Carlsson's coming at the end of August 1853 to September 1, 1854, 114 new members had been received and 7 had been confirmed, so that the number of communicants had grown from 36 to 157. But 31 had moved and 10 had died, so that after a year the congregation numbered 116 communicants.

During the first years when the congregation used the church jointly with the Norwegian congregation, only one worship service could be held on Sundays, at 2 o'clock in the afternoon. This was an inconvenience, of course, but it was the best possible arrangement. On December 12, 1854 Pastor Carlsson wrote: "We have now bought the Norwegian church and lots for $2500". When it is said on p. 101 of the history (in *Korsbaneret*) that the congregation obtained its own building in 1856, the explanation is that the Norwegians had been granted the use of the building up to that date, when the Swedish congregation received exclusive right to it. This frame church was 52 feet long and 36 feet wide. It was in some disrepair, and improvements were made in the spring of 1855, costing $257.75. A voluntary subscription to pay for the church was begun and during 1855 and 1856 a sum of $969.98 was realized. The building was resting close to the ground on blocks and had to be raised to avoid rotting. At congregational meetings on August 19 and November 3, 1859 it was decided to raise the building 10 feet, to build a story of brick underneath, and to line the church walls with boards and plastering, and to paint the church. Also gas was to be piped into the building so that both church and basement could be lit with gas. The addition and repairs cost $1,074.17. But contributions for the project hardly reached half that sum.

The basement proved very useful. It provided an office for the pastor, two large rooms were rented to the Swedish Lutheran Publication Society, which for 10 years had here its book store and printing shop, and on the south end 3 rooms were rented for the home of a family. In time the income from rents more than paid for the enlargement. At the congregational meeting February 1, 1860 the church had a debt of $1628.90, considered large in those days. Immigration began to grow, and during the next 5 years the membership increased by 305. Now the church became altogether too small. It could not accommodate its own members, much less have room for the throngs of newcomers, who crowded in to hear the Word of God. The congregation decided therefore early in 1865 to add 20 feet to the length of the church, adding $2,398.54 to the debt. Yet when completed the church was as crowded as ever. To alleviate the situation services were started on the South Side, and at the same hour. P. Erikson was made assistant to the pastor and was in charge of these services—laying the foundation for the Salem Church.[1] But I have already gone beyond the limits of this history's first part.

THE IMMANUEL CHURCH, CHICAGO.

[1]*Korsbaneret* 1881, 92, 93

The Reception of New Members

On January 27, 1854 the congregation adopted a provisional constitution which included rules for the reception of new members, thereby establishing a very important principle regarding the formulation of a congregation and the taking in of new members. The section reads as follows:

"As to the receiving of new members it was resolved that no one should be accepted in the congregation who has been or is known as guilty of an un-Christian and wicked life. Those who wish to unite with the congregation should make this known to the pastor, who through personal interview and in consultation with the church council will inform himself of the applicants' Christian faith and moral character. If there is nothing to hinder their acceptance they shall be received at an ordinary service, or, preferably, at the service preparatory for the Holy Supper, in this way:

"Those who are to be received into membership shall present themselves at the altar as their names are called. The pastor shall say a prayer then address them thus:

"Dear friends, you have asked to become members of this our Evangelical Lutheran congregation. Since you have been born and nourished within the Lutheran Church we do not require any new profession of faith. We desire only to know if also in this land you will remain true to our ancient unforgettable faith and teaching. On behalf of the congregation I therefore ask if with sincerity of heart you will faithfully adhere to the Confession you have already made at the altar of the Lord (in confirmation), and accordingly will hold to the unaltered Augsburg Confession?

"Answer: Yes

"Do you also promise properly to meet those obligations which this Confession in general and membership in the congregation particularly place on you?

"Answer: Yes

"In accordance with your promises I now declare you to be members of this our congregation, having like ourselves free and open access to the treasures of God's kingdom and the use of the sacraments. The Lord give you grace to make use of this privilege to the salvation of your souls and eternal blessedness. Amen. (Prayer and the Apostolic benediction)

First and foremost we find here the principle which the whole Augustana Synod has followed in this matter. It is a golden mean between the indiscriminating nature of membership in the State Church and the attempt of the sects to form here on earth congregations of only perfect members. This formula with few alterations is almost word for word the one adopted by Synod 10 years later at the Rockford Convention and used in all our congregations. This method of receiving members has not only in its way protected the congregation from having rotten timbers in the walls of the temple, but it has made for a clear distinction between members and non-members, giving rise, if nothing else, from the very beginning to a consciousness of the fact of membership. It has given and still gives a suitable opportunity to present to newcomers the significance of membership in the congregation, and to impress on their hearts the concern and seriousness of the congregation.[1]

Baptism. The formula for baptism followed with very few changes that in the Manual of the Church of Sweden. As unfortunately is the custom in the city churches, baptisms are seldom performed in the church but either in the parents' home or in the parsonage. Many parents here had no relatives, hardly any acquaintances, so baptism was often delayed until the mother could be present and the parents thus themselves acted as Godparents.

During the first year, or up to October 1, 1854, the pastor baptized 46 children, of whom only 16 had been born in Chicago. The second year, up to October 1, 1855, 94 children were baptized, only 38 born in Chicago. In general only about one-half of the number of parents, who had their children baptized, were members of the congregation. Of the others some have been newcomers not yet members, some have continued their journey to other places, some, though not members, were desirous of having their children baptized.[1]

1854 and 1857 — Years of Suffering

Quoting from the aforementioned historical article in *Korsbaneret*:

"The year 1854 was a year of trial, yes, a terrible year in the history both of the Immanuel congregation and of immigration.

[1]*Ibid* 1881, 110-21

This was the year when the cholera epidemic ravaged so dreadfully among the population in general but especially among the immigrants. About one-tenth of the older members of the congregation and even a greater proportion of children were carried away. The newly arrived of our countrymen suffered worst in this plague. Only a few stayed in Chicago. As quickly as possible they were directed to other cities and settlements where the epidemic was less violent. Most of those (the newly arrived) who stayed in Chicago were swept away within a few days or weeks. Often the immigrants themselves carried sickness and death with them. A large party from Värmland, especially from Karlskoga and Bjurkärn, had 5 corpses when the train arrived at the Michigan Central Station in Chicago. 17 members of the party were stricken, were brought immediately to the hospital; more than half died before morning.

"Another quite large group from Linneryd, Elmboda, and other parishes on the border between Småland and Blekinge, were sent on at once from Chicago, after one of its members, a daughter of Gustaf Collin of Elmboda, was buried. This party was headed for Chisago Lake, Minnesota, but many died of cholera on the trip up the Mississippi River. The captain of the steamer did not want to bring these immigrants with their pestilence to Taylor's Falls, so he left them several miles south of that place, on the river bank, where there were neither people nor houses, except a miserable hut used by lumbermen, but now empty. Here many of the party died, and were buried in the sand as best they could be without shovels and caskets. After a few days the rumor of these newcomer Swedes reached Chisago Lake, and countrymen and relatives came to rescue the few survivors. The baggage which had been stored in the hut was burned by the Americans — the corpses were dug up and eaten by prairie wolves. Some members of this large group had remained in Moline and Rock Island, but also among these sickness and death took terrible toll. When, later, Pastor Carlsson visited them, he found only a few still alive, and of these a group of widows and children were housed in an engine shed in Rock Island. Among them was a woman who had lost her husband and was now destitute with her small children — one was Ingrid Maria, 6 years old, who later became the wife of Pastor J. Telleen.

"The suffering and misery of the immigrants during these very trying times defy description. The worst was in Chicago whither they all came, whether they landed in Quebec, Boston,

New York or Philadelphia. Though every effort was made to send as many as possible off to other places, many had to stop there for they had no means to continue. No one can imagine what efforts, sacrifices and deprivation a pastor in such a place as Chicago had to endure under these circumstances. Pastor Carlsson was occupied early and late in giving comfort, counsel, and help not only to the sick and dying but also to those who survived, but in sorrow, poverty, and need."

In early autumn he himself was taken ill with cholera. No one expected that he would live through the dread disease. But by the grace of God his life was spared, so that he could yet for many years serve his poor countrymen who needed him badly. After a few weeks rest in Geneva he recovered enough to give himself again to the over-exerting task.

"It is commonly assumed that 2/3 of the immigrants who came that year to America were carried away by death. The survivors had to contend with sickness, poverty and much misery. The natural result of the suffering and hardships of this year for the newcomers was that for several years immigration almost totally ceased."

In letters to Pastor Carlsson from various persons one can discern the mood of this sad period. For instance, Carl Peterson from Blekinge, possibly a member of the aforementioned large party from Småland and Blekinge, wrote from Rock Island to his friends remaining in Chicago in a letter of October 26, 1854 to Pastor Carlsson, that he and those with him arrived in Rock Island but had extreme difficulty in finding rooms. An acquaintance, Ola Jonsson (now in Chisago Lake) had however taken him in and done what he could for the others. Cholera had broken out among them, some were already dead, as Holjer Anderson, Hokan Jakobson, Swen Nilson and others. After describing in detail their miserable condition he wrote, "Dear friends, by all means don't come here now, but remain where you are, for however you have it, it cannot be worse than it is here. Here it is a terrible time for us poor immigrants, may God have mercy on us." November 15 he wrote again, " Most of our party are down in sickness, 23 are dead, the rest are for the most part unable to work, and our meager resources are exhausted; without means, unable for the present to work, and winter at the door.—we have no one else to turn to than the pastor for our physical needs."

Returning to the historical article:

"Then came the general crisis in the business world in the Fall of 1857. Almost all the banks in the country collapsed, their paper valueless, with the result that commerce and circulation almost ceased altogether for a long time. In Chicago were streets where every other house was vacant. People could not live on empty streets. They moved to the country hoping to survive by planting potatoes and corn.

"Hardly any new members arrived, many of the older ones moved, and those who were left had to contend with poverty and want. One or another of the members of the congregation now in comfortable circumstances no doubt recalls those hard times when the father of the household with a saw horse around his neck and an axe in his hand went up and down the streets looking for a small job in sawing wood in order to help support himself and his family. The great mercy of God enabled the congregation and its pastor to pass through this trial. The members were poor—the pastor gladly shared their wants and their agony. For the first three years he had no fixed salary. It consisted of voluntary gifts and offerings. In 1854 these totalled $116, in 1855 to $180, and for 1856 to $240—according to the records of the congregational meeting January 6, 1857. At this meeting the salary was set at $400 for 1857, but the pastor said he could manage with $350."

It was true in Chicago as in other city congregations at that time that the young women were, comparatively, the most important economic mainstay of the church. They had incomes when the men often were without work and they were both willing and sacrificial.

The Liturgy in the Immanuel Church

It would be correct to say that the Immanuel congregation set the standard for our other congregations in regard to order of worship, church practices and pastoral acts. Certainly the central location of Chicago contributed to this fact, for all pastors had at least visited Chicago and were familiar with the Swedish Evangelical Lutheran Church there and its customs. But the real reason is found in its first pastor. He came from Sweden as a Lutheran churchman without a bias in any direction, and for him it was natural to take for granted that he should continue in much the same way. Firm in doctrine and practice, devoted to good church order and possessing ability and strength to establish and maintain it, he fostered the congregation from the beginning to become a Christian but also an orderly church organization. A union of these elements makes for a strong congregation.

PASTOR ERLAND CARLSSON.

"The same week that Pastor Carlsson arrived, before the first service, some of the leaders of the congregation met with him to discuss how services should be held, singing, etc. Cautiously someone asked him if he intended to use the ministerial gown and collar. When he replied that this was his intention, they expressed their great satisfaction. They explained that neither Pastor Hasselquist nor Esbjörn used them when they preached in Chicago, whereupon Pastor Unonius and his friends had claimed they were not Lutheran, but had departed from the Lutheran Church."[1] We have already seen why Hasselquist and Esbjörn had not worn the gown and collar. "Pastor Carlsson however used gown and collar at all worship services (högmessa) and the Handbook at all pastoral acts, not because he wanted to prove to others that he was a Lutheran pastor, but because he thought it best to follow a tradition in which he saw

[1]*Ibid* 100-101

nothing wrong." After a few years a compromise was agreed upon, in that Pastor Carlsson ceased to use the gown and the other brethren began to use the clerical collar (bands) and the Handbook, unconcerned about what the Methodists and Episcopalians had to say. This has become the custom rather generally within the Synod."

Public Worship

After the congregation in 1856 obtained full use of the building it had shared from 1853 the liturgical worship service was held in the morning, Sunday School in the afternoon, and a vesper service in the evening. The morning service followed the liturgy of the Church of Sweden with such minor changes as the Synod had recommended. In the evening the sermon usually was based on the Epistle of the day, preceded and followed by a free prayer, without any altar service. Each Tuesday evening there was a prayer meeting, when the pastor led in Scripture reading and prayer, and then gave an exposition of a passage of Scripture. One or more of the members would then participate in prayer, sometimes adding words or exhortation and encouragement. On Thursday evenings a service, similar in form to the Vespers of Sunday evening, included study of the Bible by continuing through one of its books.[1] The only new element for Lutherans in this schedule consisted of the prayer meetings, common in the Reformed churches here but not of the same content as in the gatherings of Christians in Sweden for edification. The way these prayer meetings sometimes develop here leads one to doubt that such a form of devotion is healthy. But prayer meetings have become a regular activity in many of our congregations.

Church Music

"The Swedish *Psalmbok* (Hymnal) as revised by Thomander and Wieselgren has been used at the Sunday morning services; in the evening spiritual songs, especially *Hemlandssånger* (Songs of the Homeland) have been sung. The leader in singing was the shoemaker C.J. Anderson, from the beginning of the congregation until July 1, 1856. There was no instrument, but a melodion, or small Hamlin and Mason, was purchased for $45, and an organ student, Johan

[1]*Ibid* 101-102

August Anderson from Korsberga, Kronoberg County, was elected organist."

"He was succeeded by the school teacher Magnus Munter from Grenna, who played by numerals, Ludwig Miller, C.J. Anderson, and J.A. Esbjörn, until January 1, 1863 when Jonas Engberg was chosen—he held the position until 1867. In his period church music was raised to a higher level. A large fine organ, with bass and pedal, costing $400, was obtained. A choir was organized under the direction of Engberg and Lars Lindberg, which greatly improved the congregational singing and added to the festive nature of the worship services."

Confirmation

An annual confirmation service in the Swedish Lutheran Immanuel church was preceded by 6 months of instruction by the pastor, using Barth's *Bible History* and Luther's *Small Catechism* as texts. There were 7 in the first class, 2 boys: Johannes Swenson and Karl Gustaf R. Fagerstrom, and 5 girls: Johanna Wall, Mathilda Kristina Lundahl, Kjersten Gisselsdotter, Lotta Johannesdotter and Kajsa Larsdotter. They were confirmed April 17, 1854 (day after Easter) and were admitted to the Lord's Supper the following Sunday. Pastor Carlsson tells about this confirmation in a letter to a friend. "A feeling of depression in being a stranger, or of being here in a strange land, has followed me daily, even in the temple, but yesterday when we here held confirmation, I completely forgot that I was in America. It was indeed a blessed day for my heart, and inasmuch as it was the first confirmation service among our people here it became a high holiday for the congregation. There were seven in the class—a sacred number. May the Lord save them for his heavenly kingdom."

The act of confirmation followed the formula recommended in the 1854 Swedish Handbook. It was always in Swedish except in 1863 where both the instruction and the service were in English. The reason was quite unique. During the hard cholera year of 1854 several fatherless and motherless children had been placed in "The Protestant Orphans' Asylum" in Chicago. The children were not kept here, but were left with families all over the country who would care for them, furnish food and clothes and an elementary education. The laws of the state obligated the children to remain with and serve these so-called foster parents (really slave owners) until they became of age, girls 18 years, boys 21. When some of these children reached the age usual for confirmation they were seized by an irresistible longing to return to their countrymen and be confirmed. A brother and a sister of Kajsa Larsdotter, a member of the first class, whose father had died in Sweden and the mother in Chicago, of cholera in 1854, had been placed in Sangamon County near Springfield, Illinois, near enough to each other so that they could meet occasionally. They made plans to run away, but when they reached Chicago, a telegram had alerted the authorities and a policeman was at the railroad station to take them back before they could see or speak to a single Swede. But after a while they disappeared again. This time instead of staying on the train to the station they got off at a station outside the city and went by foot into the city, eluding the police. One of these children was Hanna Larsdotter, who became a member of the confirmation class of 1865. Later she married Peter Olin, the tailor. Another girl, Emma Karolina, sister of L.M. Melander, the photographer, had been sent from the "Orphans Asylum" to an American family in the vicinity of Bloomington, Illinois, but had returned about this time to Chicago. Since these children had forgotten their mother tongue, or at least had not been taught to read it, they asked to be instructed and confirmed in English. The others in the class understood English and easily read it, so the pastor decided to use English in order to avoid having to employ both languages. It has become a custom in the congregation that those confirmed should continue to be taught in the Sunday School, where they formed a special Bible class, from which not a few of the teachers in the school have been recruited.[1]

The Lord's Supper

The first celebration of the Lord's Supper occurred October 9, 1853. As a rule it was held once a month, and the order was that of the Church of Sweden—a preparatory sermon, confession of sins and absolution preceding the communion. A change was made in the formula of absolution already the first year, resulting in the following declaration: "If this your confession of sins is sincere, so that you feel and acknowledge yourself to be a poor, lost sinner before God, and it is your fervent longing and desire to be saved and freed from all your

[1] *Ibid* 93-96

sins through Jesus Christ, I, as a minister of Jesus Christ, assure you that God in mercy and for the sake of Christ has forgiven you all your sins and this merciful forgiveness of your sins I proclaim and declare to you in the name of God, the Father, the Son, and the Holy Spirit. Amen." —The custom of making known one's intention to commune has been followed, and in later years this took the form of writing one's name on a printed card, and the date of communion, as well as the name of the native parish in Sweden, and present address.[1]

IMMANUEL CHURCH SCHOOL HOUSE.

The Church School or the Instruction of Children and Youth in Christianity

From its beginning the congregation laid great emphasis on the instruction of children in the Word of God and Christianity, making great sacrifices for this purpose. Already in the Fall, six weeks after Pastor Carlsson's coming, a Swedish school for Christian instruction was established. It was held in a small church or school house on

[1]*Ibid* 104

Chicago Avenue, between Sedgwick and Townsend Streets, which at that time stood rather solitary out on the plain. It belonged to the Elling congregation, a group of Norwegians. Elling himself preached there now and then. Immanuel's first school teacher was Eric Norelius (later pastor in Vasa, Minnesota), a student at Capital University, Columbus, Ohio, who taught for a while in order to obtain means to go on with his studies. The pupils were Swedish and Norwegian children, the subjects taught were Christianity and the Swedish and Norwegian languages. One might ask, how could the congregation, so poor and new, pay for a school teacher? The old English proverb says, where there is a will there is a way. Each child paid 1 dollar a month—the balance was raised by voluntary subscription, in which single persons and parents without children gladly participated.

In April 1854 A. Anderson (later Pastor A. Andrén) then in New York was called to conduct the school, at the same time serving as assistant to the pastor. From the president of the Synod he received a catechist's license. He left after a year for the "Illinois State University" in Springfield to study for the ministry. He was succeeded by Magnus Munter from West Point, Indiana, as school teacher, and Munter held that position with satisfaction to all for a number of years.

It soon became apparent that the congregation needed its own school building, and as early as 1856 such was erected back of the church, 24 ft. wide, 32 ft. long, and two stories in height, and cost $600. Only the lower story was used by the school. The rooms on the upper story were rented out and soon paid for the cost of the whole. This house is remarkable in that it was the first home of the Swedish Lutheran Publishing Society. For a while the printing press of *Hemlandet* was lodged in the school room, and the book store in one of the upstairs rooms. But even more remarkable is the fact that this house can be termed the cradle of our institution, Augustana College and Theological Seminary. For when Professor L.P. Esbjörn left the State University in Springfield with his 17 Scandinavian students, at the end of March 1860, he came to Chicago and the school house was opened to him and the young men. Then the first floor became lecture rooms, and the second story a dormitory.[1]

The Christian day school and the Sunday School went hand in

---

[1] *Korsbaneret* 1882, 157-8. This article is a continuation of the one in 1881.

hand. While the Swedish and Norwegian congregations used the church jointly the Swedish children attended the Norwegian Sunday School and were taught in English. Even after 1856 when the Immanuel congregation had sole use of the building English continued to be the language of instruction. The reason was two-fold: the children had become accustomed to this in the Norwegian Sunday School, and both parents and children at first considered it important, the children easily learning the new language. But after English had become the every-day language, its importance in Sunday School diminished and a greater interest developed in the Swedish heritage, so that gradually Swedish gained a place there. The Sunday School gained in value especially after 1860 as the teaching force increased. The curriculum was based on the Bible, more particularly the New Testament.[1]

Christian Life and Discipline

From the beginning the Swedish Lutheran congregation in Chicago had a few serious and committed Christians. Love, unity, and confidence characterized their relations to each other and to their pastor. All of them were poor in earthly goods, so their life was plain and frugal. Separated from family and Christian friends in Sweden, they felt the necessity of meeting with each other frequently and trustingly. They did not pass the time in feasting or party strife. They sought edification in reading old familiar writings, such as those of Luther, Johan Arndt, Nohrborg, Hoofs, etc. They sang spiritual songs, particularly "The songs of Moses and the Lamb," and "Songs of Zion." Individual and collective prayer were cherished. At the weekly service and prayer meeting someone read from a devotional book known to all. The reading might be interrupted by questions and comments. Usually two or three would pray publicly. Women would pray thus only when only women were present, as in sewing society meetings. They were interested only in edification, not in innovations. These were simple, pleasant times, when there was unity of heart and soul among the children of God, and the stream of Christian life flowed quietly but also more deeply.

The Fall of 1857 and winter of 1858 were a specially gracious and delightful period, for the congregation experienced a powerful

[1]*Ibid* 160-161

spiritual movement. Many souls awakened and found life and peace through faith in the Crucified Savior. This awakening was quite general and profound. Almost every evening Bible classes and prayer meetings were held here and there in the homes. The movement did not take on a fanatical or unwholesome character.

A wide-spread and blessed spiritual activity developed early in the congregation. The center was the church council, in which there have constantly been faithful and praying members, who have been zealous for the cause of the Lord and active in seeking to carry out their duties. To be able in a large city to arouse and maintain Christian and churchly interest and lead the congregation requires a church council with open mind and skill in organization. One can claim that this was the case within the Immanuel church from the start, and credit belongs primarily to the pastor. The council met regularly every other week to consider the spiritual state of the congregation and what could be done, and how, to improve it. An inner mission was started early, later called "The Immanuel Church Tract Society." Its activity branched out in a) house visits and tract distribution, b) visits in hospitals and charitable institutions, c) branch Sunday Schools, sometimes developing into independent congregations, d) devotional meetings, especially in more remote areas from the church. Surely the congregation has not been inactive in good deeds, but rather has distinguished itself from the start both for inner and foreign missions, for care of the sick and the poor, for the support of impoverished students, and for a variety of causes.

As to Christian discipline the congregation made decisions already at the first congregational meeting, January 27, 1854, and later adopted the following paragraph in its constitution: "Should the unhappy circumstance arise that any member of the congregation forsakes, falsely interprets or openly denies the sacred faith and teaching of the congregation, or falls into a sinful and unrighteous life, such as intoxication, adultery, cursing, breaking the Sabbath, quarrelsomeness, malicious slander, or in any other way causes general offense or grief to the church of God, then it shall be the duty of the council to exercise discipline (Matt. 18:15-18, 1 Cor. 5)."[1] This principle guided the congregation from the beginning in the matter of discipline and met with success. Most of the persons excommunicated were guilty of habitual drunkenness or other obvious and

[1] *Ibid* 162-174

offensive sins. There have been differences of opinion as to whether discipline was too loose or too strict, but the congregation did try, faithfully and conscientiously, to follow its own constitution, and to observe the rule of the apostolic church.

Statistical summary: From October 1, 1853 to June 1860 children baptized 247; confirmed 89; members received 369 communicants; removed 240; deaths 59 children, 23 communicants; excommunicated 11; married 57 couples; membership increase, from 36 to 220.

The Relationship of the Swedish and Norwegian Congregations to Each Other

Something should be said about the relationship of these two congregations. We have already seen the part Pastor Andersen played in the organization of the Swedish congregation. Both he and his congregation continued to show a friendly and fraternal attitude to the Swedish congregation, to which the Swedish members responded in friendship and gratitude. Both used the same building until March 1856. By that time the Norwegian church was sufficiently ready for its congregation to move in. Dr. Hasselquist described the event in *Hemlandet*: "The editor had the pleasure to take part in the dedication of the new Norwegian church in Chicago last March 2 (1856) and would like to report and make some comments on the event. On the previous Saturday evening the Norwegians bade farewell to their old building and turned it over completely to the Swedish congregation. It was indeed a festive moment for all in attendance, but especially for those members who had fought hard from the beginning to make the old temple a reality. It is a miracle that they succeeded, but even more that He who holds the seven stars in his hand had so often made His presence felt through the power of grace and here brought so many of His children to life. The preacher, brother Andersen, reminded all of this, and expressed the desire and prayer that the Lord would similarly and even in greater measure be present in the new house they would take over on the morrow, or else "not let them come away from the old place." Brother Carlsson spoke warmly of the debt of the Swedes to their Norwegian brethren who had so readily opened their church to them before they had their own, and were in fact "homeless" in Chicago. We part from them, he said, wishing them blessing and success."

Then he described the festivities of the dedication on Sunday, when 6 Norwegian and Swedish pastors were present, also Dr. W.A. Passavant and Dr. Harkey. In the evening there was another service in the new church. The church was termed a "stately brick building," and it was that in those days. It cost around $18,000. Then the report adds, "the former Norwegian church now belongs entirely to the Swedish Lutheran congregation in Chicago—It has cost the present owners about $3,000, and during the year the congregation has raised about $1200.—It is of interest to note that while the others barely advance the two Scandinavian Lutheran congregations have progressed steadily and improved both inwardly and outwardly."[1]

[1] *Hemlandet* 1856: no. 6.

Chapter 6

The Swedish Lutheran Congregations in
St. Charles, Geneva, De Kalb, Illinois

These familiar places St. Charles, Geneva, Batavia, Aurora, and Elgin, where Swedes located early, border the Fox River in Kane County, Illinois. A colony of Americans from Indiana settled here already in 1833 and one from New York came the following year. The county, organized in 1836, was named for Elias K. Kane, one of the first senators from Illinois in Congress. In 1840 the county had a population of 6,500, in 1860, 30,062.[1] The Fox River runs through the county, creating a pleasing landscape of woods and open fields of grass and crops. In the small towns along the river shops and factories were established quite early, in which many Swedes found employment. Fertile fields on either side of the river were available for those who wished to rent them, and gradually the Swedes acquired small tracts especially in the wooded area around Geneva and St. Charles.

As to the first Swedes in St. Charles and Geneva — places only a couple of miles apart — *Svenskarne i Illinois*, Part I, chapter 2, p. 193 has this account: "In 1849 Jonas Anderson, now living in Princeton —and his party came to St. Charles on their way west from Chicago. They had then been two days on their uncertain way, and since the place looked pleasant and alive, they decided to remain and see what could be done. They soon discovered that they were not the first Swedes there. Before them had come Nils Johnson, who owned a shop (not long afterwards he was killed by lightning out in the country), another by the name of Bjorkman, a merchant, and a third who changed his name of Baker to Clark, also a merchant, who went bankrupt about this time and betook himself to Chicago. This was but the beginning of the small Swedish colony now in the town."

This Jonas Anderson came from Färila in Helsingland 1849. From St. Charles he went on to Wisconsin, worked there a while, then came back to St. Charles, where he stayed until 1853, when he removed to Princeton. He has remained there and been active and successful in the building trade.

Nils Johnson, according to Mrs. A.W. Carlson, a daughter of Sven Thim, now in Cannon Falls, Minnesota, was from Hörby in Skåne and had come as a youth to America around 1830. He had

[1] *Svenskarne i Illinois*

been in Mexico among many other places, was a heavy drinker and an adventurer of sorts, but on occasion was helpful to his fellow countrymen. Able in English, he assumed a sort of guardianship of the Swedes in St. Charles, arranged for the building of a small church, and thought of himself as their spiritual leader. His wife seems to have been a devout woman, often exhorting him. On the morning of the day in which he was struck by lightning she had asked how it would go with his soul if he did not repent and prepare for his death. He is supposed to have replied that she should not worry on that account, for he would not need more than half a day to prepare. The date of his death, however, was somewhat later than stated in *Svenskarne i Illinois*.

It was really Anders Anderson from Timmelhed, or, as he was called, the smith from Anderstorp, who was responsible for so many from Vestergötland coming to this area. He came to America in 1851, and because of his letters home many joined him after 1852 and following years. He himself moved after a few years to Taylor's Falls, Minnesota, where he died. He was survived by two daughters, of whom one married Daniel Fredin in the vicinity of Taylor's Falls, one married Pastor Erland Carlsson.

Among those who came in 1852 were Lars Frenn, from Timmelhed, born in Wing, and his brothers Sven Thim, Anders Larson, and a half-brother Karl Larson. Lars Frenn lived one year in St. Charles, then moved to Wayne Station, near Geneva, but belonged to the St. Charles congregation and was active in its affairs. In 1864 he moved to Vasa, Minnesota where he was known for his honesty and ability in all his dealings, and where he remained a faithful member of the congregation until his death in 1880, at an age of over 61 years. His three surviving sons, Per Johan, Anders Josef, and Karl August and their families are highly esteemed in community and church.

Thim died in Geneva. Anders Larson moved to Red Wing around 1855-6 and died in Vasa 1871, almost 59 years old. Two daughters survive him, Mrs. Erik Johnson in Vasa and Mrs. Charles Swenson in Red Wing. A daughter of Thim lives in Cannon Falls, a widow of A.W. Carlson, a wainwright, and another married to an American, Spears, lives in St. Jose, California.

Among the two parties of immigrants who came in 1852 cholera broke out in the beginning of July. The Americans in St. Charles distinquished themselves through their kindness and sacrifices for the Swedish sick. A temporary shelter was built on Aldrich place on the edge of town. A number of women volunteered to nurse and care for the sick. Every effort was made to stem the plague, but it did not subside until 75 persons had died, including one of the nurses. "In the Kane County history there is an account of a large, powerfully built Swedish immigrant of about 50 years who was stricken with cholera, but refused all human help in the form of medicine or care. He depended entirely on the power of Providence and of water. He stretched his hands heavenward, stepped into the river, but was carried away by the current. Rescued from the stream he died a few moments later from the cholera."[1]

From the same source and others we have the following names of early Swedes in St. Charles: a Bowman, who served in the War, his stepson P.G. Bowman, who moved to Chicago, and a J. Sannquist. Karl Samuelson came in 1852 from the Timmelhed region, and also Karl Sjoman. These were God-fearing men, disciples of Hoof, and the former became a spiritual leader in this area, still living in Elgin. The latter finally settled around McGregor, Iowa. Abram Swenson and his sister, now Mrs. Ostergren, both living in Hastings. Anders Swenson from Rängedala and his brother-in-law Hedelin, now in the vicinity of Faribault, Minnesota. All these came in 1852, most with families. Jonas Hokanson was also among the first, though the date is unknown. Presumably he later moved to Rockford. In 1853 Peter Lundgren came from Bottnaryd, Jönköping County, John Carlson from Askeryd, the same County, and Peter Lundquist who moved to Rockford. Rumor has it that Lundquist's wife was unusually strong and could easily whip a man if the occasion demanded it. Also Fr. Peterson and August Nord-Peterson moved to Nebraska, Nord remained in St. Charles working as a plasterer. There were many others in St. Charles at this time, but their names are not recorded. *Svenskarne i Illinois* states that "around 1880 there were 25 Swedish families there, the men working in the local factories. All own small, neat homes."

In Geneva the following names occur among the first Swedes there: D. Lindstrom, now in Paxton, his son John P. Lindstrom, now in Moline, and his son A.P. Lindstrom, pastor in Chandlers Valley, Pennsylvania. They came from Böne in Elfsborg County in 1852. Goran Swenson and family, originally members of the Immanuel congregation in Chicago, were here in 1854. G. Lindgren and Sam

Ibid p. 192.

Peterson, who moved to Aurora; John Rystrom who moved to Oregon, Illinois; Gustaf Peterson, who moved to Chicago; B. Kindblad and A.P. Anderson, moved to Batavia; Julius Esping, an anchorsmith, who moved to Freemount, Kansas, and died there a few years ago; Sven Anderson, moved to Elgin; C.P. Gronberg, now deceased; Jonas M. Peterson, who died in Galesburg, Olof Swenson, a shoemaker, died in Geneva; John Peterson from Gällaryd in Småland, who is known as the oldest Swede in Geneva.

The Swedish Lutheran Congregation in Geneva and St. Charles

Hemlandet[1], 1856, number 12 carried an article by Pastor E. Carlsson on the Swedes in Geneva and vicinity and their church. "About six years ago our countrymen began to settle in St. Charles on the banks of the lovely Fox River. In time they decided to build a church. 'A subscription for a Scandinavian Lutheran Meeting-house' was begun, and a building was erected in 1852.[2] Yet no congregation was organized. Ministers of other denominations made occasional visits before two Lutheran pastors [Hasselquist and the Norwegian Paul Andersen] made a visit early in 1853 and organized an Evangelical Lutheran congregation. There were some 40 members, but the number grew as newcomers arrived. The congregation joined with the Chicago congregation in calling Pastor Erland Carlsson of Sweden, who came in the Fall of 1853. He assumed care of the St. Charles church and has regularly visited it the first Sunday of each month. Two circumstances made it necessary to think of a new building. First, the place was too small, so that in the summer of 1854 a good part of the congregation had to stand outside during the service. The other was more unique. There was a debt of over $150 on the building, which the trustees had borrowed on a note, with the provision that it would be paid when receipts were on hand for the material and labor involved and a deed was turned over for the lot on which the building stood. The congregation refused to pay until these conditions were met. In fact the deed could not be given for the simple reason that the land had been sold to a railroad company.

"Meanwhile some Swedish families had settled in Geneva, which lies two miles to the south on the same river. It was now proposed to

---

[1] *Svenskarne i Illinois*
[2] By the aforementioned Nils Johnson

build a church in this town. The idea arose from the fact that right in the middle of this little attractive town was a rather large stone building, built five years earlier as a tavern or hotel, but never finished. Satisfied with the condition of the building and finding it available the congregation at a meeting in St. Charles November 22, 1854 decided to buy the property at a sum not to exceed $2,000 and to make it suitable for services. All, regardless of whether they lived in Geneva or St. Charles, promised to do what they could. A subscription was started that very evening and netted over $400. In general each one promised a month's salary toward the new church. The amount later grew to $1200, of which very few subscriptions remained unpaid. On November 24, 1854 a contract was signed. A down-payment of $400 was made, on March 30 $600 interest and $1,000 principal was to be paid, and $100 interest on Nov. 24, 1855. A week later work was begun, and by the first Sunday in December, 1854, the house had been so far repaired that services could be held there. A sore trial was encountered last summer when a severe storm tore off the roof, and the repairs cost the congregation another $200. Including this expense, and the cost of furnishings, $1420.66, and the initial price plus interest, the total amounted to $3,540.66. When the church was finished the congregation had a debt of $1000, which was reduced by a collection of $160 on Pentecost morning and $20 in the afternoon. From the sale of land not needed $150 was realized, and some help was received from Americans in town. Yet one cannot but be amazed at the sacrifices made by this poor and new congregation in so short a time for their church. And their satisfaction has still never been greater or their economic condition been better than at present. What say you who seldom or never ventures a widow's mite for such a purpose?

"At present there are 250 members, of whom 140 are communicants. Some are farmers, some mechanics, some day-laborers.

"Remarkable are the wonderful ways in which the Lord has helped in many a quandary. When the second payment was due there was no prospect for finding the money. Every possible attempt was made, but to no avail. But a few days before payment was due a draft came to a man of their acquaintance. He immediately made a loan of $500 to the church, so they were rescued in that dilemma. But the largest sum to be paid, $1100, was the last. By then the congregation had spent so much on the furnishings that many feared that it would not be possible to meet this outlay and therefore everything, church and property, would be forfeited. It was a delight to witness the sacrifices then undertaken. My eyes fill with tears when I think of it. Many who had acquired real estate came with deed in hand and said, 'Take this, if needed, and loan what money you can on it.' But we did not have to use this expedient, since those of our countrymen with money were ready to give, and the amount was raised without difficulty. The congregation received the deed, so that it is established more firmly than is the case in St. Charles. There we lost the church, hopefully not forever, but until the congregation can arrange its affairs. It expects to bring charges against the person who in such a deceitful and cruel manner attacked and ruined the church. Meanwhile our people in and around St. Charles attend services in Geneva, and consider themselves as only one congregation."

To complete this record I quote from a letter Pastor Carlsson wrote me Dec. 12, 1854: "In Geneva we have bought a large stone building, built as a court-house[1] five years ago but never completed as such. It is quite large, 27 × 45 feet within walls, and 19 feet from floor to ceiling. Ten days ago it was roofed, and we hope to have it quite finished by New Year. The house is located in the most pleasant place in town, and it and the whole block was bought for $2000. Furnishings will cost around $500. Our countrymen are willing to do not only what they can, but even beyond. Those with work have pledged from $15 to $20 a year to the church, day laborers from $10-$20, and servant girls from $4 to $8. But they will need much more. We need the help of others. Indeed it seems dark, but I am certain that God will help us. Do you think that anything could be done for our congregations among the brethren of our faith in Columbus and Ohio?"

By selling lots which the congregation did not need for the building and parsonage, however, the property turned out not to be so expensive. Pastor Carlsson built a house on one of the lots, around 1858, and lived in it a few summers. A few years later it was destroyed, presumably by arson, because of feeling against an American minister who had rented it and was about to move in.

Evidently the congregation lost out on the small building in St. Charles. An Irish-American, or whatever he was, by the name of Marvin who had claims against the building took it almost by force from the Swedes. In 1854 when they came there to celebrate "Julotta"

---

[1] The *Hemlandet* article said "hotel" — which is correct is uncertain.

(Christmas morning) they found it nailed shut. One of the members, Jonas Peter Magnusson, broke it open so that they could come in. When they came there at Easter, they found the building had been rolled away. Marvin seems to have retained it.

A Great Holiday in Geneva — the Dedication of the Church.

Pastor Hasselquist wrote in *Hemlandet*, 1856, number 11, this account: "Geneva, Illinois May 8-12. These days were truly pleasant and happy ones. We hope to tell our readers about what happened these days, as well as something about the conditions of our countrymen in this area. Even the weather was agreeable. It rained on our trip to Geneva the 7th, as if the heavens were open, and Monday the 12th it began again to prepare for wet weather, which indeed broke out the following day with incredible force. But from the 8 to the 12th there was sunshine and warmth.

"Geneva's situation is one of the loveliest one will see in Illinois. The town itself lies on a prairie sloping toward the East and the Fox River, but also on the east side of the river city lots are laid out and a few homes already built. It is on this side, which is wooded, that almost all the Swedes have settled. The river banks were now green, and the river runs almost straight. Northward, about two miles, one could see the white houses in St. Charles, and southward, about the same distance, something of Batavia was visible. There is a slight fall here in the river, which may be the reason for the town's location, since it was anticipated that mills might be built, as indeed a start has been made. The growth of the town will be aided by a railroad passing through and the building of the county court-house, to be built on the west side of the river.

"19 Swedes have bought lots in Geneva, and built houses which with lots are valued from $200 to $800 each. Two own houses without lots, and some have bought lots, planning gradually to build homes, if desire does not draw them in other directions.

"12 Swedes have acquired larger and smaller farms around St. Charles and Geneva, which are of considerable value. 5 rent from owners. Because of the church Geneva is now a center for Swedes over a large area. Many have settled in small places along the railroad, who turn to Geneva when services are held.

"Two circumstances in particular have brought us together at this time, one is the extra meeting of our Synod, the other the festive dedication of the new church. Dr. Harkey stayed with us over Sunday, even though the synodical meeting ended on Saturday. He seemed to enjoy being with us, and we had many pleasant and interesting hours together, both in and out of the church, so that we missed him after he left. Brother Harkey [the Synod president] preached three times, in English of course. His sermons were more evangelical than one usually hears in this country, yet he did not please some of the Americans present, who, we were told, were Disciples. Some of them had approached the Swedes on Saturday and expressed their displeasure. — Now something about the church and its dedication. It is located in one of the best parts of town, is built of stone, 47 feet long and 36 feet wide, inside, and 18 feet from floor to ceiling. It is more Swedish than usual in this country in that it has round arched windows and a high balcony extending into the church. There are 30 benches on the floor and a number in the balcony; able to seat over 300 in this light and high temple. We received a deep and pleasant impression when on Wednesday evening May 7th we came out of the dark and stormy evening into the place of worship, lit by 6 large oil lamps and a great number of candles. The attendance grew with each service. On Sunday morning Bergenlund gave the communion address, and, in the dedication the 5 Swedish pastors [Esbjörn, Hasselquist, Erl. Carlsson, Bergenlund, E. Norelius] participated, mainly in accord with the Handbook of the Swedish Church. Dr. Harkey closed the act by reading in English the prayer of Solomon at the dedication of the Jerusalem temple. Then followed the Sunday worship service [högmessa]. 1 Kings, Ch. 19 was read, which tells what happened outside the cave where Elijah was lodged. The sermon, based on the gospel lesson of Pentecost, had as topic, 'Evidences of the presence of the Spirit of God and its work in the human heart.' Finally a goodly number of guests received the Lord's Supper. The large congregation present followed what was done with close attention despite the long service of over 5 hours.

"We must not forget to mention that our countrymen here are not only hearers of the Word but also doers. What they have done to acquire this church and to complete it brings honor to the Swedes in this place and is an encouragement to those in other places to go and do likewise, where the need exists. I must add that when Pastor Esbjörn spoke as the Synod's representative for the professorship in Springfield he received between $70 and $80 in subscriptions from

to do away with it, and in its place adopted an annual dues of 75 cents per communicant for current expenses, to be paid at the same time as the pastor's salary was collected. The latter was fixed, on August 24, 1856, at $3 per man and $2 per woman, annually except for newly arrived immigrants and those unable to pay.

A Ladies' Sewing Society dates from 1853, its first year's income was $20.40. Mrs. Elna Mattson was leader in the cholera year 1854, when income was $32.12. This money was used for a number of benevolent causes.

The Congregation during the Pastorate of O.C.T. Andrén

A new period of development began with the arrival of Pastor Andrén — It was a new, poor congregation to which he came. Prospects were neither great nor bright, on the contrary, but he seems not to have expected anything great, and was prepared to sacrifice, work and suffer. Rock Island and Moline constituted one congregation for many years. He also served Geneseo and other places. It is not known how many members were in his pastorate when he came, but the following year (1857) they numbered 172.

I have the following contribution to the history of the Swedes in Moline and Rock Island from Pastor O.C.T. Andrén. Since it is based on knowledge of the subject and is written on the spot, I include it here before going on in my narrative.

"Moline, or 'the city of the Mills' is situated just where the Mississippi River stretches out its arm to embrace the lovely, 3 mile long, 1/4 mile wide Rock Island, across whose western end the city of Rock Island, in Illinois and the rapidly growing city of Davenport in Iowa are located. The land on which Moline is situated was first occupied 1832 and 1833 and used by farmers until 1841, when a company comprised of John W. Spencer, David B. Sears and Spencer H. White began the installation of a water power mill. Since then Moline has gone forward by small but steady steps. At present (1859) the population numbers around 3,000. When capital succeeds, though now only in an initial stage, of making use of the mighty volume of water, Moline may become one of the largest manufacturing cities in the West. At present four factories are run by steam. Water power is used by 4 flour mills and 13 factories. As soon as weather and the river level permit the present dam will be so enlarged this year that 15 to 20 factories can be built near it. Moline's site is attractive and advan-

the pastors present. On Friday afternoon he did the same before the congregation, though not very many members could attend, and then received about $190 in pledges. This was not all. An offering was received after the service on Pentecost Sunday, and brought in over $160 in cash and pledges."

All of this shows the strong churchly and Christian interest found in this congregation, despite the fact that just at this time many were on the point of moving to other places.

Something of the Inner History of the Congregation

As mentioned Pastor Carlsson was present the first Sunday of each month. On the other Sundays the service was conducted by the deacons, especially Karl Samuelson, and one while by P. Carlson [later Pastor Peter Carlson]. They would read a sermon and add their own exhortation. In the congregation were a number of strong Christians, meetings for mutual edification were held in the homes, and a spiritual movement made itself felt 1857-58. Sometimes not everything in this movement was healthy and favorable. The awakened ones were in some cases influenced by Methodist tendencies, but not to the point of harm to the congregation. One while before 1860, when the members had to meet large expenses of the church and were affected by a unsound spirituality, one group became dissatisfied with the pastor. They thought the lay leaders could do more to convert people than the pastor did, and that they could get along without a pastor, and more cheaply. When Pastor Carlsson called a meeting the storm broke. A short man, "Shoemaker Ola" was spokesman for the dissenters. Ola was not a mean individual, on the contrary pious, though narrow. He had a big mouth, and now he filled it with real big words, at this moment bold, for he thought he had the congregation with him. Otherwise Ola was not very brave. Pastor Carlsson let him keep on until he had said all he wanted to, and then sat down. Whereupon Pastor Carlsson began, and those who were present have told me that they have never forgotten that tense moment. While he spoke in gripping, serious, words Ola sank down in his bench, deeper and deeper, until at last only his large mouth stuck up over the top of the seat. Apparently the condition of the congregation improved after this and the correction was a healthy event.

The organization and liturgy of the congregation was much the same as that in Chicago and other places. One while A. Andrén was assistant to Pastor Carlsson in Chicago and often preached in Geneva. I [Norelius] too preached there, both while I lived there a short time, in the Fall of 1858 and while I was in Chicago as editor of *Hemlandet* in 1859. Not infrequently all our pastors were there for meetings or on other occasions.

The Church School

The congregation was concerned very early for the instruction of the children in the Christian faith, in Swedish. The first one engaged as teacher was Jon Pehrson, later a pastor in the Synod. He came from Jemshög in Blekinge to America in 1854 and lived in Geneva a few years, as teacher to Swedish children, until he left for the seminary in Springfield. If I remember aright he had taken the school teachers' examination in Sweden. The school in Geneva was held in a home, the children were few, the salary small. But it was a beginning.

M. Munter was the next teacher. Apparently one while he alternated between Chicago and Geneva. Later he conducted schools in Illinois, Indiana, and Iowa. In Iowa his name has been perpetuated in the village of Munterville, post office address, Wapello County, where he died a few years ago. The praise he received in Chicago does not seem to agree with the testimony of former pupils, both in Sweden and America, as to his competence. Towards the boys he was tyrannical, and his learning was meager. As an example of what could happen in a Swedish school in those days some of his former boys report that one day Munter brought a sheep into the school-room, slaughtered and cut it up while the school work went on as usual.

In Geneva Munter was succeeded by a woman, known by every one as "School Mary," who was highly thought of. Later she moved to Freemount, Kansas, where she is probably still living.

In 1860 the congregation had 140 communicants, and current expenditures for the year were $260.

Before 1860 there was no Swedish Methodist church in Geneva, though there were occasional visits by Swedish Methodist preachers. Nor was there any other Swedish congregation.

Batavia and Aurora had no Swedish Lutheran congregation before 1860. There were few Swedish people in both places, but when they attended services or requested pastoral help they turned to Geneva. This was also the situation in Elgin.

De Kalb, Malta, and Sycamore had some Swedish settlers after 1853, and were preaching points quite early. Only De Kalb had an organized congregation by 1860. There were communities where Pastor Carlsson and his assistants held services at times, in private homes. The congregation in De Kalb was organized by Pastor Carlsson in 1859, with 40 communicants.

According to *Svenskarne i Illinois* the first Swedes in De Kalb were: Jonas Olson, the very first one. He had owned a farm near Dixon, and came to De Kalb in 1850. Soon afterwards his brother came, along with two sons of a minister named Bark. The Olsons came from Slätthög in Kronoberg County; Nils Magnus Jonson, Johan Johanson, Jonas Johnson, and John Olson of Hjortsberg also came in 1853 — all from the same county. Later Goran Swenson and family from Ulricehamn arrived — we have met him in Chicago and Geneva, Peter Monson from Vislanda came in 1854; he built the first Swedish house in De Kalb, later moved to Kansas. In the same year Peter Johnson came from the same parish. In Malta, A.T. Engstrom, son-in-law of Goran Swenson, lived for many years. These are but some of the earliest Swedes in this area. These, as the Swedes generally everywhere, had to contend with poverty, sickness, and many hardships the first years. As an example I had a trustworthy man tell me that when he was in De Kalb 1854 or 1855, he was acquainted with a man who had lost his wife and was helpless, with several children. He was persuaded to sell two of them to Americans, the boy for $25, the girl for $75.

Chapter 7

The Swedish Evangelical Lutheran Congregations in
Rockford and Pecatonica

Rockford

The Swedes of Rockford, 1885 Historical Notes, Collected and Published by George Kaeding is a valuable treatise of 121 pages, printed by Alfred Lindell Company, Chicago 1885. I draw from it a number of facts about the history of Rockford and the Swedes there:

When Illinois was admitted to the Union as a state, the northern part was occupied by the Winnebago Indians, and the present Winnebago County, in which Rockford is located, was an open prairie. This part of the country became better known after the Black Hawk War of 1832. Soldiers who had participated spread word about the beautiful Rock River Valley, and soon white settlers made their homes there. Ira Baker is supposed to have been the first white man to visit the area where Rockford now is situated — that was in 1824. He came from Terre Haute, Indiana. After the Black Hawk War the martyr president Abraham Lincoln visited the spot in company with some government officials. Not until 1834 was there any growth in population. The place was called Midway, since it was half way between Galena and Chicago. Mr. Ephraim Wyman, born in Lancaster, Massachusetts 1809, and possibly even now alive, was among the first to settle here, in 1835. "At that date," he says, "there were only 3 log houses in this place — When I first came to Rockford there were about 750 Potawatomie Indians in the woods on the east side of the river, and along the Pecatonica river about 700 Winnebagos. They were very peaceful and quiet." In 1850 Rockford had 1500 inhabitants. It is beautifully situated on both sides of the Rock River in a fertile and scenic farming region. During the past 20 years the city has developed rapidly, due to a great number of factories, and is now the home of thousands of Swedes.

The First Swedes in Rockford

It was around 1852 that the first Swedes settled in and around Rockford. John Nelson, the inventor of the stocking-knitting machine (we remember him from the Chicago story) visited Rockford 1852 and found a few Swedish families who had been there a short while. Among them were Abram Anderson and family and a young man named Clark, possibly the same person mentioned in the St. Charles section. Soon thereafter Anderson left for Minnesota, Nelson had come from St. Charles, went to Elgin after a couple of months, then in the Spring of 1853, to Chicago. I became acquainted with him in the Fall of that year, and we lived together for a few months, and during the winter he was one of the pupils in the private English school I conducted in Chicago. Later in 1854 he returned to Rockford in company with an Anders Johnson. Since his previous stay there a number of families and single persons had arrived here. These included: Swen August Johnson, from Wing in Elfsborg County, who came to America in 1852 — one of Rockford's prominent business men and among the oldest members of the Lutheran congregation; Peter Johnson; C.J. Carlson and P. Peterson, both tailors, with their families from Wing in Vestergötland; Lindgren and Lundbeck, who moved to Minnesota where they died long ago; Jonas Larson, born in Ölmstad in Småland May 9, 1825, emigrated 1853, came that year to Rockford, elected a deacon at the organization of the First Lutheran congregation, now belongs to the Zion church where he is a teacher in primary grades; Johan Sparf, from the same parish, a member of the same emigrant group. Jonas Larson tells that when he arrived in the Fall of 1853 in Rockford he found only a few Swedes, in very distressing circumstances. Poor food, even poorer housing, sickness and unemployment, was the picture that met the eyes of the immigrants as they finally reached their destination, after a journey of 6 months filled with a thousand troubles and all kinds of suffering. They had embarked in Gothenburg on a small sailing boat, crowded and dirty, and devoid of all comfort for the emigrants. — They sailed north of Scotland and ran into terrific storms. The ship was driven toward the Irish coast and they feared momentary death. The point was reached where the cook refused to give any food. When the emigrants complained they received the reply, "you don't need any more food, before dawn we will all be on the bottom of the ocean." They realized that they could do nothing else than prepare for death, for they were sure that the ship could be driven ashore and crushed in the surf. But the wind died down, so that after 5 weeks at sea they could enter the harbor of Cork in Ireland. Here they had to remain 2 1/2 months while the ship was unloaded and repaired. Afterwards it took 10 weeks to cross the Atlantic with almost equally stormy weather. In Rockford they found it hard to get work. Wages ranged from 50 to 25 cents a day, but expenses were in proportion. Butter could be bought for 5 cents a pound, meat for 3-4 cents, board for a working man cost $1.50 for a week. Jonas Larson and J. Sparf rented rooms together for $3 a month near the present 'public square.' J. Sparf is now a wealthy farmer near Cherry Valley, 7 miles from Rockford. We would note too: Isak Petterson, born in Bellö June 16, 1820, mentioned in our story of Chicago, where it is said that he moved to Rockford 1854, but here said to have come in 1855; Johannes Anderson, from Esperöd, with family, also known in Chicago, who came to Rockford 1854.

1854-55 many Swedish immigrants came direct from Sweden, some from Chicago and other places where they had stayed temporarily. Among these: John Erlander, born in Slätthög in Kronoberg county, April 7, 1826, a tailor in Sweden, came to America in 1854 with an older brother, P. Erlander, and a sister, staying in Chicago until the Spring of 1855. He has had a very successful business career, all the while being one of the most active of the members of the First Lutheran church; Peter Lindahl, grain broker; A.P. Peterson from Östergötland, machinist; G. Bergquist, from Vermland, painter; Gustaf Berglund, same province, dyer; Isak Lindgren, G. Scott, John Abramson, A. Johnson, all of them going on to other places; Adolf Anderson, killed in the Civil War; Peter Hokanson, died 1880; A.C. Johnson, born in Törneryd, Blekinge, August 16, 1836, came together with his father, Carl Jonson, three brothers and a sister from Näsum in Skåne, to America in 1854, first in St. Charles, then to Rockford 1855, where he has been in furniture-manufacturing on a large scale and enjoyed much success, also a member of the Lutheran congregation.

The largest Swedish migration to Rockford took place in the decade 1856-66. At the latter year the number of Swedes in Rockford was around 2,000 — Now it may be between 8 and 10 thousand. They are from various parts of Sweden but the majority are likely from Vestergötland and Småland. Some came long ago to this country but have not been so long in Rockford, for instance Martin Hilliard, born in Stockholm September 25, 1818, emigrated 1842, was at sea 1842-51, visiting many foreign lands, was in the Army of the U.S. 1851-1856, finally as an officer. He managed a business in Key West, Florida 1856, 1857, then tried his success in Chicago, went by ox-cart to California 1859, where he dug for gold until 1870 when he came to

Rockford and opened a store in 1873. His lovely wife, Emily Long, from Adellöf Småland died 1878.

The Cholera Year

As in many other places cholera claimed many victims here in 1854. Without means and knowledge of the language as these countrymen were, their conditions during this terrible year were lamentable. "The effects of cholera could be very rapid. Persons literally walked and died. Johannes Anderson visited a woman one morning who seemed perfectly well and busy with laundry — in the evening he received a request to provide a coffin for her — cholera had taken her. An old immigrant came home one day with a piece of pork, muttering as he put it in a pan, "now that we are in America we ought to have pork." On the next morning he was a cholera corpse and was carried to the cemetery. The story is told of the present Mrs. Erlander, who then worked in the home of an American family, that one day she saw in the window the body of a cholera victim being carried away — she was not aware that the coffin contained her own mother. Out of consideration she had not been told that the mother was even sick. The father died at the same time, and she was not told for several days. She herself had a slight attack, but soon recovered."

But from this period come also stories that reveal self-sacrificing love to fellowman, and most often mentioned are the names of John Nelson, August Johnson, Clark. They also were the ones who could speak English. An old school house, near the East side Public Square was furnished as a temporary hospital. A Colonel Marsch opened a barn he owned for a similar purpose.

Towards the end of winter 1854 the disease subsided, and in general the economic picture brightened. The Swedes were indeed poor, but they were industrious and thrifty, so that they met their daily needs and put aside some savings. Their workmanship and honesty won them the confidence of the Americans.

The Religious Needs

"The Swedish people" states *The Swedes of Rockford*, "have learned from childhood to show love and respect for the Church and Religion, especially in rural regions where almost the only schooling is instruction in religion. These traits followed the emigrants across the sea and were as deeply rooted in their hearts here as in Sweden. Even though years may have passed since they heard a Swedish sermon the thought of it evoked in the hearts of most a sense of deep loss and desire for it."

The first Swedish preacher to visit the Swedes in Rockford seems to have been G. Unonius from Chicago, though the year is not recorded. But very likely it was late in the summer of 1852, since Unonius made a visit to Minnesota in September and he probably went there by way of Rockford. *The Swedes of Rockford* states that several Methodist ministers, among them Pastors Westergren and Shogren, visited the first Swedes in Rockford. None of them made any attempt to organize a congregation.

From the same source we have the notice of the first Christmas service (Julotta) celebrated by the Swedes in Rockford, though the date is not mentioned. "The few who are still alive and were then present describe it as a gripping event. There was no temple in which to gather, where one could hear the mother tongue; no bells rang out for morning worship and Christmas joy — yet every Swedish heart felt the call to celebrate Christmas. A small group gathered in a cottage, where a Christmas tree was in place and candles burned at the windows; there was even a distribution of gifts. Here they now held a service, and however simple and unpretentious, it made so profound an impression on those present that in tears they embraced each other. They felt that such a devotional hour was meant to unite in friendship and brotherhood."

It must have been in October 1855 that Pastor Erl. Carlsson first visited Rockford and became acquainted with the Swedes there. I recall and have a notation in my diary that he came back to Chicago from this trip, on October 23rd. He had attended the synodical meeting in Galesburg, October 13-16, then started out by river for Minnesota via Rock Island, but because of low water did not get beyond Galena. So he decided to return to Chicago, taking the stage coach from Galena to Rockford. Unable to distinguish between the English words "folks" and "foxes," he began to ask Americans if there were any Swedish foxes (folks) in the town. The hunt was successful, and the countrymen rejoiced at the hunter's appearing.

Organization of the First Lutheran Congregation
in Rockford

The United Chicago and Mississippi Ev. Luth. Conference met

in Chicago January 4-9, 1854. The countrymen in Rockford had sent a representative to this meeting to lay before the Conference their spiritual and churchly needs. We read in the *Minutes* of this meeting, p. 9: "When John Lundbeck from Rockford, who had been elected by our countrymen there as a representative to the Conference, presented himself, he was made a member of the Conference. To the request for pastoral help which he had been authorized to convey, the following reply was given: Since Pastor E. Carlsson intends to visit our countrymen in Rockford next Sunday, all Swedish and Norwegian brethren in and around the town are urged to come together to counsel with him and make such agreements and reach such decisions as will contribute to the ordering of the congregation and its spiritual welfare."

Accordingly Pastor Erl. Carlsson visited Rockford Sunday January 15, 1854. Following a service with the Lord's Supper, a congregation was organized, with the name, "The Scandinavian Evangelical Lutheran Congregation in Rockford." The constitution adopted was similar to that adopted by the Chicago church and by others organized by Pastor Carlsson. The first deacons were: Jonas Larson and Johan Peterson; the trustees: Johan Lundbeck and Josef Lindgren. Of the original 77 members 32 were children. Others than the officers included: Johannes Anderson and family, Carl and Johan Sparf, the widow Anna Lisa Johansdotter from Näfvelsjö, Andrew G. Anderson from Torpa in Östergotland, Gustaf Anderson from Odh in Vestergötland, Jacob Rassmusson and family from Katslösa in Skåne (died in Vasa, Minnesota, Dec. 5, 1879), Sven August Johnson; John Larson; A.G. Edberg and family; C.M. Peterson and family, and Lars Gronlund from Ringstad in Vestergötland (drowned in Rockford July 24, 1877). Pastor Carlsson or his assistant A. Andrén visited the congregation 4 Sundays a year and the first Monday of each month.

"The first annual meeting was held March 5, 1855. The reports showed the following enlightening figures: Income $10.49, expenses $4.56. In those days one was satisfied with small sums. As deacons Carl Samuelson, Johannes Anderson and Jonas Larson were elected, as trustees Isak Peterson, Carl J. Carlsson and John Nelson (the inventor). Late in the summer it was decided to build a church. Jonas Larson and John Nelson were elected to gather the funds. Lars Gronlund and G.P. Johnson agreed to erect the building in accordance with plans drawn by Pastor Carlsson for a sum of $775."

In this connection it should be stated that Pastor A. Andrén did as much as anyone, if not more, to obtain the money for the proposed building and to get the work done. In a letter to me, dated Chicago July 27, 1856 he wrote: "My health is still good, praise the Lord, but I am very busy here. Since I came here I have mostly had to travel. I was away 14 days in various places, largely the usual ones. I came back the 14th and on the 19th went to Rockford, where I have been 8 days, except one evening when I visited Pecatonica. The Swedish congregation in Rockford is trying to build a church, if the Lord helps them. Of the Swedes there we have received $300 in pledges, hoping they will pay. Now for several days I have gone to Americans with a beggar's list, and gotten $400 in promises, so that we have now around $700. A lot has been purchased for $325, and a first payment of $108 made thereon. You can imagine how occupied I have been with such errands and holding services and meetings."

I remember very well how things appeared among our countrymen in Rockford when I paid a visit there at the end of September 1855 on my way back from Minnesota. They were poor and lived in inferior houses. Most of them were to be found on the East side of the river, then heavily wooded. Still they were full of hope and cheered by better times. They were eager to hear the Word of God and some of them were delightful Christians. We held a service in an old school house. I recall that some of the window panes were broken and it was cold, stormy and uncomfortable, but they were happy to be able to get together somewhere. In the afternoon I performed the marriage ceremony of G. Bergquist, who became a brother-in-law of Jonas Larson.[1]

When I left directly for the meeting of Synod in Waverly, I carried with me this message from the congregation: "The Swedish Ev. Lutheran congregation in Rockford, Winnebago County, Illinois to the honorable Synod, now meeting in Waverly, October 4, 1855,

Grace and Peace!"

"We humbly request the honorable synod to be granted a resident pastor in this place. Our beloved pastor, Erland Carlsson, who visits us once a month has through the grace of God done and still does everything for the good and welfare of the congregation that his brief times allows. But since, because of his other congregations, his poor health, and many other obligations, he cannot give us the care that is needed now that the congregation is rather large, we have hoped

[1] "My Reminiscences" *Korsbaneret* 1889

that Synod would be pleased to send us a pastor who can reside here and break for us the bread of life.

"Among those we would like to have here is A. Andrén, in case he should not object to become our pastor. But we will be content with whoever God ordains and the Synod sends us, meanwhile sincerely praying that the Lord will steer everything for the best. If we should not succeed in getting a pastor here for us, we hope that our beloved pastor would continue to visit us, as hitherto. It is our prayer and hope that God's rich grace and blessing might rest on the Synod and that all its actions might redound to the glory of His name and the advancement of His kingdom on earth!

Rockford, Ill. Oct. 2, 1855. On behalf of the congregation
   Johannes Anderson)   John Nelson   )
                   Deacons
   Jonas Larson   )   Isac Petterson)   Trustees[1]
                          C.J. Carlson)"

Andrén had received a temporary license in the Spring of 1855, but spent the Fall term, 1855 and the Spring term 1856 at the school in Springfield. During vacations he continued as Pastor Carlsson's assistant and often visited the countrymen in Rockford. It seems that he was called as pastor during that winter or in the Spring, 1856. On August 18, 1856 he moved there as pastor.

The building proceeded under Andrén's supervision and leadership, was completed in the Fall and was dedicated November 23rd. It stood on the corner of North 1st and Rock Street, was constructed of wood, 45 ft. long, 28 ft. wide and 28 ft. high. Pastor Hasselquist, who conducted the service of dedication has this to say about the church and the dedication, in *Hemlandet*, no. 25, 1856: "We are happy to announce that also our countrymen in Rockford have their own church, completely ready, and very attractive, presumably the finest now owned by the Swedes in America. —Underneath about half the length of the church is quite a large room, intended for a school for which it is well suited, though probably a little low. The site of the church is very lovely. It lies East of the river on a spot from which the ground slopes gently down toward the river. One can get a fine view of the part of town on the other side of the river — the part

[1]Norelius drafted the appeal — now in Carlsson archives.

most built up — and of the fruitfull valley northward, through which the river flows. On entering the church one is inevitably filled with a feeling of joy at the delightful impression made by the attractive sight of the house. The painting was done in fine style by a Mr. Bergquist from Vermland. —Not least was the effect in the interior made by the carpets which covered the aisles and the floor under the altar and pulpit.

PASTOR A. ANDRÉN.

"On Saturday, the day before the dedication, November 23rd, two devotional hours were held, one in Swedish in the afternoon, one in English in the evening when a local American minister preached. Partly because of the bad weather the preceding week, partly because of sickness, only one visiting pastor was present, namely the editor of *Hemlandet*. Consequently he and pastor Andrén had to fulfill the Sunday program.

"The Sunday morning services began with a hymn. The sermon

emphasized the importance of a church, as based on the story of Jacob's dream in Genesis 28: 10-16. After a number of Scripture passages had been read, the whole congregation stood as the words of dedication were proclaimed. Truly a festive moment!

"After the service the needs of the congregation were explained and those present joined in a free-will offering towards the payment of the debt of the church. Can our readers guess what this small group of poor Swedish immigrants raised? Yes, not less than $125. — The lot and building have cost about $1600 — the unpaid balance is $400-500. The Rockford Americans had already contributed over $500, and had promised to do more if needed. — "The congregation was also in the process of acquiring a home for the pastor. Brother Andrén had made an arrangement by which he could himself build a house on the church property, which the church could by a certain date take over for what it cost to build or else sign over, for a set price, the lot on which it stood. — The house is already built and partially furnished." Then the editor praises the pastor and congregation for the love and kindness which characterizes their relationship, and adds, "We very much enjoyed being among these friendly people. We had more invitations to their homes than we could possibly accept. We were happy most of all because there was not that partisan spirit that divides our people elsewhere. Probably just on that account there were many seeking and saved souls."

This church, which could seat around 300 persons, continued to be used until the beginning of 1870, when the first brick church was sufficiently ready to be used.

On November 4, 1858 the name of the church was changed from "Scandinavian" to the Swedish Evangelical Lutheran Church, since only Swedish members then belonged.

In May 1860 the congregation along with the other Swedish Lutheran churches decided to withdraw from the Synod of Northern Illinois and to join the Augustana Synod then being formed. The congregation at that time had 115 communicants and the expenses of the preceding year amounted to $300.

The Church School

As early as 1856 a school was started for instruction in Christianity and the Swedish language. The familiar Magnus Munter was the first teacher here too. The school still exists. The beginning was small, but during Pastor Peters years progress was steady.

The Sunday School dates from Andrén's time, possibly even earlier. I recall that one while it was in some way connected with Congregationalists. Eventually it became exclusively Lutheran.

The Order of Service and Christian Life in the Congregation.

This followed closely the general condition in our congregations. Committed Christians were found in it from the start, and a Christian and churchly spirit prevailed. The preaching of the Word bore fruit in the awakening and confirming of the spiritual life. Warm interest was maintained in missions, the temperance cause, our college and seminary and other Christian activities. Discord and dissension were absent in this period, and it can be said that the congregation was sincerely concerned about its character.

Pastor A. Andrén, the first resident pastor, served until 1860 when he moved to Attica, Indiana. He was followed by Pastor A.W. Dahlsten, who stayed two years, to 1863, then moved to Galesburg. Pastor G. Peters was called, and entered on his ministry here a cold New Year's Day 1864. He worked tirelessly 22 1/2 years — a period of unexpected growth and development not only in the city but especially in the Swedish colony and congregation. But his era lies beyond the confines of this book.

Pecatonica

This place lies about 14 miles northwest of Rockford on the Pecatonica river in a fertile area. It was only a large village when the Swedes began to settle there. *Svenskarne i Illinois* states that C.M. Peterson was the pioneer of this Swedish settlement, that he came to America in 1854, and in the Fall of that year together with another Swede by the name of Jacobson bought a farm alongside the village.

"Before these two" the account goes on, "many other countrymen had been at this place but only as workers on the building of the Northwestern Railroad and then gone on as the work was finished. Jacobson moved to Paxton, where he died long ago. He was married to the widow of Anders Anderson, another of the first Swedes in Pecatonica. — The master tailor L. Segerstrom, dead 1879, came here in 1855 and for many years was successful in his trade. He and C.M. Peterson (from Vadstena) were along at the organization of the

Lutheran congregation in 1857, which took place under the leadership of Pastor A. Andrén of Rockford." Before 1856 the following Swedes had lived in Pecatonica: Jacob Rassmusson (mentioned among the Rockford names) or Robertson as he called himself the whole time in Vasa, Minnesota; Jonas Jonason and family from Sandsjö in Småland, who lived many years in Cannon River, Minnesota and died there; Jacob Anderson and family from Böne, Elfsborg County, now in Vasa. An article in *Hemlandet*, May 22, 1858, informs us that these persons lived in Pecatonica: Johan P. Anderson, Johan Peterson, Johan P. Peterson, Gustaf Peterson, Anders G. Anderson, C.J. Johnson, Gustaf Anderson, the aforementioned C.M. Peterson, L. Segerstrom, also A. Frysberg and August Lindblad, but I do not know where they came from and when.

Pastor Erl. Carlsson and the later pastor A. Andrén, were the first to preach in this place and begin a spiritual ministry among these countrymen, but I do not know how early. However it is certain that Andrén organized an Evangelical Lutheran congregation here in 1857 and that under his leadership a church was built, which was dedicated in October. We find a report in the October number, 1857, of the *Olive Branch* (edited by S. Harkey), also published in *Hemlandet*, No. 23, 3rd year: "On Sunday, October 11th a small, neat, Swedish Lutheran church building was dedicated in Pecatonica, Winnebago County, Illinois in Pastor A. Andrén's pastorate. The church is a well built frame structure, 36 × 24 feet, costs around $600 and is almost paid for. It was built by a handfull of poor Swedish folk from Sweden, aided by their American neighbors. It is the second church built this year in Brother Andrén's pastorate. God has richly blessed this young brother's endeavors this past year." Then the report adds items about his work in Rockford. We learn that Dr. Harkey was present at the Pecatonica dedication, for he writes that "We were greatly encouraged by what we heard and saw among these people." "Pecatonica," he adds, "is pleasantly situated in a splendid tract along the Chicago-Galena Railroad. It is a growing community and in the not distant future will develop into a city. Our old friend John Garver, whose hospitality I enjoyed while there, deserves praise for the help he has given our Swedish brethren in erecting this house of worship. Without him they would hardly have succeeded at this time."

Later in the Fall a painful controversy arose, as we learn from an article published in *Hemlandet*, 1858, no. 12. Segerstrom the tailor had sent an article to the *Swedish Republican* (Den Svenske Republikanen) in the Fall of 1857, wherein he claimed that pastor Andrén had not had any part in the building of the church, though he had taken credit for it. The well-disposed members had not intended to reply, for it was so well-known and recognized that Andrén had done what he could, and urged others, particularly his congregation in Rockford to give assistance, which they did. The effort to demean him came only from an embittered person. But when another article appeared in *The Swedish Repubican*, 1858, no. 13, signed by three Pecatonica persons, the other members sent a reply through *Hemlandet*. From this we learn that at the annual meeting of the congregation on March 16 Segerstedt rendered a report on church funds he was responsible for during the previous year, and the report was approved. Segerstedt claimed that some persons, whom he would not name, had charged him with improper handling of the church building fund, and he volunteered to give an oath before a civil judge that he was right. Pastor Andrén then admonished him that it was not just to charge the whole congregation in a matter wherein it had already approved him. The pastor asked him to turn to those individuals who had accused him. Furthermore a public oath would not silence those who had complained, whether they had reason or not to do so. A simple Yes or No, an honest manner and firm character, were the best means against such. Someone thought S. would not have acted so hastily, if he had succeeded in persuading the Pecatonica people to forsake Pastor Andrén and accept Unonius. Be that as it may, it is certain that Andrén's opponents could not tolerate his strict sermons and demand for a living Christian faith. The drinking group insinuated that Andrén drank, though he was known for his zealous efforts for temperance. They even made fun of him since in Sweden he had been a tailor's apprentice.

To this his friends responded "to the charge that Mr. Andrén used intoxicating liquor we need say nothing since everybody knows that it is a complete falsehood. But that some of the worthy contributors to the *Republican* now and then have emptied both 3 and 7 quarts is evident from the fact that members of their households have come to us roughly treated and asked for shelter and protection from father who has returned in violent manner from the saloon." To the other accusation they replied, "We are of that class that pay no attention to origin or occupation when honorable. We know that A. Andrén and A. Lindblad come from the same place in Sweden, and were schoolmates in younger years. True, Andrén was a poor, tailor's apprentice. Lindblom came from wealthy parents who provided him with the opportunity of becoming an officer in the Swedish military, where he spent a short period. But it seems that he served with great merit in inland sea battles on land. Both emigrated to America at the same time and each has made considerable progress in his career. A. Andrén has risen to become a capable minister, A. Lindblom, a wood-sawer. Far from envying them let us encourage the minister to continue zealous and the sawyer to be zealous, then the minister will probably get the salary the congregation can afford and the sawyer his agreed price per cord."

I have dwelt on this matter longer than it deserves. But it depicts the character of the times and explains the cause of the lack of unity and the consequent small progress made by the congregation for several years. Later it was a different story. In 1860 it counted only 24 communicant members, and the current expenditures for the year was $25. For many years it was an annex to the Rockford congregation.

Chapter 8

The Swedish Evangelical Lutheran Congregation in Princeton, Ill.

Sixty years ago Bureau County was a wilderness or prairie. The first white man to build a house there was Henry Thomas, in May 1828. It is believed that there were 2000 Indians in this county in 1830, while a year later there were only 15 white families. When the Black Hawk War broke out in 1832 the whites fled. Indian attacks continued through 1833. Some of the whites were killed, for example Elias Philips, a farmer, and James Sample who with his wife were burned alive 1/2 mile west of Princeton. Bureau was organized as a county in February 1837. Railroads began to cross this landscape after 1851. Princeton, the county seat, is now a growing town and a good many Swedes live here and in the vicinity."

The First Swedes in the Princeton Area.

According to *Svenskarne i Illinois* the oldest Swede here was A.P. Anderson from Horn in Östergötland. He came to America in 1849, and went first to Andover where he expected to meet relatives, but found that they had died. Then he brought his family to Princeton in the summer of 1850, where he was still living 10 years ago, healthy and spry. His oldest son moved to California many years ago." Before A. there were 5 Swedes in Princeton. One of them was a Mr. Burgeson, now living in Andover, the first one there. He had come with Rev. Pillsbury, for whom he worked.[1] At the same time a Swedish youth was working for the famous abolitionist Owen Lovejoy. A Swedish girl was working in the town's hotel — she must have been Sigrid Norell, from Bergsjö in Helsingland, who married A.J. Field, from Linköping county (presumably the fourth of the group). The fifth was Eric Wester, who appeared in Princeton in 1850."

Eric Wester, according to *Svenskarne i Illinois*, had the name Westergren. It is not known when he left Sweden, but rumor has it that he was a guard at the Swedish Bank in Stockholm, was sent to Helsingör once to buy a large supply of material for the paper factory at Tumba where the bank's paper was manufactured, and that he

---

[1] Probably the one referred to in Chapter 1, who helped the Swedish party involved in the fatal accident near Princeton.

absconded to America with the money. His career in America is in accord. He seems to have appeared first in New Orleans. There he shaved Scandinavian seamen — on his barber shop the sign read — "Come let us test how Swedish steel bites." In 1848 he was in Bishop Hill but didn't stay very long. Then to Pine Lake, Wisconsin where, according to Unonius, he gave the impression for a short time of being spiritually interested. From Wisconsin he moved to Princeton and opened a barber shop. "He was," says *Svenskarne i Illinois* "full of initiative and tricks, and he soon discovered that Princeton was as good a place as any to use these traits. A rich tradesman helped him get a stock of cigars, and he opened business in a shanty. Watered with whisky the plant took root, blossomed and bore fruit. As the affair took on greater dimensions it required soon larger space. Now it included almost everything: clothes, food, shoes, hardware, tobacco, whiskey." It progressed, a branch was established in Galesburg, he joined the Bishop Hill colony in a bank deal. Then he failed. He tried his luck again in 1858, but with no better success. In 1859 he declared bankruptcy, but seems to have had enough to pay his debts." With $1700 and a trunk full of revolvers he set off for Chicago, he said, but landed in Dallas, Texas. He is supposed now (1880) to be there, in poor circumstances." Were one to write about Swedish adventurers in America, Eric Wester would certainly deserve a chapter in it.

The next Swedes to come to Princeton were those who were in my party from Sweden, in the Fall of 1850, and I have already mentioned some in Chap. 1. They were not all from Bergsjö, as *Svenskarne i Illinois* has it. Hans Kamel, Olof Jonson, Staffan Berglof, Anders Nord, and their families were from Bergsjö. Anders Larson was from Torp in Medelpad; Olof Nilson and Simeon from Attmar; Pehr Soderstrom from Norrbo or Bjuråker in Helsingland; Hans Smitt from Hassela. The Kamel family is said to be dead, the others moved to various places, many are now gone. In 1851 Lars Magnus Spak, Nils Johan Nilson from Djursdala in Småland, came, and Jacob Nyman from Tjäderstad in Linköping County. The number grew significantly in 1852. Among the newcomers were: C.M. Skold, tailor, from Vestra Ryd; And. P. Damm, with 6 children from Åsby in Östergötland; from Skåne, Oke Nilson and family, S. Frid from Wä, Nils Lindeblad and family, Pehr Fagercrantz; from Elfsborg County: Pehr Christian Anderson, Lars Anderson from Gingrid; from Stockholm: Johan Anderson, Henric Norman; Johan A. West-

man from Börstig in Skaraborg County; Joh. Gabriel Stohl and family from Jönköping County; And. P. Larson from Vadstena; J.O.
Lundblad from Linköping County. In 1853 Jonas Anderson from
Färila (already noted in St. Charles story) came, and A.A. Shenlund
from Vestergötland. Shenlund started to work on a farm. "Then he
took the wood-sawer's degree," and later he helped in E. Wester's
store. There he did not like Wester's loose business methods, so he set
up his own grocery store and gradually worked himself up through
his honesty and business ability. He died several years ago.

From this point it is not possible to track down the many who
came in the following years.

The countrymen in Princeton obtained a livelihood for themselves, some even affluence, but before 1860 they were in general in
poor economic circumstances. Though one and another adventurer
and worthless character appeared among them, they enjoyed usually
a good reputation among the Americans, and some of them were
honored by being elected to public office.

The Swedish Evangelical Lutheran Congregation in Princeton

In our narrative about Moline and Rock Island we saw that the
Licentiate C.J. Valentin left these places in the summer of 1853 and
went to Princeton to start religious activity. It is not clear whether he
was the first to minister to the countrymen in Princeton or if Esbjörn
or Hasselquist may have been there sometime earlier. But it is certain
that Valentin was the first to stay there for any length of time as a
pastor.

At the meeting of the Synod of Northern Illinois in Peru 1854
the president, Pastor C.B. Thümmel, said in his annual report, "I
was informed by Brother Esbjörn on June 22nd that he had assisted
Brother Valentin in organizing a Lutheran congregation in Princeton,
Bureau County, which persumably will apply at this session for
membership in the Synod." And elsewhere in these *Minutes* we read,
"The Swedish Lutheran Church in Princeton applied for membership and on motion was received into this Synod."

Thus, in early June 1854 the Swedish Evangelical Lutheran
congregation had been organized. Who the first members were and
what resolutions were adopted at the organization I cannot say, for I
have not had the opportunity to investigage the matter. But *Svenskarne i Illinois* reports that the charter members of the first Swedish

Lutheran congregation in Princeton were: P. Fagercrantz, N.P. Lindquist, Eric Wester, Jacob Nyman, N. Lindeblad, S. Frid, and Lars
Anderson." We can take for granted that the organization followed
the same principles that were observed in other congregations organized by Esbjörn.

Valentin seems to have left the congregation in the Fall of 1854
without any permission, and gone to Sweden. At the conference
meeting in Andover, December 1 that year Per Pihlstrom was present
as a delegate from the Princeton congregation, with an urgent appeal for a pastor. The *Minutes*[1] give this report: "Delegate Pihlstrom
presented the congregation's urgent appeal that the Conference in
some possible way secure a pastor for Princeton, or at least make arrangements whereby the congregation would be visited by other
pastors. The matter was postponed to the next day. —Saturday,
December 2: Following prayer the matter of pastor for the Princeton
congregation was taken up, and considered in connection with a
question that had been raised about the possibility of the delegate
from Galesburg, Cederstam, being given license to serve as pastor
and making use thus of his studies and God-given talents in a more
fruitful manner. After a long discussion and with the close attention
that such an important subject required, it was decided that Per
Cederstam should be examined by the examination committee and if
the result was satisfactory the president of the Conference should
recommend to the president of the Synod that Cederstam be given
license to serve as assistant to Pastor Hasselquist, on condition that
one or another of these brethren visit the congregation in Princeton
every other Sunday, and that the Princeton church thus be under the
supervision of Pastor Hasselquist, and pay Cederstam a fair salary,
the amount to be agreed on by the congregation and Pastor Erland
Carlsson, the Conference president, when he visits Princeton next
week. The Conference considered that Pastor Hasselquist in taking
on this added responsibility would be compensated by receiving a
regular assistant."[2]

The examination committee consisted of Esbjörn and Hasselquist,
and the examination of Cederstam took place between New Years
and March, for the president of the Synod stated in his annual report
1855, "March 2, 1855 I sent a temporary license to Mr. Peter A. Ced-

---

[1]*Minutes* of the Ev. Luth. Synod of No. Ill. 1854, Sept. 7-10, pp 3, 4.
[2]*Hemlandet* 1 year, no. 2.

erstam, in accordance with the decision of the Mississippi Conference of this Synod which had been given me by Brother Carlsson." But Cederstam's service in Princeton was brief. In April that year The United Chicago and Mississippi Conference sent him to Minnesota, since the need of pastors was even greater there. Already on May 20th he was in St. Paul. The congregation in Princeton remained under Carlsson's care.

The Christian element in the congregation seems to have been weak from the beginning. But there was a kind of churchly interest and a certain effort to have a Lutheran congregation, pastor and church.

During the winter or Spring 1856, while Esbjörn was travelling as an agent for the Scandinavian professorship in Springfield, he also visited Princeton and the congregation called him as pastor. He accepted the call and began his service before Pentecost. He continued to travel and was not there uninterruptedly, moving there in August. In a letter to Erl. Carlsson, Aug. 4, 1856 he wrote, "I am now moving everything to Princeton. But I will be going home to Andover next week, and, God willing, will be back the following week."

As soon as Esbjörn had accepted the call the congregation began to work for a church building. Esbjörn wrote to E. Carlsson on June 11, 1856: "Here in Princeton things are proceeding favorably. Through subscription we have raised $540 among the Americans, $340 among the Swedes, for a building. One Methodist and one Baptist minister have been here and looked around, since I came, but prospects are slight, so I have not heard anything about their return."

By November 23rd (1856) the building had reached a stage where it could be used for the first time for a service. But it was not dedicated until Sunday, September 12, 1858, in connection with a Conference meeting then held in Princeton. We read in the *Minutes* of proceedings at this meeting: "Sunday September 12th the Swedish Evangelical Lutheran Church in Princeton celebrated its dedication in the forenoon, when Pastor A. Trimper from Mendota preached in English. Pastor Hasselquist preached in the afternoon, and another service, was held in the evening. A collection for the building amounted to $50 or $60. The church is a nice frame building, 30 × 42 feet and very pleasingly furnished. It costs between $1600-$1700, and to the honor of the congregation not more than about $400 of that sum is debt. We rejoice hearily with our friends in Princeton that they now have a splendid temple of the Lord where they can quietly worship the Lord Sabaoth. May the Lord soon send them a faithful shepherd to break the bread of life and take the place of their beloved pastor, now professor Esbjörn, whom He has called to an even more significant place in His vineyard."[1] The statement in *Svenskarne i Illinois* that the church, presumably with the lot, cost $5000 must be a reference to a later church building.

Though Esbjörn's ministry in Princeton was brief, and abbreviated further by a serious, protracted neuralgia and other illnesses afflicting him, it was not without fruit. The people became more churchly and listened to his preaching. The singing improved greatly due to the rehearsals which he encouraged, and in other respects there were changes for the better.

On September 10, 1857 the congregation accepted "the constitution for Swedish Lutheran congregations in America" as proposed by the Conference, after considering various amendments and changes, and proceeding quite carefully and comprehensively. A committee was first appointed to examine the proposal closely and make suggestions for changes at various points. In its report to the congregation full reasons are given for the recommended alterations in a manner that clearly reveals the hand of the pastor. The procedure is described in a remarkable article in *Minnesota Posten*, 1857, no. 2, to which I would like to return in another connection, but here I would quote this: "When the work of the committee was completed, the congregation held a special meeting, when members were given an opportunity to make suggestions which the committee took into consideration and which led in some cases to changes in their report. The modified and altered constitution was now presented to the congregation on the above mentioned date, and read article by article. After each article any one might comment, and no one objecting the article was unanimously adopted. Thus the members had the satisfaction of having the constitution, after careful consideration, adopted unanimously and without a single objection, in a printed form as already amended. The whole congregation was moved by a deep sense of the importance and meaning of this action for its present and future welfare, at the close, when the congregation arose and sang the verse "Praise be to Thee, O God" there were tears in many eyes at the thought of coming generations who would dwell in the shade of the tree the fathers now had planted."

---

[1]*Hemlandet*, 4th year, no. 21.

None of our congregation has adopted its constitution as deliberately and as festively as the congregation in Princeton.

Again a Vacancy.

At the beginning of October 1858 Esbjörn entered on the duties of his professorship at "Illinois State University." Thus a vacancy occurred again in Princeton until the summer of 1860 when John Johnson, who had been ordained at the organization of the Augustana Synod, was called and moved there as its pastor.

During the vacancy the neighboring pastors visited the congregation as often as possible, but it could not in this way receive the necessary care, and it suffered decline. Several attempts were made to secure a pastor. In October 1858 three candidates were nominated, E. Norelius, P. Beckman, and A. Andrén. The first two declined candidacy, and A. Andrén was elected. When he did not accept there was considerable interest in calling P. Nymanson in Sweden, but this did not materialize. In 1859 a son of the well-known Per Nyman came there and at first found acceptance and even looked on as pastor, though the Swedish Conference had no confidence in him and had given him no commission. Esbjörn wrote about the situation from Springfield on Sept. 2, 1859 — "You were likely right in not saying anything (in the paper) about Nyman in Princeton. They will realize alright their mistake. I fear he has succeeded in getting a considerable following, since his acceptance clearly shows that the congregation has gone against its earlier decision not to take any one not approved by the Conference." Esbjörn's prediction proved true, for it did not take long before Nyman revealed his true character and after that the congregation would have nothing to do with him. It was a time of sore scarcity of pastors and an episode such as the following could take place.

Pastor Vossner's Attempt to become Pastor in Princeton.

It was in this period, or 1859, that a minister from Sweden, C.J. Vossner, tried to become pastor in Princeton. If I have been rightly informed Pastor Vossner came from the Eksjö area, had been regularly ordained in the church of Sweden and for some time taught in a technological institute in his native land. Why and when he came here is unclear, but from a letter to Pastor E. Carlsson he seems to have come in 1855. From this letter, dated White River, Oceana County, Michigan, July 31, 1855 we learn that he had already been in Chicago, was acquainted with Pastor Carlsson, and was now making certain requests of him, among other things asking help in recovering some of his lost baggage. He gave this information about himself and his residence: "On my arrival I bought a neat little house from a Norwegian travelling companion, Hansen by name, where I have been living and holding services on Sunday, as often as the members of my congregation, some Swedes and Norwegians, come together, which I regret is not very often. It is pleasant here and I get along though I earn but little. My house is on Congress land and has an enclosed 3 or 4 acres under cultivation. The house lies on a hill by White River at its juncture with a smaller stream, Superior Creek, forming a series of canals. At the foot of the hill is a spring with the purest water I have ever drunk. The climate, too, is quite healthful and the earth fertile. This year within my fence I have raised corn and potatoes, a very nice harvest. If only I had here a God-fearing, kind and considerate wife I would be very content and get along excellently." But these idyllic prospects were to be clouded by future setbacks. His so-called "congregation" was made up of undependable persons, single as himself, who worked at a sawmill and gave our dear Vossner a pretty thin slice of bread. There was no organized congregation, and the apparent agreement was that the pastor was to receive an offering every time there was a celebration of the Lord's Supper. When Vossner began to hold this all too often, in their estimation, they began to disappear and leave the minister alone. Things went bad for V. and he is said to have lived mostly on corn and molasses. When he heard that there was a vacancy in the Swedish congregation in Princeton he appears to have written Erik Wester offering to become its pastor and to have received a favorable reply. He loaded all his belongings — clothes, clay pots, wash tub, wooden shovel, rifle — on to a wheelbarrow and started on the adventurous journey, first by boat across Lake Michigan and then by train to Princeton where he arrived safely and well. E. Wester was enthusiastic and did all he could to have him accepted by the congregation. Vossner read his old, yellowing sermons, and Wester turned around in his bench to see what was the effect on the members, groaning when he noted that they were not impressed. When Vossner went up to Wester to learn what his prospects were he received the crushing reply that they were poor. Walking back and forth on the floor, in his dressing gown, he told him, "I regret it. Pastor, I feel sorry for you Pastor, but the people don't like you, they say the pastor preaches trash." The poor Vossner had to depart as he came, taking along his wheelbarrow to Chicago. Yet the Princeton people gathered together about $18 for him for his trouble. He stayed a while in Chicago and probably elsewhere, practicing medicine, and finally, as far as I know, returned to Sweden. The man was undoubtedly naturally well-intentioned and honest, but he did not fit in here. Probably he lacked, too, the temperament necessary for service in the congregation.

At the 1860 meeting of Synod this congregation had 149 Communicants.

Chapter 9

The Swedes and the Swedish Lutheran Congregations in Indiana
before 1860.

The Swedish Lutheran Congregation in Attica, Indiana.

The first Swedish immigration into La Fayette, Indiana and
vicinity was described in Chapter 1. As mentioned there Johannes
Peterson from Örserum, Grenna, and erstwhile councilman Carl
Peter Moberg from Grenna were the pioneers in this part of Indiana.
Correspondence with friends at home resulted in large groups coming
over between 1852 and 1854. They settled in La Fayette, in Yorktown,
14 miles away, in West Point, 10 miles, and Attica, 22 miles, and
around Milford, on the west side of the Wabash River half-way between La Fayette and Attica. This place was variously named Milford, Montmorency, or simply "Plank Road." This area of Tippecanoe
County (with its memorable battle ground, near La Fayette, from
the days of Gen. W.H. Harrison), and Fountain County, had been
populated around 30 years before the Swedes came. The Wabash
valley with its open prairies and wooded sections and fertile soil is a
lush landscape. The Swedes who came here did not come to an empty
wilderness, but to a rich land already well settled, where they could
easily find work and earn a living. On the other hand the land was
already expensive and therefore beyond the reach of our countrymen
without means.

During the first years sickness was rampant among the Swedes,
especially in the cholera year 1854 when quite a few died. Many
families were broken up, the children, becoming orphans, were placed in the American homes and brought up ignorant of their ancestry.
Many succeeded economically, many had to endure much suffering.

The Swedes who made their homes here were from the following parishes: Grenna, Vireda, Ölmstad, Adelöf, Skärstad, Svenarum,
Rogberga, Bälaryd, Linderås, Ödestugu, St. Åby, Lommaryd, Rinna,
Kumla, all in Östergötland, and a few from V. Vingåker in Nerike.
By far the greater number were young, single persons, alert and willing to work, with few exceptions sober and uncorrupted, and well
liked by the Americans. Very few had any means, but they quickly
found work on the farms, and though the pay was small in those days
they got along quite well. At most a dozen had acquired any real

estate in 1855. At the beginning of that year there were probably 400-500 Swedes in this region. The majority lived in and around West Point, which was their center. This place lay about a mile from the railroad station that now bears the name West Point.

These Swedes all considered themselves Lutheran and were well disposed to the Church of Sweden. They were not strangers to spiritual movements. On the contrary they had been influenced by them and, as they put it, they wanted to hear a living Word of God. In their native land they had listened to such leaders as Dr. Fjellstedt, J.M. Lindblad, J. Colliander, Sandén, Oskar Ahnfelt, C.J. Lindberg, and others. Some had in the beginning been strict followers of Murbäck and then came to a more evangelical position in a rich spiritual experience. Among these was P. Peterson from Öresrum, Grenna, who was considered a spiritual father among them and in whose house in West Point they often gathered for reading of God's Word, song, and prayer. He was greatly missed after falling a quick victim to cholera in the fall of 1854. Like him in spirit and influence were his sister Louisa Peterson, now Mrs. A. Jackson in West Union, Minnesota, and Mrs. N. Hokanson (Eva Stina from Grankärr, Vireda, died in Cannon Falls, Minn. 1889) and others, men and women.

Soon after their arrival in Indiana they were visited by "Father" Newman, a Methodist preacher, from Chicago. They did think he acted a bit peculiar, but not suspicious they let him enlist almost all of them in the Methodist's six months probation plan. They did not know what Methodism was, and when they asked they received the reply that Methodists were what in Sweden were called "readers" (läsare) or "awakened folk" (väckt folk), and of these they were not afraid. Newman visited them as often as he could, and sometimes one of his assistants came. He even confirmed some of the children. But gradually the more experienced began to discern the difference between Newman's and Lutheran teaching, especially when they began to study the literature and tracts he had left. Then they became suspicious, and understood they had been misled. They wanted eagerly to hear a Lutheran pastor. Their wish was soon fulfilled, for during the summer of 1854 they received visits from Chicago, first by Pastor Erland Carlsson, and then by his assistant A. Andrén. I too made visits there in the Fall of that year and at Christmas. I found no sympathizers of Methodism there except one person in Attica, namely John Wigren, a mason from Grenna, who later became a Methodist preacher. They asked me, on the second visit, to write to Pastor Carlsson and beg him urgently to come as soon as he could to organize a Lutheran congregation, which he did. On February 18, 1855 Pastor Carlsson conducted a festive service in West Point and organized "The Swedish Ev. Lutheran Congregation in Indiana."[1] This congregation included all the five places named above.

I quote here the *Minutes* of this meeting in full because of its lasting historical importance. It tells us not only about the congregations which Pastor Erland Carlsson himself organized, but reveals at the same time the roots of the congregational constitution which was common to all our congregations in America.[2]

"*Minutes* of the meeting in West Point, Tippecanoe County, Indiana, February 18, 1855, of Swedes living in this place and vicinity.

"The Swedish people living here had felt a deep need of an orderly church life, and in order to satisfy this in some degree asked that I should visit them both to proclaim the Word of God and administer the sacrament of the Lord's Supper, and to reach an agreement on the formation of an Evangelical Lutheran congregation. Consequently a visit was made and a date set for a meeting that afternoon. At this meeting, after Bible reading and prayer, the following resolutions were adopted:

"1. We here assembled unite in one congregation, with the name of the Swedish Evangelical Lutheran congregation in Indiana.

"2. As a Christian body in general and particularly Evangelical Lutheran, this congregation acknowledges that the Holy Scriptures as the Word of God are the only sufficient and infallible rule and standard of faith and practice, and also accepts not only the three oldest symbols (the Apostolic, the Nicene and the Athanasian) but also the unaltered Augsburg Confession as a short and correct summary of the principal Christian doctrines.

"3. Regarding the reception of members: Children or unbaptized adults are received in accordance with the directions

---

[1] *Korsbaneret*, 1889.
[2] The original of these *Minutes* came into my hands the Spring of this year (1889) in an unusual way. I could never find it during my time in Indiana. It must have been among Carlsson's papers in Chicago until long after I had moved from Indiana. It may have been sent to Attica when Pastor Tornquist was there and after his death been included in the books sent to Minnesota, to his brother-in-law Pastor J. Fremling, from whom I received it. It is written by J. Engberg in Chicago and signed by Pastor Erl. Carlsson.

and rubrics in our Swedish Lutheran Handbook. If some one who is baptized and confirmed wishes to join this congregation, he shall notify the pastor, who through personal interview and consultation with the deacons of the congregation, shall become assured of the person's faith and moral character. No one who has become known as un-Christian and profligate shall be received as member. If there is no obstacle for his reception, it may take place at the regular service, or preferably at the preparatory service for Holy Communion, in this manner: The person or persons to be received come to the altar when called, and, after a brief prayer by the pastor, addressed by him thus: Dear friends, inasmuch as you have asked to be received as members of this congregation and you have been born and nourished within the Lutheran Church, we do not ask you now to affirm again your faith. We only wish to know if also in this land you wish to be loyal to our ancient, enduring faith and doctrine. In the name of the congregation I therefore ask you, if with sincere heart you wish to adhere to the confession which you already have made before the altar of the Lord (at confirmation), in accordance with it be loyal to Augsburg Confession? Answer: Yes.

"Do you promise honestly to observe the duties to which this confession in general and membership in the congregation especially obligates you? Answer: Yes.

"In response to this your promise I now declare you members of this our Evangelical Lutheran Church, with free and open access to the riches of God's grace and the use of the sacraments. May God grant you grace regularly and faithfully to use these privileges to the salvation of your souls and eternal blessedness! Amen. (concludes with benediction and a Scripture verse).

"4. Should the deplorable condition arise that a member of the congregation falls into a sinful and godless life, such as drunkenness, swearing, quarrelsomeness, foul slander, or such, which leads to general indignation and distress in God's church, and to the question of excommunication, it was agreed to follow the resolutions which the Conference adopted at its meeting in Chicago January 4-9, 1854, in regard to such an event. That resolution reads as follows: No one may be excluded from a congregation until the charge has been carefully examined and the guilty one has received both privately and publicly considerate and serious warnings and exhortations, in accordance with Matt. 18: 15-18. To make such admonitions is the duty of each Christian, but it is a special duty of the pastor and the deacons to exhort with love and severity and warn the immoral. If this does not have the desired effect it is of the utmost importance that such persons not be allowed to remain as members as are guilty of public offense and sinful behavior. Circumstances in this country make action necessary, but one should not in the beginning be too severe. If it be necessary to excommunicate anyone it is desirable that it be an act not of the pastor but of the congregation. In any case it must be an act in which congregation and pastor combine.

"5. Two deacons and trustees are to be elected annually. The latter are responsible for the finances of the congregation. The deacons are to lead the worship service in the absence of the pastor, supervise the conditions in the church, visit and procure help for the poor and sick, and receive contributions for the pastor's salary. Nils Hokanson, West Point, and Anders Peterson, Milford, were elected deacons, Carl Johnson, La Fayette and Johan Wigren, Attica, trustees.

"6. The greatest desire of the congregation now is to obtain its own pastor. Until this happens the undersigned and E. Norelius, student in Columbus, Ohio, have promised to visit them occasionally.

"Members subscribed their names, 230 total, 155 communicants

Ut supra in fidem, Erl. Carlsson,
chairman."

In the Spring I came to this congregation, and made a list of the members. Consequently I can give the names of many of the first members, and in some cases their later experiences.

West Point

Nils Hokanson with wife and children, from Grankärr, Vireda parish; moved to Minnesota 1856, he and wife died in Cannon Falls 1889, eldest son died in the War, other children residing in Minnesota.

Anna Brita Peterson, widow of P. Peterson, from Örserum, Grenna, and 5 children, moved to Red Wing, Minn. 1856; she died 1869.

Lovisa Peterson, from ditto, moved to Minnesota 1856, married Pastor A. Jackson in East Union.

Fredrika Svenson, from Grenna, present address unknown.

Inga Maja Anderson, from ditto, died in Vasa, Minn.

Johan Jonasson from Reaby, Grenna; wife Johanna and 7 children; moved to Paxton.

Adolf and Carl G. Elmberg, and their wives, from Vireda, now probably in Paxton.

Gustaf Frans Westman and wife Stina Greta Brage, from Grankärr, Vireda, moved to Rusheby, Minn., then to Cannon Falls; both dead.

Johannes Monsson and wife Eva Stina Rehnberg, from Grenna, 3 children; present address unknown.

Niles Monsson from Ölmstad and wife Sara Lisa, from Grenna, one son; present address unknown.

Johan Brage and wife Maja Svensdotter, 4 children, moved to Chisago Lake; he is dead.

Jons Skepp from Svenarum and wife Anna Helena Svenson from Ödestugu, sister of the preacher C.J. Lindberg, 4 children. Parents dead. Some of children probably still live in Attica.

Joh. Gabr. Alvin (Ringkarl's Johan) and wife Inga Lotta, with 7 daughters, from Grenna. Both dead.

Jonas Lindvall and wife Anna Lovisa and one child, from Adelöf, moved to Taylor's Falls, Minn.

Johan Peter Jonsson and wife Maja Stina, from Vireda. Present address unknown.

Magnus N. Tornquist, from Ölmstad, probably same farmhand who drowned in Cannon Falls many years ago.

Lars Nilson from Ånaryd, Ölmstad; present address unknown.

Swen Bjork and wife Anna Kristina, 2 daughters, from Vireda; he died many years ago.

Lars Fred Peterson from Hof, Skärstad; moved 1857 to Vista, Waseca County, Minn.

Carl Bjorklund, a former drummer, from Grenna and daughters, Sara, Stina, and Juliana. He and youngest daughter dead. Sara is married to a Mr. Peterson, near La Porte. The sons lived in other places in the congregation: Frans now in Welch, Minn.; Gottfrid and Anders finally came to Idaho, Territory, where they have become wealthy and prominent citizens.

Attica

Erik Anderson, master mason, and his brother Johan from Skärstad; the former died early.

Johan Peterson and wife Lovisa from Reaby, Grenna, (known to many as "Sörs."), 6 children. The parents are dead, also some of the children. The son Carl Gustaf Peterson, wainwright, married to Kristin from Mörstorp, Grenna, is one of the leading men in Attica and has long been a pillar in the Lutheran congregation. A sister, Anna Sofia, is married to W. Lindberg, a merchant, who is a nephew of the preacher C.J. Lindberg in Stockholm.

Carl Er. Tolf and wife Kristina from Grenna and a daughter have been a long time in Red Wing. A brother John Tolf, married to Thilda Sörs, is long since dead.

Carl Fr. Peterson from Grusholmen, Grenna, and wife Kristina Larson from Ölmstad, moved to Paxton.

Lars Peter Nilson from Bråxvik, Grenna, later married and now living in Salemsborg, Kansas.

Joh. Fröjd and wife Stina Larson from Vireda. He died long ago, she and 3 children moved to Paxton.

Brita Stina Larson, a widow, and son Carl Edvard from Grenna, moved to Andover, Ill. where she married and now living in Friends Home, Kansas.

Brita Wigren, a widow, and daughters Maria, Johanna and Lotta. She and one of the daughters are dead, the others live in Attica. The son, Joh. Wigren, and wife later became Methodists.

Maria Johansdotter from Grenna.

John Janson, from Ljusdahl, Helsingland.

Peter Larson from Ölmstad, a tailor, married Lovisa Jacobsdotter from Fruktnötet, Linderås, moved to Paxton. He is dead.

Anna Lotta Carlsdotter from Grenna.

Heda Johansdotter from Askarp, ditto; moved to Minnesota, married to Olof Peterson, a cobbler, and long since dead.

Maja Stina Johansdotter from ditto.

Anna Brita Johansdotter from ditto.

Stina Greta Andersdotter from Adelöf.

Pehr Peterson and Olof Larson from Vestra Vingåker: probably still in Attica. Etc.

Yorktown

C.P. Moberg, former councilman, and wife Maria Sofia, 7 children from Grenna; he is dead.

And. E. Nylander and wife Hedvig Elisabeth, 4 children, from Kumla in Östergötland.

C. Saf, former soldier, his wife, and son Carl P. Saf, originally from Grenna; moved to Spring Garden. Wife now dead.

Carl Johnson, cobbler, and wife. Soon moved. Etc.

Montmorency or "Plank Road"

Lars Anderson and wife Anna Lisa, 6 children, from Gunne-målen, Grenna, moved to Paxton. The parents are dead. His brother, Jonas, a widower, from Kaxtorp with 2 daughters and 1 son. The latter and younger daughter, dead. The older daughter, widow of a Bergquist, lives in Chicago.

Anders Person and wife Johanna Sofia Long, one son, from St. Åby. He is dead, she remarried to C.J.S. Fager, and living around Paxton.

Carl Johan Swenson Fager, from Bjäkebäck, Grenna.

Magnus Monsson, widower, and daughter Maria, from Udderyd, Ölmstad.

Adolf Monson, from same area.

Carl Jonasson from Ingefrearp, Grenna, moved to Minnesota 1857 and lives in Vista.

Johan Persson from Skärstad; moved to Minnesota.

Swen Swenson, from Skogseryd, Bälaryd; to Minnesota.

Peter Jonsson and wife Eva Cathr., from Stora Åby; dead.

Jonas Jonsson and wife, Maja Stina, from Brahehus, Grenna; later became Methodists.

Johan Jönson and sister Lotta, from Melby, Grenna.

Carl Jönsson, from Siringe, Skärstad; moved to Minnesota and lives near Murdock.

Anders Johnson and wife Anna Sofia from Ingersbyn, Ölmstad; now in Beaver, Ill. A sister, Maja, married an Irishman near La Fayette. A brother Johan Johnson and wife.

Johan N. Lof and wife Anna Stina, 7 children, from Grenna. She died 1860, and others likely in Attica.

Carl Hammerstedt and wife Maria, 4 children, from Grenna. He is dead; the others lived in Attica.

Sven Bergren, a widower, with 2 sons, Carl and Per, from Örserum, Grenna. He remarried, lived a few years in Attica, then moved to Minnesota, where the family, except Per, live near Cannon Falls, etc.

La Fayette

Sven Jonsson and wife Sara Lena and a daughter, from Svenstorp, Grenna. All three are dead.

And. Wilhelm Peterson and wife Eva Carolina and a daughter from St. Åby.

Carl Adolf Peterson and a sister Gustava Johanna, from Rinna.

Sven Joh. Person, from Skärstad.

Johan Lindgren and wife Kristina, from Grenna; moved to Paxton.

It was in mid-April 1855 when I came to the congregation as their pastor, without call, without instructions, only by direction from the Conference. I can't say that I was embarrassed; in my mind I wasn't bound to any forms or any rules. I couldn't find any documents of organization (the reason is given above), nor list of members or officers. The first service was announced to be held at West Point, the third Sunday after Easter. There we could use an old Methodist church, or else a Campbellite church, which were hardly used, due to the low religious state of the native Americans. There was a rather good representation at this first service from all the places except Yorktown. The service followed the Swedish Handbook, the sermon was based on the Gospel lesson for the day, St. John 16: 16-22, with the topic: The testing of Christians, needed and useful on the way to the heavenly Canaan.

After the service I explained my mission among them. I said, "I have come here on the advice of the Scandinavian Luth. Conference to preach the Word of God and administer the sacraments among you, if you so desire. I ask you to tell me what you desire." They then expressed their great joy and gratitude and wanted me to stay with them. We agreed on a rotation of services whereby each of the 5 places would be visited every fifth Sunday. Something was said about starting a voluntary subscription for my salary. The question of further organization was left to the future and circumstances. All seemed well-intentioned, no one raised objections. So I considered myself properly called (rite vocatus) and installed in my first pastorate.

I was to have my residence in West Point, but I could not be there much since I had to visit and divide my time with the other four places. There was then no railroad between them so either I had to hire a horse or else go by foot which wasn't always so pleasant in the hot summer or when rain made the road nearly bottomless.

Shortly after I came to Indiana "father" Newman and his assistants began to make frequent visits and be troublesome. Newman said pointedly that I had forced myself into his congregation, and he preached mightily against the dead Lutheran ministers. In view of what had taken place here I had no feeling of guilt in taking over the spiritual care of the people, so cheerfully continued my work. When the Methodists made a great ado about the clerical robe and collar, though I had neither, I provided myself with robe and collar and used them as long as they preached against them. When they had quieted, I put them aside. There are times when one must emphasize secondary things in order not to deny the truth. In time we had more peace from the Methodists. The only ones that went over to them were a few in Attica, among them the aforementioned Johan Wigren, who later became a Methodist preacher. It was with them that we had the hottest disputes.

Of all the five places the makings of a Lutheran congregation were slimmest in Yorktown. Mr. Moberg had been, and I hope is, a committed Christian, though his spiritual life was quite depressed. But there were a group of adventurers who had escaped from Sweden, a former tavern-keeper from Jönköping, a former member of Parliament from Östergötland, a number of others, drunkards and ne'er-do-wells. The Americans there, moreover, were a dismal lot, and the village itself was dilapidated and like a den of thieves. When I first came there and announced my purpose I found the tavern keeper ploughing in the field, sweat running copiously down his brow. He was outspoken, and when I introduced myself as a minister and said I wanted to hold services for the countrymen in the place, he replied, "That was damned fine, then we can have the Lord's Supper too. We haven't had a Swedish service since we came. Also there are some children that should be baptized." Puffing and wiping the sweat from his brow, he went on "I'll tell you this is different from standing at the bar. Here in America you have to work so that the sweat runs off you." The man was not unapproachable, and not a conscious blasphemer of Christianity. But he was altogether a stranger to religious things, as was the case with the majority in the place. I held no communion service that time. I wanted first to see if they could be awakened to their spiritual need. I continued to preach there in a school house as long as I remained in Indiana. But the membership remained small.

In La Fayette we held services in a German Lutheran Church which was generously opened to us. The congregation belonged to the Missouri Synod, but both pastor and people were very kind to us.

A small episode occurred in this place in the summer of 1855 which deserves mention as a trait of pioneer life in those early years. There lived here an older widower, called the "Swedish old man," and likewise an older widow, called "the Swedish old woman." They had gotten the idea to be married. The date of the wedding was set, and guests were assembled, and I had come to perform the marriage. Then an uninvited guest appeared. A countryman from West Point was there to press for payment of a debt which the bridegroom owed him for having paid his passage to America. He knew well enough that if he didn't get paid before the old man got married there was little hope that he would get it later. When the bride heard that the groom was encumbered with debt she was in doubt what to do. Everybody sat around the house on the stumps — it was a new clearing — while negotiations went on. Finally I got tired of waiting, arose and said, "Is it the intention to have a wedding? Otherwise I can't wait longer but have to go." The bride was in the cabin, but door and windows were open. Then the groom yelled from the stump where he sat, calling her by name, "Do you want that we now do anything about this, then it will have to be before the minister goes." "Yes, sure I want to," she replied. The marriage proceeded. The creditor probably never got his money afterward. This kind of serio-comic happenings were not so rare in pioneer days.

In West Point we had our services in an old Methodist or an old Campbellite church, seldom used by the Americans. Here we had our best attended gatherings, for it was easier to come here from the surrounding places than to any other spot in the pastorate. The Americans in the area got around a great deal by riding horse-back, and the Swedes were not slow in adopting this custom, especially since the people for whom they worked generously allowed them the use of their riding horses. Both men and women came to church riding, often in a good sized cavalcade. Usually there were two services on a Sunday, one in the morning, one in the afternoon. Mostly the people stayed for both. Some would eat dinner at the inn, but the majority would be invited to the few families who lived there. This was no small sacrifice on their part, but they did it willingly and gladly. On such occasions it was a joy to see the assembled fellow countrymen. They showed a warm interest for each other, treated each other as relatives and were as one family. They told each other about letters or news that they had received from Sweden and from acquaintances in other parts of this country, and shared confidently both their spiritual and physical experiences. Pride and vanity hardly appeared. Generally all were in poor and limited circumstances. No one had much to vaunt over another.

In Attica we started to have our services in whatever church was kindly opened to us, but most often in an old brick school house in the southern part of town, near the cemetery. Later we had our own church. The countrymen in Attica early began to buy real estate, so they felt themselves more stablized than in the other locations. Some families had their own homes as early as the end of 1854, and their members gradually increased.

In the Fall of 1855 I could report to Synod 135 communicants and 172 unconfirmed children, a total of 307 in the entire pastorate.

In regard to the salary of the pastor it was first decided that it come from a voluntary subscription, but later it was agreed that each communicant should give $2 a year. Had this decision been realized the sum would have been $270, but it was far from being reached. Since I had to rent my house and received no money for the travelling I did, if I did not prefer to go by foot, the salary was pretty small. In view of this the congregation turned in 1855 to the Ev. Lutheran Home Missionary Society in Baltimore with a petition for help in payment of the pastor's salary. The Society generously voted $100, and $50 of this came to me for my service in Indiana.

The Church School

Despite its poverty the congregation was desirous of having their children instructed in Christianity in their mother tongue. As early as April 29, after a service in West Point, it was decided to hold a school and to have it move from place to place where there were children, that the charge be 25 cents per child per week, that student J. Engberg from Chicago should be called as teacher, and that the school should begin in West Point. These decisions were carried out as rapidly as possible. Nils Hokanson provided an old, decrepit cabin, and Engberg held school for a few weeks, but poverty prevented continuation of the school at the other places.

A small attempt was also made at a Sunday School in Attica, La Fayette, and even in West Point. But the lack of teachers and the scattered membership prevented further development.

Christian Life in the Congregation

In general the people were such as willingly heard the Word of God, and they walked or rode, many even up to 15-20 miles, to attend services. They found edification in the public worship, conducted in the usual Swedish order, or in the Bible study sessions held here and there in the homes, as often as time and circumstances permitted, at which there was singing of spiritual songs. There were no prayer meetings of the modern kind and they would certainly have aroused questions had they occurred. The people were artless, uncorrupted, had a childlike loyalty to the Lutheran Confessions, church and pastors, innocent still of the unholy spirit of sectarianism. For many Christianity was not yet a serious matter and one that went to the depths of the person, but there were many also who in word and deed manifested a Christian mind and Christian experience. Of others it might be said in general that they were not far from the kingdom. Though a few had taste for strong drink, the moral condition as a whole was good.

Thoughts of Moving

The prospect for an established congregation were not bright. The people were too widely scattered. Property was expensive and few possessed means to purchase such. Nor was the health situation satisfactory, for at that time almost everyone suffered from intermittent fever. Along toward the summer of 1855 there was growing talk of moving to some other place, where land was cheaper and the climate more healthful, and where they could live closer together. Several meetings were held and the question was discussed. The majority favored removal but few were in a position to undertake it. The result of the discussion was that I and someone else should make a trip, at the end of summer, to Minnesota for the purpose of selecting a suitable spot to which we could eventually move.

Such a trip was undertaken at the end of August by myself and Nils Hokanson of West Point. We visited the settlements of Swedes in Goodhue and Chisago Counties, and because suitable land was available in this region we felt that in all respects it was more advantageous for our countrymen in Indiana to find sites in these settlements than to strike out for altogether unoccupied tracts. At the end of the year I received a call from the Swedish Lutheran congregations in Red Wing and Vasa, Minn. which I had organized that Fall. I accepted this call and moved from Indiana in May 1856 after having served the congregation one year. It was hard to leave these dear people, but I needed to change climate for my health was poor, due to a persistent intermittent fever. Furthermore the prospects for a stable congregation at this time were poor. So I thought it best to move, and advised the others to do the same. But our thoughts and ways are not always the Lord's. Some of the friends in Indiana did indeed follow me gradually and settled in Goodhue, Chisago, and Waseca County where they founded the Vista settlement. Others moved elsewhere, but quite many stayed in Indiana, gradually drawing together in and around Attica.

In the beginning of September 1856 Pastor Hasselquist paid a visit to this part of Indiana. In *Hemlandet*, 2nd year, No. 18, he gave this account of the countrymen there: "Last week the editor of *Hemlandet* had an opportunity to make a quick trip through that part of Indiana where fellow countrymen have settled. On account of time I could not gather complete information about these places and the prospects of our Swedish people for the future. Nor was this necessary since as far as I could learn, very few of them have bought any property, either in town or in the country. In West Point, Tippecanoe County, several families reside, but some of these were ready, when I was there, to undertake the long journey to Minnesota, and others wished to follow them. Most of those remaining were scattered around the farms where they rented or worked. The same situation, I believe, prevails in La Fayette and Montmorency; Attica, however, may become a permanent home for some Swedes. Only two had yet bought lots and built homes, as far as I could learn, but the town has advantages that may keep many there and probably attract others. Not yet large, the town is experiencing a significant growth. Lots are not yet so exorbitant in price but that even poor people can become owners and gradually provide themselves with a home. Industry is active and growing, and thereby opportunities for work increase. A canal for boats, drawn by horses, flows past the town, as well as the Wabash River on which through much of the year large steamers reach the town and, often, to La Fayette. A railroad, Lake Erie, Wabash and St. Louis, will soon run through Attica, thus greatly increasing business. Attica, like most towns in a river valley, has the disadvantage of being subject to illness, especially the miserable ague, or intermittent fever. I could not ascertain the number of Swedes living here."

About this time Pastor A. Andrén visited the countrymen in Attica, and in 1858 reorganized the Swedish Ev. Lutheran congregation, because the old organization, "The Sw. Ev. Luth. congregation in Indiana" was considered dissolved. The people numbered around

200. Andrén had worked diligently for a church building and gathered around $1000 in pledges. The intention was to start building that Fall. Work was begun and continued until it was completed and dedicated Christmas Day, 1859.

Serving Anew in Indiana

In December 1858 I was back in Chicago as editor of *Hemlandet*, and it fell to my lot to visit the Attica congregation. I was happy to meet again my old friends and to preach for them. Very few new people had come, but those who before had been scattered in the area had moved to Attica, bought lots in town and small plots in the vicinity on both sides of the river. Everything seemed now more promising. I spent Christmas with them and we had a very edifying holiday. I continued to visit the congregation regularly once a month as long as I was in Chicago. From the *Minutes* of the United Conference meeting in Andover June 1-4, 1859, I quote: "Brother Norelius reported that he had visited Attica once every month, and confirmed 11 children. The congregation now has a large, fine church on a beautiful site. Work is still progressing on it and it should be ready this summer. The countrymen there hunger for God's Word. But the persistent efforts of the sects to lead them away from our church makes the need of a resident pastor all the more apparent. Until this need can be met Brother Norelius will continue to visit Attica once a month.[1]

Combined with this need was my serious health condition, which made it impossible for me to return to the more demanding mission field in Minnesota, wherefore I was attracted to a call from the Attica church. I accepted for the time being, and moved there in October 1859. I stayed for one year, to the first of October, 1860.

At the dedication of the church both Prof. Esbjörn and S.W. Harkey were present, and I shall let them give their impressions of the congregation and the event.[2]

Church Dedication in Attica

"Attica is a pleasant town on the shores of the Wabash River, where the Great Western Railroad crosses the stream, in Fountain

[1]*Hemlandet*, 5th year, No. 23.
[2]*Olive Branch*, January 1860, *Hemlandet*, 6th year, No. 2.

County, Indiana. It has a population of about 2,000, and has considerable business. A canal which connects the Great Lakes with the Ohio River flows through the town, and when the river is high steamboats can reach here. Swedes began to come here a few years ago, but until now have been undecided about a permanent settlement. Some have moved to Minnesota and other places, the rest have concentrated in and around Attica. Brother Norelius has united them in one congregation, and they have now built a permanent frame church, 50 ft. long, 34 ft. wide, and surmounted by a steeple. There are 54 benches and seats for 250 persons. Carpets cover the floor in the pulpit and before the altar. The whole building has an inviting appearance. The congregation has 120 communicants with prospects of a significant increase. Church and lot together cost almost $2000, and on the morning of dedication day there was a debt of $700 resting on them. An effort was made during the day to cover the debt with the result that about $600 was raised in cash and pledges, leaving no doubt that all would be paid. This small, generous congregation rejoiced greatly at the outcome. The dedication festivities took place on Christmas Day 1859, services being held in both Swedish and English with professors Esbjörn and Harkey assisting the pastor.

"Brother Norelius is highly esteemed by his countrymen. He has suffered ill health but we are happy to report that he is on the way to recovery. He is able to preach in English and will do so as his health improves. May it please God to restore him fully and spare him to work long in the Master's vineyard! We were very satisfied with our visit in Attica, and our prayer is that the richest blessings of God may rest over pastor and people. (*Olive Branch*)

"The undersigned wishes to add to the foregoing that we had a very edifying Christmas on this occasion. Brother Norelius and I combined, as far as strength allowed, to proclaim the Word of God, and the people showed a gladdening desire to listen, and no one seems to have been kept from coming to the house of God by the severe cold weather. On Christmas day there were two Swedish and two English services, and the day of the Saviour's birth was the more glorious because the congregation for the first time could celebrate services in the building for which pastor and worshippers had worked so hard, and which they therefore appreciated so much more. As example we only mention that Brother Norelius, in addition to the work and worry that the building of a church always imposes on the pastor, dug with his own hands the holes and planted the trees that adorn the church lot. What the members have done and still are able to do is evidenced by the fact that of the $1300 which has already been paid for the building and lot only $200 have been contributed by Americans in town, and of the $600 which was raised on the day of dedication $400 came from the members themselves. Furthermore they have received no support from any other church in Attica, even from a Swedish Methodist church, though many Lutherans helped when this was built. Despite all, the congregation has given of its means to other charitable causes, such as contributing to a student aid fund, etc. and showing utmost hospitality to Christian visitors at the dedication. May a rich measure of the Lord's blessing be granted these people, and may they long have the pleasure for which they are so grateful, to have the leadership of the present pastor, who gives them the pure Word of God and sacraments.

L. P. E."

During the building John Fröja, one of the members and officers of the congregation met with an accident. He fell from a scaffold in the steeple and broke a leg. This was the only untoward happening.

It can be truthfully said that the congregation appreciated its new church, attended often and kept it clean and neat. The salary of the pastor for one year, from October 1, 1859 to October 1, 1860, was $287.01, with no provision for house. I hired an old decrepit house down by the canal, which didn't cost much. By the help of Dr. Passavant the congregation received a contribution of $125 from St. John's Lutheran Church in Philadelphia, whose pastor Dr. Seiss took an interest in the matter. The gift came through the Ev. Luth. H. M. S. in Baltimore. Thus the salary amounted to $412.01, then considered fairly good, but the necessary expenses were not much less that at present.

The conditions within the congregation at this time were generally favorable and peaceful, and the Word of God seemed to bear fruit in both young and old. A church school was conducted by M. Munter during a part of the Fall 1858 and winter 1859. Later I conducted an evening school and Sunday School. One class was instructed and confirmed. There was little trouble from other denominations. The Methodists had now a small congregation also and a building, but we lived together more peacefully than before.

When the question of leaving the Synod of Northern Illinois arose the congregation was quickly in favor and sent a delegate along with the pastor to the organization meeting in June 1860. The membership at that time consisted of 126 communicants.

My moving so soon from Attica was occasioned by a call from the synod's mission board to become a travelling missionary in Minnesota, where the spiritual need was indeed much greater than in Indiana but certainly not the comforts or the income. Fortunately the congregation did not have to remain vacant longer than to the end of the year (1860), when Pastor A. Andrén became my successor.

Baileytown and La Porte, Indiana

Congregations were organized in both of these places in 1857 by Pastor Erland Carlsson, who was the first Sw. Luth. pastor to visit the countrymen there. While Pastor A. Andrén was Carlsson's assistant he also visited them early, and during the winter of 1859 and later that year I went there several times. In the beginning of September 1856 Pastor T.N. Hasselquist, on his trip to Attica, went home by way of La Porte and Baileytown, and in *Hemlandet* 2nd year, No. 18, under the title "A Short Visit in Indiana" gave a brief report on these places. I quote it here inasmuch as it is the first mention in print at that time:

"In the northern part of Indiana are two other places where a part of the population is likely to consist of Swedes. The one is La Porte, where already some Swedes have settled and seem to be doing well. A couple have bought lots and are preparing to build their homes. The town has an exceptionally attractive situation. There is a small lake with forest on one side and fruitful cultivated land on the other. It is expanding rapidly. Already several additions have been made by converting surrounding farm land into lots. Next October 23rd a tract of 200 lots is to be sold on unusually favorable terms. The owner said he would be willing to contribute a good site if the Swedes wanted to build a church for themselves. Many Americans expressed the desire to have Swedes move in — they considered them the best of the immigrants who had settled here. Opportunities for work are plentiful and will increase, but I believe the wages are not as high as in at least some other places. The persons I talked to were very contented with the place. P. Palmblad was the first Swede to make a home in La Porte, and he is still here. The town is on the railroad to Chicago, 58 miles away.

"About 40 miles east of Chicago in Indiana lies a small Swedish settlement which may prove the most enduring. As a rule the land is covered by a forest, in part, with large and old trees. The owners are well paid when selling to the network of railroads. The ground is probably low here and there, but where seeded it has shown itself highly fruitful. Almost a score of larger and smaller landowners live here, mainly from Östergötland and Ekeby parish. Some of them own 100 or more acres, some 80 and 75 acres, and less, down to 2 1/2 acres of one couple. Their houses are yet of inferior quality, of the kind found among new-comers, but soon will be exchanged, one after another, for better and more convenient accommodations. Surprisingly one could find himself in a wild forest in America and there come upon Swedish families cultivating the earth around their small houses. Undoubtedly they have difficulties to contend with, but seemingly the satisfaction of seeing their plots enlarging bit by bit and their fields expanding, makes everything easy, especially since they can call it their own. They paid from $6 to $12 per acre, but prices have risen so that now one can demand $15 and over, even $50 per acre. Some land, however, it was said, could still be gotten for as low prices as formerly."

We treat now each of these places. A well-written article in *Hemlandet*, 5th year, No. 17, signed by E. (presumably E. Carlsson) give us information on

"The Swedes in La Porte

"La Porte is a small, attractive and lively town in the northern part of Indiana. The important railroad 'Michigan Southern and Northern Indiana' runs through the place. A branch line, 'Plymouth Road,' connects with another major railroad to the East, namely 'The Pittsburg, Ft. Wayne and Chicago R.R.' The location is favorable: to the south and southeast, fine land for farming, hilly and alternating between groves and plains, to the west and northwest thick woods. A very pretty lake lies north of town. Business is good, and few places in the West have felt the pressure of hard times as little as this town.

"The incident that led the first Swedes to come and settle here was the presence here of a servant girl, Christina Westberg, who worked for an American family in Chicago that moved here early in the Spring of 1853. Soon thereafter her parents, Johannes Westberg and wife, followed with the other children.

They were from Eriksberg parish, Elfsborg County. The same
Spring P. Palmblad and family, from Ljunga, Jönköping County,
came, and in the summer Anders Johnson from Hjertlanda, Jönköping County, and Johan Peterson from Örberga, Linköping
County. The same year brought Peter Backstrom and John Till-
strom from Lannaskede.

"The number of Swedes was significantly augmented in the
Spring of 1855. A group of 30 newcomers had come to Plymouth,
Marshall County, Ind. the previous summer to work on the rail-
road. After working 7 months without pay the majority in dis-
satisfaction left and went to La Porte, the others soon following.
Most of them were from Kronoberg County, namely, Daniel
Anderson, Johan Anderson, and Carl Dolk from Slätthög, Swen
Johnson from Ohs, Jonas Anderson and Swen Peterson from
Wrigstad, Jönköping County. Five were from Helsingborg: Carl
L. Wais, Malte Möller, Johan Olsson, Theodore Scher and
Anders Jonsson. Another increase came in the Fall, 1856,
through people from La Fayette or West Point. Most of these
were servant girls from Grenna, Jönköping County — among
them the sisters Sara and Juliana Bjorklund. Meanwhile many
relatives and acquaintances of those already settled joined them
— for example Carl Larsson and his brother-in-law Sven Lind,
from Daretorp, Skaraborg County, Gustav A. Wais from Helsingborg, etc.

"Of those who have come only a very few have moved away
to other places. And in 4 1/2 years, until the end of 1858, only
one adult, Johannes Westberg, and 4 small children have died.
The place is one of the most healthful to be found here in the
West.

"At present (April 1859) there are 20 families, or 76 persons, 15 farm hands and 6 servant girls, making the Swedish
population here 97 altogether.

"Few of the Swedes here are farmers. The greatest number
work in town for wages, some as mechanics, some as manual
laborers. Only one person has his own business. A Captain
Edmund Johnson has been of great help to our countrymen. He
was born in northern Sweden, left home at the age of 10 as a
cabin boy, sailed 5 years on the Atlantic and 10 years on the
Great Lakes, then settled in La Porte 15 years ago. His honesty
and capability have gained him much confidence, and he was
generally considered an American until the other Swedes came
and he became acquainted with them. He has forgotten his
mother-tongue completely but he has remembered some Swedish

songs which he learned as a child and which on some occasion
he is said to have sung for his countrymen, towards whom he has
always shown a special affection. He has himself given work to
many, or else recommended them to good positions. When they
have had difficulties he has assisted them with counsel and aid,
especially when it was a matter of getting proper pay for their
work or when they had just claims.

"When one considers that none of our countrymen who settled here had anything to start with, that they have not been
here many years, and that especially the recent years have been
hard, we believe that in this place and under these circumstances
they not only have done well in temporal things but also done
something for their future, as well as or even better than they
could have done anywhere else here in the West. Six have purchased land hereabouts, from 10 to 40 acres each, and 8 have
property in town. They are sincerely convinced that with all the
sweat and toil of a lifetime they would never have been able in
Sweden to acquire such homes and security for the future as they
have here.

"That which they have felt most in need of is that they have
not had a pastor among them. They have indeed had occasional
visits by pastors, especially Erland Carlsson of Chicago. But
however happy they are to receive a visit of our church teachers
several times a year, this is not sufficient for the guidance, instruction, and edification that are needed. It is impossible for
each small settlement to hire its own pastor, partly because of
the great lack of pastors, partly because the number of members
is so small. There is, however, another Swedish settlement 20
miles distant, where a larger number of countrymen have made
their homes, and it is hoped that these two places might unite on
one pastor, thus soon meeting their needs.

"With this hope the people in La Porte have taken serious
steps to obtain their own church building. In order to secure a
deed for a church lot trustees would have to be legally elected,
and on September 17, 1857 this was effected, when Gustaf A.
Wais, Swen Lind, Charles Wais, Charles Larsson and Charles
Dolk were named trustees. In October Erland Carlsson presided
at a congregational meeting, when it was unanimously decided
to build a frame church. After some discussion as to size, it was
agreed to make it 45 ft. long 28 ft. wide, and 16 ft. high. Bids
were received on November 10, and for $590 the building would
be erected and roofed and have two coats of paint on the exterior.
The contract also called for windows and doors and laying of

the floor, which is here termed "to have it enclosed." The contract was very cheap and favorable, especially since the builder was to furnish all materials. Work progressed to the point where services could be held there last summer (1858). The interior has not yet been completed. The building in its present condition, including a good brick foundation, has cost around $600, two thirds of which has been collected from Americans, one third from the Swedish people themselves.

"Most of the Swedes here have remained in the Lutheran Church. But they have suffered their part of the sectarianism in this country. About 2 years ago P. Palmblad and his family were drawn into a new, peculiar sect called "The Third Angel's Messengers." They have their own baptism, observe Saturday instead of Sunday, and are remarkable for their very extravagant notions of the Millenium. At first they caused confusion and strife. But as their most radical views became known, as for instance that the soul sleeps with the body in the grave, that after the Last Judgment both evil spirits and persons will be burned and annihilated, etc. all but the most fanatical drew back, and the controversy has now all but subsided.[1]

"It is quite necessary that our countrymen here receive greater spiritual care. The nearest pastor lives 50 miles away, and is so over-burdened that he can rarely come. Both the other two settlements in Indiana are larger than La Porte (Attica and Baileytown). If for the time being all three could combine to call a pastor, their need would partly be fulfilled and the possibility of providing his support be enhanced.

"One is happy to see the concern and sacrifice of our countrymen in most places for a church and pastor in their midst. May the Lord in his mercy also help us not to lose the benefits of His Kingdom in this land, and may we, in sincere repentance, in true faith, in a heavenly mind and holy life, seriously seek for an inheritance in the mansions of light!

E."

The Dedication of the Church

Saturday, August 25, 1860 the Chicago Conference met in La Porte, and the delegates were received by a very happy and friendly

[1]Norelius identifies the sect as Seventh Day Adventists, with headquarters in Battle Creek, Mich.

congregation. The proceedings began in the morning with a sermon by Prof. L.P. Esbjörn. On the following day, Sunday, August 26th, the church was solemnly dedicated. The building was simply but suitably and tastefully decorated, and a large gathering of countrymen in and around La Porte were in attendance. The service began at 9:30 in the morning. Prof. Esbjörn and Pastor Hasselquist went before the altar, and the former read the prescribed prayer in the Handbook and some verses from the prayer of Solomon in 2 Kings 6. Pastor Hasselquist gave the dedicatory sermon, based on Isaiah 55:10-11, emphasizing how the Lord comes to us with His Word in the places we dedicate to His service. There followed the regular worship service, when Pastor Erl. Carlsson preached. In the afternoon E. Norelius preached in English for a good sized audience. The offering which was then received for the building came to $70. The building was now out of debt, but the $1,091 owed on the lot could be paid in 7 years with 6% interest.

Especially beautiful music was on the program of the English service. A Swedish music teacher was in La Porte, a Mr. Owen, son of the well-known Englishman Owen in Stockholm. He led in the singing, along with a fine American choir. The congregation rejoiced in now having completed the building and in hearing so many pastors, yet felt the more the lack of its own pastor.[1]

Both the congregation in La Porte and the one in Baileytown were under Pastor Carlsson's care the rest of the year, and under Pastor A. Andrén and several other pastors, until in 1873 when G. Lundahl accepted a call and became the first resident pastor.

In later years the congregation in La Porte has proved to be, I almost said, a model for a Lutheran congregation, so one is tempted to ask if it had unusual favorable elements from the beginning lacking in other congregations. I don't believe this can be maintained. Everything we know about La Porte before 1860 and some years after indicates that it was a rather stony field. A certain churchly interest was present, but also ungodly conduct. There was much drunkenness, church discipline could not be exercised, with few exceptions there was no spiritual life. Besides the pastoral visits there were at times students who during their vacation preached and conducted Christianity schools in Swedish, but pastoral care was inadequate. What happened since is a wonder to our eyes, but this belongs to a later period. In 1860 the congregation had only 28 communicants.

[1]*Hemlandet*, 6th year, No. 36.

Baileytown

According to one story I heard the name derives from a French-man, Bailey, who was married to an Indian woman and lived originally in this place. This was down near the sand dunes of Lake Michigan, quite a distance from Porter Station where the Baileytown Church now stands. It included a saw-mill, a store, and a few other houses, and was often called Slab City from the refuse of the mill. A brook flowed through the place, called Coffee Creek, and a post-office there bore that name, so that the area was called Coffee Creek as well. As mentioned it was about 40 miles from Chicago, if we mean the old Baileytown. We have already given Pastor Hasselquist's description of the landscape and the soil. Its proximity to Chicago doubtless afforded advantages for our impoverished countrymen.

I have not been able to find out who were the first Swedes to locate here. It is said that they were penniless workers who came from Chicago and found work in the woods and in tree cutting around the sawmill in Baileytown. Then they started to acquire small plots of land on which they built their homes. Among early settlers were these: Johan Swenson, Samuel Eriksson, Gustaf Danielson, John Johnson, Jonas Eriksson, Johan Berg, Gustaf Carlsson, F. Bjurstrom, Vistrand. In Calumet, now Chesterton, were John Flod, Pet. Anderson, D. Lindahl, etc. The majority, as Hasselquist noted, were from Östergötland, but the Högsby area and other parts of Sweden were also represented.

The Spiritual and Churchly Concerns

Pastor E. Carlsson, and A. Andrén while he was Carlsson's assistant, were the first Lutheran pastors to visit the countrymen in Baileytown to gather them around the Word of God. I cannot give the exact date, but it was probably not before 1855. In spiritual matters there was a good deal of apathy among Baileytown's Swedes and not a small number loved the bottle. The story is told that Andrén on one of his visits came to his quarters after the service, and found that his host and some others had hurried home before him and placed a small pan of brandy on the stove and lit a flame on it to provide thus a "church drink." As Andrén entered blue flames arose in the pan. Taking an innocent look of fright he opened the window and threw out the pan and its contents, then happily remarked, "It was fortunate that I came or there could have been a fire," or something similar. The fellows kept a straight face in a poor play, but said later that this was a dumb and inexperienced minister who didn't know what a burning brandy was.

Conditions improved slowly and in 1857 Carlsson was able to organize a congregation. But I do not know the circumstances or who were the first members and officers. The old store in Baileytown or "Slab City" was purchased at a low price, and was fitted as a church with pulpit and benches. I preached a few times in this building in 1859 and remember that it was long and narrow and the ceiling was low. But it served the purpose until the congregation could afford a better structure. This happened in 1861 when Pastor Andrén moved here and became the first resident pastor. The new church and a parsonage was built near the railroad at Porter Station.

When the congregation was organized there were undoubtedly some rules adopted for its maintenance and guidance, as was the practice generally. But on August 1, 1859 at a properly called meeting the congregation adopted the proposed constitution for Swedish Lutheran congregations, as recommended by the United Conference, and elected officers. At this meeting Pastor Carlsson was present and conducted the business. He had also preached and celebrated the Lord's Supper in the old church on the preceding Sunday. On Tuesday, August 2nd, he held a service in La Porte.[1]

At the organization of the Augustana Synod in 1860 the congregation had 44 communicant members.

[1]*Hemlandet* 5: no. 30.

Chapter 10

The Swedish Settlements and Lutheran Congregations in Hessle
Valley (Sugar Grove) Pennsylvania and Jamestown, New York

These places are situated on the border between the states of
New York and Pennsylvania, Jamestown in Chautauqua County,
N.Y., at the southeastern end of the lake with the same name and
about 30 miles south of Dunkirk, on Lake Erie; Hessle Valley or
Sugar Grove in Warren County, Pa., about 14 miles south of James-
town. The land, formerly covered with forests of leaf-trees and pine,
is hilly and uneven, requiring much toil and work to break the sod.
Undeniably the landscape is very attractive, especially the shores of
the beautiful Lake Chautauqua, which stretches from Jamestown to
Mayville, 22 miles long and with little variation in width. In recent
times these shores have become well-known for their tourist resorts.
Here is also the headquarters of the famous educational association,
Chautauqua, which attracts large crowds in summer to attend the
lectures of notable persons in almost every branch of knowledge.

The land south of Jamestown, in Warren County, consists of
high, wooded ridges, and deep valleys rich in springs and streams.
The soil in this region is clay, in many places mixed with gravel, and
in spots in the valley there is bog. Grassland and fruit orchards make
grazing and fruit growing the most profitable occupation for the
farmers. Lately many factories have started up in and around
Jamestown and the renowned oil fields are nearby, so people have
been able to find employment and markets for farm products. The
forests meanwhile have increased in value.

The healthful climate wins praise. The winters are long, with
much snow, but the cold is not as severe as in the Northwest. Many
of our countrymen have made their homes here widely spread out
from the two original locations, and organized many congregations.
But we are concerned here only with Hessle Valley and Jamestown.

In the story of the beginnings of the Swedish movement to these
places I would refer to Chapter 1. As we saw there, the first Swedes
who located here were from Kisa in Östergötland, Hessleby in Jönköping County, Lönneberga and other parishes in Kalmar County.
We noted that Germund Johnson from Kisa was the first one to come,
with his family, to Sugar Grove and how others followed him from
Buffalo. We now turn to each separately.

Hessle Valley

This place lies 2 or 3 miles south of Sugar Grove, Warren County, Pa. from which sometimes the whole region gets its name. The name Hessle Valley comes from the 3 brothers, Fredrik, Carl and Anders P. Johnson from Hessleby parish who apparently were the first Swedes to settle here and to begin to clear the forest and break the sod in this valley. As far as I know the first mentioned still lives there. Others among the first to locate here and in the vicinity were: Anders Peter Gelm, who later moved to Jamestown; J. Lanz, Samuel Samuelson, M. Hultberg, Erik Anderson from Vestra Ryd, Linköping County and wife Helena Lovisa Peterson from Lönneberga; Sven P. Peterson from Kisa and wife Brita Lisa from Oppeby; Abram Swenson and wife Anna from Kisa, John Sundell and family. After 1855 these 4 last named families one by one moved to Vasa, Minn. There were many others from long ago whose names I do not have. To begin with they endured poverty and hardship simply to keep alive, but they worked hard, sacrificed heroically, and patiently forced from the stubborn earth if not a superfluous still a frugal livelihood.

The Church Situation

From a letter of B.G.P. Bergenlund to Hasselquist early in 1853 we learn of some Methodist activity among the Swedes both here and in Jamestown, for he wrote: "I find some Swedes working here to draw them to other denominations. O that they would work as hard to bring them to faith in Jesus Christ as they do to enroll them in their books." In any case he was the first to serve the Lutheran cause, though with a want of judgment. In the same letter he wrote, "There are several hundred Swedes in the Jamestown area and some want me to remain here, but they are very destitute and some few belong to the Methodist Church." He adds, "Will Pastor Hasselquist kindly answer and advise me what I should do when some ask me to administer the sacrament? They cannot go to American ministers nor to Swedish Lutherans, and they desire services in Swedish and according to the Swedish Order. In the American churches they miss especially the confession of sins and the Creed. I have been here 3 weeks and feel that they, at least some of them, are hungry for the Word of Life." From this letter we thus discover that at least some of them felt a conscious spiritual need which they sought to satisfy by attending services in American churches, but that they missed the Swedish Lutheran worship as well as their mother tongue.

In a later letter he informs us, "In Sugar Grove there are 3 churches, Methodist, Presbyterian and Congregationalist. The Swedes can borrow either the Methodist or the Presbyterian church. In Jamestown, too, there are three churches."

In my account of Andover I have already told of Bergenlund's activity in Hessle Valley and Jamestown, and will not repeat it here. He invited Pastor Hasselquist in the Spring of 1853 to visit Jamestown and Hessle Valley, and in a letter from H. to his wife, dated Chicago, May 30, 1853, I find that he went there by train to Dunkirk and then by stage to Jamestown. He expected to be back in Chicago June 7. His stay there was brief. He preached and held communion in both places, but he did not have time to organize them as congregations.

As already noted Bergenlund received a license at the meeting of the Synod of Northern Illinois in Galesburg the Fall of 1853 to serve as pastor in Sugar Grove (Hessle Valley) and Jamestown, and he worked there until the Spring of 1855. The statistical table of the Synod indicates that the congregation in Hessle Valley was organized 1854. This must have happened under Bergenlund's leadership, unless one can assume that it took place while Hasselquist was there on a second visit, in late Fall 1854. What occasioned this visit was this: The president of the No. Ill. Synod, Pastor C.B. Thümmel, had received complaints against Bergenlund from some of the members of the Hessle Valley congregation, which were presented at the meeting of Synod in Peru, 1854. None of the Swedish pastors, except M.F. Hokanson were present at the meeting. A committee, consisting of O. Andrewson, O.J. Hatlestad, and the lay delegate from Andover, P.W. Holm, considered the matter and then reported thus: "your committee has examined the various documents referred to us and find that they describe certain misunderstandings between the Rev. B.G.P. Bergenlund and some few members of the Swedish congregation in his pastorate in Sugar Grove, Warren County, Pa. But the evidence submitted in these documents is not sufficiently clear to warrant this Synod to take any decisive action. The committee would therefore recommend to the Synod that Pastor T.N. Hasselquist be appointed as a committee to visit said congregation, examine the situation, and report to the president on the result of such examination. The congregation requests such an examination and promises to pay the expenses for this visit."

In the report of the president (Dr. Harkey, elected in the Fall of 1854) the following year (1855) we read: "My official acts as president during the year have been: On October 24, 1854 I received a letter from Brother L.P. Esbjörn, asking that I authorize, in accordance with the decision of Synod, Brother Hasselquist to visit Sugar Grove, Warren County, Pa., in order to investigate the dissension between the pastor, Rev. B.G.P. Bergenlund and some members of the Swedish Lutheran congregation in that place. I sent Brother Hasselquist a certificate of his appointment by Synod. At the meeting of the Mississippi Conference in Chicago last April Brother Hasselquist informed me that he had visited Sugar Grove and held a sort of examination of the complaints against Bergenlund, but could not come to any clear decision — further, that Bergenlund had moved and the congregation in Hessle Valley was now vacant."

Hasselquist made the visit toward the end of November or in the early part of December 1854, for it took place on his trip to New York and Boston when he was looking for type for his proposed paper *Hemlandet*. In view of the brief time it is hardly likely that he organized the Hessle Valley congregation — Bergenlund must have done this. The *Minutes* of 1854 state that Bergenlund was in charge of 2 congregations, but this is an error, for the congregation in Jamestown was not organized until after the arrival of Pastor J. Swensson. It is possible that some kind of provisional organization had been effected in Jamestown.

The First Vacancy, from the Spring of 1855 until the Coming of Pastor J. Swensson

We derive the following information from *Hemlandet*, 1st year, No. 14: "A letter from Sugar Grove speaks of a different kind of harvest. It makes one sick of heart that so many who thirst for the pure milk of the Gospel, who are without guile, have to be in want, despite all pleas and prayers. These brethren have not only raised money by voluntary gifts and built a spacious church on an attractive spot in the valley a couple of miles from the small town of Sugar Grove, but also bought a small property for a parsonage and about 25 acres of land. The land, it is true, is not yet cultivated to any great extent, but cattle can graze on the uncultivated part and wood is free. To these friends I can only reply that a pastor in Sweden has been urged to come and care for them and be their leader in the Lord's name. We do not yet know if the call will be accepted. Pray to Him who leads the hearts of men as rivers of water and sends workers into His harvest to persuade those called to forsake what there is to be forsaken and come over here to break the bread of life for the hungry.

"The letter reads thus: 'Pray for the brothers and sisters redeemed with you in Christ. The harvest is at hand, but workers in the good grain are far from us. Lord, healer of Israel, Those who art able to do beyond what we can pray for or think, send us a shepherd of Thy will! O, Lord God, let not Thy churches stand empty of teachers or hearers. Be merciful to us and hear the sighs of our hearts. Man does not live by bread alone, but by each and every Word from the mouth of God. Send us Thy Word and Thy Spirit. Yes, send us what can save and make blessed our poor souls. Here we need a daily encouragement to go in the school of Jesus and there grow. When the watchman is absent the deceitful tempter is not soon or easily unmasked. The bypaths are many and appear so alluring to the unexperienced traveller. Many go the evil paths, and my heart bleeds bitterly for them. Therefore I pray, help us before we perish! It would give us great joy if we could hear that there is any prospect of getting a pastor this summer. Give me a reply to this.' "

At the same time the congregation here as well as the countrymen in Jamestown were troubled by the proselyting of Methodism. The first Swedish Methodist preacher in this area seems to have been a man by the name of Hammerin, but he died early. J. Bredberg followed him, and I believe about this time. Since I had the opportunity of learning to know him quite intimately I have difficulty in believing that he became a Methodist by conviction. "Of the dead only good" said the ancients, and I certainly do not want to become judge of this person who has passed away. But it is the duty of the writer of history to tell the truth about even a deceased individual if it serves to throw light on an historical situation. Bredberg was a minister in the Skara diocese in Sweden. He came to America in 1853, unhappily as a fugitive. The cause I do not know, but could be found in the records of the Skara diocese if anyone took the trouble to discover. I met him in New York just as he stepped on land, and it was my fate to live with him for about six weeks. He wore a Swedish ministerial garb and had a few theological books with him, including Martensen's *Dogmatics*. He never admitted to me that he had been a minister, but claimed to be a journalist. But it was clear that he had been a minister, for it showed in more ways than one, not as a servant of Christ but as a caricature. He was in poor circumstances and needed at once to find means of support. For this purpose he soon looked up Pastor O.G. Hedstrom on the Bethel Ship. He knew how to get next to him by regular attendance at services, class and prayer meetings, and displaying a religious spirit. He found work translating some English material to Swedish for which he received some remuneration. Still lacking in English he often asked for my help, which I did not withhold if I had time. This was not blameworthy but it was blameworthy that before Hedstrom and on the Bethel Ship he acted piously and pretended to be converted while at the same time he made fun of Hedstrom behind his back, and in daily life drank heavily and in every other word swore and misused the name of God. I reproached him directly for his falsehood, but this didn't seem to trouble his conscience. Afterwards for a year he corresponded with me and his letters certainly did not reveal that he was an honorable, convinced Methodist. Meanwhile he succeeded in gaining a reputation as a Methodist convert and after a while became a preacher in the Methodist Church. He was sent to Jamestown where as mentioned he confused the Swedes with his new light. Then he came to Illinois, and when he found a better opportunity for his temperament among Episcopalians he went over to the Episcopal Church and was made rector for the Swedish Ansgarius congregation there. He remained in this position until his death some years ago. That unworthy persons insinuate themselves in every communion we well know, but this should teach those concerned to speak more cautiously about their own purity and excellence.

During this difficult period of 1 1/2 years there doesn't seem to have been any visits by our pastors in Hessle Valley and Jamestown. The field in the West grew larger each year and there were too few pastors to allow for an extension of activity in the Eastern states. The vacancy was surely not good for the congregation. Some were drawn to the Methodists, some moved away, but the congregation survived. Some faithful men and women held fast to the Word of God and their Confessions, waiting patiently for better times and retaining confidence in their brethren in the West.

The Jonas Swensson Period

First an explanation of how he came to accept the call to serve the countrymen in these places. (In another section of his book Norelius has a long biography of Jonas Swensson with some information on his work in Hessle Valley and Jamestown, wherefore the account here is comparatively brief.)

Jonas Swensson wrote to Pastor Erland Carlsson from on-board the ship *Minona*, June 27, 1856. He told about his ministry, his trials, and the serious illness from which he had a remarkable recovery, then goes on: "In the middle of May (1855) I read in the journal *Väktaren* a letter from you to someone I do not know who, in which you mention that there was talk of calling me to America. For several days I was torn as to what I should reply in case the call came, for I had no inclination to leave. But I soon comforted myself that there would be no call, since the long delay (the date of the letter in the paper was erroneous). If, however, a call should come, I would decline, I said. A year ago now your call did come (June 24). That indeed led to conflict. I thought to say "No," for I did not want to go. As in the case of Jonah, flesh and blood trembled in view of the difficulties. I searched for many reasons to satisfy myself if I declined. But I was thrown into the depths of the sea, filled with a terrible anguish and inner torment which would not cease as long as I wanted to escape the call. Prayer both privately and together with some Christian friends was my only refuge, for there was little help in counselling with fellow-men in this matter. After a few weeks I became so strongly convinced that the call was from the Lord that my own will gave way and I decided to accept the call. Then I found inner peace and courage to meet whatever were the difficulties. This assurance of God's will has since upheld me constantly, and is still my comfort though I do not anticipate anything else than that difficulties of many kinds await me. The Lord's guidance in this journey has been wonderful. To name only the means necessary. As you know I had no means of my own. It was not easy even to think of getting a loan for such a voyage, and I could not bring myself to ask for it. 1 1/2 months after I had decided to leave I did not know where the money would come from. But in His grace the Lord had given me a firm assurance that He would provide the travel expenses when needed, so that I could be quiet and not anxious about the means. Only a few close friends knew of my feelings, otherwise people might have looked on me as simply crazy in not worrying about money. On top of this after deciding to leave I had also decided, following the Lord's clear guidance, to get married before leaving. The bride was also without resources, so the costs now naturally increased. (I do not know if you who know conditions there look on this as a wise step but for my part I am sure of God's will and I thank the Lord who has selected for me a helpmate with whom I can be one in the Lord and who also is willing to meet with me all suffering and sacrifices.) That the Lord keeps His promise I experienced, praised be His name. Just before leaving, the Lord provided me, even without my asking, partly by loan, partly otherwise, what I needed for the voyage. This is only for the voyage, not beyond, so that if I arrive safely I will be almost penniless. But I am not anxious. He who has cared for me hitherto will do so also hereafter. I am more anxious now how I shall fulfill my call pleasing to the Lord. Yet I know that even this must be a gift of grace. I would need to be informed on many things and therefore had hoped to meet you as soon as possible. Of course it can't happen now. As long as I was in Sweden I was so occupied in my work, especially the last 3/4 year, that I could not make much preparation for the trip. Consequently I lack knowledge of English. — We left Gothenburg May 21 on the Swedish boat *Minona*, captain Rhyden. The ship has made good time, otherwise we would have a large part of the distance ahead of us. More than half the time we have had stiff contrary winds. Since the 27th we have been only a couple of days from New York. Going against the wind we are now, July 1st, not much closer. But today the wind is more favorable. There are about 130 emigrants on board, most of them bound for Minnesota, so they will pass through Chicago. I pity the poor people, for they surely don't know their own welfare. They are from various regions, and I only know them from here on the boat. But judged by their conduct most of them, if not all, live without God in the world. At least I haven't found anything but sin and ungodliness, and the greatest indifference among them toward spiritual things. Many times my heart has been heavy. When circumstances and weather have permitted I have held morning and evening prayers and on Sundays a service in the ship's hold. It has been depressing because of the great indifference, and many times storms and the ship's motion have prevented meetings. Nevertheless I hope that you who are used to troubles with immigrants will be able to help them when they pass through (Chicago) since none of them understands a word of English —." Then he expresses the hope to see Brother Carlsson soon, and asks many questions about the books used in services, worship forms, etc.

This letter alone reveals something of the man who now became pastor in Hessle Valley and Jamestown. We can understand the zeal he had for his work in the Lord.

Swensson lived in the small, simple house, similar to a crofter's cottage in Sweden, near the Hessle Valley church. There was born his eldest son, Carl Aron, now pastor in Lindsborg, Kansas, in 1857. In general it may be said that he had a hard time with much poverty and privation. Beside Hessle Valley and Jamestown he visited several other localities where Swedes had begun to settle. In the Fall of 1856 it was reported that he served two congregations and three preaching places, with a combined communicant membership of 184. The salary they could give him was indeed small. It is possible that they may have had some help from the Home Missionary Society in Baltimore, though I have no information.

Jamestown

A contributor to *Hemlandet* 5th year, No. 13, thus described this town and its Swedes: "It is 56 years ago (1802) since the first house — a log cabin — was built here, now there is a population of about 4000 souls. The town is situated 30 miles south of Dunkirk at the outlet of Chautauqua Lake. There are 10 mills along the river of the same name, some quite important. Five or six factories are driven by steam, among them a clothes manufacturing plant with 40 employees, another similar one is run by water. In these factories many Swedes have found work.

"The first Swedes arrived here 9 or 10 years ago, but most came in 1852, and after that some have come every year. With very few exceptions we are all doing well. The climate is healthful, water is fresh and pure, and forests are more than plentiful. If rightly cultivated the soil produces a good yield. Some of the Swedes have bought houses and lots, some are buying land on which to build, some buy land that is under cultivation. Laws and ordinances are strictly enforced. Only two Swedes have been found guilty of violations, and that for intoxication. The Americans on the whole are very friendly to us. I would guess that there are some 250 Swedes in this place. What is sad I have not mentioned, namely, that we have not been united in our religious faith. Though all of us have promised loyalty to and steadfastness in the one same Confession, a number of Swedes have formed a Methodist congregation, though not very large. Whether it is right and necessary for us Swedes to adopt another religion in order to be saved I leave to better Christians than I to decide, but I believe, for my part, that what is written in Chapters 23 and 24 of Matthew can be applied to these religious controversies.

C."

The Swedish Lutheran Congregation

As already noted some sort of beginning of a congregation must have existed when Bergenlund visited the Swedes in Jamestown. But the synodical records indicate that the congregation here was formally organized in Pastor Swensson's time, or 1857. It may be that he found the organization so faulty that he deemed it necessary to reorganize it in proper fashion, but I am not acquainted with the circumstances nor with the names of the first members or first officers. In 1860 we are told by Pastor J. Peterson, that these were members of the church council: C. Rydberg, C. Flink, A. Anderson, C. Klang, Norin. The congregation had no church of its own until 1866. Since the pastor did not live in the place he could not give it the care it needed. As a rule he visited here every other Sunday and on weekdays when time permitted. His work was indeed not in vain, but much work and patience were required to establish an ordered church among a people who had lacked strong leadership before and also been subjected to sectarian influences.

Pastor Swensson served these congregations a little over two years. He had a very difficult time to decide to move and assuredly it was not because of impatience or inconsiderateness. (Norelius refers here to his biography of Swensson where he went into detail about the move). Pastor Swensson moved early in the Fall, and the congregations again became vacant. At the meeting of the United Conference in Princeton in September 1858 there was regret that no pastor could be sent them and that the prospects in this area were not bright. Twenty-eight families, it was reported, belonged to the congregation in Sugar Grove and in the surrounding area were a few other scattered families. In Jamestown around 30 families were members of the Lutheran congregation, with some scattered persons there also.[1]

Evil disposed persons interpreted Swensson's moving in a malicious manner, even saying that these congregations no longer wanted to belong to the Lutheran Church and that Swensson's work accom-

[1] cf. *Hemlandet* 4th year, No. 20.

plished nothing. But I give here a communication from Jamestown to the Mississippi Conference meeting in Chicago December 6-7, 1858 as a refutation of these rumors and an illustration of the situation there shortly after Swensson's removal. The *Minutes* report: "The Swedish Lutheran congregation in Jamestown, N.Y. had written to the Conference about the necessity of a pastor in that place and vicinity. We quote important parts of this letter, so that everyone may understand the nature of the rumors officiously spread around in Illinois concerning the congregations Pastor Swensson felt himself forced to leave. The rumors, born and nourished by individual letters, one of the worst of which has come to our attention, would give the impression that Brother Swensson's labors were altogether fruitless, if not worse, when in fact the letter shows the truth is just the opposite.

'Revered and honored pastors and other conference delegates! The grace and peace of God the Father and His Son, Jesus Christ and of the Holy Spirit be with you now and always, and especially at this important meeting. May he crown your counsel and decisions with His blessing, to the glory of His holy name and the extension of His kingdom and to the advance of our church and its growth in the word of truth here in this strange land!

'We wish hereby to thank the worthy members of the Conference for their concern for us at your last meeting and that you sympathized with us in our great loss through the removal of our dear pastor. We note that you haven't forgotten us, though it was not now possible to repair this loss. We pray and humbly ask that your dear pastors and friends would continue to have us in mind and at the first possible opportunity send us a pastor who, with the word of truth and the life-giving dew of the Holy Spirit, would refresh the planting which our dear pastor, now so missed by us, with great toil but with the help of God started. We must and will confess, since God delights in the truth, that this tireless pastor often had to fulfill his office among us with sighing and not joy. For he came to a field that not only had been barren but planted with seed which cannot bear the fruit of eternal life. That seed was and still is, alleged, to be of the best quality, but it showed itself not to be so now when this sower came who took unmixed seed out of the good and certain store. His work was made more difficult in this condition, for flesh and blood always wants to go byways.

'Again we renew our desire and plead that the Conference will continue to have us, poor wilderness wanderers, in kind remembrance and, as mentioned, send us highly needed help as soon as possible. Our congregation, moreover, is more united than might be expected at our dear pastor's moving. Almost all of us come together every Sunday for a service at which we use some good Postil that has a sermon for the day. We have not been without the blessing of God even in this simple manner. However we feel that we are less fortunate than vacant congregations in the West. For they can be and often are visited by servants of the Word of God and can receive the Lord's Supper, which we cannot do here. They have many other advantages in spiritual matters which we lack. We leave ourselves and your dear pastors and other friends as well as all brethren in the faith in the care and protection of our most beloved Over Shepherd, also in this new church year, etc.

Jamestown, November 28, 1858'
(Signed by a large part of the membership of the congregation)

"Surely it was painful for the Conference not to be able to satisfy these dear brothers' need and desire but under present circumstances this was impossible. It was, however, decided that one of the pastors here should visit the countrymen in Jamestown and Sugar Grove and surrounding places, also that one of the older students at our university in Springfield should be encouraged at the end of the next term to go there for a longer or shorter period to serve them as best he can."[1]

"I made a visit there in May 1859 and wrote an article in *Hemlandet* 5th year, No. 21, which may serve to give a picture of the places: "The land in this region is not suited for extensive or profitable farming, and the kind of grain fields we have in the West are not found here. On the other hand it is favorable for dairy farming, sheep raising, and manufacturing. Pure and fresh water flows down from innumerable springs in the hills. Forests as well as hills stand in the way for farming. One finds a large number of stubble fields, 10-12 years old. The clay soil is mixed with stone, and looked thin, but is said to give good yield if wisely and expensively cultivated. A person from the West is most impressed by a sort of wattle fence very common in this region. The roots of trees are broken up and set on end, making a fence with all kinds of horns.

[1]*Hemlandet* 4, no. 26.

"Forests and hills abound around Sugar Grove. The Swedish Lutheran church, 3 miles south of the village of Sugar Grove, lies between two high hills, one covered with leafy trees, one with pine. In this area are several hundred Swedes, some of whom have been here as long as 10 years or more, but most, 5 or 6 years. As far as farming is concerned it is clear that they could have found more profitable locations if they had gone West. But they live here, and many have purchased property — houses, lots, and small tracts — and very likely intend to stay here.

"As many of *Hemlandet's* readers know, our countrymen in this region are organized into two congregations, one here in Sugar Grove, one in Jamestown. Since Pastor Swensson moved away last Fall they have been without a pastor, making for a sad situation. In Jamestown the congregation has indeed not diminished, rather it has grown and under the circumstances possesses a praise-worthy unity. They have not yet been able to build a church. The Sugar Grove congregation, on the other hand, has for several years had a neat frame building, 32 × 40 ft., which cost around $800, and a parsonage valued at $250. One while there were 36 families belonging to the congregation, but partly because of removals, partly because of the activity of the sects, especially lately, the number has decreased significantly, so that at present there are hardly more than 16-18 families in the Lutheran Church. What our people in this region therefore deeply need is a shepherd of souls, who would uninterruptedly serve them with zeal, wisdom, and understanding. For such they are praying fervently to the Lord of the harvest. Pastor Swensson's name is held in dear remembrance in these congregations, and I was deeply moved when I heard many remark that his leaving was a day of misfortune and heartfelt sorrow. I am convinced that their period of fasting has taught and prepared them to heartily welcome and value the pastor that the Lord may see fit to send them — In Jamestown there is also a Swedish Methodist church and a small congregation. In Sugar Grove and the vicinity a few families have gone over to the Methodists. Their minister is a former pastor from the Skara diocese, whose former and present history speaks for itself. For the benefit of him and his like I would say that those who live in glass houses should be careful of throwing stones on others.

E. Norelius"

In Sugar Grove the congregation suffere
could not resolve. Some of the members there
to the Mississippi Conference meeting in Andov
ing the Conference for help. The Conferen
Hasselquist, Swensson and O.C.T. Andrén as
municate with the congregation about the mat
far they succeeded, but apparently the seed of ⟨
for about two years later Hasselquist as Synod ⟨
make peace. At the aforementioned meeting J⟨
in Springfield, Ill. was asked to go to Jamestown and Sugar Grove at
the end of the school term, to proclaim the Word of God among our
countrymen there. This he promptly did.

The John Pehrson Period

In his biographical notes which are enlightening for an understanding of the times, Pehrson states: "In June 1859 I came to Jamestown, N.Y. and Sugar Grove, Pa. to work as a student in the preaching of the Word of God. After September 9 I had permission as a
licentiate to perform other duties of the ministry, and on June 10,
1860 I returned as an ordained pastor."

Pehrson remained until the summer of 1862, residing in Jamestown, from which he made visits to Sugar Grove and other places.
Despite his worthwhile sermons, devout and upright character, he
does not seem to have evoked any marked sympathy in these places.
Probably the reason lay in the differences in natural mood and spiritual upbringing that separated him from the majority in these congregations. Strenuous efforts, also, were made by the Methodists to win
as many Swedes as possible, especially while "Father" Newman was
stationed there. The congregations, however, remained quite station-
ary, even if one cannot say that they made any progress. At the end of
Pehrson's ministry the congregation in Jamestown had 82 and Hessle
Valley (Sugar Grove) 77 communicants. The pastor's salary while he
was there was about $300. Convinced that he could serve with more
blessing on some other field, Pastor P. resigned and moved away before the Synod meeting of 1862. The ensuing vacancy lasted until 1864
when Pastor C.O. Hultgren was called. He has remained faithful at
his post now over 25 years.

Chapter 11

Minnesota

Louis Hennepin, the French explorer in 1680 was the first white man to traverse the upper Mississippi River, to reach St. Anthony Falls, giving them their name, and to penetrate some 200 miles farther northwest. His compatriot Nicholas Perrot in 1683 built some log forts at the end of Lake Pepin, near Frontenac, and on Prairie Island (1695) and other points. But a long time elapsed before white men took possession of and settled the land within the boundaries of Minnesota. The Dakota and Ojibwa tribes, both strong, inhabited the territory, each on opposite sides of the Mississippi and traditionally at war with each other. Fort Snelling was begun in 1819 when a military post from Ft. Crawford at Prairie du Chien was established there. The first white inhabitants, Swiss by nationality, occupied land between St. Paul and Ft. Snelling, but were expelled by soldiers since they were on what was considered a part of the military reservation. No steamboat had come to the Upper Mississippi before 1823, and only 15 steamboats had navigated the Father of Waters as far as Ft. Snelling by May 26, 1826. The Minnesota Territory was organized in 1849 and even then settlements were few and far between. The Indians owned and occupied the land west of the Mississippi and north of Iowa to the borders of British America. Here and there some adventurers had settled down among the Indians and carried on trade with them. In such and other places missionaries had begun to work for the conversion of the heathen, and there white settlements began to arise. Among them were Wabasha, Red Wing, Point Douglas, Red Rock, St. Paul, Stillwater.

When early in 1849 the Minnesota Territory was formed Alexander Ramsay from Pennsylvania was named its first governor. A census of June that year revealed that the territory then had 4,780 white persons, of which number 317 were soldiers, women and children at Ft. Snelling. St. Paul was chosen as the seat of government.

Fredrika Bremer visited St. Paul on her travels, in October 1850. She gave this description of the place, "Scarcely had we touched the shore when the governor of Minnesota, Mr. Alexander Ramsay, and his pretty young wife, came on board, and invited me to take up my quarters at their house. And there I am now, happy with these kind people, and with them I make excursions into the neighborhood. The town is one of the youngest infants of the Great West, scarcely eighteen months old, and yet it has in this short time increased to a population of two thousand persons, and in a very few years it will certainly be possessed of twenty-two thousand, for its situation is as remarkable for beauty and healthiness as it is advantageous for trade."

"As yet, however, the town is but in its infancy, and people manage with such dwellings as they can get. The drawing-room in Governor Ramsay's house is also his office, and Indians and workpeople, and ladies and gentlemen, are all alike admitted. In the meantime Mr. Ramsay is building himself a handsome, spacious house, upon a hill, a little out of the city, with beautiful trees around it, and commanding a grand view over the river. If I were to live on the Mississippi it would be here. It is a hilly region, and on all hands extend beautiful and varying landscapes.

"The city is thronged with Indians. The men, for the most part, go about grandly ornamented, and with naked hatchets, the shafts of which serve them as pipes. They paint themselves so utterly without any taste that it is incredible. — Here comes an Indian who has painted a great red spot in the middle of his nose; here another who has painted the whole of his forehead in small lines of yellow and black; there a third with coal-black rings round his eyes. — The women are less painted, and with better taste then the men. Generally with merely one deep red little spot in the middle of the cheeks, and the parting of the hair on the forehead is died purple. — There goes an Indian with his proud step, bearing aloft his plumed head. He carries only his pipe, and when he is on a journey, perhaps a long staff in his hand. After him with bowed head and stooping shoulders, follows his wife, bending under the burden which she bears on her back. — Above the burden peeps forth a little round faced child, with beautiful dark eyes. —"
[translation in Mary Harriet's *Women in the New World*]

Missions among the Indians

The Roman Catholics were the first to attempt to extend Christianity among the Indians. They were French and accompanied the fur traders who roamed across the country before the beginning of this century. Small log chapels were built beside Lake Pepin, at St. Paul, Mendota and several other places.

The American Board had a number of missionary posts in the

northern part of the state. One mission was begun in 1832 at Sandy
Lake with Edmund F. Ely as teacher; at Leech Lake, 1835, with
Wm. T. Boutwell as missionary; at Fond du Lac on Lake Superior
1834; at Pokegoma (Snake River) 1835. These missions were among
the Chippewa or Ojibwa Indians.

In 1835 Dr. Williamson, father of Prof. Williamson at Augustana
College, Rock Island, Ill. came to Minnesota to start a mission
among the powerful Sioux or Dakota Indians, and soon thereafter, in
cooperation with the four brothers Pond, Stevens, Riggs and Huggins,
missions were begun in Lac qvi Parle, Traverse des Sioux, and other
places along the Minnesota River, then called the St. Peter River.
Also missions were established among the same tribes by the American
Board at Red Wing and Kaposia.

The persistent and almost superhuman efforts of Doctors Riggs
and Williamson in translating the Bible into the language of the
Dakotas are a beautiful example of Christian patience and perser-
vance. Among the Dakota Christians they are deservedly honored as
apostles.

The Episcopal Methodists established missions among the Dakota
Indians in Kaposia and St. Peter, 1837, with Alfred Brunson and
David King as missionaries. In 1839 Sam Spates, Huddleston, Cop-
way and John Johnson were sent to Crow Wing and Sandy lake to
work among the Chippewas. The Kaposia mission was moved in 1842
to Red Rock, below St. Paul.

Presbyterians from Oberlin, Ohio, began work among the Chippewa tribe at Red Lake, Cass Lake, and Little Lake Winnepeg, in
northern Minnesota, in 1843, with Spencer, Wright, Barnard and Dr.
Lewis as missionaries. These missions were functioning as recently as
1851.

The Swiss mission which started at Mt. Trempeleau in 1837
moved to Red Wing in 1838, Danton and Gavan serving as missionaries. When Danton's health failed in 1846 the mission was turned
over to The American Board and its missionaries John Alton and
Joseph W. Hancock. The latter carried on in some measure until the
Indians were removed in 1853 — he still lives, in Red Wing.

The first church activity among the white settlers in Minnesota
took place in the following order. We have noted that the Catholics
were the pioneers, along with the French voyageurs.

The Methodists started in 1844 when Rev. Hurlbut arrived. The
Baptists date from 1849 when Rev. Parsons was stationed in St. Paul.

In the same year and place the Presbyterians came, as Rev. E.D. Neill began work.

The Episcopalian missionaries, Breck, Wilcoxen and Merick, made St. Paul their center in 1850. The Swedish Lutherans' first congregations date from 1854.

I have considered it best to give these brief historical notes before turning to the Swedes in this their most Swedish state. I refer those interested to Rev. E.D. Neill's *History of Minnesota* as the best and most reliable source for the early history of Minnesota.

The First Swede in Minnesota

Some of our older Swedish settlers may be acquainted with the name Fahlstrom. He lived on a farm near Afton, Washington County, was married to an Indian woman who was said to be half Chippewa, half negro, and his grown-up children were considered to be, as they really were, "half breeds." They spoke Chippewa in the home, otherwise English, and when the Swedes came to the area the old man revived some of his Swedish, which he had long ago forgotten. Undoubtedly Fahlstrom was the first Swede in Minnesota. But whence and when had he come here, and what was his history? To answer these questions I can only report the information I received in 1867 from an old American by name Bolton, who had been a farmer-missionary at the Methodist Indian Mission in Red Rock in the early 1840's.

Bolton and his wife were well acquainted with Fahlstrom, and of his early history had learned that as a youth he had come over on a vessel that sailed on Hudson Bay. For some reason he had left the boat and living many years among the Indians had learned 7 different Indian languages. He had endured many dangers and hardships. In manner and customs as well as in language he had become as an Indian. Year after year he moved southward and finally in company with Indians had reached Ft. Snelling. Such was the information they had gotten about him before he came to Ft. Snelling. There they got personally acquainted with him. They saw him as another Indian tramp who lived near the fort and carried on a wild life. As a result of the work of the missionaries and other preachers a religious revival occurred at Ft. Snelling and near-by places, and not a few, both whites and Indians, were awakened to spiritual concern, including Fahlstrom. He spent much time around the mission in Red Rock, and was presumably converted there. He then got the notion that he wanted to get married, and against the advice of his friends went and married the above-mentioned woman. Later he settled down near Afton. He was not altogether satisfied with his Christian life, and characteristically retained his Indian customs. His acquaintances judged him charitably and hoped that despite all his faults he still was a Christian. He used to go out and preach for the Chippewa Indians in the forests and could often be gone several weeks. He was very hardy — one might see him in the depth of frigid winter wrap a blanket about him and lie down in the snow under a tree in the woods and sleep soundly. After the Swedes moved into Minnesota it sometimes happened that he appeared at Methodist meetings and tried to speak in Swedish, but the result was not very fortunate. The old fellow died a few years ago, but his sons still bear his name.

The first Swedish settlers in Minnesota came in the spring and summer of 1851 and made their homes in Chisago Lake, Chisago County, and Marine, Washington County. In 1853 Swedes moved into Goodhue County and a little later into Carver County. E.U. Nordberg, whom we know from the Bishop Hill story, was the first to direct the attention of the Swedes to Minnesota. At least he was at the St. Croix River at the beginning of 1851 and corresponded with a group of Swedes in Moline, Ill. This led to the first Swedish migration into Minnesota the Spring of that year. From this small beginning the Swedish population in Minnesota has grown to that point where no other state of the Union has so many Swedes as this state. The reasons for this are its location in the North, its climate and nature, the availability of land, and the favorable communications which were of no little significance during the early years of immigration. The Swedes who came to America 1850 and 1851 and later, could buy land at the government price of $1.25 per acre in many parts of Illinois, but many would not have taken the best farm as a gift if they were compelled to live there. They yearned instinctively towards the North, to the forests and lakes and to a climate more similar to that of the land of their childhood on the other side of the Atlantic, even though they knew that they would have to contend with a harsher nature than that farther south. And in those days one could find no more direct route to Minnesota from Illinois than on nature's waterway — the Mississippi River.

Chapter 12

Chisago Lake

It was here that the first Swedish settlement in Minnesota had its beginning. Lake Chisago, which lies in the southern part of the county by the same name, has the shape somewhat of a snowplow, pointed towards the north, stretching southward in two branches, the western one larger and longest. The shores would measure 40 miles were one to include all the bays and arms, nowhere is there a broad expanse of water. The water level is not as high now as in the early days when the Swedish pioneers settled here. In general the land in the Northwest has dried significantly. In many places where 25-40 years ago there were pools and ponds there are now bogs and meadows. The reason is to be found in the clearing of the woods and the cultivation of the earth. There are a number of smaller lakes around Chisago Lake which undoubtedly originally were connected with it. To the west and southwest are Sunrise and Green Lakes, to the northeast Little Lake, and Long Lake to the southeast. The entire area between the St. Croix and Sunrise rivers down towards Marine is a leafy wood on hilly ground, but a few miles beyond the St. Croix the land becomes more level, interspersed with knolls, swamps, and lakes. In some bogs there was an abundance of tamarack (Larix Americana), a tree useful for many purposes. In the center of this wooded area, about 9 miles west of Taylor's Falls on the St. Croix River, lies Chisago Lake, for a long time hidden in the forest. Human cultivation has of course brought new elements of beauty to these shores, but not everywhere has nature been improved on. Anyone who saw this landscape panorama in all its virgin state, when the shores, promontories and lakes gloried in the various kinds of leafy trees and here and there a pine, will hardly forget the view, and willingly admit that Nature excels art. This lake now serves as a center for a large Swedish population. In recent years it has become renowned as a place of summer recreation, and many wealthy American families are beginning to spend summers here. Whether it will be an advantage or a liability for the former, simple rural life, remains to be seen. Center City is now the county seat. It has a railroad, county offices, hotel, bath houses and boats for use or pleasure. There stands too, after the fire, the stately Lutheran Church and a smaller Methodist church. But we are not now concerned about Chisago Lake as it is today, but with this community as it came to be and its early history.

Chisago Lake's First Colonists

Among those who spent the winter 1850-51 in Andover and Moline, Ill. was Per Anderson from Hassela parish, Helsingland. We have already met him in Chapter 1 and saw that he was leader of one of the immigrant groups that came to America in the autumn of 1850. In his native place he was always called Jorris Pelle, from Jorris, the name of the farm he owned and lived on, a comfortable Finn home in the western part of the parish where the people were of Finnish origin. Thus he was a Finn woods peasant. A Finn woods peasant considers it an almost absolute necessity of this life to have plenty of space, large forests, lakes, fishing, hunting grounds, and an inexhaustible source of fresh air; good farming land he considers of less value. So it is not to be wondered at that Per Anderson did not want to stay in Illinois under any terms, though Esbjörn and some of his fellow travellers tried to persuade him to do so. Economically he was well off in Sweden, and though he had a large family and beyond that helped many others to come to America he still had quite a few hundred dollars on his arrival here. To characterize him further one could say that he was well-versed in his class, had read widely and was able to write and count readily, but he was a poor farmer and business man. In temperament he was very amenable, in fact too much so, unselfish, and helpful to such a degree that he hurt himself. He was clear in his understanding of God's Word and did not lack Christian experience.

During the winter of 1851 while he was in Moline he began to exchange letters with E.U. Nordberg, who, as we have seen, was then in the St. Croix valley, and I still remember the tempting letters, along with a map of the Chisago Lake, that he received from him. Thus is was that Per Anderson reached the firm resolve to travel to Minnesota the next Spring and find the said lake.

So in the Spring of 1851 Per Anderson and family, together with a hired hand, Daniel Rattig — now in Colorado, — (another of his servants, Peter Sjolin, now in Cambridge, Isanti County came during the summer by a different route) and several other families journeyed up the Mississippi northward. Two of these families, Anders Ersson from Grängsjö in Gnarp and Anders Anderson from Torp parish in Medelpad, stopped near Lansing, Iowa, where some of their acquaintances had settled the year before. According to Per Anderson the two families who accompanied him to Chisago Lake were those of Per Berg from Högs parish, who had come over with the "old man of Stenbo," and P. Wicklund from Ångermanland. Pastor Cederstam (*Hemlandet*, 2 year, no. 6) says that beside these three there was a fourth family, from Östergötland, which came to Chisago Lake from Illinois. In the following letter, the first that Per Anderson wrote to me after his moving to Chisago Lake, no mention is made of the fourth family. Nevertheless it is certain that such a family came at the same time, and according to some, along with him, for they joined the other three on the same boat at Galena. In a letter addressed to "E.U. Nordberg, Chisago Lake, Taylor's Falls County, Minnesota Terr." dated "Bishop Hill August 21, 1851" and signed by J. Hellsen, inquiry is made about a specified family from "Östergyllen." The family is supposed to have come from St. Louis and been somehow involved with a widow who had come to Bishop Hill from St. Louis. Nordberg is therefore asked to "spy out" if the family was in his neighborhood.

In the aforementioned article in *Hemlandet* Pastor Cederstam writes: "Nordberg on account of whose letters they had struck out to find this lake, met them in Taylor's Falls and helped them to find the lake and to clear a way for them from Taylor's Falls. N. stayed here until Fall that year, then suddenly left the place and since then has not been seen in the settlement."

According to the information which I received in 1854 when I was there and wrote down and then published in *Hemlandet* 1855, the small party had a difficult time in locating the lake. They had to spend one night in the forest and only on the second day discovered the lake. From this I concluded that Nordberg was not with them, for it is only 9 miles from Taylor's Falls to the lake. Had he been at the lake before and been able to describe it, he would not have needed to get lost in the woods. But probably it only proves that he had not himself been at the lake before, or maybe only once, and so was not sure of the way to find it.

Only a few houses were then to be found in Taylor's Falls, and our colonists had a hard time getting a roof over their heads while a path was being cleared to the lake. It took 10 days before a way could be made through forest and over swamps and they could transport women, children, and their baggage to the lake. A small cabin was hastily constructed below the present Lutheran parsonage toward the bay, right in the thick forest. So they were at the goal of their journey.

Per Anderson's First Letter from and about Chisago Lake.

"Chisago Lake, Sept. 7, 1851.

My thoughts have often been of you this summer, but I have not been able to write you since I haven't had your address. However I received both of your most welcome letters eight days ago. Both I and my family were very happy to see that you are alive both in body and soul. Time did not allow me to send a reply by the earlier mail, which goes and comes every Tuesday. But now I want to write and tell you that all of us are alive and have been blessed with good health since we parted in Moline up to the present. — We now have our home beside the large lake in Minnesota which last winter we saw on E.U. Nordberg's map. Its natural shape is more remarkable than was shown on the map, with a great many isles and peninsulas. It is well suited for living space and spacious enough for a large settlement. The earth is quite good and fruitful. The land is wooded — no dry prairies, but fit for cultivation, with many moist places luxuriant in grass. The fine woods provide for all the needs of the farmer. On the whole the land is level, somewhat hillier and sloping towards the lake.

"There are now 10 of us who started farming this summer, 9 Swedes and 1 American. Only 3 of us have families, P. Wiklund, P. Berg, and I. The others are single men, but I hope that before long the population will increase significantly, for here is room for several parishes and the climate is healthful and splendid. Of course there will be some difficulties the first year to get everything in order in this wilderness. It is 10 miles to the closest neighbors, who are new settlers. They have been on their farms 3 or 4 years and are now in good circumstances. Food is more expensive here than in Illinois. A barrel of flour here costs 5-6 dollars, meat is 10-12 cents a pound. A laborer is paid 20, 25, 30 dollars a month almost any month of the year. We expect to work our farms with good success if we have health and all goes well. In a word, as I see it, we have the most suitable place for Swedes to settle, not for the first year, but for the future. There is no lack of good fishing and hunting. As for churchly matters I must say that it is depressing at present, because there are so few, almost none, to talk with about the unmerited grace in Christ — There are indeed here no controversies, but rather everything religious is dead. But my hope is in the Lord that He will soon establish a congregation here." He mentions also that letters from Burlington (Iowa) tell of several Swedes coming from there as well as from Lansing, and that they had written to immigrants arriving in New York advising them to come to Chisago Lake, etc.

Life in the Wilderness

"These 4 families" wrote Cederstam, "lived about two years in this solitude. Two are still here, the others have moved closer to Taylor's Falls.[1] The first house built still stands (1856), it is 10 ft. square and 8 ft. from floor (earth) to roof. This log cabin served during the first summer and autumn 15-16 persons as to what was necessary indoors. No one had any great means. One of the families was in debt for the journey from Illinois and owned beside necessary clothing only, as the expression goes, "an axe and a knife." They lived mainly on the rich yields of lake and forest which have made it possible for poor Swedes to make their way here."

From other excerpts of letters from Per Anderson I can give further details of life in the wilderness during these pioneer days. Jan. 1, 1853 he wrote: "We have been overwhelmed by all the work and toil to get house and necessary provisions for the winter. We completed our new house sufficiently in mid-November to be able to move in. It is not a large building — square in shape, with attic, put together in Swedish manner. We had church service here for the first time on Advent Sunday — the first time indoors, we had service earlier in the summer. We have, in all simplicity, celebrated here the birth of our Saviour. Also today we have had a service, and intend so to continue until our congregation grows and the Lord sends servants in His vineyard. I hope this will not take too long, since our settlement has increased somewhat already and now consists of 16 newly started farms. If all come who intend to come in the Spring it will mean a considerable addition. One Swede came in the Fall from Burlington, Iowa, and has taken land here. He says that many in that settlement expect to come here in the spring. As you said, I have written to my acquaintances in various places encouraging them to move here. — Jonas Westerlund and his cousin Anders Westerlund came in the Fall, found land and began to work. Erik Westerlund (the elder) will

---

[1]Norelius thinks the "two" should be "three still here" and only one, Wiklund, had moved.

come in the Spring, and others. — I learned long ago that G. Palmquist had come (to America), but I have not had his address, so I
could not write to him, — but I have heard that he plans to come
here in the summer."

"Chisago Lake, January 18, 1852 — I can tell that since the
middle of December we have had a steady cold period, but neither
bitter winds nor storms. Snow fell at the end of November and has
remained on the ground, giving us very pleasant sleighing. The snow
is now 5-6 inches deep, and I like the winter better here than in
Illinois."

"Chisago Lake, March 21, 1852. — I must complain that I am
depressed as to my spiritual life. Though I have, thanks and praise to
God, the Word of God, I miss brethren in the faith with whom I can
freely speak of the secrets of the soul and the grace in Christ. I look
for G. Palmquist as the bird waits for dawn, but I am fearful that
there may be hindrances, for Sandman and his comrades (in Lansing, Iowa) cannot be persuaded to come here this spring. They say
that they have no desire ever to come here if Palmquist agrees to stay
there."

"Chisago Lake, May 23, 1852. — The whole Spring has been
very wet, so we have had great difficulty in burning the timber we
cut during the winter where we intend to plant for the summer. Now
we have a lovely summer and a charming nature. The water glitters
from the sunbeams through the groves filled with leaves and flowers. If
the church and congregation were as flourishing in spiritual things I
would consider the area vastly more valuable. May the Lord guide to
the best! My hope is in Him, for I know that He is able to do more
than we can pray for or think." Then he goes on to repeat how Palmquist is awaited.

August 18, 1852 he writes about a trip he took to the Lansing
area in Iowa, to meet Sandman and his neighbors and to find out
about Palmquist, as well as to induce them to come to Chisago Lake.
But there he got sad news. "Had I come 14 days earlier it would have
been better, for then I would have had a chance to speak to your
brother, H. Smitt and Palmquist, who at that time were on their excursion, if I may so call it. H. Smitt went back from Columbus (near
Lansing), Palmquist and E. Sund from Stillwater, since there was no
boat to Taylor's Falls, and they dared not undertake the 30 miles by
land." Thus nothing came of the hope that the many acquaintances,
who were expected, would come to Chisago Lake. Even sadder was

this information: "I read a letter from Palmquist when I was in Iowa, which upset me greatly — the news that Palmquist had gone over completely to the Baptists. It seemed to me that in this matter the devil was the whitest he had ever been or could be. For all the friends and brethren in the faith who truly are enlightened in the Word and who had heard Palmquist preach, claim that never before had they heard any one who proclaimed the Word so purely and truly as he, and who so carefully distinguished between justification [by faith] and false self-righteousness. In a word, of those I had met he was considered a chosen vessel of God, and I fear that many take him as a model and without further searching in the Word will accept the Baptist doctrine. — Palmquist says among other things in the letter where he tells of his entrance into the new church, 'This was the most blessed day I have experienced. Before, I was a child of God and saved, but now I have experienced what it means to be risen with Christ through baptism unto death' — From this and similar words I understand that he now first had discovered the right spiritual life, and presumably he says what he believes. I understand that he has written to you and describes his conviction, but I cannot but let you know what I learned, since I consider the matter important and would like to hear your explanation and testimony about it. I consider my baptism completely valid on account of the commandment and promise of Christ, and if any children are born in this neighborhood I would see it as my duty to bring them to baptism without delay. For the Word says clearly that unless one is born of water and the Spirit he cannot see the kingdom of God."

The First Visit of a Pastor at Chisago Lake

He wrote about this on September 17, 1852: "Today we had the honor of having for the first time a pastor at Chisago Lake. Unonius from Chicago has been here and administered the Lord's Supper. It was of course festive, but one thing was missing, namely the mystery of the Gospel, which exceeds all human understanding. He preached the Word of God just well enough and defended the sacraments altogether according to our Confessions, but in all respects just like the State Church of Sweden. — He strongly exhorted us not to depart from our Confessions and warned us carefully against the Baptists and other sects. He claimed that no one not ordained had the right to perform pastoral acts, for example, baptism and told us to turn to

English speaking pastors of the Episcopal Church if such acts were needed. To me this is not important, for I value the commandment and word of Christ more than ordination and clerical robe, if an emergency occurs. But there really are many who would object if we should venture to do anything of this sort. Be kind and give me some advice on this when next you write.

"Unonius will surely push for a rapid settlement of this region, and this Fall the population seems to have increased considerably. Five or six families are now on the way who are expected today or tomorrow, and Unonius said he would direct a large number here next Spring. He has even asked the governor in St. Paul to reserve the land adjoining the settlement for prospective Swedish settlers and this has been granted. If there were some 30 families here next summer there would be space for a Swedish colony. He promised, or rather offered, to arrange for a pastor to come as soon as possible and planned to make a trip to Sweden next Spring to secure pastors there to come to this country. I could not oppose him, but thought to myself, "Lord send Those workers in Thy vineyard, Thou knowest who are most fit."

One can conclude from this that Unonius had expressed himself in this manner and what were his ideas. Possibly too he may have spoken to the governor about reserving land around Chisago Lake for Swedish settlers, but certainly the governor could do nothing of this kind directly, wherefore the above must be interpreted more as a pious wish than as a contract. The same letter gives us this information: "It has been a very dry summer, but I can still say that our crops have suffered very little. But now, in the night between the 13 and 14th we had frost. This damaged the corn and what had been planted late — what had been planted at the right time was ripe and mostly harvested, so that we do not count on a failure." Returning to the religious matter, he wrote: "I can mention that Unonius read your letter and declared your refutation of the Baptists entirely satisfactory and advised all to learn from it." On November 21, 1852 he gave information on events and conditions in the settlement, for instance Daniel Rattig had been down in Rock Island and Moline and come back with a number of persons who thus added to the small community; that a daughter had been born in his own family, whom he had asked Carl Carlsson from Thorbjörnstorp, a former church vestryman who was then in Chisago Lake, to baptize, but he declined whereupon Per Anderson himself performed the baptism according to the rite in the old Swedish Psalmbook and Lectionary, and called her Kristina. This was the first Swedish child born and baptized at Chisago Lake. He adds that, from what he had heard, next Spring they should be prepared for an attack by the Baptist contingent down in Illinois, but he comforted himself because "the Lord alone is mighty to preserve and keep His Word and teaching uncorrupted, wherever He pleases, even if the devil and all false spirits were ten times as strong and deceitful as they are." To several direct questions he answered, "Undoubtedly wheat will grow here. The land in our neighborhood is settled by only 10-12 new farmers around Taylor's Falls, and they are mostly from the states of Maine and New York, 2 or 3 Germans, no Frenchmen as far as I know. The forests here consist principally of linden, oak, elm, ash, sugar maple, walnut, etc. Money has been scarce this year because the river has been so low that timber could not be floated out to market. A cow costs $30, a horse $100, a barrel flour 5-6 dollars, 1 bushel corn 75 cents to a dollar, 1 bushel potatoes $1, a coat from $5 to $15, boots $4-$5. We have already had more snow than at any time the former winter."

For further light on conditions during 1853 I would add still more excerpts from Per Anderson's letters. On February 9, 1853 he wrote from Rice River Camp, 60 miles northwest of Chisago Lake, where he was spending the winter in cutting lumber: "We have here had almost 4 feet of snow this winter and rather severe cold some days, but not as evenly cold as last winter. — You ask what guarantee we have on the land we have taken possession of. To this I shall have to reply that none of us have yet taken legal preemption on our land, since there has not been any question of trouble with Americans who might want to force us out. We intend to delay as long as possible in order to postpone the time of payment. The place is not close to the highway or the town, so there is unoccupied land for several miles in all directions from us. — We know that we cannot lay claim to more than 160 acres per person, but I have no fear that there won't be enough Swedes here." He always had something to say about religious matters, and principally he spoke about his fears of the intrusions the Baptists might attempt. In this letter there is mention too of Unonius. "I have again had a letter from Unonius," he says, and "he offers to become our pastor next Fall. I have not answered him, but I declare frankly that I do not agree with this, though the majority around me favor him."

"Chisago Lake May 18, 1853. There have been many people the whole time. I do not recall a day when the family has been by itself since I came home in the Spring, on March 25th." Several single persons and families of his acquaintances and companions on the voyage from Sweden came up from Illinois in the Spring, but most of them were Baptists or Baptist inclined so this did not give him much joy. He mentions too that his brother Daniel Lindstrom and many others were expected in the Fall, direct from Sweden. He is planning how to accommodate them, especially if they come late in the Fall.

June 7, 1853 he wrote on the same topic and as I was soon leaving for New York he asked me to guide the party that was awaited from Sweden to Chisago Lake. Again he wrote me, on August 7th, when I was in New York, and expressed his misgivings about finding room for a large group over the winter, especially if there were many without means. Many had come during the summer, especially from Småland, so there was a scarcity of lodging and not much surplus food, for the land was new and not yet extensively cultivated. The party did come so late that it was necessary to spend the winter in Illinois, but the following Spring and Summer many continued on to Chisago Lake. As I myself accompanied them from Rock Island and for the first time saw Chisago Lake, staying there from May 24 to September 11, 1854, I can from my own observations describe the settlement as it then appeared. There were few houses in Taylor's Falls. As far as I can remember no Swedish family lived there then, but at a distance from the town towards the lake there were some Swedes, Anders Anderson the wainwright and his son-in-law Daniel Fredin, Peter Wiklund who had moved here from the lake, and a brother, and a Bylund, all three from Ångermanland — possibly some others. Fred Lammers, whose wife was Swedish — a daughter of Daniel Nilson in Marine, — also lived here, but closer to town. The road to the lake did not then go where it does now, but in many bends and was extremely bad. It was very difficult to drive with a load, but then there were not many that drove. What one bought in town one carried on one's back or in one's hands. Between A. Anderson's place and the lake there were yet no tenants. The first house one came to was Per Anderson's, south of the road, diagonally across from P. Shelins towards the bay. A little westward P. Berg lived, on the land of the present parsonage, on the south side of the road. This was the site of the first house at Chisago Lake — the above mentioned log cabin, which remained many years. On the peninsula, where

Centre City and the Church now stand — long called the Nordberg-holm after E.U. Nordberg, the first to possess it — Frans Mobeck had his home and possibly also Anders Swensson. North of P. Berg's place a path led through the woods to Little Lake. On that path was Hans Smitt's home and close by that of P. Norelius. North of Little Lake and towards the west was Daniel Peterson who later moved to the New London area. On the south shore of Little Lake were the homes of P. Kron and B. Franklin, who later sold his place to Peter Swenson from Elleholm in Blekinge. On the west shore of the same lake was the home of Peter Lund, who moved to Grove City. On the north side were Hokan Swedberg, A.P. Norelius, and some whose names I do not remember. Returning to the large lake we find Magnus Olsson and A.M. Ahlstrom and others toward the north. On the east shore by the bay Peter Johanson lived next to Per Anderson, and towards the south were Anders Molin and Peter Svenson. Among well known places on the southeast and south sides were those of Magnus Jonasson, Glader, Garberg, and on the so-called "clamp" — the peninsula between the two branches of the lake — were the homes of Nord, Nojd, D. Lindstrom, et. al. The many who arrived in the summer took land everywhere in the woods around the lake in all directions. They cleared small plots around the log cabins, burned up the wood, hacked up the earth between the stubs and planted whatever they could.

A vital factor in the establishment of the economic strength of the Chisago Lake was the necessity of "cutting your coat according to your cloth." It was a long way to any city and in the little village of Taylor's Falls no one enjoyed any credit, even for five cents. This forced people to live frugally to get along with the fewest possible necessities, and to cultivate inventiveness in meeting the first, natural needs. They built their homes of timber that grew on their own property, made their furniture of the same material, often using wooden pins in place of nails. So also they wrought their simple tools. They cut their grain with a scythe and threshed it with a hand flail, sometimes, in the early days using the ice as threshing floor. They did not think of earning money by their farming, they strove to keep alive. Clothing was simple, quite often they used home made wooden shoes — the Americans called them the "Wooden Shoe People." But in a few years it turned out that those who looked with contempt on the wooden shoes had to give up their farms while the wooden shoe people stayed on. This happens many a time. The Chisago Lake people tugged slowly ahead this way and learned to economize strictly. Thus they also learned how to be independent and self-sustaining, and the Chisago folk have retained this trait probably more than many other Swedish settlements, even when they have become affluent.

The surrounding country, especially to the Northwest, was even at that time largely unknown, and I remember with what delight I undertook small exploratory trips in the wilderness. Thus Sunrise Lake, Sunrise River, and Sunrise Prairies were discovered. Of course some had found them before, but they were unknown by the greater part of the new settlers. East of Sunrise Lake, in the very heart of the thick forest, I came across the solitary cabin of a hermit. When the Swedes first came to Chisago Lake they found on a forest-clad island in the lake one lone cabin, inhabited by an American named Van Raensler. The island, which contains about 7 acres and lies near the railroad station, was in those days unusually lovely. The forest has long since been cut down and now the place is altogether prosaic. Van Raensler was no longer happy with people around, so he moved farther into the wilderness, where I now came across his new cabin. Many years later I learned that he had overcome his shyness and begun again to live among other people.

We return now to the account of Pastor Cederstam in *Hemlandet* for 1856: "In 1853 and 1854 the settlement received its largest increase of immigrants from various parts of Sweden, from Ångermanland to the southern areas of Skåne. Undoubtedly the Chisago settlement is among those of rapid growth. This is clear when we compare the present with what the situation was a few years ago. From 4 families it has grown to over 500 persons, according to a census, and in wealth from nothing to almost $20,000. This fact alone speaks for itself if we recall that nearly all came here without money, and some in debt. To be noted, too, is that a number, both of single persons and families, have come here since the census of last summer. We can be very hopeful as to the future as the settlement becomes known and gets into communication with neighbors and surrounding places — hitherto we have been hidden from everybody. We have had only one road, and that a poor one, to Taylor's Falls, the closest place for us to buy necessities. There we have had to pay at very high prices, while receiving only what it pleased the buyer to give for what we had to sell. This has now changed and we have reason to believe that we have come to a better land as far as temporal affairs are concerned.

More roads have been opened up, so more tradesmen have found the way to us, both to buy what we had produced and to bring in what we may have needed. The result is that many of the oldest settlers have now exchanged their log houses for quite comfortable homes, built in old Swedish style, and many other conveniences, hitherto unknown, have found their way here.

"In another respect the community has reason to be proud, for probably in no other place in the United States, with the exception of Bishop Hill in Illinois, is there a colony that has its own election district with Swedish judges and clerks, and Swedish justices, etc. so that controversies can be settled in our native language, when such arise. — In a word, given a few years the settlement will hardly recognize itself. Beyond doubt there will be within five years a railroad from St. Paul to Lake Superior, and will go on one side or the other of Chisago Lake — the land on both sides has already been surveyed for this purpose. A highway has already been voted to run between St. Anthony Falls and Taylor's Falls, which will go through the center of the settlement. Work has already begun on two towns, one on the east, one on the west. There is a store in the eastern location (Centre City?). By next summer there will be a shop, saw-mill and steam engine in the western location (Chisago City?). There will be several mills within 10 miles. All of this will be to the advantage of the settlement. The land around the lake has all been bought up, but within 1 or 2 miles north and northeast of the settlement there are still areas just as attractive, in the opinion of some, even more so, than the lake property, at $1.25 per acre.

"I could tell of a number of remarkable things here but will mention only a few, in order not to tire the reader. At a small channel in Chisago Lake there are two unusual, round mounds across from each other on either side of the straits, one on an island, the other on the mainland. They are conical in shape and clearly indicate that they were raised by human hands. Some of the Swedes living here opened one of the mounds in March 1854 to discover the contents. From the top they dug a hole about 12 feet down, and found that it was a burial mound. For at a depth of about 6 feet they began to find human bones. The deeper they dug the earth became looser, so that they could easily insert rods to the right or left of the sides of the mound. The earth inside was filled with fine roots or vines plaited together into a sort of turf. Between these clumps were parts of skulls and other parts of human skeletons. Most of the bones however were crumbled into dust.

It looked as if the corpses had been laid carefully one layer above another. These mounds are now entirely covered with thick leafy trees. The mounds are around 20 feet in height and 36 feet in diameter. A little distance from these there is one of the lake's many islets, this one measuring about 3 acres of cultivable land, with plainly marked traces of ancient cultivation. Here and there are small heaps of stones in order, indicating fenced off portions, on the sides and slopes of the island. When the Swedes came this island had just as thick forest as the rest of the area around this lovely and remarkable lake. Who piled up these mounds? Who had planted on this island?"

We give herewith a list of the oldest settlers at Chisago Lake and the places in Sweden from which they came, but only of those who had come from Sweden before 1855. The names are copied from the old record book of the Swedish Lutheran Church, compiled by Pastor Cederstam 1855. Since the greater part of the people belonged to the Lutheran congregation we may suppose that there were few at that time not on the list. I remember some of them, but after a few years they had left the place, such as Hans Smitt and family, Jonas Norell, Per Norell, and many others.

Arrived in America 1850

Per Anderson and family from Hassela in Helsingland
Daniel Rattig and wife from Hassela in Helsingland
L.P. Sjolin from Hassela in Helsingland
Per Berg and family from Hög in Helsingland
Anders Swensson and family from Kittilstad, Linköping County
L.J. Stark from Lidköping
    wife Amalia C. Lengquist from Karlshaun

1851

Johan Smith from Örtomta in Linköping County
Jonas Anderson from Örtomta in Linköping County
Claes Dahlhjelm jr from Wallerstad, Linköping County
A.M. Dahlhjelm sr. from Wallerstad, Linköping County
Magnus Olsson and wife from Brunflo in Jämtland

1852

Peter Joh. Kron from Algutsboda in Kronoberg County
Mathis Bengtson from Örkened in Kristianstad County
Per Joh. Lund from Oppmanna in Kristianstad County
    wife from Wånga in Kristianstad County
Eric Abrahamsson and wife from Wårdsnäs in Östergötland

Carl Jonasson Lind from Hoffmanstorp in Kronoberg County
Carl Mag. Petersson and wife from Nöbbeled in Kronoberg County
Truls Lindquist from Örkened in Kristianstad County
Anders Peter Andersson and family from Örtomta, Linköping County
Magnus Jonasson from Linneryd, wife and children from
    Hoffmanstorp in Kronoberg County
Joh. P. Back from Gårdsby, his wife Inga Lena Swensdotter
    from Wist in Östergötland
Anders Peter Andersson from Örtomta in Linköping County
Frans Mobeck and family from Stenberga in Kronoberg County
                          1853
Anders P. Norelius and family from Hassela in Helsingland
P. Norelius and family from Hassela in Helsingland
Jonas Norelius and family from Hassela in Helsingland
Tufve Pehrsson and family from Glimåkra in Kristianstad County
Nils Pehrsson and wife Nilla from Glimåkra in Kristianstad County
Johan P. Abrahamsson and wife from Långasjö in Kronoberg County
Johannes J. Lonnquist from Dädesjö in Kronoberg County
    wife from Östra Thorsås in Kronoberg County
Erik Garberg and wife from Linneryd in Kronoberg County
Nils Hokansson and family from Algutsboda in Kronoberg County
Petr. Magnus Johansson and family from Algutsboda in Kronoberg
    County
Joh. Petersson Stenberg and family from Algutsboda in Kronoberg
    County
Peter Joh. Carlsson from Hoffmanstorp in Kronoberg County
    wife from Elmeboda in Kronoberg County
Anders Swensson Ogren and wife from Hoffmanstorp in Kronoberg
    County
Daniel Petersson and family from Ö. Thorsås in Kronoberg County
Joh. Helin from Hoffmanstorp in Kronoberg County
    and family from Dädesjö in Kronoberg County
Peter Johansson and family from Algutsboda in Kronoberg County
Joh. Johnson and wife Maria Petersson from Algutsboda in
    Kronoberg County
Daniel Nilsson from Ö Thorsås in Kronoberg County
Hokan Larsson Swedberg and family from Backaryd in Blekinge
    County
And. Mag. Ahlstrom and family from Elghult in Kronoberg County
Joh. Hokansson, former teacher from Wexiö rural parish

Daniel Lindstrom and wife from Hassela in Helsingland
John Johnsson from Hinneryd in Kronoberg County
And. G. Blom from Ö Thorsås in Kronoberg County
Peter Johansson and family from Ö Thorsås in Kronoberg County
Joh. Jonasson Lind and wife from Hoffmanstorp in Kronobreg
       County
Swen Mag. Peterson and family from Algutsboda in Kronoberg
       County
And. Janssons from Täfvelsås in Kronoberg County
       wife Helena Nilsdotter from Furuby in Kronoberg County
Carl J. Lind's wife Lena Kajsa Jonasdotter from Hoffmanstorp
       in Kronoberg County
Claes Dahlhjelm's wife Eva Karlsdotter from Dädesjö, Kronoberg
       County
And. Peter Jonasson Lind from Hoffmanstorp in Kronoberg County
Nils Nilsson from Gammalstorp in Blekinge
Joh. Pet. Qvarfot from Ljuder in Kronoberg County
Joh. Okesson from Hofby in Blekinge
Mans Okesson from Hofby in Blekinge
Ola Jonasson and wife from Tving
Anders Pet. Glader and family from Hoffmanstorp in Kronoberg
       County
Carl Svensson Ek from Dädesjö
Nicol. Jonasson and family from Elmeboda
Carl Peter Dolk and family from Dädesjö
Johan Johansson and wife from Hoffmanstorp and Östra Thorsås in
       Kronoberg County
Swen Magnusson from Wexiö
Gustaf Jonsson Hultqvist from Ingatorp, Jonköping County
       wife from Sund in Linköping County
Jonas Magnus Molin and wife from Asarum in Blekinge
Caroline Molin from Asarum in Blekinge
Carl Israelson and wife from Tving
Erik Magnussons wife Johanna Jonasdotter from Hoffmanstorp
Carl Abrahamson's family from Långasjö in Kronoberg County
Peter Gustaf Gustafson and family from Elmeboda in Kronoberg
       County
Lorens Johansson and family from Hoffmanstorp in Kronoberg
       County
Tufve Pehrsson from Brody

family from Glimåkra in Kristianstad County
Otto Ferd. Makrill from Linneryd
    family from Tving in Blekinge
Oke Johnsson and family from Asarum in Blekinge
Pater Magnus Petterson and wife from Hoffmanstorp and Linneryd
Carl Gustaf Pehrson and wife from Linneryd and Ronneby
And. M. Molins wife Stina Svensdotter with children from former
    marriage from Algutsboda in Kronoberg County
And. Janson Porters wife Helena Nilsdotter from Furuby in
    Kronoberg County
John Carlsson, hired hand from Furuby in Kronoberg County
                            1854
Swen Nilsson and family from Örkened in Kristianstad County
Nils Hokan Bystrom from Hofby in Blekinge
    wife from Wäckelsång in Kronoberg County
Jons Nilson and family from Hjersås and Vånga in Kristianstad
    County
Samuel Peterson and wife from Elmeboda and Furuby in Kronoberg
    County
Peter Peterson from Elmeboda and Furuby in Kronoberg County
Helena Magnusdotter, widow and family from Elmeboda in
    Kronoberg County
Tufve Trulson from Knisslinge in Kristianstad County
Peter Swenson and family from Jemshög in Blekinge
Gustaf Collin and family from Elmeboda in Kronoberg County
Peter Person and family from Dädesjö in Kronoberg County
Johan Jonasson from Dädesjö in Kronoberg County
Anders Carlsson and wife from Hoffmanstorp in Kronoberg County
Carl Gustaf Paulsson from Hoffmanstorp in Kronoberg County
Elias P. Fast and wife from Nöbbeled in Kronoberg County
Peter Anderson from Herråkra in Kronoberg County
Johannes Pehrson and family from Dädesjö in Kronoberg County
Frans O. Moqvist from Hoffmanstorp in Kronoberg County
Carl Gustaf Johansson and wife from Östra Thorsås in Kronoberg
    County
Sven Carlson Kron and wife from Dädesjö in Kronoberg County
J. Helins wife Sara Eriksdotter from Dädesjö in Kronoberg County
    her sons in former marriage Carl and Jacob from Dädesjö in
    Kronoberg County
David Pehrson and wife from Elmeboda and Linneryd in Kronoberg

County
Kajsa Erengisslesdotter, widow and children from Linneryd in
    Kronoberg County
John Smith's wife Maja Lena Jonasdotter from Elmeboda
Mathis Bengtson's wife Hanna Nilsdotter from Örkened in
    Kristianstad County
John Johnson's wife Kajsa Petersdotter from Elmeboda in
    Kronoberg County
Nils Daniel Andersson and family from Furuby in Kronoberg County
Jonas Eriksson and family from Dädesjö and Gårdsby in Kronoberg
    County
Mathis Mickelson and family from Asarum and Dädesjö in
    Kronoberg County
Jonas J. Nojd and wife from Örtomta in Linköping County
Jons Olsson from Ronneby in Blekinge
Johannes J. Elmqvist and family from Elmeboda in Kronoberg
    County
Magnus Peterson and wife from Dädesjö and Täfvelsås in Kronoberg
    County
Mag. Magnusson from Elmeboda in Kronoberg County
Kristina Peterson from Dädesjö in Kronoberg County
Johan Hokanson and family from Furuby in Kronoberg County
And. P. Lind's wife Stina Peterson from Dädesjö in Kronoberg
    County
Swen Nilsson and family from Hemsjö in Kronoberg County
Carl Samuelson and family from Örtomta in Linköping County
Joh. J. Brage and family from Ölmstad in Jönköping County
Carl P. Bolin and wife from Ronneby in Blekinge
Carl Joh. Korsberg from Furuby in Kronoberg County
Carl J. Ljungqvist from Asarum in Blekinge
Peter Swensson from Asarum in Blekinge
Johan Olsson and family from Ronneby in Blekinge
Truls Lindqvist's wife Sissa Mattson from Oppmanna in Kristianstad
    County
Ola Thomasson from Oppmanna in Kristianstad County
Pehr Mattson from Oppmanna in Kristianstad County
Johan Pet. Nilsson and family from Ö. Thorsås in Kronoberg
    County
Peter Jonsson and family from Ö. Thorsås in Kronoberg County
Carl Jonasson from Ö. Thorsås in Kronoberg County

Peter O. Pettersson and wife from Däsesjö in Kronoberg County
Martha Kajsa Petersdotter from Furuby in Kronoberg County
Gustaf Johanneson from Dädesjö in Kronoberg County
Oke S. Dahlberg and wife from Ronneby and Hofby, Blekinge
Ola Anderson from Backaryd, Blekinge
Carl Johansson from Ö. Thorsås in Kronoberg County
Carl P. Vigren from Långasjö in Kronoberg County
Erik Magnusson from Ö. Thorsås in Kronoberg County
Johannes P. Peterson from Gårdsby in Kronoberg County
Eva Kristina Petersdotter from Hoffmanstorp in Kronoberg County
P.G. Gustafson's wife Sara C. Israelsdotter from Elmeboda in
    Kronoberg County
And. P. Wallmark from Asige in Halland
P.J. Folin and wife from Karlshamn
Hokan J. Dahlstrom and wife from Backaryd in Blekinge
Israel Jonasson from Hoffmanstorp in Kronoberg County
Pehr Masson and family from Oppmanna and Wånga in Kristianstad
    County
Anders Nilsson and wife from Österlöf, Kristianstad County
Jonas Johansson from Jäf in Kronoberg County
Anna Maria Magni from Sandsjö in Kronoberg County
Eskel Trulsson and wife from Knisslinge in Kristianstad County and
    Elmeboda in Kronoberg County
Pet. Joh. Johansson and wife from Furuby and Dädesjö in Kronoberg
    County
Gustaf J. Melander from Ö Thorsås in Kronoberg County
Carl G. Pehrsson's wife Kajsa Nilsdotter from Ronneby in Blekinge
John T. Lindahl and family from V. Thorsås, Kronoberg County
And. P. Anderson's wife Martha Magni from Thorsås, Kronoberg
    County
Johanna Magni from Thorsås, Kronoberg County
Anders Magnus Molin from Asarum in Blekinge
Anders J. Porter and family from Täfvelsäs in Kronoberg County
Otto Alex. Bernh Wallmark and wife from Asige, Halland County
    and Kronoberg County
Johan Magnusson and wife from Nöbbeled in Kronoberg County

The increase in 1855 was very small, almost none at all, because the cholera epidemic of the previous year frightened people from emigrating. A considerable influx occurred between 1856 to 1860, but space does not permit a listing of their names.

The Religious Needs

As the community grew so did its need of satisfying churchly desires. The people as a whole probably felt no deep need of pastoral care, but always there were some who took their Christian faith seriously. And even the rest were accustomed to having a church, pastor, and the sacraments, and were not yet infected by a later period's unbelief and denial. As we have noted a large number came in 1853 and many of them had been in Pastor Erland Carlsson's party from Sweden. When provision had been made for the most pressing demands of physical life and people began to reflect a bit, the church and spiritual needs began more and more to be felt. As yet there was no Lutheran pastor in Minnesota to whom they could turn. So naturally they turned first to Pastor Erl. Carlsson in Chicago with whom many of them were acquainted.

January 27, 1854 Daniel Peterson, in a letter to Pastor Erl. Carlsson, wrote: "We have what we need for our bodily life but we need help for our spiritual life. We come together every Sunday, read and sing, but we need more edification for our souls. A minister by the name of Agrelius has been up here and proclaimed the Word of God satisfactorily, but since he was of another denomination we did not in general go to communion. We look forward to Pastor Carlsson's visit in the Spring. I do hope that Pastor will come — we will of course take care of expenses. I wish that you would stay in our home when you come to the settlement." Agrelius who was a Methodist, was thus the second Swedish minister to visit Chisago Lake. We shall return to him.

In this connection is a curious letter written to pastor E. Carlsson at the same time by A.M. Dalhjelm. I give it in full because of the information it contains about the religous situation at Chisago Lake. He wrote in a grandiloquent style and gives the impression that the writer is pastor in Chisago Lake.

"Most learned and dearest brother in Christ!

Brother's more than welcome letter of last November 24 came to me on the following 12th of December, and I respectfully thank you for it! Long before I had had in mind to write to Brother, but as a Methodist minister has been on his way to this Swedish settlement, I have waited until he had been here. Now he has been here, and his name is Aurelius (Agrelius). I did not go to listen to him, for I only get a troubled conscience from these false teachers' exposition of Holy Scripture. I was confi-

dent that this small, Christian, Lutheran congregation was so
united that he would not be able to deceive any one. But what
happened? He celebrated the Lord's Supper and by his eloquence
misled the following persons to come forward [to the Lord's
table], the old man from Sandsjö, his wife and daughter, Carl
Peterson and his wife, and Glad with his wife, but not his son.
Though they had been strongly dissuaded they could not refrain.
I think they were blind in not seeing the difference in the ceremony. In the distribution of the elements he has not addressed
each one alike, but to one he said one word, to a second, another.
Poor people! I have reproached them and said that no minister
of the Christian, Lutheran faith can condone such a procedure.
I close with the statement that all the religious controversies
here have ceased. Baptists have their own services; once in a
while they may come to ours, but they conduct themselves quiet
and peaceable. Ever since I held a service last Fall and used as
text, 'We preach the Crucified Christ, a stumbling block to Jews
and folly to Gentiles' 1 Cor. 1, 23, and had as theme for the
whole sermon, 'Christ is preached as a stumbling-block to Christians'; the Baptists were present, but since then they have not
ventured to open their mouths, and every thing is calm (!)

"Yes, my brother in Christ, for a year and a half I have now
proclaimed the uncorrupted Word of God for this small Christian
congregation every Sunday and holiday according to the creed
of our forefathers and following the Swedish Church Manual.
Last Christmas I had two services, the first one [ottesång] beginning at 5 o'clock in the morning, with a pretty large attendance.
After the service I received an offering of $6.69 — this was my
salary for the whole period of service. I declined the money for I
am more than willing to preach the Word of God without any
payment. I am no longer able to go on with this work, for I am
weary of years and of life — and because of Jesus my Saviour's
merit I am assured of being able soon to move to the imperish-
able fatherland in heaven.

"During this time of conducting services I have baptized 5
children — one has died — and buried 3. The Lord has called
the small children hence. Blessed be the name of the Lord —
they could leave this perverted world at the right time.

"The faith and confession of our church here rests unshake-
ably on the stone which the builders discarded, and by the
gracious help of Jesus I believe that the gates of hell will not
overthrow it.

"All the Swedes here bid brother welcome here in the Spring,
as early as possible, to prepare them to receive the Lord's Supper—."

He mentions further that "a plan for a church has been drawn up, and that probably during the winter timber will be assembled so that building might start in the Spring." He adds information how Carlsson should travel to Chisago Lake, etc.

Chisago City February 4, 1854 A.M. Dahlhjelm"

D. was undoubtedly in his way a well-intentioned individual, but his unlimited self-confidence and zeal especially for superficial forms spoiled it all. Maybe he had received some general commission from the settlers to lead in their assemblies, but it seems that he went far beyond what they intended. The arrangements that Pastor Carlsson made for the organization of the congregation were seemingly not to his taste, and he assumed a critical attitude when it was formed. Through the whole summer of 1854 when I was there he attended only one service. In Sweden he had been somewhat more than a common soldier and he was unusually well-read. He suffered greatly in his final illness and one dares hope that the dross was refined away before he died.

The Organization of the Congregation

"In the spring of 1854 the Swedes here had a visit by Pastor Erl. Carlsson of Chicago, and on this occasion the present Swedish Lutheran congregation was formed, on May 12, 1854, with around 100 communicant members. And it should here be noted that Pastor E. Carlsson was the first Swedish Lutheran minister to preach the saving Word of God in the Minnesota Territory." (*Hemlandet*, 2nd year, no. 27)

The *Minutes* of this meeting reveal that the same articles of organization which we know from Chicago, Ill. and Attica, Indiana, were adopted here. Pastor Carlsson presided, and the secretary was a former school teacher, John Hokanson, now in Red Wing. The first council consisted of A.M. Dahlhjelm, Per Berg, and Anders Swensson, trustees, and Hokan L. Swedberg, Per Anderson, and Carl Peterson, deacons. John Hokanson was appointed secretary and A.M. Ahlstrom, sexton.

Article 7 of the *Minutes* reads: "Though Mr. Berg graciously promised the use of his house for the regular church gatherings, it was thought best to procure a separate place. Consequently it was resolved to build a Swedish Lutheran 'meeting house' by next summer.

It was to be built on the site already selected whose owner, Anders Fredrik Swensson had promised to sell to the congregation from 1 to 4 acres of land at the government price, and to give a deed to the trustees of the congregation on payment for the land. The building should be 18 yards long, 14 yards wide, and 15 yards high — inside measurements.[1] The lumber was to be secured and the labor and expenses were to be evenly divided between all who were or wanted to be members."

Pastor Carlsson was unable to stay long in Chisago Lake. About a week after he left I arrived with the intention of spending the summer there with my relatives. It was agreed that I should preach for the congregation on Sundays and for a while conduct a school on week-days. The room then was P. Berg's hay barn, built of undressed logs and situated near the present residence, not far from the present Hedengran family home.

Events within the Congregation the summer of 1854.

On May 25, Ascension Day, I preached for the first time at Chisago Lake and continued almost every Sunday until Sept. 10th. In the afternoons I walked to the vicinity of Taylor's Falls and preached for the Swedes living there, then usually returned in the evening. The road through the woods was miserable and the mosquitos so bad that one could manage only by wearing a net before the face. I started a school June 12th — the first such an attempt at Chisago Lake.

On Sunday June 4th when I came to the barn to conduct services I found before me a stately grey-haired man who introduced himself as Pastor Agrelius, a minister from Sweden, now a Methodist preacher. It probably would have been courteous of me to invite him to preach in my place, but I could not do so from personal conviction nor did I have the right on behalf of the congregation to do it. So I preached as usual, but hardly had I ended before Agrelius arose and gave a sermon or address. I did not want to have a scene, so there was nothing else to do but patiently endure him. Patience indeed was necessary to listen long to such twaddle as he dished up. All respect for old gray haired Agrelius, former assistant pastor in Pelarne! But his speech was beneath all criticism. Its substance was, how fortunate the Swedes were who came to America. Here they could

[1]The Swedish word is "alnar" — the aln probably about 24 inches. Trans.

fear God as much as they wished. Fear reigned in Sweden, especially for the Russian bear. For Russia adjoined Sweden north of the Bottnik Gulf and some fine day, the old man believed, the Russian bear would come that way and embrace Sweden between its paws — then it would be good to be away from there. His political musings anent the Russian bear were probably not too far off, but they were meager food for spiritual fare. He continued to be troublesome during most of the summer, attending our services and making his speeches afterwards. If he announced any services of his own he got practically nobody. People tired of him. Creed and custom didn't bother him much. He could offer his services to people in this wise: "If you want it in the Methodist way you can have it, if you want the Lutheran way I can serve you. I know how, for I have been minister in Sweden for 26 years." At least it is reported that he so said on several occasions, and I consider it quite possible, for he had no firm ideas about doctrines. As for his moral character I never heard anything unfavorable about him, and though there was some mystery about his leaving Sweden no one had heard that he was a fugitive from the law. He probably arrived about 1851. He had tried to start a Swedish Lutheran congregation in New York, but he was not the man for such a project. When he failed he had gone over to the Methodists, been converted by Hedstrom, then sent west to work among Scandinavians. This church which he tried so faithfully to serve did not for a long time afford him any support when he became incapacitated, and many years later I heard complaints more than once about this, from non partisan persons. Agrelius lived many years after his travelling around, at Big Lake in the settlement at Marine, Minnesota — probably is there now.

On Sunday June 17 as I had finished the service a stranger stood up and announced a service in the afternoon though he had said nothing to me or to any of the officers of the congregation about it. I had arranged for a service that afternoon at Taylor's Falls and had to leave at once in order to be there. The man was a Baptist preacher Fredrik Nilson. He has a place in the history of the Church of Sweden since he was the first to introduce the Baptist doctrine in Sweden, for which he was exiled. Bishop C.A. Cornelius, in his *Manual of Swedish Church History* says of him, "A seaman of Halland, by name of F.O. Nilson, had been converted to the Baptist sect in America and been baptized again in Hamburg (1847). He returned to his native place and worked there and in Gothenburg as a missionary, succeeding in rebaptizing around 50 persons. The penalty for his proselytizing was exile" — very likely the last such punishment because of religion in Sweden.

To me, however, Nilson was not a stranger. I had met him and Pastor A. Viberg in New York the year before and had a rather serious encounter. During the winter he had been in Illinois and Iowa, gaining not a little success in Iowa. Now he came to Chisago Lake to proselytize. But the self-conceited way in which he obtruded himself among us did not work to his advantage. He was not particularly gifted as a speaker, but he could present his thoughts coherently. He gained no success on this visit and after a week's stay he left. I again met Nilson in 1868 in Gothenburg, to which he had returned after the strict religious laws of Sweden had been modified. He seemed sickly and gloomy, the ardor had greatly subsided. But he was to return to America and play out his last role. Why is it that so many of the Baptists end up as free-thinkers? I would be able to name many of my acquaintances who have moved in that direction — thus also it went with Fr. Nilson. Sad to relate, he became an associate of the notorious "doctor" Erikson and led a dissolute life. A few years ago he died in Houston, Minnesota, only God knows in what a condition! How many had been disturbed in their childhood's faith by that man! And finally he himself cast off his Christian faith altogether and died in this pitiable state. What a warning!

During the summer we had a couple meetings to discuss and to decide the location of the future church building and the erection of the proposed school. It was difficult to reach agreement and the discussions proved fruitless. Yet later in the Fall the school house was built. Many new immigrants from Sweden came during the summer, and the settlement grew rapidly in area and population. For my work that summer I was compensated with $25.[1]

The Calling of a Pastor

In the *Minutes* of organization, section 5, we read, "Since the congregation is without pastor and it is very important to obtain one, it was resolved to join with the Lutheran congregation in St. Paul in extending a call to Pastor Carl Magnus Swensson of the Vexiö diocese to come and assume the spiritual leadership of these congregations.

[1]Cf. "My Reminiscences" in *Korsbaneret*, 1888.

Meanwhile, as hitherto the congregation will meet every Sunday for mutual edification, uniting in faithful prayer to God that in his mercy He will soon send them a faithful shepherd and carer of souls." Pastor Swensson was called but declined, leaving the matter of pastor still open. Early in November the congregation was encouraged by the visit, though short, of Pastor T.N. Hasselquist. Per Anderson took the opportunity of writing about this visit, on Nov. 8, 1854: "His visit here was very brief. He came on Monday evening and was here but one day, going on the following Wednesday morning. He had three services, one on Monday evening, one on Tuesday morning, one in the afternoon, also celebrating the Lord's Supper. At the latter he used Luke 15 as text, giving a wonderful exposition. He told about the Prodigal Son's position and thinking both on his departure from and return to the father's house, in such glowing colors and evangelical spirit that the gables of the new school house could have melted, but I am afraid that not many hearts were moved. Oh, how depraved the human heart is. I cannot forget the formula he used for the absolution at communion, for I felt it was so appropriate and biblical. After the customary confession of sins he said, 'If now your confession of sins agrees with or is similar to that of the Prodigal Son when he came back to the Father's house, then I proclaim etc.' Oh, would that the Lord might bless the dear seed of life which has been sown among us!"

He wrote again on December 10th: "Our church situation is the same as before. We come together every Sunday in the school-house and a sermon is read, which I hope is not without fruit altogether, for God will surely keep his promise, that his Word will not return vain, and I have observed that some of the newcomers listen attentively and reverently. Would to God that we were all thus! It has now been suggested that we call Hasselquist as pastor. A meeting has been called for that purpose on the day after Christmas, to draft a letter and propose what salary the settlement could offer, etc. Everybody seems to want him, and I will not object, for I was very well satisfied with the sermons he gave here, as you remember I mentioned. — I do not know the circumstances and whether or not he can leave the congregations down there. He said nothing about it when he was here, but on his way back he is supposed to have said to H. Swedberg in St. Paul that he would enjoy to live up here. This has led us to call him." He states also that there had been a good deal of sickness that Fall in the settlement.

The call was not accepted. One while it was proposed to send A. Andrén to Chisago Lake for the time being. But Andrén, who was assistant to Pastor Carlsson in Chicago, could not be spared.

The call to Pastor C.M. Swensson [in Sweden] had been sent to Dr. Fjellstedt with authorization to send it to some one else if S. did not accept. This explains how missionary Lundgren was called to become pastor at Chisago Lake. This is evident from a letter by missionary Lundgren to Pastor Carlsson:

> "Tranquebar, November 15, 1854
> Pastor Carlsson:
> My dear Brother!
> My health is failing. I am not able to do the Lord's work in these lands, and must leave India. The physician declared, what I long suspected, that I could not take the tropical climate. Pastor Fjellstedt sent me a letter in your familiar handwriting with your beloved name, containing a call to Pastor Swensson from a congregation in America to become its pastor. Since he declined Fjellstedt transferred the call to me. I accept gladly, if the people in America want me. — I will leave India January 9th, and be in South Hampton February 9th. Write as soon as you get this and give me directions. —
>
> Faithfully yours,
> G.E. Lundgren"

For reasons I do not know Lundgren did not come to America but returned to Sweden. It was during this hopeless awaiting a reply that Hasselquist finally was called. And when he was not able to accept, the prospect of a pastor for the congregation was not bright. When the Conference met in Chicago, the Spring of 1855, it had a letter from Hokan Swedberg on behalf of the congregation with an urgent plea for a pastor. In response the Conference sent "Brother P.A. Cederstam, who had received the Synod's license to exercise the pastoral office, to the fellow countrymen in Minnesota."[1] I return now to his own account.

> "After the congregation here and countrymen in Minnesota had appealed for a long time and loudly to pastors in Sweden and to some in this county to come here and break the bread of

[1] *Hemlandet*, 1st year, no. 7.

life among them, but always in vain, a plea was sent to the Conference which met in Chicago April 11-17, 1855. When the Conference was not in a position to send an older and experienced pastor, who naturally in all respects was needed, they sent me who had just a few months earlier been entrusted with the office of the holy ministry by the authorities of our Church.

"I appeared before this congregation for the first time on Pentecost 1855, and since then have worked here most of the time. A school house was built here in the Fall of 1854, but so small that not a third of the people can find room in it. So we have often had difficulties, but in a new country you cannot expect to have everything convenient. We have often talked about building a church, but for a number of reasons no decisions have been made until this winter. If no accident prevents we will build a church next Spring and Summer, (1856). Contracts have been let, and a start will be made in the middle of June. The building will be 48 feet long, 36 feet wide, and the walls will be 18 feet high, with a vaulted ceiling. — A subscription among ourselves has netted $430 in pledges and I think with a little effort I can double this. We have ourselves cut and donated the lumber (for sills, beams, etc.), to the value of almost $500. The church will be as close as possible to the center of the settlement on a lovely peninsula south of the present school-house, where we have bought two acres of land for the church and a cemetery. I should mention that we have just bought 80 acres of land as church property."

—"The Swedish Evangelical Lutheran congregation here at Chisago Lake consists at present of some over 200 communicants. In my judgment since I came here these members and the people in general have conducted themselves in an honorable manner." He has this to say about the spiritual state: "Of course one can often observe in the lives of many that their hearts are unbroken and hence full of evil and of love to the earthly, but there are also those who are troubled because of this evil and seek help against it."

The Congregation during Cederstam's Pastorate

Laying the foundation of a congregation is of great and inestimable importance for a large part of its history, because it sets the direction of its development. A congregation can consider itself fortunate if this fundamental work is done well and points in a sound direction — unfortunate if otherwise. Pastor Cederstam did a fine

PASTOR P.A. CEDERSTAM.

work at Chisago Lake — only later was it fully appreciated. He himself admitted that he was young and inexperienced. But this was not the main obstacle he had to contend with: A severe handicap lay in the fact that his call was indefinite or temporary. What pastor can pursue his calling in a congregation with a proper boldness in such a situation? He felt that most of the leaders wanted a pastor from Sweden and that he was only an interim leader. Yet no word or act of his can be interpreted as an attempt to alter his attitude for his own benefit. Rather, he sincerely accepted the notion that he was serving the congregation in the meantime and he stood ready to leave as soon as some one else was obtained. When we realize with what interest, self-sacrifice and self-denial he worked under these circumstances our admiration is excited. At the congregational meeting September 9, 1856 when Pastor E. Carlsson was present and was elected as chairman pro. tem. the following resolution was adopted: "Since the term of the one year call to Pastor Cederstam to serve this congregation expires on October 1st, the question of pastor of the congregation was taken up, and by a unanimous vote it was decided that Pastor P.A. Cederstam continue in this office at least for one more year." From the meeting of the congregation December 8th, 1857 we learn: "Then followed the subject of a call to become pastor of the congregation. Pastor Cederstam reminded them that he had been sent here in the Spring of 1855 by the United Chicago and Mississippi Conference, that on September 9, 1856 he had been elected as pastor for at least one year, counting from October 1st and that at the beginning of this year, 1857, he had again been elected for an indefinite period, from October 1st. He declared that he wished to leave the congregation next Spring (1858) and when no objection was raised, it was unanimously resolved to call some other pastor, etc." From these resolutions one can understand the difficulties of his position, as indicated above.

Besides it was not easy to get the people to unite on the site of the church and the building. This subject has in many a rural congregation been one of serious and grievous strife, leading to dissension and discord. It was so in Chisago Lake. No congregational meeting was held from the date of organization May 12, 1854 until July 4, 1855, which was the first one attended by Cederstam. The meeting was held to decide the church site. According to the *Minutes*: "After much discussion and contention about the location for a church building it was decided to accept the offer of Mr. P. Anderson and Mr. Daniel Rattig of a lot for the church at the northeastern corner of the present fenced property of Mr. P. Berg. No objection was made by those present except Mr. P. Johanson and Mr. A. Wallmark. But it was resolved that the congregation should erect the building on this site despite the objections of these two." Yet at a meeting of September 12th, with no mention of the rescinding of the former decision, another resolution was adopted, namely "that the two acres of F. Mobeck on the large opened area on the so-called Nordbeck peninsula be acquired for $50 and this be the church site." The people were unaccustomed to self-government and self-taxation, and it was no easy task to achieve a Christian community order, parliamentary procedure, respect for already agreed on decisions, interest in the church, or willingness to contribute to building of church or other common congregational endeavors. With patience and persistent effort Cederstam succeeded in gradually laying a good foundation for church order and in creating interest in the church. An evidence of this lay in the incorporation of the congregation on

December 5, 1855. The first trustees elected were Peter Anderson for 1 year, Daniel Peterson for 2 years, Hokan Swedberg for 3 years. Presiding at the election were the deacons who were called "Elders" — not a Lutheran term. Further evidence of Cederstam's success was the noteworthy church edifice which was undertaken and accomplished, requiring gifts of money, material, and labor, in amounts very considerable in those days. Cederstam spared no effort in gaining the goal and many were the miles he covered in attaining it. The interior was not furnished during his period but services were held in the building.

In the matter of doctrine there were of course differing tendencies, one toward legalism, one more evangelical. Cederstam had the confidence of both groups, and the differences led to no serious divisions. On July 8, 1855 the congregation decided that in the absence of the pastor the deacons should conduct the service in accordance with the Manual of the Swedish Church, and "since we are Lutherans" a sermon of Luther, preferably from the Postil, should be read. Also, "it was unanimously agreed that in the absence of an Evangelical Lutheran pastor, no pastor or layman of another denomination than the Evangelical Lutheran Synod of Northern Illinois who may be present and wishes to speak or preach shall be permitted to do so before the service as already prescribed shall be concluded." Hokan Swedberg was expressly named as the leader at that time in case of the pastor's absence.

In March 1856 a controversy arose within the congregation regarding ceremonies, and in particular some objected that the pastor, in conformity with a decision of the United Conference, used the word resurrection of the "body" in reciting the Creed. A.M. Dahlhjelm expressed his feelings toward the congregation, the pastor, and the Swedish pastors in America in a series of articles which were read. To get action D. called the members together in a meeting April 20, 1856. It was held at a time the pastor was away. The resolution adopted at the meeting seems to have deflated the intended protest. It read, "the congregation decided to abide with the constitution that Pastor E. Carlsson set up May 12, 1854. If there be any one who does not accept this constitution he will be considered as having left the Lutheran Church in Chisago Lake."

Church discipline presented a more difficult problem. This word "church discipline" was detested in Chisago Lake and in all our congregations in this country because in Sweden the word was associated with legal fines and church-law penalties. There the true Christian discipline had long been neglected and the people had no idea of its meaning. When here pastor or deacons reproached anyone for word or deed it was considered an improper attack on one's personal liberty and an interference in a matter not of someone else's concern. To belong to the congregation, to go to church and listen to the pastor and to receive communion, to have the children baptized and to pay one's dues, etc. was all good and proper, but to be warned, exhorted or spoken to for his behavior beyond this was considered impertinent. If any one did any wrong the civil law was to apply and punish. So it is not to be wondered at that resentment and opposition would greet any attempt at Christian discipline of the members of the congregation. There are a number of examples in the records of the Chisago Lake Lutheran congregation. On midsummer day afternoon 1856 a large crowd had arranged a dance in a wooded place and indulged in drinking. Cederstam had gotten wind of the party, had warned and exhorted zealously against it. More than that he, probably questionably, got some of the deacons to go with him to the place to forestall the party — they were received with abusive language and throwing of sticks. This was not the end, but the matter was seriously discussed in the church council and the guilty individuals were required to confess the error of their ways within a certain date or be subject to excommunication. One finds cases of individuals being warned for unChristian conduct, and being unwilling to change they were excluded from the church. The first incident of excommunication took place September 7, 1856. Gradually members came to understand that a Christian congregation cannot exist without Christian discipline. Usually such persons were elected to office in the council as in some degree were known for more serious Christian character and who would support the pastor in promoting Christian discipline and order. A Sunday school was started July 4, 1855. Gustaf Collin, F. Mobeck and N.H. Bystrom were selected as leaders. No attempt at a daily church school appears until Hedengran's time. On the other hand an English district school was begun soon after the erection of the school-house in the Fall of 1854. A.M. Ahlstrom was the first leader of singing in the congregation. On March 24, 1856 P. Sjolin, a former teacher and organist was elected sexton, whose remuneration was in the form of voluntary gifts and collections. Ever since he has served as the church organist.

The 80 acres which on Cederstram's initiative had been purchased in May 1856 for residence purposes were offered for sale in
the following November. The land was considered too distant from
the church. Sale went slowly, but when finally made the congregation
bought P. Berg's place. Its 29 acres after some time were plotted for a
cemetery and the parsonage. Compensation for all including the
pastor was minimal. The records give no information on the pastor's
salary, its amount or how raised. In the *Minutes* of the annual meeting
December 18, 1857 there is this resolution: "7. regarding the salary of
the pastor, it was decided that the present pastor C.A. Cederstam's
salary for a half year, beginning with October 1 shall be 1 dollar for
each communicant member, and that these sums shall be paid in by
April 1, 1858." If we may figure on the same basis for the two previous
years the salary would be about $400 per year at Chisago Lake, if all
paid which is doubtful. Cederstam had to provide his own lodging,
and most of the time this was at Daniel Peterson's home, north of
Little Bay. The janitor service came cheap, as we learn from the
same *Minutes*. "8. on the question of finding some one who would
make fire in the stove for the regular services and meetings in the
church during the winter, as long as this was necessary, as well as
take care that dogs did not come in, etc. Johannes Helin agreed to do
this at a compensation of $2.75." The following year the salary went
down to $2.50 when Nils Hokanson stopped at the lowest offer — for
the job was auctioned off.

That Cederstam had no chance for laziness as pastor at Chisago
Lake is sufficiently attested when we remember that he had not only
the congregation there, with all its cares and building of a church,
but also the congregation in Marine and St. Paul, along with preaching places as Taylor's Falls, Rusheby, Carver, in a word, the whole
area East of the Mississippi where there were Swedes. Not infrequently he walked the whole way in all kinds of weather. In addition
there were the meetings of the Synod in Illinois he attended, and for
several weeks he sat in the Minnesota state's constitutional convention
in St. Paul the summer of 1857 as delegate from Chisago County — as
many duties as can fall to one man's lot.

Again Concerns about a Pastor

When, as mentioned, Cederstam had told the congregation at
its meeting December 8, 1857 that he firmly intended to move the

following Spring the question of a pastor was again raised. After lengthy discussion the following resolution was adopted: "Inasmuch as no one knew any Swedish Lutheran pastor here in America who would and could accept a call from the congregation it was unanimously decided to turn to the United Chicago and Mississippi Conference with a request and plea that without delay a call be issued on behalf of this congregation in accordance with the following: Because we have ourselves experienced and have learned from *Hemlandet* that it is difficult to find and call a pastor in Sweden, who is both willing and suitable, to come here and break the bread of life for countrymen in need; and in order that the congregation may not be without a leader for a long time, it has been decided 1) to propose three names, whereupon J.F. Hörberg of Vexio diocese was placed first on the list — pastor Magni of Vexio diocese in second place, and Haimunt (Helmer) of Ronneby, Lund diocese, in third place. 2) In case none of the above should accept the call, the Conference authorize Dr. P. Fjellstedt to give the call to some other pastor.

"Further it was resolved that this congregation promises to pay the pastor who comes as stated above a salary of $500 a year, starting from the date he leaves Sweden, free parsonage and use of 29 acres of land, in addition to whatever the congregation in Marine and the countrymen at Taylor's Falls can contribute. If desired the congregation promises to send travelling money with the understanding that it be deducted from the annual salary."

In April 1858 Cederstam left and moved to Scandian Grove.

Chisago Lake during the Vacancy

The vacancy lasted from the beginning of April 1858 until October 1859. It was a period of waiting and testing, but also beneficial. A congregation that expected too much of its pastor or believed that it could obtain almost any pastor that it was pleased to call had to learn in some measure during this period that it is the Lord who sends laborers into the harvest and a congregation must learn to be content with whom He sends. The congregation had been well enough organized to show itself strong enough to maintain itself and continue in good order even without a pastor, a proof that a good foundation had been laid. The records of the ten congregational meetings held during the vacancy tell us something of what went on. Most of the meetings were chaired by Carl Peter Bolin. Occasionally a visiting pastor was asked to preside. The various activities of the congregation were cared for, officers were elected as usual, the economic matters were managed, etc. but mainly the question concerned the need of pastoral care and the securing of a resident pastor.

In September 1858 the congregation promised to pay $25 a year for 4 years "towards a fund whose interest would go to the payment of the salary of a professor absolutely essential in this country for the education of pastors for the many congregations in need of them." A letter from Pastor E. Carlsson to the congregation had prompted this decision. It was not, however, the intention to build up an endowment fund by these annual contributions from congregations, but rather simply to pay the salary of the Scandinavian professorship in Springfield, Illinois. Still the decision, which was carried out, reflected the good will and synodical consciousness of the Chisago Lake congregation. The years 1857-1859 were among the most financially difficult years in this country, and Minnesota as a new and undeveloped region suffered in a double measure in the crisis. Both individuals and corporations had a hard time. The following is an example. On January 23, 1859 the congregation met to discuss and decide about its debts which had been incurred mainly through purchase of land. The *Minutes* say, "the chairman informed the congregation of the sad state of its debts, and that Anders Johnsson was on the point of going to court for what the congregation owed him, unless it gave him guaranteed security and interest at the rate of 2 per cent monthly, and 3 per cent interest monthly if he had no security. It was resolved that the trustees should have authority to give Anders Johnsson a guaranteed security of payment from the congregation's common assets in real estate and to pay him 2 per cent interest monthly, but not beyond next May 1st." In many cases the fixed dues of members were not paid in, and draconian resolutions were passed to enforce payment by delinquents. One might expect that the measures taken to ensure the financial condition of the congregation would have broken it up. But this was not the result, and few, if any, left because of these obligations. On the contrary the church building was completed, a parsonage was built, and other improvements made. It reveals that Swedish people are quite conservative, and that religious faith is deeply imbedded in their consciousness. This was especially the case at Chisago Lake.

The main problem was yet how the congregation should receive pastoral care and find a pastor. The following were some of the measures taken in this matter.

The Minnesota Conference was organized at an appointed meeting at Chisago Lake October 7-9, 1858. The local congregation enjoyed the edification and encouragement afforded by the event, and was the subject of resolutions regarding continued pastoral care, in so far as circumstances permitted. The *Minutes* record "the Conference went on to consider the need of vacant congregations for spiritual care. Regarding Chisago Lake and the St. Croix Valley as a whole, since the congregation at Chisago Lake has no prospect of receiving a permanent pastor during the coming winter or next half year, and since its need of pastor is very great and should not be ignored, it was resolved 1) that Brother Borén remain here after today until the end of October, and if he cannot stay longer Brothers P. Carlson, P. Beckman and J.P.C. Borén regularly visit the congregation in this order each month at least until Spring; 2) that Brother Borén during the weeks he spend here also visit the Swedes at Rush Lake and other nearby places."

The congregation was grateful for these decisions and gladly on its part voted on October 27, 1858 to make arrangements to meet the provisions of the Conference. We read, "the congregation must agree to pay pastors for these visits and for their stay here. It was decided that every family which is a member of the congregation, be it large or small, contribute one dollar and every single individual pay 50 cents, to defray these expenses." From this income the treasurer Daniel Peterson was to pay "first, Pastor Borén for the time he has spent here $25, Borén himself taking care of his board, and then $15 to each pastor coming here during the vacancy, plus an offering while here. Room and board each one can obtain at Daniel Peterson, whom the congregation will compensate in the amount of a bill he will keep and present. D. Peterson will receive and pay out the money as long as its lasts, after which another decision will be made." At this same meeting preliminary steps were taken toward the building of a parsonage.

In accordance with these arrangements the pastors named visited the congregation during the vacancy. Pastor Borén stayed a few weeks after first having made a trip home to Red Wing. P. Carlson came in December, and conducted the annual meeting December 13, 1858, etc. At that time and under these circumstances it was no easy task to visit Chisago Lake. Borén and Beckman were 90 miles distant, P. Carlson almost as far. The roads were poor, the weather and road conditions often difficult, and means of transportation nothing to brag about. I need not mention that there were no railroads then in Minnesota. In addition to Chisago Lake they also included Taylor's Falls, Marine, Stillwater and St. Paul — each trip requiring about two weeks' time.

Meanwhile the hope of securing a pastor from Sweden faded more and more. It seems that Hörberg declined the call and no reply came from Pastor Magni. We quote from the *Minutes* of the congregational meeting April 25, 1859: "Inasmuch as the congregation has waited over a year for a reply from Pastor Magni and fears that the answer will be negative, it was decided to hold a new election. Then the question was raised whether the congregation should call some one from Sweden or choose some one in America. No one knew of any one in Sweden, willing and suitable, who would come here, so it was resolved to turn to our Swedish Lutheran pastors in America. Three names were proposed, namely, T.N. Hasselquist in Galesburg, Pastor E. Norelius in Chicago, both in Illinois, and Pastor P. Carlson in the Union settlement, Carver County, Minnesota. Since all three pastors were well known in the congregation, it did not seem necessary to ask them to come this far to give a trial sermon, and the congregation proceeded at once to vote in this wise, each voting member voted on all three in order of preference. The nominee who received the majority of first place votes should be called. If he declined the call would be sent immediately to the one in second place, etc. Before the election it was decided to change, for this occasion, section 2, paragraph 8 of the constitution, which provided for the election of the one receiving 2/3 of the votes, to read that a simple majority would be determinative.

"The voting resulted thus: Pastor P. Carlson received 51 votes in first place, 26 in second, 5 in third place. Pastor T.N. Hasselquist received 31 first place, 37 second place and 12 third place votes. Pastor E. Norelius received no first place votes, 17 second place and 65 third place votes."

To act in this manner, especially in an arbitrary way to change the constitution in direct contradiction to its own provisions, was of course a breach of order and made the whole procedure illegal. But evidently no one realized it at the time.

The terms of salary included "free use of 29 acres of land," $200 in cash, and 200 bushels grain of various kinds." But he was not to receive compensation for "baptism of children, the churching of women, and burial of the dead, provided that baptisms and churching of women shall take place as far as possible in church and on Sundays."

At the same time the membership fee was set at $1 per year, the same for men and women.

How the Congregation Received a Pastor.

Hasselquist had been called and had declined; the majority believed it was useless to call Norelius, for they thought he would not accept; nothing is said about P. Carlson — probably he had verbally declined. So a new election was held August 25, 1859, and "Pastor A. Andrén of Rockford, Pastor Borén in Red Wing and Mr. Carl August Hedengran in the Union settlement, Carver County, Minnesota, were proposed as candidates. The congregation continued to follow the decision made at the previous election that a simple majority constituted an election."

In the election 81 votes were cast, one vote for Andrén, none for Borén, and 80 for Hedengran. The determining factor seems to have been some hope that Mr. Hedengran might accept while there was little that any of the others would. Hedengran was not yet ordained, but on a visit there together with Pastor P. Carlson he had made a favorable impression on the congregation as a man serious in his Christianity and able to proclaim the truths of God's Word in a clear and attractive style. We may suppose that he was warmly recommended by P. Carlson to the congregation.

The salary arrangements were the same as those determined at the previous election, and decision was reached to begin work on the parsonage next October. It was two stories high, built of dressed logs, and located on the slope beside the church. A few years later it was moved and replaced by a building on the old property of P. Berg, on the 29 acres owned by the church.

Representatives of the congregation in Marine were present at the meeting and requested that the prospective pastor might visit their congregation once a month. This was agreed to, without any reduction of salary from Chisago Lake.

At the Synod meeting in October 1859, in Chicago, Hedengran was given an examination and received a pastor's license, whereupon he moved to Chisago Lake. He presided at his first congregational meeting November 18, 1859, and we learn that his first concern was the establishment of a church school, so that the children might be properly instructed in the Christian faith and in the Swedish language. "The congregation was asked if it desired to have a Swedish teacher and the answer was 'Yes.' " A Johan Petersson was chosen as school teacher; the instruction was to cover 6 months and be given at four different places in the parish. For the present the salary consisted of board for each month of school, "8 bushels of rye and corn, plus $4 in cash, to be contributed equally by the parents, according to the number of children."

Nothing unusual occurred during Hedengran's first year. Everything went on quietly and peaceably. There were signs of a considerable hunger for the Word of God, and that Word was effective both in awakening to and confirming souls in the grace of God. The spiritual program was marked by a strict churchliness. The worship service and all churchly ceremonies followed closely the Swedish Manual and and traditional forms. A small bell was purchased in January 1860 for the church and it was rung according to a fixed schedule. Hedengran was given a 3 months leave in the Spring and Summer to spend in Moline where he continued study with Pastor O.C.T. Andrén. He was ordained at the organization meeting of the Augustana Synod in June 1860 at Jefferson Prairie, Wisconsin.

On May 28, 1860 the congregation voted to join our other Swedish Lutheran congregations in leaving the Synod of Northern Illinois and enter the new (Augustana) Synod. Lack of money prevented the sending of a delegate to the constituting convention. For some unknown reason the question of joining the Synod came up again at a congregational meeting September 30, 1860.

For many years the parish had been divided into 6 districts (rotar) — these were now better defined.

There had also been 4 burial sites, in 1860 regulations were adopted regarding the users of each.

The first was located by the church. At first some graves were dug on the church lot, but when the parsonage was to be built there the burial place was moved to the foot of the slope, though there the ground was rather low. A second cemetery was near Daniel Lindstrom's place, the third East of the lake near Carl and David Peterson's, and the fourth south of the Lake on land belonging to P. Glader.

From the beginning the congregation exhibited a strong loyalty to the Synod. We have seen how it turned to the United Conference with its problems, especially in seeking a pastor from Sweden. The proposed congregational constitution recommended by the Conference was adopted October 11, 1857. Delegates were sent to Conference and Synod meetings, as far as means permitted. The congregation contributed to the establishment and support of the Scandinavian professorship at the school in Springfield, etc.

The statistics of June 1860 show that the congregation had a debt of $320; 370 communicant members; 49 baptisms since the previous synod meeting in October 1859; 20 confirmed during the year; 35 received by letter; 6 deaths — 3 children, 3 adults; 6 marriages; 1 church school; contributions of $1.95 to Inner Missions; and other expenditures of the year $373.

Chapter 13

Marine — St. Paul — Taylor's Falls — Rusheby

Marine

This settlement, about 3 miles northwest of the village of Marine Mills on the St. Croix River, was started the same year as Chisago Lake. Along the river the land is sandy and hilly, but a few miles beyond it becomes more level, and the soil better, though still mostly thin. The area is primarily forest, with some larger, some smaller lakes, and bogs. In general it resembles the Chisago Lake area. The distance between the two, measured from the center of each is about 14 miles.

The First and Older Swedes

Daniel Nilsson from Norrbo in Helsingland and his family are, as far as we know, the first Swedish family to make a home in this area. He came to America in the brig *Sofie* in 1850, spending the first winter in Moline. He set out for Minnesota in the Spring of 1851 and came directly to Marine Mills. It is possible, but not certain, that one or more of his party from Sweden accompanied him. But it wasn't long before others followed. For a while Nilsson worked for an American in Marine Mills, and found a place for himself by a small lake on the edge of a thick forest and there in the depth of the woods he settled down. He was an ambitious worker and a true wood-cutter. I had seen an example of this the year before, when on the bluffs of the Rock River near Moline he had in a short time cut and split 1500 oak fence-staves for a cow, which later was honored to be taken along to Minnesota. In the wilderness of his new place he cleared a rather large plot in a few years, put together a well-made and spacious house of Swedish style, built barn and stable and other places. He belonged to that generation that wanted a separate house for each purpose or need. In a word he was an unusual worker, the whole family sharing his zeal. The Lord blessed them with health and success so that after a few years they found themselves in comfortable circumstances. Their home was for years the gathering place for worship services and lodging place for visiting pastors. Later the family moved to Kandiyohi County and made their home on the west shore of Green Lake, where he ended his days.

Nearby the Nilsson place those early years an Englund from Enånger lived, on the same side of the lake. One while, on the south side, lived a prominent Prussian nobleman who had been a Councillor, but gotten into trouble in the 1848 revolution and escaped from his country, as was the fate of many other Germans those days. His name was von Kustis, or something similar. They were very well-behaved and peaceable people, the children even learned Swedish and some of them were confirmed. Ohlin and others from Medelpad had places north of the lake, and farther west Anders Larson and family from Enånger, more recently arrived. These constituted the oldest populated part of the settlement. There were many others whose names I do not now recall. Leaving Ohlin's place and following a path in a northerly or northwestern direction one came to the spot where the church now stands. There was the home of Olof Hansson from Skåne, just where the old parsonage stood at the bottom of the slope. Then continuing through the woods towards the northeast one came across an old man from Blekinge, John Bengtson, now long since dead.

Six miles north of Marine Mills one reached the road to Taylor's Falls, where some people from Kronoberg County had located — they call the place Islycke. Among them were Johannes Peterson, and Erland Peterson. This northern section later attracted many, but already in 1854 there were quite a number, and this became the most important part of the settlement. Most of those who came before 1860 seemed to have been from Kronoberg County. Here, as elsewhere, our countrymen had few if any resources, and they struggled to survive and break a path in a forbidding nature those first years. Courage, patience and persistence were required of both men and women to win out in this battle. True, hunting and fishing satisfied some of life's necessities, but these were often shared with Indians who were not far away. The cutting of timber and floating of logs to saw-mills afforded some opportunities for making money, but while the men were gone wives and children had to care for themselves.

Church Matters and the Organization of the Swedish Evangelical Lutheran Congregation

Here too was an early recognition of the religious needs and thought given to meet them. It is not clear who was the first minister to visit the settlement, but it was probably the Methodist preacher Agrelius, for he was already living there in the summer of 1854 and undoubtedly he had been there before he made his home here. There was, however, no organized Methodist congregation that year in this place. In May, in connection with his journey to Chisago Lake, Pastor Erl. Carlsson visited the settlement, preached and celebrated the Lord's Supper and organized an Evangelical Lutheran congregation. This took place in Daniel Nilsson's home. I cannot now tell how many joined and who they were, or who were the first councilmen. The Lutheran group probably did not exceed 100 persons. Some of our countrymen had already lost interest in the church, others were indifferent. In general it was felt that sufficient religious interest was lacking for the building of a vital Christian congregation. At least that was my impression when I was there later in the summer of 1854. Nor had there been much change when I came there again a year later.

After coming to Chisago Lake (Spring 1855) Cederstam visited Marine regularly one Sunday a month, for the congregation was a part of his extensive pastorate. *Hemlandet* (1st year, no. 6) contained the first published report on the place. "Countrymen living 3 miles west of Marine Mills, Washington County, have long felt the need of a building where they could come together on Sundays and other occasions to edify each other in their Christian faith and piety. No one has a house with room beyond personal needs, so people as well as pastor have been troubled and uncomfortable at the services of the congregation. Had they been united they could easily have built a house of worship, but party strife has ever been a foe of harmony and unity, so that concord in this matter took wing and flew far from this place. For some weeks the prospect looked pretty dark for those who wanted to belong to a distinctive congregation, namely the Lutheran. They might have to choose to go on as before or join with the Methodists and those who want to please everybody. Only a few, and most of them poor, were determined despite their poverty and the labor, to gather lumber for a building. They have met success in their endeavor, and now have the material and almost $200 in pledges. With voluntary labor they hope soon to have a small church. Two acres have been contributed for the site, and a building of 30 by 20 feet is planned. So by the help of God we hope soon to have our church, as we have wanted ever since we came here, and that despite all the deceitfulness of our opponents. We have no resident pastor but one Sunday every month Pastor Cederstam of Chisago Lake visits us. On the other Sundays we still meet and encourage each other as best we can. Some go and listen to the Methodist minister Agrelius, who lives here. But most of those who want to belong to our Lutheran Congregation have decided to stay with a definite church as against a less distinctive one." This was written in May 1856.

This first church in the settlement was a little south of Daniel Nilsson's place on the south side of the road. It was a primitive, log, affair and looked like a haybarn. But it served the same purpose as a more splendid building and was used as late as 1860 or 1861. Few if any of the people in the northern sector participated in its erection, for they thought it was located far from them. When finally a new church site was agreed on between the north and south sections at Olof Hansson's place, the old building was sold for a district school house, taken down and moved farther to the East, south of the small lake. If I am not mistaken it came later into the possession of the Methodists, or possibly they only used it for their services.

The new church, a frame building erected in 1861, was about 50 by 36 feet and cost $1400. It stood in the cemetery, right across the road from the site of the present church.

Our statistical reports differ in regard to the year of organization. For many years after the beginning of the Augustana Synod the date is 1855, later the date was 1857. In fact the congregation, as we have noted, was formed in 1854, but it was reorganized by Pastor Cederstam in 1857.

Pastoral Care

Any congregation, especially a new one, that lacks for a long period the care of a pastor will not meet the requirements essential for a healthy growth. Such was the case in Marine and the congregation suffered because of it. While Cederstam was at Chisago Lake and during the first two years of Hedengran's time the congregation received visits about once a month, but this was insufficient. Chisago Lake was vacant from the Spring of 1858 until the Fall of 1859, and Marine had only occasional visits by Borén, Beckman, and P. Carlson. Preachers of other faiths appeared, making for increased confusion and disunity. Bergenlund, whom we have met elsewhere, preached and conducted a school here 1859-1861, exciting at least at first some enthusiasm among the people. On one occasion P. Carlson ran into

Bergenlund's wrath. A violent dispute arose by the old church in the woods. Carlson saw no gain in continuing the controversy and started to leave. Bergenlund pursued him yelling loudly, asserting "I don't care about the symbolical books (of the Lutheran Confession), I cast the whole collection to h . . ." Bergenlund soon wore out his welcome and the people of the place were glad to see him go.

It was 1863 before the congregation obtained a resident pastor. Unfortunately he left too soon. It is a sign of God's care that the congregation did not die out under such unfavorable conditions and survived. Any signs of a deep Christian conviction were admittedly not apparent in those days, yet there lay under the surface a sense of spiritual need among most, and this expressed itself in many ways. And here and there were individual souls who not only sorrowed over their condition but took seriously the question of salvation. The brighter seasons of this congregation came later. There was then no congregation in Marine Mills in this period, though a few Swedish families had settled there before 1860, among them very likely O. Westergren, a blacksmith.

In 1860 the Marine congregation had 75 communicants, with expenditures of about $200. The whole Swedish population in the settlement probably did not exceed 300.

Taylor's Falls

This place lies in a northern, wildly romantic Nature, at the Falls of the St. Croix River, and had just begun to be settled when the Swedes came to this region. Some Swedes soon located here, but their number has never been large. Since there was a congregation here when the Augustana Synod was organized a reference to it should be included. Prior to 1860 when the organization took place the congregation was a preaching annex to Chisago Lake, and from its beginning until 1872 it was an annex to the Chisago Lake church whose pastor cared for it. The majority of the members in this small group were then, and very likely even now, the Swedish farmers who had chosen places in the forest 2 miles west of town, towards Chisago Lake. Among the earliest certainly were P. Viklund and his relatives whom we are acquainted with from our account of Moline and Chisago Lake. Later A. Anderson, the wainwright, whom we met in St. Charles, came here but after a while moved into town, as well as his son-in-law Daniel Fredin, from Hassela in Helsingland, and Tufve from Skåne. Another was Fred Lammars, a German by birth, son-in-law of Daniel Nilsson in Marine — he later moved to Marine.

Pastor Hedengran organized a congregation of 24 communicants in 1860, and a small frame church was built on the western edge of town. The congregation has existed through the years but never grew very large, because of the sparse population.

Rusheby

Thirty miles north of Taylor's Falls lay Rusheby, about 20 miles directly north of Chisago Lake, in Town 37 N. of R. 21 in Chisago County. It must have been in the vicinity of the present Rush City.

In the Fall of 1856 some Swedes from around La Fayette, Indiana, migrated up here and made their home in the wild forests. Among them was Gustaf Westman from Vireda, Frans and Fredrik Bjorklund from Grenna, Jonas Lindwall from Adelöf, with their families. Afterwards P. Berg and wife from Madesjö and his brother Johannes Berg followed. Almost all of this original group moved sooner or later, and now live in scattered places or have died. John Berg is probably the only one of them still in the area. Others later took their places.

A letter of G. Westman, dated May 3, 1857, tells us something about the place in those early days. "We are well satisfied with our temporal possessions, but we lack the best part, namely the preaching of the Word of God, and this makes life heavy. When we came here we thought we might soon be able to have a church and pastor, but now we realize this cannot be, for we are so few, and the small group is divided — some are attracted to the Baptists and others to their own "ism." Furthermore persons of other nationalities are claiming the land around us, so that we are almost surrounded by them. I do not know why the land is being taken up so rapidly. Many have chosen their claims in the middle of winter without inquiring as to the nature of the land. When we came last Fall there was a great amount of unclaimed land, now there is little or none. I can tell this of our location. The township is 37 North of Range 21, Chisago County. My claim is in section 27, three quarters of a mile from the government road which runs from Taylor's Falls to Superior City. Here the land is remarkably good and attractive. — I hope that as soon as all the land has been taken up we can then be able to sell, if we wish. Some have already sold and gotten good returns. A town is to be laid out here (Rush City?). There are excellent opportunities for gainful work in the woods in winter time and in floating of timber on the St. Croix River in Spring and Summer.

"The winter has been very severe with unusually heavy snowfall. Provisions are and have been quite expensive: flour, $12-$15 a barrel, meat 20 cents a pound, potatoes $1 a bushel, etc. We are about 20 miles from the Swedish settlement of Chisago Lake, by the road over Sunrise, but one cannot travel by carriage on it. — Only on a couple of occasions have we heard God's Word proclaimed by Pastor Cederstam. We miss Indiana — there were difficulties but there we at least often had opportunity to hear preaching of the Word of God. — I talked with a Swedish farm-hand who lives in Superior, Wisconsin. He said there were 25 Swedish farm-hands and 3 or 4 families that had moved there last winter."

It was not easy for our pastors to visit this hidden corner of the earth, but the cries for help of our countrymen compelled them. Cederstam was the first to come several times, often on foot, but the trip could be at the peril of one's life or of injury to health. Pastor Borén was there in the Fall of 1858. Later Hedengran made several trips and organized a congregation of 11 families, in 1860. I made a visit there early in the spring of 1861 and learned that a trip to Rusheby was no excursion. It was in the period of spring rains, with much snow and water on roads worse than miserable. In some places the corduroy road floated on the water. I succeeded in crossing because I had a blind horse who responded perfectly to the driver, otherwise I would not have made it. Night had come before I reached there, and only with difficulty could I find my way through darkness, the thick forest, the mud and the water, to the cabins of the settlers. A service was held the following day in the home of P. Berg (now in Spring Garden) and it was a scene to behold the happiness with which the poor people gathered for worship. Most of them came by foot on the terrible roads, some rode on sleds drawn by oxen through the mud and water which reached up to the seats — every body wanted to be along. At a certain time in the life of each pioneer there is a hunger that finds some degree of expression, and that is the time to begin a spiritual activity. If that time passes and people begin a habit of being without the Word and sacraments, then hearts become hard and resist spiritual motions, and the spiritual earth turns to stone.

This little congregation had no long existence, for most of the members moved away. Then after a few years others came and in time there were two Swedish congregations in this area, one in Rush Lake, organized 1870, and one in Rush City, 1876.

St. Paul, Minnesota

When the Swedish migration to Minnesota started, St. Paul had only between one and two thousand inhabitants, and its people, according to Fredrika Bremer, lived in a motley array of primitive houses. In less than 40 years it has grown into an imposing city of almost 200,000 persons. For those who saw the place then and see it now the change is a marvel. The entire area where the first Swedish Lutheran church now stands was, even in 1854, an oak forest that stretched intermittently all the way to Stillwater. Where there were high hills the ground is now level, and here are the most stately buildings of the city. One must admit that J.W. Bond's "vision" of St. Paul and Minnesota in his *Minnesota and its Resources*, 1853, has in many respects been realized, though then it was considered a phantasy.

The First Swedes in St. Paul

N.P. Ofelt, now living in Vasa, Goodhue County, has contributed the following information about the first Swedes in St. Paul. Mr. Ofelt, from Färlöf in Kristianstad County came to America in May 1852, arriving in Boston on July 17th. His party from Sweden included: Johan Johanson and three children from Östergötland; Swen Rosenquist, a shoemaker, and family, from Lund, one while as farmer near Afton, but now in River Falls, Wis.; Nils Nyberg, also a shoemaker, from Färlöf, and Carl Bjarstedt, from the same parish, both of these single men. Henry Russel and family joined the party in Boston. R. had been a seaman and lived 12 years in Boston. J. Tidlund and family from Vestergötland had come over the previous year, and joined Russel — both were tailors. In Chicago two members were added: Ringdahl, a tailor from Vestergötland, and P.M. Anderson from the same area, who had arrived in America a year ago. All these formed one company and came to St. Paul where they stayed the first winter. Before them there were two Swedes in St. Paul, and only two as far as Ofelt knew. These two were Nils Nilson from Östergötland, or the "doctor's Nils" as he was called because he worked for Dr. Sweeney, — he appears in the story of Red Wing; and A.J. Ekman, probably a business or tradesman from Gothenburg, who was reputed to have fled the country — he died around 1856. These were the first Swedes in St. Paul.

Ofelt met Fahlstrom, the above mentioned first Swede in Minnesota, in 1852, when he came to St. Paul. Fahlstrom claimed he had then been here 27 years, had been twice married both times with Indian women, that he could speak 7 languages, that he had a Swedish Bible and had found his Saviour at the Minnesota River (mission). He spoke Swedish tolerably well, but had forgotten some words. In 1853 there was an influx of Swedes, mainly from Östergötland. Ofelt remembers some who came — Johan Johansson from Umeå, a tailor, John Johnson, a carpenter, now in Galesburg, and the minister Agrelius. In those days Tidlund and Russel became zealous Methodists.

Church Affairs and the Organization of the Lutheran Congregation, and its History until 1860

It is possible that G. Unonius on his visit to Chisago Lake in 1852 also had religious meetings with the Swedes in St. Paul, but information of such is lacking. On the other hand it is known that Agrelius and Tidlund had carried on Methodist meetings before any Lutheran pastor had visited St. Paul.

The first information we have regarding steps toward the formation of a Swedish Lutheran congregation in St. Paul appears in the following letter which I include here in its entirety:

"St. Paul, Minnesota Terrace,
March 15, 1854.

Pastor T.N. Hasselquist!

We take the liberty of turning to you for information on a matter of great significance for us Scandinavians who live here in St. Paul. On Sunday, February 26th, there was a public meeting of Swedes and Norwegians at which a Scandinavian Lutheran congregation was organized. The undersigned were elected as its trustees.

"But our congregation is without a pastor, and our first duty is to fill this need. On motion of one of our members, Frank Mobeck, we take the liberty of turning to you for counsel and enlightenment in this matter. There are indeed two Scandinavian ministers here, pastor Agrelius and Mr. Tidlund, an ex-tailor recently ordained as a preacher; but since they belong to the Methodist denomination and we do not wish to become members of their church and much less wish to leave our good old Evangelical Lutheran faith in which our fathers in our native land for centuries have lived piously and died blessed, and which faith we ourselves once before God and the Church freely promised to support, willingly and sincerely, all our lives, it is highly important for us to obtain, the sooner the better, a zealous pastor who can preach the Word of God in a manner we are accustomed to hear and who can teach our children so that they may get a sound foundation for our holy faith.

"We consider it important to mention that the Scandinavian population in Minnesota is estimated to be about 600, including 200 at the Chisago Lake settlement, 100 in Marine, 150 in St. Paul, 150 in scattered places.[1] Only a few have joined the Methodist churches. As far as we know no Swedish Lutheran pastor has been stationed in Minnesota. We do not know to what authorities we should go for obtaining a pastor. Therefore we seek your help in this matter and ask you to present our need and petition to the proper persons. As to the support of a pastor we are encouraged by the hope of receiving a subsidy of 300-500 dollars from the American Home Missionary Society. In addition we have offered to share a pastor with our countrymen at Chisago Lake and to participate in his salary, until each of our congregations is strong enough to have its own. These amounts together with voluntary gifts ought to be sufficient to compensate a minister who is moderate in his expectations.

"We want also to express our sincere desire and plea to have you visit us as soon as possible, if you can, and to stay with us for a while. There are many reasons for our wish to have you come. The main reason is that we would have the opportunity of being edified by your instructive sermons, and being stimulated in our zeal for church and religion which suffers from a lack of a pastor. We do come together meanwhile to read our postils (books of sermons), but if we have to be without a pastor a long time we will lose many to the fanatical Methodists and the congregation may face dissolution. We believe that your presence, even for a brief time, would do much to increase, and assist in the progress of, the congregation. We are happy to report that whereas we had only 21 members at the time of organization we already have 72 members and many others have declared that they want to join with us. Knowing of your zeal for religion and the Lutheran Church we have ventured to present our desires to you and to ask for an early reply. Wishing you the grace of God and His blessing, we sign on behalf of the congregation, humbly, Frank Mobeck, C.J. Lindstrom, C.A. Hedengran, P.M. Andersson, A.J. Ekman"

---

[1] This must refer to the Swedes in Minnesota and to only those Norwegians who were in St. Paul, for far larger numbers of Norwegians were then in southern Minnesota.

Three of these are familiar names. Fr. Mobeck moved to Chisago Lake, C.A. Hedengran (later a pastor) moved that summer to East Union, A.J. Ekman, the merchant from Gothenberg and probably the writer of the letter, died not long afterwards. The letter was received very sympathetically by the Illinois pastors and moved them to undertake a mission in Minnesota. Pastor E. Carlsson had already promised to make a trip to Chisago Lake, so Hasselquist, not wanting to interfere with that visit, postponed his going there.

We have already described Carlsson's journey to Minnesota in April and May 1854. On May 6th at a public meeting of Scandinavians he organized a Scandinavian Evangelical Lutheran congregation in St. Paul, which has ever since continued, through many changes and trials. What of the former organization? The *Minutes* of the May 6th meeting tell us: "Scandinavian Lutherans who had felt a deep need of a religious community and ordered church life and wanted to satisfy said need had held a public meeting on February 26th and decided to organize as a body with the name, The Scandinavian Evangelical Lutheran Congregation of St. Paul. Members subscribed their names — at present to the number of 76 — and elected officers, namely Frank Mobeck, C.A. Hedengran, C. Lindstrom, P. Andersson, C. Sorensen, Julius Jansen. Since no constitution had been prepared for the congregation or adopted, another meeting was announced for this date, to determine the character of the congregation as Evangelical Lutheran, the conditions for membership, etc. which all had to do with the welfare and progress of the congregation, leading to the following resolutions." These resolutions consisted of the usual articles of organization which Pastor Carlsson employed at the organization of congregations and have already been described.[1] In these *Minutes* we also read: For the coming year three trustees were elected, C. Sorensen, Julius Jansen, C.A. Hedengran, and three deacons, Frank Mobeck, J.P. Andersson, C. Lindstrom. A.J. Ekman was elected secretary and sexton of the congregation.

"As the congregation is in great need of its own pastor, all those present unanimously decided to authorize E. Carlsson the Lutheran pastor from Chicago, who at the time was visiting his brethren in the faith here, to transmit the congregation's call through Dr. P. Fjellstedt in Lund to Pastor C.M. Swensson of the Vexiö diocese, requesting him to come and assume the spiritual leadership and care of the

---

[1] In treating the history of the Immanuel Church, Chicago, and in more detail in the story of the Indiana congregations.

newly formed congregation. Instead of writing direct to Pastor Swensson it seemed best in this important matter to turn to Dr. Fjellstedt, so that in case Pastor Swensson was hindered from accepting the call could then be forwarded by Fjellstedt to some other minister whom he would approve for this important position. Pastor Carlsson promised to formulate the call and read it to the congregation Monday evening, the 8th, when the minutes would be approved. Meanwhile the congregation will unite in faithful and urgent prayer that the Chief Shepherd might in grace soon send here a faithful and good steward." Signed by "Erl. Carlsson, serving as chairman, pro tem., on request. A.J. Ekman, secretary."

Another meeting was held May 27 when the *Minutes* were approved. Thus it was not on the 8th as expected at the former session. There were other matters to deal with, proposed by the Norwegian members. These were the decisions: Worship services were to be held every Sunday morning and evening; every other service was to be in Norwegian, alternating with the Swedish; since there was at present no Norwegian or Danish member elected as deacon, Mr. P.E. Lome was to serve as deacon at the Norwegian services until other arrangements are made; that the devotions at this present meeting be in Norwegian, then the plan outlined above take effect; that collections be taken each month as often as necessary to meet the economic demands of the congregation; that two subscriptions be circulated annually, one in May, one in October, for the building of a church treasury. "Read and approved June 18, 1854, and certified on behalf of the congregation, Frank Mobeck, Carl J. Sorensen, P.J. Andersson, Andreas Andersson, C.J. Lindstrom."

I was then in St. Paul for the first time, and would like to share with readers my memories of impressions of the place and of the Swedes who were there then. I arrived in St. Paul on May 21st after 6 full days on the journey from Moline. The neat little town of 6000 inhabitants, five years old, lay high and dry on the prominent sandstone bluff, looking around on the then almost unknown surrounding world, unconscious of what it would one day become. It was a Sunday afternoon, and at the landing I met some countrymen. From them I learned that Pastor Carlsson had already been here and organized a congregation. He was expected on his way back. They suggested that I preach in the evening and brought me to Frank Mobeck. The service was in a primitive school house on Jackson Street which at that time had few houses above Seventh Street. There was quite a good attendance and people seemed happy and hopeful.

There is no record of any congregational meeting from May 27, 1854 to March 18, 1855. A meeting on the latter date adopted these resolutions: "That A.J. Ekman be chairman; that Mr. J.A. Hellstrom be elected as trustee to take the place of Mr. Julius Jansen, who had resigned; that J.P. Schonbeck for the present replace C.A. Hedengran who had moved away last summer; that the trustees be empowered by the congregation to come to an agreement on buying a lot in St. Paul on which to build a church in the future; that the lot offered by Mr. Vital Guerrin for this purpose, lot No. 6 in block 20, seemed suitable, his price of $300 and terms of payment satisfactory; that money for this purpose be raised through a subscription, which had already been started and on which a sufficient amount had been paid so that the first payment of $50 could be made on the lot; that the trustees, if they wished, should be recompensed for their time at $1 per day." The *Minutes* are signed by the chairman, A.J. Ekman — who was secretary as well, and "were read, approved and signed this day in the presence of the congregation, witnessed to on March 25, 1855, in St. Paul, by Frank Mobeck, A.J. Hellstrom, J.P. Ofelt."

Nothing came of the proposed purchase of a church site. Little money was in the treasury, but this was almost all lost in a way we will describe later. From this time Swedes began to move away from St. Paul to seek homesteads on land where there already were settlements or new ones arose. Only a few of the original members remained and the congregation was almost dissolved. A principal contributing factor was the lack of a pastor. When Pastor Cederstam was sent to Chisago Lake it was the intention that he would also serve St. Paul, but he could not possibly do more than pay it occassional visits. Once in a while another pastor might come, as Esbjörn, E. Carlsson, and E. Norelius, but this was not enough. Meanwhile a number of new families arrived, mostly Norwegian and Danish, among whom were some independent individuals and some whose sympathies were with the "Norwegian Lutheran Synod in America." They tried to change the weak congregation to their ideas, but went about it so subtly that at first the members were unaware of any evil purpose. A series of 10 meetings were held from November 29, 1857 to May 13, 1858, and it became clear what was their goal. Using the original record book they entered the decisions of the meetings under the heading, "Minutes of the meetings of an association to organize a Scandinavian Evangelical Lutheran church body in St. Paul, Minnesota Terr." (in Norwegian). Usually at these meetings P. Lund served as chairman and C. Lipke as secretary. Of the original members of the congregation who attended we find such names as John Johnsson, Johan Johansson, Martin Nilsen and Andrew Eriksson. Occasionally the old missionary, Father Heyer, a German Lutheran pastor, was present and sought to give his counsel. Finally on May 13th, 1858 a constitution was completed and revealed what the usurpers had in mind. This seems to have prompted the original congregation to call a meeting for May 17, 1858 to decide what measures should be taken. Pastor Cederstam served as chairman. It was this session that saved the church, and its *Minutes* deserve to be quoted. Cederstam wrote the report: "After the opening of the meeting the chairman read the call for a meeting, namely, We the undersigned hereby make known that we cannot approve the congregational constitution which was adopted last Friday evening at a meeting in Mr. Jorgensen's home, in that it prohibits pastors of the Northern Illinois Synod to speak or preach here. Consequently we hereby invite all Scandinavians in St. Paul who wish to work with us to build up a pure Lutheran congregation not only in name and form but also in spirit, to meet with us at Mr. Johansson's tomorrow evening, Monday the 17th at 7:30 p.m. to deliberate with each other concerning steps to be taken for the success of the project. St. Paul, May 15, 1858. John Johansson, Johan Johansson, M. Nilsen."

At that meeting discussion led to the following result: "This congregation, organized May 6, 1854 by the Lutheran Pastor E. Carlsson of Chicago, Illinois, has been without pastoral leadership except for occasional visits by Swedish pastors from Minnesota or Illinois. The larger part of the membership has moved away and few Scandinavians have stayed here lately. As a result the maintenance of the congregation has been neglected too long. Yet the remaining members have continued to hold worship services almost every Sunday, and on week days when possible. The attendance has fluctuated. Last Fall the number of Scandinavians in St. Paul was augmented by a few Norwegians and Danish families who seemed interested in our poor Zion. A public meeting was announced for the ordering of our church affairs, and several meetings for the purpose were held during the winter. From the beginning there has been disagreement between the congregation and the recently arrived Scandinavians, not concerning faith and Confessions, but as to the synod we should belong to. The congregation's members have been hopeful for unity and until now have attended these meetings. On May 13th at a meeting at Mr. Jorgensen's some of the recent Scandinavians without any commission to do so presented a proposed constitution which they demanded the congregation should adopt. Since one of the unalterable articles prescribed that ministers belonging to the Synod of Northern Illinois should never be permitted to speak or preach or have any relationship to the congregation, the members refused under any circumstances to accept such a rule, first because they considered it un-Christian, and in violation of the liberty of this country. (Norelius adds: a poor argument), and despite the fact that it is well known that the pastors of the Northern Illinois Synod are permitted, and by synodical decision, required to believe and teach in accordance with the fundamental doctrines of the Lutheran Church, which this congregation has accepted; secondly, because this congregation was organized by Pastor E. Carlsson, who was and still is, a member of this Synod, and because the pastors of this Synod are the only ones who have done anything to assist us. We consider it un-Christian to exclude these pastors from the congregation, especially as long as we are without pastor and they want to visit us. When now those who have drawn up and want to force this constitution on us are unwilling to change it, and since these persons have never been received as members in accordance with the constitution, it was unanimously resolved that for the present the congregation will abide by the constitution adopted May 6, 1854. Further it was decided to elect two deacons for one year, Johan Johansson and John Johnsson then being elected, and that the congregation be incorporated under the laws of the state, as soon as possible." The *Minutes* were read and approved at the next meeting, on the 24th of May.

The latter meeting was held in Martin Nilsen's home, with Johan Johansson evidently serving as chairman and John Johnsson as secretary. Two resolutions were adopted, that those who wish to be members of the congregation should subscribe their names in the church record book, and that the name of the congregation be changed to First Scandinavian Lutheran Church in St. Paul. Those who signed their names as members were: John Johnsson and wife Kristina and daughters Emma and Charlotta Maria; Johan Johansson and wife Hedvig C.; Martin Nilsen and wife Kristina and daughter Lovisa Kristina; Hokan Olsson. Bengt Jonsson, T. Nygren. We note thus that the group was small. We have some information on them: John Johnsson, a nephew of Dr. Hasselquist, moved to Galesburg in the 1860's where he still lives. Johan Johansson and wife are both dead. Johansson was born in Umeå, and had been a master tailor many years in Stockholm. He belonged to the so-called Norrland Luther-readers, was a brother of the book-seller Johansson in Umeå, and of the prominent master-tailor Johansson in Hull, England. During the whole period of pastor vacancy he was chairman of the congregation and had the ability to lead in the devotional meetings. He was of great help to newly arrived immigrants. Toward the end of the war he got into difficulty about funds that had been entrusted to him, even being sued and imprisoned a while. Even if his crime cannot be considered a deliberate act it was nevertheless a result of sin. He came later to deep felt repentance but also to a true restoration. His last days were full of frightful pain. Cancer attacked his legs, consuming them inch by inch. His cries were so distressful that a small cabin was built for him apart from other houses, and there he ended his days in the 1870's with a firm belief in God's forgiving grace in Christ Jesus. Martin Nilsen, Danish by birth, still resides in his old place, but his wife is dead. I believe he and the rest of the family belong to the Memorial English Lutheran Church in St. Paul. His son-in-law is Herman von Stockenstrom, assistant secretary of state. Nilsen's home was long a favorite guest home for all kinds of visitors.

At the June 7th, 1858 meeting three trustees were elected. Since the date of incorporation the list of trustees has been as follows: June 7, 1858 — Johan Johansson, 3 yrs., Martin Nilsen, 2 yrs., Hokan Olsson, 1 yr. June 26, 1859 — John S. Smith, 3 yrs., Johan Johansson, 2 yrs., M. Nilsen, 1 yr. July 18, 1860 — T. Nygren, 3 yrs. Johannes Polsson, 2 yrs. — in place of Smith, who had moved, Johan Johansson, 1 yr. August 7, 1861 — Johan Johansson, 3 yrs., Andrew Eriksson, 2 yrs., in place of Nygren, resigned, Johannes Polsson, 1 yr. August 8, 1862 — Martin Nilsen, 3 yrs., Johan Johansson, 2 yrs., Andrew Eriksson, 1 yr. August 7, 1863 — John Johnsson, 3 yrs., M. Nilsen, 2 yrs., Johan Johansson 1 yr.

At several meetings between 1858-1860 the congregation debated how to recover $100 belonging to the building fund which had been deposited in the Truman Smith bank. The bank failed, but after many delays and difficulties the congregation received two grave stones which long remained unsold.

The Congregation Receives its First Regular Pastor

On October 25, 1860 the congregation met to elect a pastor and issued a call to Pastor E. Norelius. There was no promise of a salary but the congregation agreed to pay $5 a month for the pastor's rent, as well as arranging for the place. It was understood that the pastor was to have his headquarters in St. Paul and serve the congregation when he was home, otherwise he was to serve as a travelling missionary in the parts of Minnesota he was able to reach. A committee was appointed to hire a suitable place for services, and it succeeded in renting a small room, almost a closet, from a German, Henneberg, a little north of the present location of the church.

Pastor Norelius entered on his work shortly after this meeting and served the congregation for a year, until the Fall of 1861. He has many precious memories from those days, attesting to the Lord's faithfulness and grace toward the slender plant. The congregation was small, consisting of only 13 communicants in the summer of 1860, but grew slowly. Peace and unity prevailed, and the devotional hours in the small chamber were delightful and refreshing. Mr. John Johnsson led the singing, often with the help of a psalmodikon. The Christmas morning service 1860 was especially uplifting. The small pulpit was tastefully decorated, the small room was radiant with light, but the greatest joy was in the happiness with which the Word of God was received. The two most important achievements of the year were the acquiring of a lot for a church and the adoption of the normal congregational constitution.

A contract for the purchase of the corner lot on which the present church stands was made with the German Henry Schurmeier. The price was four or five hundred dollars, a sum the small group had difficulty in meeting. Yet, they succeeded, and thus acquired a very suitable place for the church. It would take a long time before any building could be erected.

On March 10, 1861 the congregation adopted the constitution which the United Chicago and Mississippi Conference had worked out and proposed to member congregations. Hitherto only those articles which had been approved when the organization took place had been in force. Through this act the congregation gained in stability and was better able to defend itself against religious adventurers.

At the last meeting before E. Norelius moved, on August 7, 1861, the financial report of the year showed income of $251.32 and expenditures of $210.20 — figures then considered encouraging.

Pastor E. Norelius submitted his resignation at this meeting. It was reluctantly accepted. Clearly the congregation, though somewhat enlarged, was not able to support a pastor by itself. It remained vacant a few years and was served by visiting pastors of the Conference.

Chapter 14

Vasa — Red Wing — Stockholm, Wisconsin

Goodhue County

That part of Minnesota which attracted the largest number of Swedish settlers, next to Chisago and Washington counties and St. Paul, was Goodhue County, especially its northern and northwestern sections. Norwegians occupy the southern and southwestern sections. Together, the Scandinavians far outnumber all other ethnic groups.

This county lies at the upper end of Lake Pepin and along the Mississippi River from a point a little above Lake City to about half way between Red Wing and Hastings, and inland to a width of 36 miles. From north to south and from east to west the distance is 36 miles, yet the shape is not a square. It embraces 24 townships, and its area 764 square miles or 488,833.84 acres. The water courses that touch or traverse the county are, the Mississippi, Vermillion, Big and Little Cannon, both branches of the Zumbro, rivers, and Prairie, Belle, Spring, Hay, and Wells, creeks. The county has no lakes. The land is a natural prairie, more level in the southwest, but in general hilly and uneven and cut up by the streams. Trees line the streams and give material for building, but across the whole prairie around the houses groves have been planted so that one nowhere sees barren stretches. Clay predominates, but sandy soil forms a small belt from Cannon Falls to the East or Southeast and occasionally comes to the surface. As a rule the earth is fertile, but for many years it suffered from irrational use. Lately more conservation-minded farming has prevailed, with good results.

In geological terms the rock formations of Goodhue County belong to the lower Silurian, beginning with the Potsdam sandstone, overlaid with a rather thick layer of magnetic limestone which emerges to the surface and stretches 6 or 7 miles inland from the streams. On top and beyond is a layer of loose sandstone, which has been called St. Peter sandstone. This layer is visible around Cannon Falls and in the southern section of Vasa where a solitary "White Rock" provides a good example. Above this is a layer of slate, in which are found most of the country's fossils, especially at Kenyon and Cannon Falls. This is visible in the higher or bluff areas which adjoin Vasa and the Town of Belle Creek, at Leon and on the heights at Cannon Falls.

Vestiges of the glacial period appear in the western and southern sections of the county, where boulders, some quite large, are scattered on the fields.

The land in this part of Minnesota belonged to the Sioux Indians until 1852 when they sold it to the United States government. But it took some years before they departed from these, their favorite, hunting grounds. As long as the Indians occupied the land there was plenty of reindeer and other wild animals, but when the whites moved in all wild life disappeared, except for wolves and rabbits. Red Wing was an old Indian village, and, as we have seen, was the site of an early mission among the Indians. Here, too, the first white inhabitants of Goodhue County, settled. The Indian name, Hhoo-pah-doo-tah meant the village of Red Wing, the chief. His grave is said to be on the top of Barn Bluff, though of this no one is certain.

Around Red Wing there are (or rather were, for now they are largely destroyed) signs of the Mound builders. A large number of mounds were found especially on Purdy's farm, 5-6 miles west of Red Wing, on the road to Vasa, near the Cannon River, and some indications yet remain, though they have been plowed over for many years.

The Coming of the First Swedes to Goodhue County

Col. Hans Mattson, at present Secretary of State in Minnesota, was the first to bring Swedes to Goodhue County. In a letter in *Hemlandet*, 2nd year, No. 8 (1856), he wrote, "In September 1853 I went with a small party of Swedish immigrants to Minnesota to look for a place where together we might start a new settlement. When we got to St. Paul, Minnesota's largest city, some of my party took jobs, while I and four others went on to look for a future home. We had been directed to Red Wing which shortly before had been laid out as a town. We were told that fertile land was to be had in this area. We got on a steamboat and headed directly for this place. Red Wing has its name from a renowned Indian chief, who lived here long ago. The place is on the banks of the great Mississippi River, 50 miles below St. Paul. When we landed we found the whole shore where the city now lies, covered with Indian tents, but could see only 4 houses, indicating that people of our own race also were here. We met immediately several Americans, who received us in a very friendly way. When they learned our errand they got a carriage for us and a driver who was at home in the surrounding wilderness, to show us the country.

We went out the following day but found nothing satisfactory until we came up on the prairie where Vasa is now located. Here on this prairie we found the most fertile ground and could see oak forests all around. We had now seen enough and went right back to St. Paul to make ready our moving.

"Already we were in October, and we anticipated a cold winter. We thought that it was impossible at this late date to get houses built suitable for the women and children, so all who had families decided to stay in St. Paul for the winter. I and two others returned in order to take claims for all of us. Back on the big prairie we had with us a cloth tent, a stove, provisions and winter tools. As soon as we had erected our tent at Belle Creek, in a grove of trees, and put our romantic home in order, we went out to explore the land around us. We took several claims (by writing names on trees). We started building a house where we could spend the approaching winter. In a few weeks two families of our party came from St. Paul, and in the following summer (1854) the number had grown to 10 families. Also there were some Swedes then in Red Wing. Now (1856) there are over 100 Swedes in Vasa, and there is reason to believe that the number will be doubled next summer. Where there was wilderness there are now large cultivated fields and comfortable houses. Two and a half years ago we seldom heard any other sounds than those of wild animals, especially the howling of the wolves. Now we hear the sound of the ax in every corner of the woods, and the "who-haw" of the ox-driver on the way from forest and house. In place of the bands of America's brown natives we saw here at first we have now seen a crowd of almost a hundred Swedes gathered in this place to hear the preaching of the Gospel. At such a meeting when Pastor Norelius from Indiana conducted the worship service, a Lutheran congregation was organized, and the place was named Vasa, in memory of the great hero Gustaf Vasa who liberated our dear fatherland from tyrannical power and introduced in it the doctrines of the Lutheran Church. The name seems a happy choice in that the Swedes of Vasa emulate the great Gustaf Vasa and his successors in their endeavors and sacrifices for the common good of their small land (Vasa). Previously the place was known among the Americans as "the Swede Prairie," or "Mattson's settlement," also White Rock because of a white sandstone rock, in shape and size resembling a small Swedish church. It is said that the Sioux Indians formerly held their assemblies at this rather remarkable rock.

"The situation and nature of the land in Vasa is very favorable. The settlement is 8-15 miles from Red Wing. The prairie has from 2 to 3 feet of black loam above a red clay base; it is level and in general undulating. Everywhere woods are only a mile away. Most of the settlers have spring — or brook-water near their homes, but some have found good water at a depth of only 4-5 yards, despite the height of the land.

"The products of the soil bring good prices. Wheat brings $2 per bushel, corn, $1. We trade in Red Wing. I have mentioned what Red Wing was when I first came. Now it is a town of 1,000 inhabitants. There is a steam saw mill, a flour mill, a university (!) with a fund of $40,000; 16 stores, a printing place, a newspaper, and plenty of manual laborers of all kinds. About 100 Swedes have their home here. Red Wing is an example of what Minnesotans can accomplish in a short period.

"As to churchly matters here, the people of Vasa, are with only a couple of exceptions, Lutherans. But in general their attitude is such that towards those who favor the religious principles of other denominations they are not disdainful or sit in judgment, as happens among Swedes in many places. As a result of this tolerance we have been free of the religious controversies which unfortunately among the Swedes elsewhere have embittered social relationships and resulted in both spiritual and physical wounds. How it will be in the future depends greatly on the pastors we have, though experience amply proves that certainly not entirely on them. One building is now nearly complete which will be used as church and school house. We have asked for Pastor Norelius in Indiana and hope he will be here by Pentecost." Thus far H. Mattson.

The first Swedes in this area were: Hans Mattson from Önnestad in Kristianstad County, and his brother-in-law, a former teacher in Sweden, S.J. Willard from Fjelkinge, the same county; Peter Sjogren, who called himself Green in this country, from Ljuder in Kronoberg County, and who came to America in 1852; Carl Roos from Långbans hyttan, Värmland, a former color sergeant and surveyor, who came in 1853; Anders Gustaf Kempe from Varola in Skaraborg County, a former tanner, who also came in 1853. Mattson and Willard took the land where A.P. Friman now lives, a 40 acre piece just south of the present Lutheran church. Each had a log house, the former where Friman's house now stands, the latter across the ravine, just south of the stable. Both are still living, Mattson in Minneapolis, Willard in

Red Wing. Roos and Kempe built where Peter Nilson now lives, next to the post office at White Rock, and shared quarters. Their wives came from Sweden a few years later. Both are now dead. Roos died May 1889, almost 89 years old. Peter Sjogren made his home by Spring Creek on the spot now occupied by Carl Carlsson, about 3 miles from Red Wing. He moved first to Featherston, then to Kandiyohi County, then back again to this county, Welch Township, where he died. More will be said below of the others who came those early years.

Such was the beginning of the Swedish movement into Goodhue County. Since then the Swedes have continued to come and increased in numbers so that they now occupy wholly or to a large extent the following townships: Red Wing, Burnside, Welch, Cannon Falls, Vasa, Featherston, Goodhue, Belle Creek, Leon. These all form a large square, with Vasa — exclusively Swedish, in the center. Here as everywhere else, our countrymen had at first very meager resources. When they came they had practically nothing and had to start from scratch. They chose a place at the edge of woods, erected small simple log cabins, and as soon as they could and in any possible manner broke up a plot of ground where they could plant some potatoes and a few vegetables.

When they needed flour or something else from Red Wing they had to carry it in bags on their back 10 or more miles over deer tracks or Indian paths for there were at first no other roads. Gradually they acquired oxen who were more essential than cows, useful in the breaking of the ground and in transportation. It was in this earliest period which may be termed the ox-age that the remarkable "shriek-carts" were built, whose terrible noise still rings in the ears of those who ever heard it. The wheels of these carts or wagons consisted of rough oak blocks in which a hole was drilled to hold a rough wooden axle. Grease was not plentiful, and if the wheel was dry and the four such wheels on each cart began to shriek, one can imagine that there was no lack of music on the prairies of Goodhue County in those days. Anyone who has mastered the art of riding in that kind of oxcart was looked up to with respect and to such one might be tempted to tip his felt hat. No wonder that H. Mattson was considered almost a king when he became owner of the first team of horses, for the life and future of the people depended on means of power. Despite the toil and sacrifices called for in the conquest of the wild nature and taming the earth to yield the necessary sustenance, the pioneers exhibited an admirable courage, patience, and even cheerfulness. They did not

complain or moan about the difficulties, but were happy and contented. The future was bright with hope.

Naturally in every pioneer beginning material interests were
preeminent in one's thoughts and feelings. But our Swedish people,
especially of rural regions, have been reared in a Christian community
and, whatever the situation, have never wholly denied their Christian
heritage and man's higher, spiritual needs. Thus we are told that the
people in Vasa and Red Wing in the very earliest days, before any
preacher had set foot here, gathered for worship in any way possible.
In Vasa H. Mattson sometimes led the service and spoke to those attending. On one occasion, probably the summer of 1855, when the
people has assembled under the oaks of Carl Carlsson and Mattson
had concluded the service, he recalled that he had forgotten to end
with the benediction. "Wait men," he cried as the congregation
broke up, "I forgot to read the benediction, you have to come back."
Carl Carlsson turned his quid and replied, "That you will have to
keep till next time." and so it ended.

The First Pastoral Visit in This Area and the Organization
of Congregations in Vasa and Red Wing

I draw on my "Reminiscenses" in *Korsbaneret*, 1889 for some of
these events. "Together with Nils Hokansson (or Nils in Grankärr, as
he was called — died in Cannon Falls 1889) of West Point, Indiana,
I undertook a journey, my second, to Minnesota, August 27, 1855, to
find a place where Swedes in Indiana might settle, and to preach for
my countrymen whom I might meet in new places. We travelled to
Chicago and then by railroad, now finished as far as Duluth, on the
Mississippi, across from Dubuque. There we took a boat up the river
and landed in Red Wing the night of August 31. As soon as it grew
light I climbed up Barn Bluff by the river bank in order to get a view
of the region. I was richly rewarded for the exertion. Red Wing was
then a new town beginning to grow and just then was being blessed
by a lively land boom. Here was the land office for this whole part of
Minnesota and the taking up of land went on at a feverish rate. People
were frantic, each one trying to get the best pieces ahead of someone
else. Lots in town were sold and bought in such a frenzy that a
stranger might be led to believe something extraordinary would happen here. Houses, or rather shacks, went up incredibly fast, and all
kinds of stores sprang up as by a turn of the hand. It was both amus-

ing and instructive to observe people and the methods they employed
to grasp at once seemingly the whole world. One man — a Swede, as
I learned — who was engaged in building a small shanty which was
to serve him as some kind of business place, attracted my attention
by his assumed comical lord-of-the-manor attitude. He had folded a
few bills lengthwise between his fingers, stuffed his pockets with
documents as if with contracts and valuable papers, put a pencil
back of his ear and a hat on the back of his head. Thus arrayed he ran
back and forth on the street, waving his dollar bills, sorting his documents, talking right and left to passers-by about his land affairs as if
her were a very rich man. I found out later that the poor fellow
probably had no more than these four dollars between his fingers,
and was so ignorant that he could hardly write his name.

"Especially in boom times material interests are so strong and
overpowering that it seems impossible to turn men's minds toward
ideal or spiritual things. Yet there are everywhere those with clearer
vision who realize that in the long run a community cannot endure
or really grow merely by material means, and therefore, if not out of
principle then in prudence, they seek to satisfy spiritual needs. Such
men were then in Red Wing, who were intent on building a brick
building, where City Park now is, as a home for 'Hamlin University'
(this Methodist school with a great name was later moved to a site
between St. Paul and Minneapolis), and in bushes East of Plum Street,
they had put together a shed out of unfinished boards to represent a
Presbyterian church. Right in the midst of the boom and the excite-
ment of the pale-faces wandered bands of red men, who in stoic
calm and disdain beheld this to their minds strange and vain rivalry
which had arisen in a dwelling ground sacred to them and innocent
of such obscenity for hundreds of years. A deep melancholy came
over me as I observed this people, shoved aside and dying.

"As soon as I had my breakfast at the hotel I hurried out to look
for Swedes. Before long I met quite many, even some acquaintances
from Illinois. Among the first with whom I spoke was Hokan Olsson
from Mjelby in Blekinge, a close friend of rector H.B. Hammar, and
a man deeply interested in the church, and who has played an important part in Red Wing and its Lutheran congregation. Without
any doubt he was the first Swede in Red Wing to do anything about
the establishment of a Lutheran church there. It was he who spread
the report that I would conduct a service that evening (September 1),
the first such by any Swedish pastor in Red Wing. I myself told as

many as I met, and all were courteous at least, except one poor fellow who said "to h-- with running after a pastor." We were allowed to use the Presbyterians' 'shanty,' after I had talked with their pastor, J.W. Hancock, a former missionary among the Indians here and assured him of my orthodoxy! That evening about 100 were present. Everything went well, and it was decided that I should hold a service again the following day, in the afternoon, which was the 13 Sunday after Trinity. This I did and even a larger number attended. The question of organizing a congregation was raised, and a meeting for this purpose was announced for Monday evening the 3rd of September.

"After the Sunday afternoon service I was approached by a man named August Johnson, who lived 12 miles west of Red Wing, on a farm. He urged me to come there, and had me ride with him, when I consented. Neither roads nor carriages were then very common. We arrived at the settlement after dark and I was lodged with Carl Carlsson from Karlskoga. That night and early the next morning the word was spread that a worship service would be held Monday morning. I believe most of the farmers in the settlement came, in any case there was a full house. After the service 'The Swedish Evangelical Lutheran Congregation in Vasa' was organized, with 87 members, including children. Four children were baptized. This all happened in Carl Carlsson's home, located hardly a half mile northeast of the present Lutheran church, but long since razed. C. now lives at Spring Creek, not a member of any church. I promised to make another visit and then hurried to Red Wing. There that same evening at a meeting in the Presbyterian church 'The Swedish Evangelical Lutheran Church in Red Wing' was organized.

"I admit that the conditions for the organization of a Christian congregation in these places were in general not favorable, and in time I regretted what was done, yet I believe that God had a hand in it and that it was well that these congregations were formed with what material was available. History has shown that gradually they were nourished and developed into Christian congregations and that the work done there had the blessing of God. The members, adult and children enrolled in Red Wing, numbered 82.

"On September 20th I was again in Vasa, and stayed with S.J. Willard, later widely known as the county auditor. There I first met H. Mattson (later Colonel) who had been away when I was on my first visit. Now a farmer he was probably enjoying his quietest days. On the 21st we had service and the Lord's Supper at the home of Nils

Peterson. He had the largest log house in the settlement, a half mile south of the present church. After I had baptized a child, given the preparatory address (for communion) and preached the sermon I was stricken with fever and had to rest. The people waited patiently until I recovered sufficiently so that I could conclude the service and administer the sacrament.

"The next day we went around and explored the area as far as time permitted. When we came to the high point in the district now called Smoland, my companion remarked, 'Now let us return. You see how much land there is. Surely it won't all be claimed in our day!' They did not then entertain very high hopes of a rapid occupation of the area. I too thought I had seen enough so that I could report to the friends in Indiana that there was plenty of room in Vasa. But a year later there were not many pieces left for those who came then."

After these general observations we can now go on to the story of the particular congregations and places that are the subjects of this chapter.

Vasa

At the organization on September 3, 1855 only such articles were adopted as were necessary on the occasion. More detailed regulations were delayed until a pastor could be procured. The article on doctrine, however, received careful attention. It is almost identical with that proposed by the United Conference in 1857, except for the addition after the words "the Unaltered Augsburg Confession" a possibly stronger statement, "as interpreted by the other symbolical books of the Lutheran Church" etc. I will not say that the congregation was aware of the confessional standpoint thus adopted, but no one showed opposition to it. Swen Jacobsson, S.J. Willard and the senior Ola Olsson were elected deacons. It was decided for the present to join with the congregation in Red Wing in securing a pastor who could serve both places.

The first members of the congregation included almost all the Swedish people in the settlement at Vasa. They were:

Carl Carlson, a former miner, his wife Lovisa Pettersdotter and 3 sons from Karlskoga, Örebro County, and foster daughter Hilda Marie Kindgren, later married to Pastor Borén. Came to America 1854. His first place was 1/2 mile northeast of the present church, in section 15.

Ola Olsson, a widower, with sons Ola, Knut, Per, and daughter Else, from Mjellby, Blekinge; came to America 1854; lived near the high point west of Belle Creek, in section 8. Their cabin was for a long time the only one, in the brush, and was often visited by Indians roaming around. The father and youngest son died some years ago.

Jon Bergdahl, a widower, and daughter Malena from Önnestad, Kristianstad County; came to America 1853; lived about a 40 acre distance straight south of the church, in section 15. He is dead, the daughter married N.P. Malmberg.

Samuel Johnson and wife Stina Lisa Pettersdotter from Algutsboda, Kronoberg County, came to America 1854; a daughter Maria, one of the first, if not the first, child born and baptized in Vasa; lived in the Smolands district, sec. 10. The parents now live in Nehalem Valley, Oregon; the daughter, on Prairie Island, Goodhue County.

Gustaf Carlsson and wife Lovisa Johansdotter, with sons Frans, August, Alfred, and Aron, from Algutsboda, Kronoberg County; came to America 1854; lived in Smoland district, sect. 10. The father was killed by a falling tree, in the forest, 1880; the mother and eldest son, who has been a sheriff, live in Red Wing, the other son lives in Hector, Renville County, and the third son in Featherston, still a member of the church.

Erik Andersson and wife Helene Lovisa Pettersdotter and daughter Martha Ellen; he from western Ryd, Linköping County, came to America 1850; she from Lönneberga, Kalmar County, came 1848; daughter born in Jamestown, N.Y. They still live in their old home in Smoland dist., sec. 2; daughter married to Gustaf Larsson in Featherston.

Swante Johan Willard and wife Anna Mattsdotter and daughter Selma Adelaide; he born in Fjelkinge, teacher in Sweden, she, in Önnestad; came to America 1853; daughter born in St. Paul, baptized in Vasa, married to a Dane, Mr. Christiansen in Rush City. Willard lives in Red Wing, County auditor 12 years; first wife died.

Jonas Fredrik Gustafson from Bjurkärn and wife Kristina Lovisa Eriksdotter, from Årsta, Örebro County; came to America, he 1853, she 1854; son Gustaf Adolf, one of the first Swedish children born in Vasa. At first they lived at Belle Creek, behind the children's home on "Jonah-land," now in Town of Belle Creek, still members of the congregation. In his younger days Jonas was famous for his strength. When the oxen had difficulty drawing a stump he laid it on his own shoulders and carried it.

Nils Petersson and wife Elna Jönsdotter; he from Stoby, she from Höginge, Kristianstad County, came to America 1854; lived one half mile south of the church, sec. 21; he died, she remarried and lives near Hallock, Red River Valley. His father

Per Nilsson and wife Pernilla, with daughters Hanna, Kjersti, Nilla and Anna; came from Stoby 1855 and lived a little east of John Nilsson's place in sec. 21. They were among the wealthiest families that came to Vasa in those days, accordingly he was known as "the rich man." The parents and Nilla are long since gone; Hanna married Erik Eriksson and now lives in Minneapolis, Kjersti married Hans Mattson, Anna last married to an American.

Nils Westerson from Hvetofta, wife Sissa Jocobsdotter from Vånga, Kristianstad County, and sons Per, Jons, Svante, and daughter Annette; came from West Karup 1854, lived a couple of miles southwest from the present church, in sec. 20. They still have their old place but often visiting elsewhere.

August Jonasson, farm hand, from Algutsboda; came 1854, died 1857; lived in the Smoland district.

Peter Johansson from Algutsboda and wife Karolina Petersdotter from Ekeberga, Kronoberg County; came to America 1854; the son Johan Wilhelm, one of the earliest born in Vasa, lived in Smoland district; wife and son died; he remarried and living in Town of Goodhue.

Swen Jacobsson from Halland County and wife Matilda Soderberg from Östergotland; came early from Sweden, year uncertain; son Joseph born in Moline, Ill.; lived on And. P. Johnson's place in Smoland district; had a child buried on the place, August 1856. After a few years moved to Moline.

Anders Nilsson from Wiby and wife Kersti Monsdotter from Trolle Ljungby, Kristianstad County. They came from Ljungby 1855 with a son Nils and a daughter Karna, lived in Skone district. The father died, the wife and Nils and younger children live on Per Nilsson's old farm south of the church; the daughter K., widow of P. Engberg, lives in Red Wing.

Swen Swensson and wife Nilla Larsdotter from Trolle Ljungby, with son Swen and daughters Karna and Bengta came here from Sweden 1855 and still live on their old place in Skone district; Swen lives in Moorhead, daughters married, live in Minneapolis.

Swen Olsson from Nymö and wife Karna Andersdotter from

Trolle Ljungby and daughter Martha. Came from Sweden 1855 and lived in Skone district, sec. 14; now live on another farm in the southern part of the township, near Potato Mound; wife died, he remarried, to Anna B. Bernsdotter; daughter Martha married to a Scotchman in Minneapolis.

Bengt Andersson from Trolle Ljungby and wife Elna Larsdotter from Fjelkestad; came here 1855 and have remained in their old home in Skone district.

Ola Swensson, farmhand, never married, lived in Smoland district, now dead.

Signild Andersdotter, housemaid, from Trolle Ljungby, came 1855, later married Anders August Johnson and moved to Bailey-town, Indiana.

Matts Mattsson, former homeowner, with sons Hans and Lars from Önnestad, Kristianstad County; came to America with son Lars 1852, spending some time in Moline; lived with sons; now dead. Hans came to America 1851 and has had a varied career, day laborer, farmer, merchant, real estate dealer, lawyer, county auditor, served in the army and mustered out with title, honor, and rank of colonel; twice secretary of state, consul general in East Indies, etc. Lars lived at Belle Creek, sec. 20; now lives near Hallock in Red River Valley.

Matias Flodquist, formerly tradesman, from Ekers parish in Nerike; came to America 1854. He and the next two named originally took claims on the land that came to be known as Jemtland. He moved away soon to unknown destination.

Carl and Gustaf Peterson, brothers, from the village of Arvika, where presumably they were merchants; came at the same time as Flodquist, moved away early in 1860's.

Olof Peterson with wife and 1 child; came in 1854 from Stoby and lived on the place where Per Mortenson now lives in Town of Belle Creek. The wife drowned in Spring Creek; he moved away and probably lives in Iowa. His brother

Niklas Peterson from Stoby and wife Helena Olsdotter from Finja, Kristianstad County; came to America 1854 and are still on their farm near White Rock.

Bonde Olsson, farm hand, no information.

Nils Ekelund, farm hand, came from Bosjö Kloster, Malmöhus County, 1854; lived on J. Norelius' old place, married a Norwegian widow — a sister of Rev. J. Johnson, and moved to Cambridge, Iowa 1865.

Bengt Kilberg, carpenter, came 1855 from Munktorp, Malmöhus County, built the old church in Vasa 1862; lives in Red Wing.

Peter Vedin, farm hand, no information.

Carl Roos with wife and two children; came from Långban-shyttan, Värmland, 1853; served in Civil War, though above age, belonging to Minn. 3 Reg. He soon left the congregation; died May 1889.

And. G. Kempe, former tannery-owner, from Varola, Skaraborg County; came to America 1853; lived with Roos, moved to Red Wing, died there.

Besides these there were some families and single persons living in Vasa or who came later in the Fall, who were not along when the congregation was organized, as Carl Himmelman and Erik Eriksson from Karlskoga, Per Larsson, a widower and his daughter from Win-slöf, Peter Andersson and family from Mjölby, Linköping County; came to America 1851; Jons Olsson and wife from Hjeräs; T.G. Pearson and wife from Stoby and Önnestad, he came in 1851, she in 1852. They lived a few years in Knoxville, Illinois before coming here. P. was a school teacher in Sweden; he has served in the state legislature and has been a justice of the peace many years. They now live near the church.

These were the original members of the Swedish Evangelical Lutheran Church in Vasa. Space does not permit listing the names of those who joined the following years up to 1860, but certain groups will be mentioned in the course of the narrative.

Some of the First Happenings in the New Congregation

Already on September 30, 1855 a congregational meeting was held to call a pastor. Pastor E. Norelius received a unanimous call. On the question of salary it had been thought that Vasa, Red Wing and the new settlement at Lake Pepin (Stockholm) could unite in of-fering $400-$500 as a yearly pastor's salary, but because of the rather great distance of the last named the arrangement was limited to the other two congregations. So Vasa decided for itself to pay $200 a year, half in cash, half in provisions. This would be raised to $300 if the pastor would conduct a 4 month district school. The Red Wing congregation cooperated by promising a salary of $200 for the year.

During the winter logs were brought together and in the Spring a house was erected at the East end of Willard's farm to serve as school house, church, and parsonage, for in the call it was stipulated that I might live there if I wished. It was a small structure, 16 ft. square, reared out of rough logs, and on my arrival it had neither floor, windows (two small openings), door or clay between the logs. This small place was used for services as late as 1862, with a small addition made of boards in 1858. In the addition there was a dirt floor, planks were laid on poles driven into the ground to serve as benches. An event as late as Christmas 1861 lives vividly in my memory. We had "Julotta" (Christmas morning service), and A.E. Bellin's wife had made a straw wreath for the occasion, decorated with some chicken feathers, and hung from the low ceiling with some candles affixed to it. The place was packed with people standing so close together that one could not move. Worst of all, the straw wreath caught fire and in the crush it was not possible to reach it to put out the flame. The place filled with smoke so we could hardly breathe, but no further misfortune was suffered. In winter snow some times blew into the loft and as the room warmed up the melted snow rained down on everything and on the people. It didn't seem worth the trouble to improve the place since every one expected that a new church would be built.

PASTOR E. NORELIUS.

As mentioned I received the call and accepted without much deliberation, prompted both by the spiritual need of the people and by a strong inner impulse to take up work in the wilderness. Fortunately I lacked both the ability to look into the future or the maturity of age to count the cost of this undertaking, otherwise flesh and blood would surely have exclaimed: don't go to the wilderness of Minnesota. Yet after more than 30 years of living and working within these boundaries I now see that God had a hand in my decision. To speak much of oneself and my own experiences is not admirable, for as Aesop says, even fools can do that, it is egotistical, I know. But in such an account as this, where I want to give a true picture of the times, it is hard to avoid speaking about oneself if I am to tell of my experiences. I want neither praise, admiration, or pity for what I have lived through of pioneer's woes. Others have undergone the same and probably fared even worse. My purpose is only to give a true account of former days, of use, possibly, for our descendants.

My wife and I arrived in Red Wing May 16, 1856, and entered on my duties by preaching in Vasa on the first Sunday after Trinity, when the gospel lesson was the parable of "the rich man and Lazarus." The service was held in Per Nilsson's home, and I did not then know that he was referred to as "the rich man" or I might have been more careful in my expression. But every thing went well and he was understanding enough not to think I was alluding to him. He allowed me to live in his house free of cost for several weeks while I was setting up our own place. We even had our services there until we got a floor in the school house. Our furniture was no hindrance — it consisted of a bureau, a stool, and a bed. While living there I had three memorable experiences. The first was a visit from a visitor from a far distance. When I came to Red Wing on Sunday, June 28th Pastor Esbjörn was there, on his mission to collect funds for the Scandinavian professorship. He preached in my place at both the morning and afternoon services, explained his errand and received not so few contributions to the professor's fund. Then in the evening we proceeded to Vasa. I had come to Red Wing on a borrowed horse. On the return trip Pastor Esbjörn rode and I led the horse, for Esbjörn was not a good horseman, it was dark and the road uncertain. We arrived safely at midnight at the place I had to return the horse, then we had a good way on foot to my quarters. Esbjörn felt so tired and bruised that he had to rest a while, before going farther. So we lay down on some boards and went to sleep. Late at night we finally got home. But my wife was non-plussed in receiving this dear guest for we had only one bed. But heart-room creates house-room, and the beloved man stayed with us the whole week. We visited almost every home in the settlement and on Sunday he preached a glorious sermon on "Christ's Transfiguration."

The second event was my discovery of another Swedish settlement near Vasa, which later became known as Spring Garden. On Sunday July 6th just as I was preparing to go to the service in the school house (which we now had begun to use), there came over the prairie from the south an unfamiliar ox-cart filled with people. There were two families, each with a small child which they wanted baptized. The one family was Magnus Edstrom, the other Johan Johnson Wanberg. From them I got my first accurate information about Spring Garden. They had not known where Vasa was, but had started out to find the place, driving many crooked roads through brush, over hills and valleys, for they had heard that a pastor had come to Vasa and they were determined to have their children baptized. They earnestly begged me to come to Spring Garden which I did as early as the 12th of that month. Thus the field of activity expanded. In June I had already paid a visit to Stockholm, Wisconsin, and promised to come there as often as I could.

The third event made a painful impression on me. I knew well enough that my congregatin did not consist of angels, but I was not prepared to be cooly invited by the members to a drinking party and card playing. The matter of Christian discipline, indeed, did give me my hardest problems. I was tempted to take radical measures, but came later to realize that you cannot go farther in discipline than the Christian consciousness of the congregation extends, and that this consciousness must first be awakened.

Meanwhile I endeavored to get my own hut to creep into. About 3 miles southwest of the school house, near White Rock where John Monsson has his home, I bought the claim rights of 160 acres for $130. Here beside a lovely spring was a small so-called "claim" cabin, 8 ft. square with turf roof and earth floor. As an addition I built a shed out of two loads of rough, unplaned boards, brought from Red Wing. This was our residence and we moved in before there were floor, roof, windows or doors, and at nights slept on a heap of chips until we had better. Soon we had roof, of a kind, for we stretched cloth to form both roof and ceiling, but since it was loose rain came through, and then we had to sleep under an umbrella. If you wonder why the congregation was not concerned about furnishing a house for the pastor, or at least helping in building one, my answer is, the congregation could not. The members were not better off themselves and had all they could do to take care of themselves. My neighbors were in similar circumstances and even worse, for some had large families to care for. To the west my nearest neighbor was T.G. Pearson and wife who began about the same time to build and live like ourselves. One mile northeast was Jacob Rassmusson, or Robertson as he called himself here, who had come and settled here during the summer. He came with his family from Pecatonica, Illinois, on ox-cart, through Wisconsin. Among other useful things he brought with him was a spinning wheel which now served as shelter. For he set it up on the ground, covered it with cloth and quilts and lay under it the first nights. Soon he dug a hole in a hillside and hung a quilt in front of the opening as a door. His daughters were then little and shy, and when anyone came they scurried off immediately into the hole, just like a bunch of small ground squirrels then so prevalent. Another example: Sven Turner and his wife came that summer to Vasa from Batavia, Illinois, and began in the same primitive way to make a home for themselves, on the same spot where they still live. They made a shed without floor or roof and spread a cloth over their bed against the rain. Here their first child, a daughter, was born on July 4th. When these conditions were general and each one had to exercise ingenuity in order to survive it was not to be expected that the congregation should provide a house for the pastor.

We got along well, however, in our little shed. We put wallpaper on the boards, laid a cheap carpet on the floor, made table and chairs with legs inserted in holes bored in boards, and tried to make everything pleasant. Finding food was the worst problem. None was here except for a chance catch of fish in the brook. As yet the land had produced nothing. Town was 15 miles away — and little with which to buy — and no conveyance. It was hard for my wife, for I had to be gone so much of the time. I had now to make my visits, on foot, to Red Wing, Vasa, Spring Garden, Cannon Falls, and Stockholm, Wisconsin.

Dr. Passavant of Pittsburgh, Pa. paid us a happy visit in late August or early September. We worried about entertaining him in our very meager house-hold. But it went better than we thought. Naturally he got to use our one bed, but unfortunately it rained that night and the roof leaked. No wonder that he dreamed that he lay at the bottom of the sea and agonized. This was his first trip to Minnesota and I remember how he conceived all kinds of thoughts and plans to advance the interests of the Lutheran Church. Among other things he pondered on buying a piece of land for a school, to serve as a mission among the Swedes. We looked at the land around White Stone for this purpose, and he liked it, but the matter never went beyond this dream.

THE OLD CHURCH IN VASA.

Later in the Fall a prairie fire swept over the area, threatening to devastate us. I was gone but by her strenuous efforts my wife managed to save the house. Some of our American neighbors to the south lost everything they had in the fire.

In October a party of our friends from Indiana arrived and during the next 3 weeks we took care of up to 20 persons in our small place. I do not now understand how room and harmony lasted so long. We continued to live in our shelter until November 4th, when snow and cold weather set in, then moved into Red Wing and resided there.

After this digression about the pastor's condition and experiences, I return to the congregation's doings and decisions in 1856, the first year of its existence.

As soon as we got a floor in the school house we began to hold our services there and as a rule I preached every other Sunday. After the first Sunday the people displayed a marked reluctance to attend. Sometimes I had only a dozen in church but on my way to the schoolhouse on a Sunday morning I would meet many headed for the fields, with ax or gun on shoulder. This gradually changed for the better, but it took time to establish even a formal, respectable churchly habit. Four congregational meetings were held during the year, two of these devoted to completion of the constitution. At the meeting on June 22nd a proposed draft was discussed and adopted. It is of historic interest for it became the basis of the congregational constitution which the United Conference prepared and recommended the following year, hence I want to give an account of it here. The proposal consisted of 8 articles: name, doctrine, membership, pastor, deacons and trustees, church council, business meeting, conclusion. The first three articles are almost identical with those Pastor Erl. Carlsson used to introduce in those congregations he organized, of which we have already treated. The following articles are new and read thus:

"Article 4. The Pastor

1. The pastor shall be elected by vote at a congregational meeting. To issue a call to a pastor a 2/3 majority vote of the congregation's voting members shall be required.
2. A pastor cannot be dismissed unless a 2/3 majority of the voting members agree.
3. The pastor shall proclaim the Word of God and administer the holy sacraments in accordance with the Confession of faith of the congregation (cf. Art. II); he shall live a Christian and edifying life; visit the sick; be concerned about Christian instruction and fostering of the youth; comfort, instruct, exhort and warn, both publicly and privately, as the Word of God prescribes (1 Tim. 3).
4. Charges against the pastor may not be made without two or three witnesses (1 Tim. 15:19). If unfortunately he be found in error in regard to life or teaching the church council shall exhort and warn him, in a friendly manner. If this does not have the desired effect the matter shall be referred to the synod to which he belongs.

5. The pastor shall be entitled to receive the salary which the congregation from time to time has promised.

"Article 5. Deacons and Trustees

1. Three deacons shall be elected yearly at a congregational meeting.

Their duties are: to conduct the service in the pastor's absence; to have a general oversight of the behaviour of the members; to visit and secure help for the poor and the sick; to assist the pastor in the exercise and maintenance of church discipline; to be of help in the church, etc.

2. According to the laws of Minnesota not less than three nor more than nine trustees shall be elected annually at a congregational meeting.

They shall take care of all church property and be responsible for the financial affairs of the congregation.

3. One of the trustees shall serve as treasurer and keep accurate account of all income and expenditures of the congregation and render a report at its annual business meeting.

4. The trustees shall be elected for a term, as follows: the first group for one year, the second for two years, the third for three years. Thus, after the first year one class will be elected each year.

5. The congregation may also elect a secretary who shall keep an accurate record of the congregational meetings and be responsible for all the books and papers of the congregation.

"Article 6. The Church Council

1. The Church Council consists of pastor, deacons and trustees.

2. The Church Council is the congregation's judiciary, and has to examine and settle matters of controversy or dissension if such unfortunately arise in the congregation; it has to call in, hear, warn and exhort accused members, in friendly manner, and to reach agreement on measures that can best advance the welfare of the congregation.

3. The Council as such shall not deal with financial matters.

4. In the absence of the pastor (when the congregation has such) the Council shall not make decisions in important matters, such as exclusion of members, etc. In any case 2/3 of the Council members shall be present when decisions are made in any matter that may come before the Council.

5. The pastor shall enter the decisions of the Council in its record book.

"Article 7. Congregational Meetings

1. A yearly business meeting shall be held June 25 every year, to elect deacons, trustees, treasurer, etc. and to receive a report on finances, etc. Reports shall be made by trustees, treasurer, and secretary, so that all members will be made acquainted with the conditions of the congregation.

2. Voting members in the business meetings are all confirmed male members who are truly members of the congregation.

3. The pastor is ex-officio chairman of the congregational meeting. The annual meeting cannot be held in his absence.

4. The pastor shall call other meetings of the congregation when circumstances require or at least 10 members demand it."

The concluding article concerns changes in the constitution.

When the proposal of the United Conferences appeared (1857) it was regularly adopted at the meeting June 25, 1858. But to return to the meeting June 22, 1856. After action on the constitution election of deacons took place, for one year. Reelected were those chosen at the organization meeting, namely Ola Ohlsson, Sven Jacobsson, S.J. Willard.

At this meeting the question of site for the prospective church was raised. Willard generously promised to set aside 10 acres of his land, on which the school house stood, as site for church, cemetery, and school house. The offer was accepted, and it was decided to build here the future church. As we shall see later the place of the church in Vasa was not thus determined.

On July 6, 1856 the congregation met again, and the first trustees were chosen in accordance with the law and the congregation was incorporated. These trustees were: Peter Nilsson, 1 year, Carl Carlsson, 2 years. Olof Peterson, 3 years.

New Arrivals

During the summer many new people arrived, some directly from Sweden, some from Illinois. Those from Sweden came from Trolle Ljungby and neighboring parishes of Kristianstad County. Among them were Lasse Pehrson and a large family; Pehr, Lars and Nils Jonsson; Jons Nilsson from Backen; Jons Nilsson from Dalen; Ola Andersson; — all from Trolle Ljungby; Jons Olsson, Jr. and family from Kiaby; Nils Pehrson, and family, ditto; Abram Nilsson from Gustaf Adolfs parish; Anders Monsson, from Fjelkinge; Per Monson from Viby. Those who came from other places in America were, Goran Johnsson and family from Frinnaryd Jönkoping County, came to America 1854; Swen Turner and wife, from Wieslanda, to America 1853, came here from Batavia, Illinois; John Johnson and wife from Ljunga, and brother And. Aug. Johnson, to America 1854; Jacob Robertsson (Rassmussen) and family from Katslösa, Malmöhus County, came to America 1852, had lived some years in Pecatonica, Illinois; Sven P. Peterson and family, he from Kisa, Linköping County, came to America 1849, here from Sugar Grove, Pa.; Nils P. and Johan Ohfelt from Färlöf came to America 1852 and here from St. Paul, the latter died in the Civil War; Nils Swenson from Fäsum, Kristianstad County, came to America 1853, here from St. Paul; Bengt Nilsson, former county official, and family from Kärda, Jönköping County, came to America 1853 and here from Illinois; Jonas Jonasson from Malmbäck, Jönköping County, and wife Johanna, from Barkeryd, and children, came from Sweden 1852 and here from Pecatonica, Illinois, settled along Cannon River in Town of Cannon Falls; at same time and place Krants, a former cavalry soldier, and family, from the same place in Sweden, settled there; Hokan Olsson, Jr. and family from Mjellby in Blekinge, came to America 1854 and here from St. Charles, Illinois; A.G. Kempe's wife and children from Varola; Carl Johansson and family from Värö in Halland, Anders Monson and wife from the same parish, all came to America 1854 and spent some time in Wisconsin before coming here. Possibly there were others who came and settled here during the summer, but I do not now recall their names.

During the Fall I undertook to go through the whole settlement to count the number and find out how many did not belong to the congregation. At the congregational meeting on November 8th I could report that there were 185 people in the place and 101 confirmed persons who wanted to belong. This number included all who already were members and wanted to join — beside this there was hardly a single Swedish inhabitant. At the same time I received pledges of $260 toward the pastor's salary, somewhat over the sum promised in the call. But at the end of the year $67 was unpaid, and never did come in.

At this meeting it was decided to hold a school in the congregation for 2 1/2 months. J. Engberg, then a student, later a book dealer in Chicago, (died January 1, 1890) was chosen as teacher with a salary of board, room, and $35 a month. The school started November 15, 1856. It indicates that the congregation was interested early in the matter. Though its career has been fraught with strife and dissension the school has maintained itself to some degree from that date to this. The roll of teachers from the beginning, in order, reads thus: J. Engberg, Lovisa Peterson, Jane Nilsson, Lars Andersson, Lundin, S.F. Westerdahl, J. Magny, A. Andersson, P.T. Lindholm, etc. The first resolution concerning the salary of the teacher was that every member between 21 and 55 years of age should pay 50 cents a year. This decision was carried out by payment with potatoes, which were left in the school room and froze. Engberg's salary was thus pretty meager. The same meeting voted to furnish the school with benches and a pulpit, and to dedicate the cemetery. The school furnishings were hardly extravagant, since it was announced that Nils Petersson would provide them at a cost of $9.50. Beyond this sum the whole building had a cash expense of $28 which was apportioned at the end of the year among the members.

The cemetery was dedicated Sunday, November 9th, 1856. The resolution to fence it in was never carried out. Through the years quite a number of persons were buried here — the first was the body of Anders Monsson's wife, Maria Andersdotter who froze to death on the prairie the night of December 13th, 1856. Later some were removed to the new cemetery, but a large number still lie in what is now a tilled field.

The first confirmation children in Vasa were Anders Johan and Maria, a son and daughter of Jonas Jonasson and wife. They walked the long way from Cannon River to White Rock for instruction and were confirmed in the Fall of 1856. In 1857 three were confirmed, Nilla Person (Mrs. Wohlfart), Anna Charlotta Kempe (Mrs. Fredricks), and Boel Robertson (Mrs. Forseli). Also in the following year there were three, but then the number increased constantly until in some years there have been over 60 confirmed.

1857 was a difficult year, and conditions were severe until the outbreak of the Civil War. They resulted from the intense speculation mania which reached even to the pioneer settlement in Vasa. People borrowed money on their land as security, partly to pay the government land office for the purchase, partly to be able to buy beasts of burden, tools, etc. When the speculation bubble burst the times turned hard and debts were unpaid. One while it looked as if the majority would lose their lands and the settlement be totally ruined. Yet with industry and sacrifice — and the Swede can sacrifice in time of need — most fought their way through these difficult days. But the congregation's development suffered. At the same time the Word of God seemed more powerful than before, and some began seriously to seek the way to life. This was the case later in the year, earlier, godlessness had been prevalent. Many lived a wild life, defied openly the Word of God and the pastor, throwing all advice and warning to the winds. The hard times came and their senses were tamed.

A considerable increase of people occurred in the summer and fall, bringing some with more spiritual interests, but also some inclined toward Methodism. The newcomers included Olof Polsson and family from Sveg in Herjeådalen; Erik Polsson from the same place; Per Sjulsson and family, also from Sveg, he was killed by lightning a few year later; Erik Jonasson and family; Jons Zakrisson and family; Olof Hansson and family; Jon Monsson and family from Storsjö and Tännäs in Herjeådalen. These came directly from Sweden, most of them making their homes in that part of the settlement which received its name from them — Jemtland. Also a former coppersmith, Anders Erik Bellin and family from Karlskoga; Johan Sundell and family from Sund in Östergötland to America in 1851 and here from Sugar Grove, Pa. Germund Johnsson and family from Kisa came to America 1846 and here from Sugar Grove; Nils Andersson and family from Essunga in Vestergötland came to America 1854 and here from Illinois; etc.

On June 25th the congregation had a meeting which I would like to consider as a starting point for its course in some of the following years. Jacob Robertson, Johan Sundell and Sven Peter Peterson were elected deacons, all for one year. This choice was the dawn of a better day. In 1858, after the adoption of the constitution recommended by the United Conference, 6 deacons were elected, namely, Carl Johnson in Spring Creek and Per Jonsson in Dalen for 3 years, Joh. Sundell and Jon Bergdahl for 2 years, and T.G. Pearson and Nils Svenson for 1 year. For many years after this only 2 deacons were elected for 3 years; 1859 T.G. Pearson and A. Vesterson, 1860 Ola Polsson and Joh Sundell, and in place of Carl Johnson who had become a Baptist, Jacob Robertson.

The original trustees were Per Nilsson, 1 year, Carl Carlsson, 2 years, Olof Peterson, 3 years. When Olof Peterson moved in 1856,

T.G. Pearson was elected in his place, November 22, 1856. In 1857 Sven Jacobsson was elected for 3 years in place of P. Nilsson, whose term expired. In 1858 Carl Carlsson was reelected for 3 years, and in 1859 T.G. Pearson and Anders Vesterson, both for 3 years. Evidently the *Minutes* are erroneous, for not more than one would be elected for three years — the other doubtlessly was elected to fill a vacancy. In 1860 Erik Erikson was elected for three years.

In those days large collections were unknown in Vasa. At the 1857 meeting a report reveals that "during the year collections have amounted to $3.15, most of which has now been expended."

Organist and Sexton

In the *Minutes* of the congregational meeting 1857 we read: "Congregation and pastor had often felt the need of a leader in singing, and when the matter was raised it was resolved to ask Nils Pehrson to assume this duty. He agreed to try, and the congregation promised to take one or more collections for him. Further measures would be taken after he had given the matter a trial." Nils Pehrson was a smart person, and tried alright, and though it did not always go so well, it went, and people were satisfied. But after a few times when it didn't go well it was apparent that congregational singing was in a low estate. In 1859 a psalmodikon was purchased, and A.J. undertook to play it and lead the singing at a salary of $15. After a year, it is reported he was satisfied with $4 if he could keep the psalmodikon which had seen its day. It was in that year that the following incident occurred. Borén was then pastor, holding service every other Sunday. When he was not there one of the deacons led. By now the Methodists had become active in Vasa, and a preacher Ahlstrom was very popular, and liked by some of the congregation. One Sunday when Borén was absent, Ahlstrom appeared in the schoolhouse, hoping to be asked to preach, as some doubtless desired. T.G. Pearson, the deacon, sat by the pulpit, waiting for the service to begin, signalling to the organist to start playing and singing. But the organist was in no hurry, and kept looking back to the Methodist preacher as if he expected him to come forward and conduct the service. Pearson then told him to begin, but he only sat and waited. Then leaning over and whispering in his ear Pearson exclaimed, "If you don't play and sing you will not get your salary." Then he started.

We do not know who was organist in 1860 but the 1861 congregational meeting reports, "Since the organist last year volunteered his services there was no question of arrears in payment. Still announcement was made that over half of the members had contributed to the person who had served in this capacity, in the amount of $16, far above what he would have requested. The new pastor has been accustomed to lead the singing himself, so there is no necessity to elect any one to the position." So pastor and cantor became the same, as at first. On October 6th, 1862 the trustees were authorized to hire a competent organist at a reasonable salary, and from that date L. Engberg served as organist until 1878 in a very satisfactory manner.

Jon Bergdahl was elected as the first sexton in 1857. The salary was minimal — he was to receive one collection. He was succeeded by Olof Polsson for a year. By the time of the congregational meeting in 1859 neither one of them had received any compensation, so it was decided to have two offerings that fall for them. At the same meeting Per Sjulsson was elected to the position at a salary of $3 for the year.

The Pastor's Salary.

At the 1857 congregational meeting it was decided to pay the salary of the pastor by voluntary pledges payable either in money or farm products. The crops were small that year and money very scarce. The people were greatly concerned about their own subsistence, so it is no wonder that the pastor's salary was small. About $200 had been pledged, but at the annual meeting 1858 $100 was unpaid and there was no prospect of meeting the balance. These provisions were then made for 1858: On the first and last days of November the members should meet in the schoolhouse to contribute what they wished of farm products, and in addition two offerings should be made for him, one on the first Sunday in January 1859, one at Easter. When I left Minnesota early in November 1858 I had received one barrel of beans and a few bushels of corn. While I could not use them, those who ate the beans claimed they could not have survived the winter without them. This indicates how hard were the years 1857 and 1858.

The salary in Pastor Borén's time, from November 1858 to the summer of 1861, was small and irregularly paid. In 1859 it was set at $200 for the year, in 1860 the trustees were asked to visit the members and gather voluntary gifts, in cash or wheat.

After my return to the congregation in September 1861 the record of salary payments read thus:

1861	salary	set	at	$200	amount	paid	$137.55
1862	"	"	"	"	"	"	200
1863	"	"	"	250	"	"	250
1864	"	"	"	300	"	"	300
1865	"	"	"	350	"	"	350
1866	"	"	"	500	"	"	500
1867	undetermined				"	"	500

For 1868 when Pastor Cederstam was vice-pastor the salary was fixed at $1000, also in 1869. In 1870 I suggested, as trial, that I would pay for the furnishings of the parsonage and all the congregation's expenditures, if the members would contribute free will gifts for both purposes. The amount paid in was $1174.20. When the expenditures, building costs, and assistance to the pastor had been taken care of, little or nothing remained for the salary. That experiment was not repeated. From 1871 to 1888 the salary had been set at $1000 for the year and been paid regularly.

Church and Church Site.

At the annual meeting 1857 the congregation decided to create a church building fund and that the schoolhouse should belong to the public school district with the provision that on certain terms the congregation have use of it. The understanding was that the school district would maintain the building. Yet in the summer of 1858 the congregation made one addition of 45 1/2 boards, 24 studdings, and 50 cents in cash. Each family donated a board. In 1858 it was again voted to establish a building fund, but since nothing was done the resolution was rescinded in 1859. In October that year the decision about the schoolhouse also was rescinded and it was resolved that henceforth it should be only church property and serve as the church. A Methodist and a Baptist congregation had come into being and each wanted to use the school for meetings, though the Lutherans had built it for their own use. This happened during Borén's pastorate and caused not a little controversy.

Here as in many another of our settlements the question of site for the church occasioned a long and bitter struggle. Probably this could have been avoided if Willard had given the deed for the 10 acres he had promised for the purpose, but he did not do this. At the meeting the congregation resolved, "Since there is no assurance as to securing title to the promised piece of land, the trustees are to ascertain as quickly as possible if Mr. Willard will give an unqualified "Warranty Deed" for this lot, and if not the congregation shall choose another location." No deed was forthcoming, so in the winter of 1858 a list was circulated as to what other place could be agreed to. Two places had been mentioned, the one in the vicinity of the school on land then owned by Olof Polsson, the other at the crossroad on Sven P. Petersson's land, where John Andersson's new house stands. At a meeting on April 10, 1858 the latter place won 6 more votes than the former, but this did not settle the matter. When Willard assured them that there was no danger in building the church on the old site, and agreement on this was possible, it was voted again to abide by that choice. But this did not last. New proposals were made, one decision contravened another. During Borén's time we cannot follow them all in the *Minutes*. At a meeting probably in the winter or spring of 1860 we read, "Since there was still no agreement on the site of the new church, a new vote was taken, and the largest number of votes favored a lot on Erik Eriksson's land." This lay some distance southeast of the school, on land now owned by P. Trolin. The intention was to move the schoolhouse there and enlarge it. But by June opinions had changed, and the proposal now was to sell the school for $60 and use the money on a building "on some spot on the east or west side of Gustaf Carl's road on a height north of the gateway to Willard's old farm." So the record reads and the church council was commissioned to negotiate the purchase of one or two acres of this place. This site must have been somewhat south of the Swedish Baptist Church. Even this decision wasn't realized. Again on January 12, 1861 a meeting was held to decide on a location. Six places were now voted on: 1) the original choice, 2) the hill beside H. Mattson's farm (The present church site), 3) the already mentioned Olof Polsson's land, 4) Sven Petersson's corner, 5) a lot on Carl Carlsson's land, 6) "north of the gateway to Willard's old place." On voting the Olof Polsson's spot received 40 "yes" against 9 "no" votes. The trustees were to secure the deed, and a building committee was established to present plans for the building. At another meeting in two weeks, the trustees reported that the Olof Polsson's land was too uneven and unsuitable for the building, so they had decided to purchase a place on Erik Ericsson's land on the same line. The congregation gave its consent and voted to buy 2 acres here. The building committee brought in its proposal, and it was decided to use brick. Now things were to move, "every settler should provide 2 logs as long as could possibly be procured." Again nothing happened. The troublesome dissension caused some to lose patience and on their own initiative they began to haul stone for a building on Sven Petersson's corner.

When I returned to the congregation in the fall of 1861 the matter was still undecided. A meeting was held September 7th and decisions were reached that finally led to results, but caution was called for in reaching the goal. A committee of 11 was named. It was to decide on the site by the first Sunday of October and its decision was to be final. The members of the committee should live at least 2 miles from the schoolhouse, hence were from the edge of the settlement in all directions. Beside the pastor, they were: Truls Johnsson, Niklas Petersson, Jons Olsson, Sr., G.M. Englund, Nils Swensson, Jona Jonasson, Erik Andersson, Goran Johnsson, Johannes Andersson, Jon F. Gustafsson. A decision was also reached to proceed with building. The committee quickly were united on the site, namely the one where the church now stands. This was undoubtedly the best in the whole settlement as far as centrality and beauty are concerned, but the land belonged to a Dr. Whitmore in Wabasha and we did not know if he would sell some of it to us. Together with Nils Swensson I visited him to negotiate. He did not want to sell unless he could sell the whole property. He wanted $320 in gold for the 80 acres, half the amount to be paid now, the other half after a year at 10% interest. We returned home, and called the committee together. All were agreed to buy the land, and advanced money for the first payment of half the cost. I then went to Wabasha and concluded the deal. At a meeting of the congregation on October 12th the committee reported, indicating the church site on top of the knoll and giving opportunity to anyone to buy more or less of the acreage. It was resolved to buy the beautiful 40 acre lot for church, cemetery and parsonage and never did it use $160 for a better purpose.

It may be added here that the old church, the present schoolhouse (1890) was erected in the spring of 1862 and furnished by the fall of that year. Not less than 6 congregational meetings were held. As soon as the site and building were determined a few families living a distance to the south left that congregation, complaining both of the location and the site of the proposed building. They formed a congregation of their own and called Borén as their pastor, a call he unwisely accepted. Sometimes we might be preaching only a mile apart. The division, however, did not deter the others from completing the building, though it was reduced in size from the original plan. The church was 40 feet long, 26 feet wide, with a 12 foot addition on the north side for a sacristy. By June 1862 it was erected and the exterior completed, so that the Augustana Synod could hold its third annual meeting in its unfinished interior. Those who had separated came back, most of them within the year. The congregation continued to grow, soon the church was too small.

Liturgy and Congregational Life

The worship services, the pastoral acts and congregational customs followed our usual Lutheran forms. After 1857 the members became more orderly in their church life and would doubtless have improved even more if I could have devoted my whole time to this congregation, which in view of my extensive field was impossible. Here and there, especially among the youth, were signs of spiritual growth, but a more serious Christian spirit was not popular. The Methodist and Baptist movements, beginning at the end of 1858, at least forced people to think more seriously of their faith, and though there was much of selfish disputation attention was turned to spiritual matters which yielded some benefit. Then too there was an awakening of a consciousness of good form, though this was revealed in being agreeable to the demands of the vigilance committee more than in loyalty to evangelical church discipline. There, for example, was the incident in 1859 where almost all the men in the community gathered and went from place to place to chastise certain individuals and execute justice. In one home a married man had committed adultery with the wife of another. The crowd moved there and whipped him properly with switches so that he felt it. Yet the punishment was so well received that all were treated to coffee. Then the procession continued on to a couple who were living together, though unmarried, and these were strictly enjoined to marry within a certain time or the group could be expected back to take appropriate measure. The warning was heeded, and on the same day the group came back the couple were off getting married. At the same time and in a similar manner they dealt with a man who was trying to defraud a widow of her property. Without further ado the man was driven off, and the group plowed, seeded, and fenced in a large plot for the widow, promising that her rights would be protected. Then the vigilantes had a few drinks and enjoyed the evening.

Civic righteousness asserted itself before the Christian sobriety demanded by the Word of God. Addiction to drunkenness was for a long time the hardest knot which church discipline had to loosen, but conditions improved with the years. In general the people were friendly and helpful to each other and to those in need. Legal suits and personal feuds were rare. In public meetings individuals could argue and dispute with each other, but without dangerous consequences. Ostentation and vanity were not yet apparent, the one thought himself as good as the next. Such was the prevalent trait before the war.

Change of Pastor

After 2 1/2 years on this field I left because of a call from the United Chicago and Mississippi Conference at its meeting in Princeton, Ill. Sept. 10-14, 1858, to travel to the East and seek help from American Lutherans for impoverished Scandinavian students at the school in Springfield. I accepted this call and moved to Chicago in the beginning of November. Because of the hard times and the approach of winter it did not seem wise to start on this errand. Instead I was given another task, namely, the editorship of *Hemlandet* which had been merged with *Minnesota Posten* and was now being moved at the end of the year from Galesburg to Chicago.

In the beginning of September, just before the Conference meeting referred to, a student J.P. Carlsson Borén had come to America on my suggestion, and at the Synod meeting in Mendota, following the Conference meeting in Princeton, he was given a license to serve a congregation. The plan was that he should be my assistant in Minnesota. When therefore I moved he was called by my congregation to take my place for a year. As I did not then return he was called to be my successor, though in Vasa only for one year from June 23, 1860.

It may be added here that Borén unfortunately was voted out in Red Wing 1861 and that I was called back to this congregation (Vasa and Red Wing) in September 1861 and served them until the beginning of 1868 when I asked to be relieved of Red Wing. I then served Vasa and the Zion congregation in Goodhue until 1879, occasionally assisted by pastors or students. I resigned from Vasa that year and

Pastor P.J. Sward succeeded me. Again called to Vasa in the summer of 1886 I served until March 1, 1889 when I left due to ill health. Pastor J. Fremling then became pastor. Altogether I have been pastor in Vasa around 25 years.

Red Wing

The preceding chapter has included information on the Swedes and the Lutheran congregation in Red Wing, so their story can be more briefly told here.

The First Swedes in Red Wing

Who the first of our countrymen were to make their home in the place cannot now be determined. But quite certainly among the first was Nils Nilsson, or "doctor's Nils" who worked for Dr. Sweeney. He never made any great fortune. P. Sjogren and his people too, were among them, but he made his home at Spring Creek, a mile from Red Wing. We have already met him. Also Johan Nilsson and family from "Östergötland — he spoke loudly because of deafness, and was nicknamed "the shrieker" or the "shrieking old fellow." Earlier he had lived in Moline and must have come to Red Wing in the summer of 1854. In any case he was likely the first Swede to build his home there, and many of the newcomers first stayed in his place. The old fellow had his peculiarities, was outspoken and somewhat rude, but in his dealings he was honest. He used to call me the "kid preacher", and though not a religious man he sometimes let us hold our services in his home before we had a church. More than once he came in his sheep-skin coat with a bag of flour in his wheel barrow to my house and exclaimed so it could be heard, "The pastor is supposed to have his tenth, isn't he?" One Sunday after I had held the service in his house and left my Bible in the window, he stood and looked in the Bible. Pretty soon he cried out, "It is a long time since I read the Bible, but I see that they know how to slaughter chickens in the Old Testament."

Those who joined the congregation when it was organized were among the oldest residents in the place, so that their names are in the list of members.

From the beginning of their coming here, even in 1856, the Swedes found work. They succeeded fairly well, built small homes, and the sober and orderly ones gradually attained temporal security, though few had their own business. Many stayed here only a short time, then moved out on farms where they bought their own land and house. Their places were taken by others, so that the number increased and by 1860 reached between three and four hundred souls.

The Lutheran Congregation

As already mentioned a congregation was organized Sept. 3rd, 1855, at the same time as one in Vasa. The first members were:

Hokan Olsson, wife and 6 children, from Mjellby, Blekinge, came to America 1854 and here from St. Charles, the spring of 1855. H. Olsson was the first to endeavor seriously to form a congregation and remained a leader for many years.

Anders Carlsson, wife and 1 child.

Peter Sundberg and wife from Kronoberg County, became a Methodist, moved to Spring Garden, then to Iowa.

Magnus Jonsson, wife and 3 children.

Bengt Andersson, wife and 2 children, moved to Spring Garden.

Carl Andersson, carpenter, from Värmland, and wife from Östergötland, moved to Minneapolis.

John Nilsson Bylo, tailor, and wife, came from Indiana, soon moved.

Morten Pehrsson, wife and 6 children from Blekinge.

Peter Johansson

Nils Kallberg, wife, and 1 child from Kronoberg County, moved to Spring Garden and then Iowa.

Anders Johan Johnsson, from Östergötland, soon left.

Nils Trulsson, wife and 2 children, from Blekinge, moved to Dakota County.

Anders Petersson

Swen Swensson

Lars Westerson, wife and 1 child from Ifvetofta.

Anders Westerson from ditto.

Anna Brita Persdotter, a widow, 2 children, from Halland.

Nils Nilsson

Peter Andersson, wife and 4 children from Mjölby, Linköping County, came to America 1851 and here from Rock Island, 1855, moved to Town of Cannon Falls.

Anders Wilhelm Jonsson, 1 child moved to Spring Garden.

Elna Persdotter, now Mrs. Mattes Pehrson, came to America from Trolle Ljungby 1855, moved to Vasa.

Inga Swensdotter, now Mrs. A. Danielson, came from same place, at same time, as preceding, also Carin Larsdotter, and Anna Nilsdotter.

Carl, and son Samuel, Beckman.

Edward Soderlund, wife and 2 children.

Peter Sjogren, wife and 5 children, came from Ljuder, Kronoberg County, 1852.

Swan Kallberg and wife, came (probably) from Hemsjö same county, 1854.

Thus a total of 84 persons, 54 of whom were communicant members. Few of these are now in Red Wing.

The first deacons were Peter Sjogren, Hokan Olsson, and Anders Carlsson. The congregation joined the one in Vasa in calling E. Norelius as pastor, in the beginning of October 1855. During the period before his arrival the people gathered in various homes on Sundays when Hokan Olsson led, and read a sermon. On Christmas 1855 they celebrated both an early service (Julotta) and full worship service. While gathered at holiday table they talked about church affairs. Among other topics they talked about *Hemlandet*, and H. Olsson recommended it warmly. John Nilsson (the shrieker) raised a question, "How many leaves do I receive then during the year for $1?" The reply was 24. "Ha," he rejoined, "if I buy a head of cabbage for 10 cents, I get far more!" That might be true, but not everybody confused cabbage leaves with the leaves of a paper.

I arrived with my wife in Red Wing May 16, 1856. In a letter to Pastor Cederstam the following day, I wrote, "Here we are, without house or home, without goods and almost without money. To judge by reason, it looks dark. There are many Swedes here and more arrive daily. May the Lord grant me wisdom to work for the building of His Kingdom here." Indeed it did seem dark, and many times since I have wondered why we did not immediately lose heart and return to Indiana, whence we had come. The Lord it was that sustained us. First, we could not find a house or even find room with someone. There were not enough houses in the town for the people. Everybody lived in crowded conditions, the houses were small and inferior. After a long and intense search for quarters with some one the high-voiced John Nilsson exclaimed, "I know of no other way than that for the present you move into my pig pen." He really meant it. For he had built a small shed in which he planned to have pigs, but it had not yet been used for this purpose. We might indeed have put up in the pig pen if Carl Andersson, the carpenter, had not allowed us to live in a tiny chamber for a couple of weeks until we could move out in the country.

The following Sunday, Trinity Sunday, I gave my introductory sermon in a half-finished store, which later became a saloon. It was hardly uplifting to have to conduct the service standing by a desk in a pile of chips, but where necessity compels one doesn't think of external conditions. Most festive it is if one senses a hunger and thirst for the Word of God. After the service a subscription was begun for a church building. $104 were pledged, and $50 had already been collected for this purpose. In such a new place it was a good start. When I came only 32 of the original 54 communicants were still here, but the number soon increased again, to 63.

During the summer we held our services in private homes, but it was crowded and inconvenient. Therefore, it became necessary to acquire our own building as soon as possible. We proceeded rapidly both with the building and the completion of the organization of the congregation. June 1st and 2nd, 1856 an important congregational meeting dealt with these two and other matters. This meeting can be considered as crucial for the history of the congregation, for at the meeting the foundation was laid for its inner organization and future development. The constitution then adopted was the same as that one later adopted in Vasa, which has already been described. In August 1857 the model constitution recommended for congregations by the United Conference was adopted without objection, for it was almost identical with the one already approved. Members subscribed their names anew at the meeting, totaling 63 communicants. A new election was held for deacons, and on June 2 an election of trustees resulted in the choice of Carl Andersson, Hokan Olsson, and Christian Berg, a Norwegian. The congregation originally called itself "Scandinavian", but this was later legally changed to "Swedish".

The First Church Building

At the aforementioned meeting this resolution was adopted: The church shall be built of boards set in a vertical position. It shall be 26 feet wide, 30 feet long with 12 feet high walls. There shall be 3 windows on each side, 5 panes high, 3 panes wide, 12 by 14 inches each. The door shall be 2 yards,[1] 6 inches wide and 4[1] yards high." So read the resolution and the church was built accordingly.

Prior to the meeting the congregation had appointed a committee to choose a site and negotiate its purchase. The committee reported that it had selected lot 1 in block 17. It belonged to C.J.F. Smith, was bought for $153. It was paid for during the summer and the deed was obtained September 30, 1856. The church was erected during the summer, but only the walls and the roof, and remained in this incomplete shape until the fall of 1857. It has the distinction of being the first Swedish church built within the boundaries of Minnesota. The winter of 1856-7 was harsh, and fortitude was required to endure through the service within these thin, plain, board walls. But it was no small joy for these people to have come far enough to gather under their own roof. To avoid being frozen stiff they bought a huge pot-belly stove, which was fired until it got red hot and burnt into the floor. All resources had been exhausted. In its unfinished condition the church cost around $600, and I remember how hard it was to find money to pay for the stove.

In the fall of 1857 the building was completed with inner board walls and furnished with benches, pulpit and altar rail. The congregation borrowed $200 from the church extension fund of the General Synod. It took several years to repay this. Also it was decided that at every communion service each guest should pay 25 cents to the building fund, but this met with disapproval, and after a year the rule was rescinded and each member henceforth was to pay 50 cents a year.

The church was never entirely completed until it had become too small and outlived its usefulness. It was never painted, never dedicated. Yet in all its simplicity it served its purpose at the time. It was the center of life of the congregation, holding it together and the scene of many festive occasions. For a long time it stood solitarily out in the plain where the Indians used to have their ceremonies in the summer, and since it resembled a barn the Americans often called it "The Swedish Barn." At Christmas time it was decorated with paper crowns, wreaths, and candles. Never shall I forget the impression made on my mind on Easter morning, 1865, when news came of the assassination of Abraham Lincoln and the church was draped in deep

---

[1]the Swedish says "aln"-ell, probably about 2 ft.

sorrow. The Swedes in Red Wing and elsewhere sincerely grieved over this noble person. Memorable too is the fact that the German Lutheran Synod under the leadership of "Father" Heyer was organized in this building, and that the Minnesota Conference school (college) was housed here during its first year.

The building still stands, though transformed and enlarged, and was used as a parsonage as late as the summer of 1889. Just to the north, on the same lot, one can see a small house which exhibits the building style of those early days. I had it erected for my own use in the fall of 1856, and it was then looked on enviously as a pastor's place. Since then it has been somewhat enlarged.

The need of a new church building was discussed at a congregational meeting on January 7, 1863. But many years elapsed before this idea was realized. That story is beyond the limits of this volume.

Pastoral Care

From the foregoing it is evident that I served the congregation from the middle of May 1856 to the beginning of November 1858, and that I divided my time between Vasa and Red Wing, as well as visiting other places. When I moved Pastor J.P.C. Borén took my place, first as vicar and then as pastor, until the congregation did not renew his call in the summer of 1861. The reason for his dismissal seems to have been the following: At a meeting of the congregation on December 12th, 1860 a discussion took place as to how the debt should be paid-for the $200 loan from the General Synod building fund had not been fully paid-and a proposal was made to rent the pews in the church. The proposal led to a hot discussion. Borén urged it vigorously, using rather strong language in a violent manner. The proposal finally carried by a vote of 21 to 12. When the seats were sold, some were bought by non-members and some of the members were left without. This and other irritations resulted in much objection to Pastor Borén. The dissatisfaction grew until on June 28, 1861 he was not recalled by a vote of 24 to 12. On the election of a new pastor, with Borén and myself as candidates, I received 27 and he 6 votes.

It is a sad situation when a pastor is dismissed from a congregation. To put the blame altogether on one party would doubtless be one-sided and unfair, for in such events there is very likely fault on both sides. Pastor Borén has now rested in his grave since March 1865, and one can judge more calmly and impartially. At the time I was openly accused of having intrigued to cause his downfall. I can now in good conscience publicly declare my position in this matter, as I did to him privately when he lived. Borén was a sincere Lutheran in his faith, and preached the Word of God aright and entirely. His insight into the doctrine of salvation was thorough. His conscience was alert and he strove to live a Christian way of life. But he had his faults as each of us has. They lay more in his natural temperament than in his opinions. He was tiringly slow in all his motions and very stubborn in his decisions. Almost always he came late. Usually the people had to wait a half hour after the time appointed for a service. He was slow in beginning and slow in concluding. His stubborness hurt him in cases where he should have yielded, for the sake of peace, as in the matter of selling the seats, and in similar financial affairs. This quality of his nature seems to have been the principal reason on his side why things went so badly. But I cannot assert that the congregation had valid reason to vote him out. Borén had to endure many trials and sufferings before he died. I fully believe that the Lord cleansed him from the inherent dross in the purifying crucible.

The pastor's salary after 1856, the first year, was about $250, for the second year $185, the third $75. During Borén's time it should have been $200 for the year, but was never fully paid. In 1861 and 1862 it was set at $75, 1862 and 1863 $175.

The Synodical Connection

When the congregation was organized no decision was made as to the Synod it was to belong to, but it was taken for granted that it should join the same Synod of which the pastor was a member, the Synod of Northern Illinois. In the summer of 1858 some German and English (speaking) Lutherans met in the Swedish church in Red Wing to organize a Lutheran Synod in Minnesota. They invited the congregation and its pastor to unite with them and thus leave their Synod. The congregation declined the invitation, for it was not prepared to cut its ties with the Northern Illinois Synod. Yet I and my brother pastors in Minnesota gave the matter much thought. Hitherto we had not had our own conference, but in October of that year one was formed.

When the Synod of Northern Illinois broke up in 1860 the question of the formation of our own Scandinavian Synod was raised. Each congregation was asked to express its wish in this matter.

On May 15, 1860 the congregation formally resolved to leave the Northern Illinois Synod and unite with the other Swedish congregations in creating their own Synod. In this way the congregation became a part of the Augustana Synod.

The Christian Instruction of the Children and the Church School

This gave us concern from the very beginning. The instruction of the young in the Christian faith had suffered greatly in the new environment. To establish a church school at once was out of consideration. Poverty, and even more, indifference, in the matter stood in the way of taking such a step. Many and probably the majority had the idea that a church school was altogether superfluous when you could send your children to the English public school.

The bitter fruits of this attitude were revealed in confirmation instruction. Children came to this instruction who could not read with understanding in either language. Instead of teaching the Christian doctrines, the pastor often had to spend most of the time in helping them to spell and read. And to refuse to confirm children all too ignorant awakened opposition.

As soon as we obtained our own church building we began as best we could to conduct a Sunday School. I could not always be present and it was difficult to find competent teachers, so this kind of school was less than satisfactory. Then too we had difficult competition in the American Sunday Schools, who lured away our children, and there were parents who out of vanity sent their children to the American schools, with the result usually that these were lost to the Lutheran Church.

A congregation that is not concerned about giving its children Christian instruction according to its faith and profession murders itself, and would do better to shorten the pain by immediately dissolving itself than to incur a lingering and troublesome death. I do not charge this congregation to have been more dilatory in this matter than others, but not until the meeting on May 16, 1862 did it begin to show a real concern about the church school, by then allocating $20 for this cause. Individuals had, it is true, tried to start such a school, but the congregation as such had not. I myself conducted a school five days a week during three winters, 1861-3. In 1862 the school was enlarged, and other pupils even from outside the congregation, could enroll and receive instruction so as to go on to higher studies. Thus it became a Christian folk-school, and from it developed the Minnesota

Conference high school (and Gustarus Adolphus college). Three of those who attended the school later became pastors in the Synod, J.G. Lagerstrom, J. Magny, and J.S. Nilsson. From this time on the school continued as a congregational school at least during part of the year.

Church Music

In the beginning we sang as best we could. Sometimes pastor, song leader, and sexton might all be one person. We were content just so it went. In the winter 1856-1857 we gained some members (especially the Engberg family) who had musical ability, loved and understood song and music. Frequently we had song rehearsals and at the service we could hear real good church singing. When these soon moved we had to find other means to improve the music. An old chamber organ was purchased from the Presbyterian Church, and John Miller, now in Spring Garden, became the first organist in the congregation. Since then there has been general satisfaction with the music in the church.

Liturgy, Discipline and Christian Life.

As to liturgy there is nothing noteworthy to report. Worship services and pastoral acts followed the customary order. A deacon led in the absence of the pastor and would read a sermon from one of our approved Postils. Services were held also on Sunday and Wednesday evenings, with a sermon. No modern type prayer meetings were held in my time.

As to discipline and Christian life the congregation at first was a spiritual wilderness, with few, but happy, exceptions. Nor could it be expected that this ground would soon bear spiritual fruit without preparatory clearing, plowing, and planting of good seed. All this had to be done in hope, and in the process one had to endure with tears and patience much that under other circumstances should not have been tolerated. The most hopeful sign was that on Sundays people at least came together for services. At the week-day service, however, it might happen that the pastor also had to be janitor and have only three or four in attendance. Yet even within a year one could perceive not a small change. At least in regard to externals there began to be more orderliness and respect for sacred things. The Word of God has not been without effect on consciences, and one could begin to use more severe measures to maintain Christian discipline and order. Improvement was gradual and even if one could not detect any general awakening the Word of God still worked quietly and individual souls became concerned about their salvation.

Though later in time than the period here considered I would remark here that the war years in general brought a spiritual apathy. This was especially the case at the close of the war. Disdain for God's Word, drunkenness and extravagance got the upper hand. I admit that I then almost despaired of the continued existence of the congregation. In the winter of 1865 I called the congregation together for a special meeting and told the members plainly, though not harshly, that the church would be ruined if they did not seriously follow the constitution and exercise a Christian discipline. I even made this a definite condition for my remaining as their pastor. The meeting had good results, and from that time on I could more emphatically insist on a Christian discipline. After that, too, the element that resisted all Christian nurture began to separate itself from the congregation.

No schism in matters of doctrine occurred in my time, though now and then some one went over to another denomination.

In 1860 there were 84 communicants.

Stockholm, Wisconsin

This is a small village with a station on the Burlington and Northern Railroad, on the shore of Lake Pepin across from Lake City. In front it has about half the length of the lake (a widening of the Mississippi River) and in back high bluffs, whose outstanding point a bit beyond the village is Maiden's Rock, named from a romantic Indian legend. The land between the lake and the bluffs is not extensive and the soil not favorable, but here the first Swedish pioneers settled. Soon they extended their boundaries up beyond the bluffs, where the earth is fertile and there were forests of oak and other trees. Now the Swedish settlement stretches out about 20 miles in length and 10 to 15 miles in width — one of the larger areas held by Swedish-Americans.

As we have already seen (Part I, chapter 2) it was Erik Peterson from Karlskoga in Värmland who first led the Swedes to this spot. Here we might add that around 1852 E. Peterson had worked as a rafter on the Mississippi and then first observed the place. While his timber float had tied up on the shore P. had climbed up on Maiden

Rock, from which there is a magnificant view, and had been enthused by the landscape. Afterwards he returned here and selected a piece of land and lived a while at the so-called Brownly's place. Then he wrote home to relatives and acquaintances. But before they could arrive he started off for Sweden and they passed each other on the ocean. They stayed in Moline, until Peterson came back in 1854 together with many others from their native place, as already mentioned. At first they thought of calling it Swedenburg, but to avoid being mistaken as Swedenborgians they gave it the name Stockholm. That part of the settlement back of the bluffs which in time comprised the Lutheran congregation received the name Sabylund. More distant parts had their own names.

Some of the first Swedes who came to Stockholm had more than average means to support themselves and suffered less in pioneer days. Many, however, were less fortunate and experienced a full share of sacrifice and suffering.

Most of the pioneers here were heads of families and at least for a while were members of the Lutheran Congregation. Among them were the following;

Erik Peterson, from Karlskoga
Jacob Peterson, from Karlskoga
Carolina Peterson, from Karlskoga
Maria Peterson, from Karlskoga
Erik Andersson, from Karlskoga
Carl Hattstrom, from Karlskoga
Jonas Erik Anderson, from Warnum
Anders Anderson, from Warnum
Peter Petersson, from Bjurkärn
Erik Eriksson, from Karlskoga
Lars Olsson, from Bjurkärn
Melker Nilsson, from Karlskoga
Jon Anderson
Carl Jonsson, from Twäryd, Elfsborg County
Peter Axel Johnson, from Josefina, Linköping County
Olof Sandstrom, from Asarum, Blekinge
Mathes Sandstrom, from Asarum, Blekinge
Bengt Sandstrom, from Asarum, Blekinge
P.N. Lund, from Kärda
Nils P. Gram, from Denmark
Nils Johnson, from Karlskoga

P.M. Lindberg, from Linderås, Jönköping County

Anders Janson, from Karlskoga

Gustaf Hedstrom

Erik Janson, from Karlskoga

Johan Goransson, from Lungsund

Jacob Jansson, from Åsarp, Elfsborg County

Abram Josefsson, from Karlskoga

Isak Nyman, from Karlskoga

Erik Larsson, from Årsunda, Gefleborg County

Lars Grund, from Årsunda Gefleborg County (died in war,
Andersonville Prison)

Johan P. Jonsson, from Finnekumla, Elfsborg County

Adolf Johansson

Johan J. Hill, from Kråkshult, Jönköping County

Johan P. Danielson, from Lemhult, Småland

Erik Peterson, from Bjurkärn, Värmland.

Organization of a Lutheran Congregation

This place was first visited by a pastor June 19th, 1856, when I was asked to come at the time of a death. The wife of Erik Petersson had died and for the burial there was no Swedish pastor closer than at Vasa. When Isak Nyman came with a carriage to get me, we drove from Vasa to Florence, a small town on the Minnesota side of Lake Pepin, and then went by row boat over to Stockholm. The funeral was held the same day, and the good pioneers had not forgotten the Swedish nectar. On the following day, June 20th, at a service 7 children were baptized, of whom 4 had been born in 1855. Inasmuch as they were the first Swedish children to be born and baptized here I include their names: Eleonora, the daughter of Erik Petersson; Aron Fredrik, a son of Jacob Peterson; Emma Fredrika, daughter of Jan Andersson; Axel, son of Melker Nilsson; Johan Erik, son of Jan Jansson; Carl Henrik, son of Frans Nilsson; Ada Desideria, daughter of Lars Olsson. Then followed the worship service and the Lord's Supper and the organization of a congregation, consisting of 70 members, adults and children. I promised to visit there as often as I could, until they could obtain their own pastor. No deeply religious elements were evident in the group at that time. The people were not certainly any worse, in general, than those at many other places. But among them were those who had been infected more or less by rationalism and denial of faith. This worked like an evil seed.

In the fall I arranged to have Brother P. Beckman come as a teacher and preacher, and occasionally I visited there when pastoral acts were performed. After a year Beckman received license from the Synod of Northern Illinois to serve as pastor in the place, and he stayed until June 1858. In his autobiography he has told of his experiences in that period. It was clear that Beckman was too churchly and religious to suit the leaders, though it is also certain that there were those who grieved over conditions. When Beckman left, the leaders advertised in the *Svenska Republikamen* for a pastor, stipulating expressly that he was not to be a "läsare prest", a pastor of revival type. The advertisement was read by a dissolute Swedish student, John Rosenberg, born in Åsarp, Elfsborg County, 1826 who was then living among some Swedes near Watertown, Minn. preaching and drinking. The son of wealthy parents, he had qualified for entrance into the university. Around 1853 and 1854 he had assisted Pastor G. Unonius in Chicago but had since practiced as apothecary and medical doctor. He married an Irish girl in Chicago, but lost his money and ruined his family by his drinking. The wife died of grief, and he went from bad to worse. Gladly he accepted the call described in the advertisement, and was in Stockholm before July 16, 1858. For on that day he held a congregational meeting, or at least served as its secretary, when there was a report on repairs on the schoolhouse, the formation of a treasury and a new listing of the membership.

Again on August 8th a meeting was held, to elect a treasurer, Rosenberg being chosen, and on the 7th of September when the *Minutes* read: "Resolved that J. Rosenberg be called as pastor of the congregation for one year, from September 20th this year to the same date 1859." The salary would consist of voluntary gifts of money or of produce payable quarterly. Since he was treasurer Rosenberg said he would look after certain repairs on the schoolhouse. The cemetery was to be cleared and fenced in by voluntary labor. The *Minutes* of September 28th, 1859 state that "the year for which J. Rosenberg was called as pastor had now elapsed, and he thanked the congregation for its friendly and fine attitude. The congregation resolved unanimously to continue and send for a pastor when opportune. J. Rosenberg offered to lead in religious instruction every other Sunday, or when convenient, without compensation. This was happily accepted."

Rosenberg preached, stayed and drank, proving that he was no "reader pastor". But after a year all respect for him as preacher had vanished. He ceased preaching, fortunately, and concentrated on medicine. Meanwhile Pastor J.P.C. Borén had visited the place, and to him the congregation turned for pastoral service.

On September 1, 1861 Borén presided at a meeting at which the congregation was reorganized. The United Conference's proposed congregational constitution was adopted, Borén was called as pastor, and officers were elected, namely as trustees, for 3 years, Carl Hattstrom, for 2 years Erik Peterson, and for 1 year, Lars Olsson, and as deacons J. Rosenberg (!) and Jacob Peterson for 3 years, Erik Andersson and Lars Olsson for 2 years, and Erik Peterson (!) and Hattstrom for 1 year. Carl Hattstrom was chosen as janitor, for which he was to receive an offering, John E. Andersson was to have six dollars a year for leading the singing. Heads of families, who wished to be members, subscribed their names after the *Minutes*. They were 34 in number, with few exceptions the same names as on earlier lists of the pioneers.

The congregation expressed a wish at a meeting on January 3, 1864, that Pastor Borén would move to Stockholm, so that his help would be more readily available. Pastor Borén agreed, and arrangements were undertaken either to buy or rent a house for him. In April a whole block was purchased for $75 and a small house for $45, which was moved onto the property and fixed in fair shape. From the price one can deduce that it was no palace. But Borén had no pretensions and was grateful for even small favors. On the whole he was liked and beloved by the congregation. His service was brief, for in March 1865 he died. His remains lie in the Lutheran cemetery in Vasa.

While what followed belongs to a later period, I add here that from the time of Borén's death until 1871, when Pastor Fremling became pastor, the congregation was the scene of religious strife and contending parties, to the detriment of the spiritual environment.

Svithiod

This place, later called Goodhue, comprised one township of Goodhue County. It adjoined the Vasa township on its northwest corner, and had a few pioneers before 1860. Originally it was partially, but thinly, wooded by scrub oak and brush. It was not rich looking and surrounding areas were earlier occupied. Later the soil turned out to be among the best in the county. The first Swedes took land in the southwest corner around 1859. Among the first was A.P. Friman from Veta, Linköping County, who came to America 1852, stopping in Chicago, St. Paul and Red Wing before coming here. He now lives near the Vasa Church. He settled on the land now owned by C.J. Fors. At the same time or shortly thereafter Samuel Johnson arrived and settled on the farm now owned by McQuine, near Friman, but in the town of Belle Creek. Paul Nilsson bought land. Gradually they were joined by Sven Nilsson, now in Templeton, Cal., J. Nordquist, Gudmund Neslund, J.G. Lagerstrom, later a pastor, Pastor Borén, C.J. Fors, P.G. Veber, Anders Swenson, Daniel Larson, etc. as well as by some Danes and Norwegians. When Pastor Borén moved there around 1862 he organized a congregation, calling it Svithiod, serving there until he moved to Stockholm. Then the congregation became a district within the Vasa Church, until 1869, when it again became an independent congregation with the name, Zion Lutheran Church, Goodhue.

PASTOR J.P.C. BORÉN

Chapter 15

Spring Garden — Cannon River and Cannon Falls

Spring Garden

Spring Garden is southwest of Vasa, and the distance between the two churches is about 9 miles. The land in Spring Garden is of the best in Goodhue County, being more level than in Vasa. Part of it was originally prairie, but most was forest and brush. The name comes from the presence of many springs. Because of cultivation the earth is much drier than it used to be.

The First Swedes in Spring Garden

Carl Andersson Haggstrom, who was born in Vrigstad, Jönköping County in 1826, emigrated with his wife, Martha Stina Jonsdotter from Voxtorp, 1854. He tells that they travelled from Chicago along with 8 other families to Geneseo. Some had acquaintances in Andover, so all went there. That was the dreadful cholera year when many of the newcomers died. There was much want and misery, and work was hard to get. In religious matters there was controversy, but they remembered gratefully Pastor Esbjörn, for he helped and comforted them both in spiritual and temporal matters. They spent the winter in Andover.

In April 1855 Haggstrom accompanied Magnus Edstrom and family from Voxtorp (who had come together from Sweden) to Red Wing. Another of their party from Sweden, Johannes Wanberg, now joined them there. They left their families in Red Wing while they went inland to find home-sites and to claim the land. In what is now the town of Leon, near its western edge, they found what they were looking for, unusually attractive and fertile level land, surrounded by fine woods and having fine water. Here they staked their claims and erected a small hut for necessities. On October 6th they brought out their families. Edstrom, who had some means and had helped others, owned a couple of steers, so he invited the others to ride. They drove from Red Wing to Belle Creek, the site of White Rock. From there to the spot they had chosen, was not even a trail, a distance of about 6 miles. "How long are we going in this fashion?"

Mrs. Haggstrom inquired, "Well," replied Edstrom, "I guess we will have to go on until we find some small cabin." So they did continue on until they came to the small "claim hut". The first three families to come to Spring Garden were thus: Magnus Edstrom, C.A. Haggstrom, and Johannes Wanberg. Later that fall came Anders Wilhelm Johnson from Torpa, Jönköping County, who had come to America earlier. Johan from Stabbarp in Grenna, Peter Jonson from Thorstuga, Jönköping County, Anders Enberg from Ignaberga, Kristianstad County and probably others. They lived in crowded conditions as best they could, suffered from ague, and had far to go for supplies, for Red Wing was the closest town, and that was almost a trackless 20 miles away. What they bought they usually had to carry home on their backs. Early in 1856 they were without flour, and it was scarce everywhere. Haggstrom however, had bought a barrel in Red Wing for 11 dollars, and paid an extra dollar to have it brought to old Chandlers at Belle Creek, but it required much toil to get it from there to the settlement 6 to 8 miles farther. Both that and the following winter Indians were plentiful. They hunted around here and visited the settlers daily. They seemed friendly, wanting, however, something to eat.

In the summer of 1856 the population rapidly increased with the arrival of two parties from different directions. One party came from Geneva, Ill. which had come there in 1854. This was the large Holm relation. The head was Johannes Holm from Habo parish. The sons were Isak, Anders (who came a few years later from Geneva), Gustaf, Carl, Johan, August, Per (died in the Civil War) and sons-in-law, Wolf, Johan Miller, P. Gustafsson, Jacob Johnson. These took the land in the eastern part of the settlement. The other party came from Butler County, Iowa, under the leadership of Anders Swenson from Dunarp, Grenna parish. He had come with relatives and friends from Sweden in 1853 and lived a while in Indiana not far from LaFayette. From there they moved to Iowa and stayed there until 1856. Not satisfied there, they moved on to Minnesota. Some remained in Spring Garden, for instance Magnus and Peter Lundell. Others settled near Cannon Falls, being some of the first Swedes in this area. In addition to these parties individual families came from various places, as Carl and Johan Lagerstrom from Geneva, Ludvig Miller from Chicago, Anders Kallberg from Slätthög, Kronoberg County; Peter Johan Johansson from Voxtorp, Bengt Anderson from Värö, Halland; Carl Säf, born in Grenna, lived one while in

Yorktown, Indiana, after 1853; Nils and Fredrik Andersson from Längserud, Dalsland, etc.

Pioneer life was possibly not harder here than in other places, but the great distance from any town during the first years made it more difficult to get necessary provisions. This may have contributed to teaching these newcomers to be as independent as possible of the whole world. They learned how to accommodate themselves, and they were in no hurry to build themselves better homes. Haggstrom's first house, as already mentioned, cost him in cash only $2.50 and this place served both as living space and as the congregational's meeting place for many years. Generally these people waited to build until they could afford it, and as a result one now finds such fine homes in Spring Garden. They were careful not to fall into debt, and few settlers are in such good economic circumstances as those here.

Church Affairs

In the Vasa story I have briefly mentioned how I discovered and visited this settlement in 1856. No organization of a congregation was attempted, but preparations were made. I continued to visit the place until Pastor P. Beckman was called in the summer of 1858, when he organized an Evangelical Lutheran congregation. Those whom I listed as the original settlers were almost all the first members, for the majority were Lutherans. There were a few from Halland who were Baptists. In 1860 the communicants numbered only 45. The first church was built in 1862, on the same site occupied by the present church.

In Beckman's time the contributions to the support of the pastor were small and insufficient. To begin with they were all poor and lived in straitened circumstances, nor were they many in number. Maybe it would have been better if he had had courage and inclination to call the situation to their attention. Then came the hard war years when all costs were high. One example may suffice. From the war years when it was still possible to pay money for a substitute, C.A. Haggstrom was called to duty, and ordered to be in St. Paul within a few days. As the only one able to support his family, he chose to hire someone to take his place, provided he could obtain the money. $300 was required and this he had to borrow at 30% interest, payable in wheat in the fall. Wheat sold at $1.75 a bushel, but he had to sell his to his creditors for $1.25 a bushel. Also he had to travel to St. Paul to report. In such times, it is clear, means did not suffice for church requirements, especially if people were little concerned about them. The congregation did, however, manage to acquire 40 acres of land for the use of the pastor, which today amounts to a valuable asset. But unfortunately the church and cemetery are in one location, the parsonage at a second, and the church land at a third.

Liturgical Forms and Christian Life

From the beginning the congregation has followed the customary order of worship, and pastoral acts such as baptism, confirmation, and others, have been conducted as in our Swedish Lutheran churches. In the absence of the pastor one of the deacons has always led in a read service, and for many years this was the lot of J.P. Gustafsson. He could be considered as the congregation's permanent supply pastor, and he has filled the position with dignity and edification.

Churchly order was maintained, obvious sins were chastised and in some degree disciplined, though here, as elsewhere, time was required to get members to see and acknowledge the necessity of a more serious Christian discipline. We have no records of the church council in the early days, but we know of some instances that give evidence of this concern.

No Christian school of the congregation existed before 1860, but as far as his time permitted the pastor instructed children and youth in the Christian faith.

To the extent that their means and situation allowed, the members participated in contributions to the Scandinavian professorship and to missionary causes.

The years 1857 and 1858 witnessed a deeper effect of the Word of God on individual souls, but no more general spiritual awakening occurred. The people as a whole exhibited an outer honorableness and decency and many were total abstainers.

Pastor Beckman served the congregation until 1869, and was succeeded by Pastor J.O. Cavallin.

Cannon Falls and Cannon River

These names now refer to two congregations, though originally they were one. The small town of Cannon Falls began to be settled by a few people in the spring of 1856. There never was any "boom" period.

The first Swedes to make their homes near Cannon Falls were a part of those who came with Anders Svenson from Iowa in 1856. Johan Peter, August Peter, Carl Johnsson and probably some others at first located on the sandy prairie just south of Cannon Falls. They did not remain there long, for the soil was not fertile. So they selected better land on the other side of the river, about 3 miles south of the town. In the fall of 1856 Nils Hokansson (Nils from Grankärr, Vireda parish) came with Carl J. Anderson from West Point, Indiana, and the two laid claim to land along Cannon River below the town, the former building his home in Cannon Falls. Soon the aforementioned And. Swensson also located there. Gustaf Westman and some others also came here, from Rusheby and Gustaf Anderson from Visingsö, with some from West Point, Indiana. In the spring of 1857 a party composed mainly of young people came from various places around LaFayette and Attica, Indiana, staying a while in Cannon Falls. They were mostly relatives of two families, one from Grenna, one from Skärstad. In the fall they moved on to Waseca County, settling near Wilton and founding the Vista settlement. Before 1860 most of the Swedes in and around Cannon Falls were from Grenna and surrounding parishes and had lived for shorter or longer periods in Indiana around LaFayette. Among the exceptions were J. Jonsson Engberg, Sr. from Bergsjö, Helsingland and A.P. Norelius and his relatives who came here from Chisago Lake. These lived in Clarkdale. Also Anders Peter Johnson who came from Elgin, Ill., and hailed from Vestergötland; P.O. Tilderquist, now in Vasa, born in Södra Rörum in Skåne; Anders Lindstrom from Gotland. A few built homes in the town, but the majority obtained land east and northeast of town on either side of the river, especially the latter. A small community grew up there, and in 1862 a small church was erected 3 or 4 miles from town. The land around Cannon Falls is very sandy in places and the soil generally poor and dry. Still the Swedes then and since have managed to gain a fair income, though by necessity they have had to learn how to economize. Before 1860 the only ones in business for themselves were a few shoemakers, tailors, and one or another carpenter and blacksmith. Someone might have a little income from hauling grain to the mill in town, or working for a merchant, but the pay was small. Still the Swedes in and around Cannon Falls were hospitable and cheerful, and sometimes it might seem that they knew how to live more light-heartedly than others.

The first Swedes in the town lived on the north side of the river, a little below the old mill, where they bought lots. But gradually they moved out into the country, leaving only a few families there.

Church Affairs

As early as 1856 as soon as there were Swedes there, I visited the place a number of times, preaching in their small cottages and continued to go until Pastor Beckman came to the area. My visit there at New Year's 1857 was memorable. I went by foot from Vasa through unusually deep snow, and ran into a very severe storm, almost losing my life. When I finally got through I had serious frost bites. But after thawing out I gathered the people for worship. The prospects in spiritual matters in Cannon Falls were not bright. There were some very fine and devout women, but in those days the men were given to strong drink and during the holiday had caroused merrily. In the spring there was improvement when the large party from Indiana came. In the town work was available where there was some building. This attracted Swedes and one while it appeared that they might settle down here. A Swedish Lutheran congregation was organized with 25 or 30 communicants. A lot was donated for a church and decision reached to go ahead at once with a building.

How a Church Changed Into a Sack of Flour

In order to strike while the iron was hot I started at once a subscription among the Swedes. Some promised money. Some volunteered various kinds of labor. The work began, a foundation was laid. Depending on the pledges, I went on foot to Hastings, 17 miles from Cannon Falls, ordered lumber and got most of it delivered. Just then the greater part of the Swedish community in Cannon Falls moved to Waseca County. Those remaining became discouraged, were unwilling to build, and criticized me for having pushed the project. The result was that no church was built, and I had myself to pay for the lumber. I had borrowed the amount and paid interest at 4% per month, so it grew to quite an amount before I could pay. Meanwhile the lumber disappeared, each one helping himself to a part. All that I ever received for the church lumber was a bag of flour which one man gave me for what he took.

So for many years there was no talk of building a church in Cannon Falls. But in 1862, in Pastor Beckman's time, a small church was built 3 or 4 miles below Cannon Falls, where most of the members lived. The church was called Cannon River. Services and meetings were often held in town, but the members living there were considered members of the Cannon River congregation until a separate congregation was formed in the town of Cannon Falls.

PASTOR P. BECKMAN.

Pastor Beckman Becomes the Pastor

Beckman served the congregation, together with Spring Garden, from the summer of 1858 until 1869. The congregation remained small as there were few new arrivals. In 1860 it had 30 communicants, 5 years later there were only 38. Economic resources were still meager and the people could contribute little to the support of the pastor. Yet they likely did what they could. The spiritual condition, on the other hand, improved in this period. Not only were the numbers more attentive to the Word of God, but not a few seemed to be truly affected, and a Christian character became dominant. Here as in most places, it was difficult to give the children Christian instruction. The congregation tried to do what it could by holding Sunday School and now and then supporting a few months of day school. Miss Louisa Peterson, now Mrs. A. Jackson, was the first to conduct a school within the congregation and she sowed many a good seed in the hearts of the children.

Chapter 16

The Union Settlement in Carver County — Gotaholm —

Union

Carver County is about 30 miles above Ft. Snelling, along the Minnesota River. Originally it was forest. Near the river the land is sometimes inferior but as you move farther from it the soil is of the best quality. The county has a number of lakes, the largest and most beautiful being Clear Lake or Waconia. Clearing the land has been slow and toilsome, because of the heavy woods, but the effort has been richly repaid.

The Beginning of the Swedish Settlement
known as East and West Union.

Soon after 1850 steamboats began to ply the Minnesota River from St. Paul, and this led the Swedes to this area. According to Joh. Hult, the first Swede to settle down here was Nils Alexanderson from Kronoberg County, followed by Hult and his family and two brothers, Anders and Peter Hult. Immediately afterward Sven Gudmundson and family from Hössna came, Jonas Carlson and family from Naum a few months later. In the fall Anders Stomberg and family arrived together with a small party from Lekåsa.

These came in 1854. It is possible that N. Alexanderson was there already at the end of 1853, for J. Hult found him there when he arrived in April 1854. All of them had come to America in 1852 and 1853 and had spent some time at other places before settling here (Cf. Part 1, Chapter 2). They chose home sites near the spot where the E. Union Church now stands, calling the place the Oscar settlement, a name changed four years later to E. Union. At the same time a number of Norwegian families began to arrive here, among them Per Kleven, Ola Paulsen, later a pastor in the Norwegian-Danish Conference, his relatives and others. As soon as they could, they wrote to their friends at home about their new settlement, and gradually, year after year, more came and established themselves in the neighborhood before other nationalities could occupy the land. Thus the woods were filled with Swedes and Norwegians and a good sized community existed here before 1860. The story of the trials, sacrifices and difficulties of all kinds in the early years, needs not be repeated here, for it is similar to that of other settlements. It is sufficient to remark that here too the Swedish industriousness and persistence won out and in a few years the people were well-off.

A Norwegian by the name of Gorgeson had already laid out the town of Carver before the first Swedes came to the area, but there was only one house. The settlement was begun about 4 miles west of Carver which in time became the central market place.

Early Events in the Pioneer Period of Church and Community

In a history of the settlement in 1868, Pastor P. Carlson, wrote: "Up to 1858 when a congregation was organized, confusion reigned among the people both in temporal and spiritual matters, as usually happens in new places, until each one finds his place. There was much evil, such as drinking and dancing, yet there were serious-minded persons, too, and on Sundays J. Hult used to read from a postil of Luther for those who came together for devotions.

"Also there were visits by our Lutheran pastors, as Esbjörn, Norelius, Cederstam, and Hasselquist."

Esbjörn visited the place in the summer of 1856 on business for the Scandinavian professorship, and conducted several services. Undoubtedly he was the first Swedish Lutheran pastor to visit there.

Some adventurers posing as pastors had already been there and one of these was still there when Esjbörn came. Pastor P. Carlson thinks that the notorious Holmgren was the first of these adventurers, but this is an error, for Holmgren did not appear in the West until January 1857, when he attended a conference meeting in Moline and deceived the whole membership. It must have been in the fall of that year that he appeared in Carver, because in the late summer he was traveling around in Minnesota practicing his tom-foolery. The first one of this kind was very likely the one who called himself Sandblad. "He preached here a while," wrote Carlson, "and gained the confidence of some. He bought a lot in Carver on credit as if to build a house, hired a worker to dig out the basement without paying him, left for St. Paul to buy lumber for the house, and as he claimed, also for a church, took along a few watches for repairs, and this was the last we heard of him."

Of the next one we learn, "the most persistent of all was a Mr. Daniel Brown. He was here a long time, roaming around with his gun and brandy keg. He hunted, fished, drank, preached, baptized, etc. At times he drank to the point he lost human dignity. In his sermons he often told his listeners to live as he taught not as he lived. Toward the end of his stay here (1857) he was to instruct children for their first communion, but he behaved so badly as to become offensive to everybody. His plan of action was to support himself by buying a piece of land, then getting people to build for him what he called a parsonage, and working it awhile. When he had played out his role as a minister, he sold his land and moved to some other market. As long as there was a lack of real leaders and pastors, he got away with it. He acted thus in East Union, in Christiania, and tried the same in Moore's Prairie and elsewhere."

It was this Brown who was in East Union 1856 when Esbjörn visited there. From what I could learn he was a sottish student from southern Sweden, well educated and a glib speaker. Esbjörn heard him preach and admitted that the sermon was fair and doctrinally sound, but he deeply deplored Brown's depravity.

My first visit to this settlement was in May 1857. As yet there was no decent road between Carver and East Union, nor was there any great need of one, for few owned oxen by which they could or needed to make the trip to town. On my way out to the country to find newcomers, I first met C.A. Hedengran, with whom I had a long conversation. He had just come through serious spiritual suffering and gained some peace of mind, but he was afraid of losing this peace. His behaviour struck me as being peculiar. Then I encountered Ola Paulsen, a brisk youth, full of life and politics, but yet a stranger to God. But something in his frank, honest nature was a prophecy of better things to come. A political election was approaching and he was out electioneering. I found my way to Johannes Hult to whom I had been referred as the best person to give me information about the spiritual and churchly situation in the settlement and as one who was concerned about religious life. I stayed here a few days, over Pentecost, preached a few times, performed baptisms and celebrated the Lord's Supper. They were just then in the process of building their first church, a log structure 30 by 36 feet, 14 feet walls. Only half of the roof was laid, but we gathered there once for a service, when I used the carpenter's bench as a pulpit and altar. Some children also were baptized. On Pentecost we had service and communion in the home of Sven Gudmundson, near the church. After the service there was a sharp clash with Brown who thus far had played the part of pastor in the settlement. The people were completely tired of him by now and wanted to get rid of him. I gave no occasion whatever for them to do so, but they made me, unwilling as I was, to become his judge, and brought one charge after another against Brown. In violent rage he tried to defend himself. Surrounded by almost the whole group and a target for one attack after another, he had to give way. Even those who loved the glass as much probably as he did, complained, "It is bad enough that we drink, but it is terrible that the minister shall drink as a pig." I could not, of course, do anything else than advise the people to have nothing at all to do with B., and as soon as a congregation is organized, to permit no unauthorized person under any circumstances to speak or conduct a service. As elsewhere so here the great spiritual dearth opened the door for such charlatans to gain access to the people. But they soon awoke to this danger and were on better guard. Before long Brown left the settlement and tried his luck in some other place. At this point there were 160 claim holders in the settlement. There were about 400 Swedes, large and small, this number increasing by another 100 in July, so that by the end of the year the Swedish population was over 500. The Norwegians numbered around 150, the Danes 9. On July 19, 1857 J. Hult wrote me, "I wrote immediately after you were here to Pastor Cederstam, but so far have not had a reply. I asked if he could possible come here and stay a few weeks to instruct those of confirmation age. Brown has left, selling his house for $110. In regard to the church and spiritual things it is as troublesome as it can be, for when there is no leader each one goes his own way. We hope to have windows, door and floor in by next Saturday, July 25th."

Pastor Cederstam came in November, instructed the children and confirmed them. He wrote on November 6th, "I now have the children, but you may believe it is no easy task. May the Lord help me! They number 14. A week from next Sunday I intend to have confirmation and the Lord's Supper."

Other denominations strove to gain a foothold at this time in the settlement. P. Carlson relates, "Among the newcomers from Skåne were some Baptists. They had some kind of minister with them by the name of Ekbom. He and the well-known Fr. Nilson in Scandia worked hard here but with little success. The Methodist minister Tidlund also appeared in the settlement and did his best, but won no foothold here."

As we have seen a Lutheran church was built here before there was any congregation. Pastor P. Carlson gives us the following information as to its location: "When the people settled here strangely enough 40 acres remained unclaimed. They then agreed, since it was a suitable piece, that these 40 acres should become church and parsonage land. But no one was able to buy or hold it for this purpose. So they left it in the hands of a neighbor, allowing him to call it his own and prevent anyone else from obtaining it. What happened? The accommodating gentleman, who was to keep it for a church, sold 40 acres of his adjoining the church land, then claimed and kept the church land for himself. The people resented such a deal and made him promise to keep 3 acres for a church and cemetery. On this promise they built a timber church in 1856, but it was never fully finished for it was at once obvious that it was too small. After I came here we began to inquire about the title to our 3 acres. It looked as if the congregation would lose the property, for we were denied the deed. The owner intended to use the church as a stable. But the Lord finally steered the matter so we got secure possession, though only after much trouble."

Right in the midst of these problems we have described a spiritual awakening started which had great significance for the settlement. "In 1856," says Carlson, "one of the pioneers, C.A. Hedengran, had his eyes opened concerning his free-thinking. He ran around with the Bible under his arm, cried, and professed, 'The Bible is God's Word. Christ is the Son of God. There is a hell!' These were the statements he had denied. He truly became a voice in the spiritual wilderness and a sign which many would reject. Through the reading of the Word of God he slowly found light and peace.

"In the fall of 1857 after a long and trying journey through the land from Iowa, I came to this settlement for the first time as a traveling colporteur for both the American Tract and the American Bible Society. I started immediately with my work which was to visit homes, sell books, and lead in devotional periods, from day to day, and the people flocked to hear God's Word. From the first there were many signs of a great need in their hearts, a need that could be satisfied only by Christ grapsed by faith."

After a brief visit in St. Paul and Scandia by Clear Lake, Carlson returned to the Union settlement and spent Christmas there, working tirelessly. "On Christmas Eve", he wrote, " I received a letter from Pastor Norelius, along with a letter of recommendation from the

Conference meeting held earlier in the fall in Rockford, Ill. I was urged to make my home up here and serve our countrymen by preaching the Word of God, according to the grace God gave me, and to extend my activity to other settlements if I could. In his private letter N. wrote, If the people in Carver (a name often referring to the whole region) want to call you as pastor, ask (the Conference) for license, in the name of the Lord, I will try to secure it for you."

The people pleaded most earnestly with Carlson to stay and become the pastor in the place. As yet no congregation had been organized, no officers existed. There was only a large number of persons who had been baptized and now confessed themselves to be Christians according to the Confessions of the Evangelical Lutheran Church. Their right to call a pastor in such fashion was never challenged, nor if in fact P. Carlson was properly called. On this call he was licensed to serve as pastor, at a Conference meeting in Galesburg, in the spring of 1858. When he left the Union settlement in January of 1858 a real awakening had begun. Many had been impressed by the Word of God, and some seem to have come to peace with God. While he was gone Hedengran and Ola Paulsen led the devotional gatherings and boldly witnessed of the Lord. Carlson spent the rest of the winter and the spring as an assistant to Pastor Erland Carlsson in Chicago in order to gain more practical experience in the exercise of his ministry.

The Organization of the Congregation

Pastor Carlson returned in May 1858 as the pastor in the settlement and preached his inaugural sermon on Trinity Sunday. On May 8th a meeting was held at which our Ev. Luth. congregation was organized. The congregational constitution prepared by the United Conference in 1857 was adopted without any alteration at a meeting on June 18th. Carlson's call was renewed, but peculiarly, for only one year, and with the provision that if either pastor or congregation wanted a change, this could take place after six months. This was probably due more to lack of experience than to any expressed principle. At this time the name of the settlement was changed to Union.

The following excerpt is from the *Minutes* of the meeting May 8th, 1858. "Pastor P. Carlson was elected chairman and C.A. Hedengran secretary. When the chairman asked if those present desired to organize a Scandinavian Ev. Lutheran congregation, the response was "yes". It was then resolved that each and every one who became a member of this congregation should promise with a sincere heart to remain loyal to that faith and confession which he had declared before the altar in his homeland, thereby acknowledging that the Holy Scriptures as the Word of God is the only sufficient and infallible norm for faith and life, and that the Augsburg Confession and Luther's Small Catechism are a brief but true summary of the main Christian doctrine.

"Resolved that occasionally the Norwegian Psalmbooks (Hymnals) should be used at the regular services.

"C.A. Hedengran and Hans Paulsen were elected deacons for a period of 3 years. Ola Paulsen and Sven Jonsson for 2 years, and Jonas Hellstrom and Anders Stomberg for 1 year.

"As trustees, all to serve for 1 year, the following were elected: Magnus Peterson, Ola Peterson, Sven Carlson, Ola Nilson and John Skone for the eastern section, Peter Flodin, Sven Johnson, Nils Lindstrom, Sten Olsen and Halvor Torkjörnsen for the western section of the settlement.

"It was resolved that the congregation should belong to the Synod of Northern Illinois."

Further, "resolved that no one either minister or lay member, shall have the right to preach or conduct any kind of meeting in the church, of whom it is not previously known that he professes the pure, Evangelical Lutheran teaching, or can show to the pastor or the deacons of the congregation a license or letter of recommendation from some Lutheran ministry."

Also, "resolved that each and every one who allows his dogs to enter the church during a service, be fined 25 cents, which goes to the treasury."

The Minutes were read and approved at the close of the meeting, and signed by the chairman and secretary. Then it was read to the whole congregation on June 13th and approved, and witnessed to by Swen Mellgren, Ola Nilsen, Ola Peterson, N.M. Alexanderson, M. Peterson, Charles Sorensen.

The First Members

According to Pastor P. Carlson, about 100 families joined the congregation. The following list, which he made, includes mostly the names of families, and had only 56 names. Evidently others were counted as members, for some of the officers elected are not found on the list, which has these names:

Swen Gudmundsson from Hössna in Vestergötland
Joh. Gustafson from Hössna in Vestergötland
Carl Abramson from Naum in Vestergötland
Anders Carlson from Naum in Vestergötland
Johannes Carlson from Naum in Vestergötland
Swen Mellgren from Naum in Vestergötland
Jonas Carlson from Naum in Vestergötland
Pehr Carlson from Naum in Vestergötland
Johannes Hult from Bitterna in Vestergötland
Anders Hult from Bitterna in Vestergötland
Peter Hult from Bitterna in Vestergötland
Kajsa Larsdotter from Bitterna in Vestergötland
Kjerstin Petersdotter from Bitterna in Vestergötland
Johannes Anderson from Lekåsa in Vestergötland
Anders Stomberg from Lekåsa in Vestergötland
Olaus Andersson from Lekåsa in Vestergötland

Sven Larsson from Lekåsa in Vestergötland
Joh. Andersson from Lekåsa in Vestergötland
Peter Lundquist from Herljunga in Vestergötland
Maja Swensdotter from Herljunga in Vestergötland
Joh. D. Skone from Herljunga in Vestergötland
Anders Wass from Wedum in Vestergötland
Lars Anderson from Wedum in Vestergötland
Otto Tapper from Wedum in Vestergötland
Peter Nilsson from Torsled in Vestergötland
Joh. Kyllerstrom from Torsled in Vestergötland
Anders Larsson from Eggvena in Vestergötland
Lars Anderson from Göteborg
Jonas Johnsson from Gammalkil in Östergötland
Carl Alm from Östergötland
C.J. Stenberg from Asby in Östergötland
Peter Swenson from Sund
C.A. Hendengran from Gödelöf in Skåne
Swen Monsson from Skåne
Swen Pehrson from Näsum in Skåne
Bengt Monsson from Gumlösa in Skåne
Ola Pehrsson from Färlöf in Skåne
Joh. Adolf Hellstrom from Jönköping
Johan Johnsson from Lekeryd in Småland
Swen Dahlberg from Åsenhöga in Småland
Anders Högstedt from Skire in Småland
Nils Alexanderson from Näfvelsjö(?) in Småland
Samuel Arvidsson from Nytja in Småland
Henrik Andersson from Ny in Wärmland
Jonas Andersson from Ny in Wärmland
Ola Paulsen from Norway
Henrik Paulsen from Norway
Paul Olsen from Norway
Lars Eriksen from Norway
Syvert Olsen from Norway
Arne Eriksen from Norway
Per Kleven from Norway
Ola Nilsen from Norway
Bjorn Aslagsen from Norway
Magnus Pedersen from Denmark
Carl Sorensen from Denmark

As mentioned, at a meeting of the congregation on June 18th the organization was completed and the constitution adopted. Again on July 4th the congregation met to arrange matters. It was held that "a school is essential for the instruction of the children if the Christian faith is not to die out". Agreement was reached to have Lars Anderson, a former school teacher, conduct a school for $8 per month and free board as compensation. It was resolved "that no one who has the least interest for the propagation of religion in the coming generation shall permit his name to be missing on this list" (of pledges toward the school). Ever since a church school has been maintained in these congregations, and much has been done for higher schools. Probably no settlement has furnished more candidates for the ministry than this one.

As to the religious situation P. Carlson reports, "The awakening which had cooled somewhat started up again and continued about 1 1/2 years. There were not many families who had not in some degree experienced the power of God's Word in their hearts. A blessed time, but, oh, one perilous to myself who, though in a concealed way, began to divide the glory with God, as I later realized." Strife and dissension were not absent. During the revival the Baptists tried persistently to draw people to themselves, but very few joined them and finally the effort ceased.

A seed of future dissension lay in the fact that the congregation was Scandinavian. Some of the Norwegians, especially those not belonging to the more emotional religious element did not feel at home in the congregation, and some Norwegians had never joined. When Norwegian ministers of other theological views came and preached, disputes and dissension arose. Prof. L. Larsen visited the settlement in the summer of 1858 and formed a congregation of four Norwegian families and one Swedish. Naturally the Swedish pastor and church council did not regard it proper to open the church for such a divisive purpose. But some members felt differently about it and were offended that Larsen was not permitted to hold his service in the church. This led to sad controversy in the congregation.

West Union Becomes a Congregation

In the summer of 1858 C.A. Hedengran made an agreement with the western section of the settlement to erect, with his own means, a small chapel there, since the people had so far to the church. The members were to supply the upright timber, bring it to the site, and donate some labor, the rest he would pay for. In the woods, near a small lake, a small structure was then built 22 × 32 ft. and 12 ft. high — this was West Union's first church. Divided into two rooms, one served for school and services, one for living quarters. Here Hedengran lived, conducted school and led in worship, until the following year when he was called to Chisago Lake. The house now is used as parsonage for West Union, after having been the church for 10 years. In the fall of 1858 a separate congregation was organized in West Union, giving the original congregation the name East Union. Hans Paulsen, a devout Norwegian, a member of the congregation, donated 4 acres of land for church and cemetery. Subsequently the congregation purchased an additional 16 acres, thus owning 20 acres for church and parsonage.

Pastor P. Carlson alone served both congregations for several years, preaching each Sunday in both places, which are about 6 miles apart. When the St. Ansgar Academy opened in East Union in 1865 he received help from Pastor Jackson, the principal of the school.

In 1860 the congregation decided to join our other congregations in leaving the Synod of Northern Illinois and becoming a part of the Augustana Synod. At the organization meeting of the new synod the pastor and Ola Paulson were present as delegates and participated in the proceedings. East Union then had 171, West Union 107 communicants.

Gotaholm

Some of the information on Gotaholm and Scandia has been furnished by Pastor J.S. Nilson who for several years was pastor there. Gotaholm is situated in Carver County, 18 miles northwest of Carver and 45 miles west of St. Paul. Like the Union settlement this place had fertile soil and forest. The southern branch of Crow River flows through the area, and by it the town of Watertown has grown up in recent years to become the center of the Swedish settlement. The church is now in Watertown, but originally was alongside the settlement.

The first Swede to settle here was Daniel Justus. He was from southern Helsingland and came here in August 1856 wandering through the woods. He laid claim to a piece of land by a small lake which later acquired the name Swede Lake. The following winter brought Jons Jonsson, Ulrik Ingemanson, and Carl Swensson but I do not know where from. Others followed including in 1858 a former member of the Swedish Parliament, Olof Andersson from Värmland. The first settlers chose places around and near the small Swede Lake. The thick woods made cultivation toilsome, but the labor paid off. On the side were small sources of other income, such as deriving sugar from the sugar maples and picking cranberries which could sometimes yield a nice price, or digging for ginseng in the woods.

The Swedish population was augmented by not a few countrymen who came here from Jamestown and Sugar Grove before 1860. Among these were Philip O. Johnson, Hendriks, Miller, Oberg, Brown.

The Swedish settlers here were from Småland, Vestergötland, Värmland, Helsingland, and elsewhere in Sweden. They had succeeded well in their work and are now in good circumstances.

In confirmation and completion of this information I include here a letter of J.P. Miller, published in *Hemlandet*, 1859, no. 4.

"Watertown, Minn., Dec. 14, 1858

"Gotaholm is the name of a Swedish settlement near Watertown, Carver County, Minn. In the summer of 1856 a family from Pennsylvania journeyed to Minnesota to look for land and a home in this great wilderness. Arriving in St. Paul they met another family from Illinois, on a similar errand. They agreed to go together and continued on to Carver and then to Clear Water Lake or Scandia. They found that all the land hereabouts had been taken, so that there was none available to them. But they were directed to a lovely little lake six miles northward, called Swede Lake by the Americans, where it was said some land was still unclaimed. They went there, were well satisfied by what they found, laid claim to properties, immediately moved there, built homes and began to cultivate the land. Thus these two families were the first to live here. A little later in the fall of the same year some Swedes came from Illinois who claimed land, built houses and then went back to bring their families in the Spring, which they did. The same Fall I too was in Minnesota to look over the country and find some available place for myself and acquaintances where we could settle together. I came across some Swedes and they recommended Clear Water Lake or Scandia. Arriving there I heard about a family that was said to have come from Pennsylvania and had been here some time earlier. I ascertained where they were, determined to find them. I found them at this lake and remarkably I recognized them as former acquaintances in Pennsylvania. I stayed a few days exploring the area which then was unclaimed, and decided the land was more fertile here than any I had seen in Minnesota. It was already November, winter was at hand, so I didn't stay to take any land, but traveled back to Pennsylvania to tell my acquaintances about the place and to prepare to move here in the Spring, which we did. Since then other families have come from Pennsylvania and Illinois and other states, as well as some direct from Sweden.

"Our settlement consists at present of 23 Swedish and 2 Norwegian families or some over 100 persons. Very likely the figure will soon be doubled for other families are expected both from Sweden and other places in America. The settlement is about 2 miles south of Watertown. This small town, on the south branch of the Crow River, was plotted only two years ago, and now has a saw mill and flour mill, two stores, and several other convenient buildings — As to the surface of the earth, it is mostly covered with various kinds of leafy trees, except for a great number of small or large meadows, with excellent grass, suitable for feed for animals. We have a surplus of woods both for building and other purposes as well as for sale.

"Small and large lakes are in our neighborhood. The soil consists of 1 to 3 feet black loam over clay. Here it is not as much mixed with sand as on the plains, and it is more productive here than there. It is probably true that the plains are easier to cultivate than the forest land and one can more quickly develop a farm. But if you consider how great the lack of forest in the plains, and what it costs to obtain wood for buildings and fencing, I believe that it is more advantageous to build a home in the woods, especially for one without means. The Swedes in the settlement own over 3000 acres, and those who have lived here one or two years have acquired a good livelihood. They are all satisfied as far as I can tell — Now one sees roads and large or small clearings, already cultivated and comfortable houses on almost every claim, everywhere in the forest only two years ago everything was wild. All the land has been claimed, but Americans hold much on speculation, and one can buy at present for 3 to 6 dollars an acre.

"As to church life all the Swedes here are Lutherans. 3 acres have been bought by the congregation situated by the lovely small Swede Lake, on the county road between Watertown and Chaska. The intention is to build next summer a school house and church, for which lumber has already been cut and hauled here. Though we have no pastor we assemble every Sunday to hear the Word of God, reading sermons from selected postils and other religious books. On the third of this month Pastor P. Carlson from the Union settlement paid us a visit and conducted services. On this occasion a Lutheran congregation was organized, the community receiving the name Gotaholm. The name Gota is due to the fact that the greater number of the settlers came from Göta rike or the Götha realm as against the parts of Sweden designated as Svearike and Holm is in memory of the Swedish missionary Holm who in the 17th century preached the Word of life to the Indians in America (the Delaware Colony). Thus the combination Gota and holm.

"In conclusion may He who has the power keep us in unity and love, so that strife, dissension or schism may not arise among us, but we may have a true love for the Word of God and for His teaching and faith into which we were baptized."

J.P. Miller"

The pious wishes of the writer seem to have been fulfilled to a great extent in this settlement.

The Lutheran Congregation

Pastor P. Carlson was the first pastor to visit and begin religious work in this place. On December 3rd, 1858 he organized an Evangelical Lutheran congregation, with 45 communicants and a total membership of 101, a number that slowly increased. From that date Pastor Carlson visited the congregation once a month and gave it care until 1866. In Olof Andersson, the former parliament member, a devout, prudent, and dependable character, the pastor had an excellent assistant. This man was a true type of the old-fashioned Swedish free-holder, a lovable personality, sensible, wise and equable. He commanded unqualified respect, yet was as humble as a child. For many years he played the part of a beloved and revered father of the whole congregation, on which he unconsciously set his stamp in loyalty to doctrine, reverent use of the means of grace and a quiet manner. In the last month of 1860 and beginning of 1861 I spent a few days as traveling missionary in this community. The temporal possessions were small and the people lived in a very simple and limited style, but everywhere I found contentment and happiness.

They willingly came evening after evening, intent on hearing the Word of God, at the meetings in the little log school house south or southwest of the lake. Of course, some especially on the fringes of the settlement were indifferent or spiritually cold, but by far the majority were upright and open to the instructions of the Word of God.

J.S. Nilson became the resident pastor in 1866, and a parsonage was built at the south or southwest shore of the lake, on the 22 acres which the congregation owned. Services continued to be held in the small log building until 1870 when a church was erected in Water-town, about 2 miles away.

Scandia

This settlement is situated on the eastern shore of Clear Water Lake, a name it merits. It is about 10 or 12 miles from the town of Carver and 5 to 6 miles from Gotaholm. The lake is unusually beautiful, as is the surrounding country, which originally was covered by luxuriant leafy trees.

A. Bergquist described the place in the September 8, 1858 issue of *Hemlandet*: "This place lies 10 miles northwest of Carver and in my opinion, is the most beautiful and best part of Carver County, by the side of one of the most beautiful of the lakes if not the most beautiful lake in the state. This judgment is often confirmed by visitors who came here. The lake is 12 square miles in size and ringed by high land covered with woods of luxuriant growth. The trees are mainly sugar maple, but mixed with other kinds. Most of the land around the lake is owned by Swedes, 14 of the claims going down to the lakeshore. Our settlement stretches east and southeast from this lake to another smaller lake where some of our people live. This, too, is a lovely lake, connected by the Six Miles Creek to Lake Minnetonka. At present the land sells for about $6 an acre.

"The Swedes who live here are from various parts of Sweden and belong partly to the Lutheran but mostly to the Baptist Church. Those of the latter group have built a place where they hold services." He goes on to tell of Gotaholm, 5 miles distant, where there were then 20-30 Swedish families.

Pastor Nilson says that it was in 1855 that 7 families settled in Scandia, and the number soon increased to 22. It is certain that some of these came from the Galesburg area. About this time a group of Baptists came from Burlington, Iowa, accompanied by their minister

Fr. O. Nilson. Supposedly they were the pioneers in this place, but there were also some Lutherans. The latter were not happy because of the religious situation, and began to sell to Germans who came in throngs to the land south of the lake. No Lutheran congregation was established here. Individual families joined the Gotaholm congregation. Pastor P. Carlson did in fact later start a congregation and visited it on his trips to Gotaholm. But it was dissolved when the people moved away. Only two families remained, namely the Sw. Swanberg and the Johannes Peterson family. Very soon afterward the Baptist church dissolved. P. Carlson explains: "For a long time we were in controversy with them, for they were always along when I preached nearby. Finally, they began to break apart, a large number hesitating what to do. The minister, Alfred Johnson, two deacons and 11 others, in all 14, left the church. Six of these, including the minister, were received on public profession in the Lutheran congregation in Gotaholm. When the four children of the former minister were to be baptized I preached on baptism, with the Baptists present. But when it came to the baptism it was more than they could endure and they walked out. This was in Johnson's own home. He took a three legged stool, placed it in the middle of the room and on it put a bowl of water. The three older children stood around, the youngest he took from the arms of the mother and fell on his knees with it, whereupon all were baptized. Then some of the children of the Baptists who had left were baptized — some over 18 years old."

In the town of Carver there were from the first some Swedes, but by 1860 no attempt had been made to form a congregation. Those interested in the church had only 4 miles to E. Union. The same was true in Jordan which later was annexed to E. Union.

Chapter 17

St. Peter-Scandian Grove

This area in Minnesota was not unknown in the good old days when the importance of the country lay in hunting and fur-trading. The name Travers de Sioux at the lower end of St. Peter reminds us of the great trail which the Indians and the Selkirk Company traders in Manitoba followed in their hunting and trading in furs. The Selkirk people used to come with their wooden carts, in which there was never a nail, from the far north down to Prairie du Chien, bringing their pelts and returning with necessities of their own. The route crossed the Minnesota River at Travers de Sioux, and the place and region were known by this name, before any whites had settled here.

Speculators hoped that the town of St. Peter, which lies along the Minnesota River at the western edge of Big Wood would become a large city, indeed the capitol of Minnesota. Interested speculators forced a law through the legislature to the effect that St. Peter was to be the capitol, but at the crucial moment someone did away with the bill, and the decision was frustrated.

An attractive, level prairie stretches west and north of St. Peter, with here and there a small lake surrounded by woods, giving the landscape a neat and splendid appearance. The soil is good, easily cultivated and the plains are rich in grass. Earlier the plains were often moist, but there is no reason now to complain.

On this plain lies the large Swedish settlement which with the years has grown to several parishes. In St. Peter we have the oldest Swedish congregation in this area and Gustavus Adolphus College, so important and promising for Minnesota and the whole Northwest. 7 or 10 miles away is the fruitful and well situated Scandian Grove, where Swedes and Norwegians get along well with each other. Ten miles west of the Swedish Church in Scandian Grove is the New Sweden Church, a center for a considerable Swedish populace. Again ten miles west of the New Sweden Church is the church and settlement of Clear Lake. About six miles north of New Sweden lies Winthrop, on the railroad, where is a throng of Swedish businessmen and Swedish farmers round about and where are both Lutheran congregation and church. Twelve miles north of Clear Lake is the settlement of Swedlanda in Renville County. In this region, thus, a very large Swedish population and a comprehensive settlement, stretching about 30 miles from east to west, in some places 15 miles wide, in others even more.

Here in general one will meet well-situated and some wealthy farmers, and persons who have gained a reputation in wider circles of both the world of business and of politics. But in this part of our story we are concerned only with the two oldest settlements and those Swedish Lutheran congregations which antedate 1860, namely St. Peter and Scandian Grove.

St. Peter

This place, 72 miles from St. Paul, on the left side of the Minnesota River, was first settled by Wm. B. Dodd, Oliver Ames and Wm. L. Ames who in 1854 laid claim to 500 acres and plotted a town. They became part of a larger land company with Governor Willis Gorman at the head. Great plans were made for the place but they never were realized. So it belongs in the company of those cities which stop growing. Still the place has an attractive, healthful, and not unfavorable situation and probably can in the future rise to greater heights. A mile from town, on the other side of the river is the very lovely little Lake Emily.

About the same time, that is around 1855, when Scandian Grove was settled the first Swedes and Norwegians came to St. Peter. The Swedes were from the Hvetlanda area in Småland. Some took land near and above the town along the river, others stayed in town and looked for work. One after the other began slowly to build their own homes. While their income was meager they managed to support themselves.

A Congregation Is Formed

The countrymen in St. Peter seem to have been concerned early about their churchly and religious needs. Almost certainly the Methodist preacher Tidlund was the first to visit the place to hold religious meetings, but the people do not seem to have had any inclinations toward Methodism. P.J. Ahlstrom was evidently the leader in religious matters and the people followed his arrangements. He had some talent for leadership and was doubtless well-meaning, but he also had some peculiar ideas. In 1857 a Lutheran congregation was organized, which adopted "The Unaltered Augsburg Confession except Article 14". The reason for such a decision may have been an exaggerated suspicion of pastors and priestly power, apparent also in some other ways. The same year a small frame church was built at the edge of town, alongside the present Swedish Lutheran parsonage, not far south of the present Swedish Lutheran church. It was slow in being furnished, later given an addition, and remained until a few years ago when it burned down. It is still remembered as being long and narrow, with a low panelled ceiling and a pulpit whose front resembled a lyre.

T.N. Hasselquist was the first Lutheran pastor to visit and preach for the Swedes in St. Peter. This was in 1857 when he traveled around in Minnesota. Pastor Cederstam spent some time here and in Scandian Grove in October and November of the same year. At this time the Scandian Grove people thought seriously of calling him as pastor, but wanted the St. Peter people to join with them in such a call. These had misgivings for they were afraid of the cost. By the beginning of January 1858 they had reached a sort of decision, one that sounds hesitant. Ahlstrom wrote to Cederstam, on January 11, 1858, and excerpts give us some idea of the situation. "I want also to convey the thanks of our small congregation for Pastor's welcome visit here last fall. If Pastor cannot accept our invitation to come here, because to begin with the income might be too small, we would still enjoy having him visit here occasionally, in case he might accept a call to some other place with greater salary, if that place be not too far from us. As soon as I had received Pastor's letter I made up a list, in which I informed the members of Pastor's interest in accepting a call, if we so wished, and added that each one who desired to have Pastor Cederstam as our pastor should write his name on the list, and in order to let him know about income, each one who subscribed was willing to contribute $4 toward the salary of the first year. This surely is not much, but as our church is not complete yet and will require more outlays, our members cannot afford to do more. Twelve members, including myself, have already signed and I believe some more will be willing to do so. We have made up a constitution and adopted it. Our church will be called The First Swedish Lutheran Church in St. Peter. Two deacons and three trustees have been legally elected." So far Ahlstrom.

The following persons had signed their names on this list, and may well be considered as the founders of the congregation.

P.J. Ahlstrom	C.J. Sandberg	G. Knudson
S.W. Johnson	Johan M. Johansson	L.J. Lundholm
I. Lundeen	Israel (illegible)	Germund Jonsson
	A.G. Petterson	C.A. Johnson

Most of them were probably heads of families.

According to the constitution which had been adopted only those could vote who had paid a certain sum during the year, and a certain number of voters had to be present for a resolution to be considered legal. In time this was changed.

P.A. Cederstam Becomes the First Pastor

In his letter of acceptance, directed to both congregations, written in March 1858, Pastor Cederstam wrote, "I have indeed had offers from other places, and if I considered the convenient and physical, at least for the present, I would prefer them and leave Minnesota. But I believe the Lord has sent me here, therefore neither advantages can induce me away nor perils and toils drive me away — Yet I will add that if it is God's will that I should come to you as your pastor, I will, as the Lord gives me grace and talent, preach and teach and administer the holy sacrament according to the unaltered Augsburg Confession as understood through its interpretation in the other symbolical books of the Lutheran Church. With the grace and help of Jesus I will so work among you that souls may be saved. If this is to happen the congregation must help and for that reason separate itself from those who live in open sinfulness — I know that you yourself realize this, therefore do not suppose that this statement of mine will cause any change in your decision. But if this should be the case, do not let your call bind you in any way, but express your opinions, frankly, and in an unrestricted and decisive manner." From this one can understand that he had resolved to exercise, from the beginning, the Christian discipline that the Word of God demands.

In May 1858 he moved to his new pastorate in Scandian Grove and served the congregation regularly until August 1862. This was the poorest and hardest part of its history, requiring work, persistence, and patience on the part of the pastor if the church was to endure. His salary, for example, in 1859 was $134.60 in Scandian Grove and $56 in St. Peter. It was of help that he could preempt 160 acres of land in Scandian Grove, but it meant toil, sacrifice and worry before he could pay for the land, cultivate it, erect necessary buildings, and derive any income from the farm.

The war broke out in 1861 and during this period of poverty and unrest, when St. Peter's Swedish Lutheran Church was an annex to Scandian Grove, as it continued to be for many years, the congregation did not much develop in either material or spiritual respects. But a good foundation had been laid and it was something that the congregation did live. Pastor Cederstam's connection with the congregation was severed by the Indian rebellion of 1862, and in the fall of 1863 John Pehrson became pastor. Separating from Scandian Grove in 1871 St. Peter became an independent congregation and Michael Sandell became its first resident pastor, until 1874. He was succeeded by Pastor J.G. Lagerstrom, under whose leadership a new church was built and growth was significant.

Scandian Grove

The beginning of this settlement is described in an article in *Hemlandet* for 1858, number 14, by A. Thorson, as follows:

"St. Peter and Torkels Lake, June 19, 1858"
"Since we Swedes in this place now have organized an Evangelical Lutheran congregation I think this happy news should become generally known. If I add further details about this region and our situation it ought not be without interest to our distant friends and countrymen who want to find a new home in the West . . .

"When I came here 3 years ago there were 10 or 12 Norwegian families. I and my family and relatives were the first Swedes to settle here. At present we are about 200 souls. Some came last year direct from Sweden and Norway, the others from other states, such as Wisconsin and Illinois. In these 3 years there has been no sickness of any kind, and there have been only 2 deaths, of children. So it must be a wonderful climate, rarely found here in America.

"Since we now have the Word of God proclaimed among us, and the scattered sheep no longer are without a shepherd, it is the desire of both myself and friends here that our countrymen in the East will seek for a home among us. I would like therefore to give as accurate information as possible to those who wish it, so that they may not be deceived by my statements. Our settlement lies 7 miles northwest of St. Peter. This latter place is already a flourishing town with 2-300 houses, and certain to grow even faster when the two railroads, which will cross each other there, are completed. Our settlement has about 1200 acres of woodland, about 400 acres are owned by Swedes, the rest by Norwegians. The price of woodland here is $16 per acre. Four miles west of these woods are several thousand acres of prairie land at the government price of $1.25 an acre. This prairie earth has from one to two feet of black loam on a clay base, is free of stone, and in the south surrounded by large forests, 10 to 12 miles from unclaimed land. Here the forest land is cheaper and one may take for granted that there will never be a scarcity of timber — We older settlers now have 1400 to 1500 acres of cultivated land, and considerable ploughing is planned for this summer."

The editor of *Hemlandet* added the following information: "The congregation referred to in this article is called, "The First Swedish Ev. Lutheran congregation in Scandian Grove, Nicolette County, Minn." In a private letter from there it is stated that "the number of members in our newly formed congregation may not be large, but the number is not so important as the fact that in love under the guidance of the Spirit of God we may work together to become a congregation to the glory of God and to our salvation and blessing". As far as I can learn there are now around 70 Swedes here, but more are expected from Illinois. They all seem very congenial and united. It is a joy to behold the friendliness and confidence with which they treat each other. Would that it would always continue thus, for unity and helpfulness are always a good trait, but especially in a new settlement. Compared to the general situation in the country, the temporal conditions of the Swedes are quite favorable, and considering their attractive farms, they will doubtless be among the more fortunate. . . ".

A Summary of the Early History

In reply to my inquiry, the first Swede in the place, A. Thorson, has given me the following information about himself and the community as a whole.

"I was born in Wää, an annex parish of Kristianstad. My father was a farmer, and when I was 14 I was apprenticed to a merchant in Kristianstad where I remained 6 years. Then I moved to Sölvisborg and worked as a bookkeeper for 5 years. What led me and two other young men to emigrate to America was a letter from a certain Igelhard to his home town, Karlshamn. He had left for America in 1845 and was in Chicago. His letters were very impressive. My two comrades and I resigned our jobs in April, and June 1, 1847 we were ready to leave. One was Lars Theorin, a minister's son from Småland, the other was Carl Hokanson, a miller's son from Blekinge — both were book-keepers in Sölvigsborg. There were no other Swedes in our party. We traveled via Helsingör to Havre de Grace, France. Then we boarded an emigrant vessel destined for New York. Our ship suffered damage in a severe storm and after a long and trying voyage we landed in Charleston, So. Car. October 7, 1847. Strangely, I had a letter of recommendation from the mayor Wickenberg in Sölvigsborg to a brother of his in Charleston, who was in wholesale business with an American. The firm's name was Klenk and Wickenberg. The brother had come as a youth to America to relatives who had probably emigrated in the 18th century. He was now old. We stayed there about 3 weeks and then continued on to New Orleans. Now our meager resources were almost exhausted, and poverty stared us in the face, and it led me to cry for both bread and work. Finally I got a job in a large hotel as a waiter and worked myself up to the position of steward. Theorin left for the Mexican war and died on the way. Hokanson found work as a lumberman. Late in the summer of 1848 I traveled to California via Chagres and Panama and worked for my passage to San Francisco. In San Francisco at that time there were not many houses, and none at all in Sacramento. I went with Americans directly to the mountains. I stayed in California, suffering much hardship, until the third year. I came away at least alive and in quite good health. Through hard work, sacrifice, and suffering, I had succeeded in saving $2000. Now I wanted to see my native land again. I traveled via San Juan del South and Nicaragua to San Juan del North, where I got on board an English warship that took me to Jamaica, Cuba, and finally New York. From there I continued on to Gothenburg and then home. Briefly this much on my first trip.

"On coming home I had a "tempting" invitation to go back to my first position. But I liked agriculture. So I rented a small property from Baron Hugo Hamilton at Areslöf near Kristian-stad, settled there and married Anna Nilsson, sister of Andrew Nilsson, now in Scandian Grove. After a two year trial I found that farming here was not to be compared with agriculture in America. I decided to emigrate with my family, especially since my wife's parents and brothers were very interested in going along. We sold our possessions and in the middle of April 1855 we set out, via Malmö, Lybeck and Hamburg. Our party consisted of 30 persons — my wife and I and 1 child, my wife's parents, and her brother, A. Nilsson, my brother Nils and sister Bengta, a cousin Anna Ostrom, together with 6 girls and 15 young men, all from the Kristianstad area. In the English Channel we collided with another vessel, but were all saved with the exception of one sailor. Our ship was towed to Dover, England, and underwent repairs for 6 weeks. Then the voyage continued to New York, Chicago, and Princeton, Ill. Some of the party remained in Chicago, others went along to Princeton, where I and some of the others had relatives we wanted to visit. Our destination was not yet determined. After a few weeks in Princeton, I and a brother-in-law, P. Benson, who had come the year before, made a trip to Minnesota. We went first to Red Wing to look around a bit, then to St. Paul. From there by foot up the Minnesota River through Carver to Henderson. Not attracted to the land, we returned to St. Paul. There we met a Swede by the name of Skonbeck, who described the fine land around St. Peter. I arranged with my brother-in-law Benson that he should go there and examine the area, while I went back to my family in Princeton.

"After a few days I received a letter from Benson, who had bought the right of a claim from a Norwegian for $300 and he urged me to get land at once. I went immediately with my family, the parents-in-law, and brother-in-law, A. Nilsson, arriving in Scandian Grove October 7, 1855. The rest of our party stayed in Princeton, though some came later. On our arrival we built a house and harvested hay for 20 cattle I had bought in St. Paul. The fall was beautiful. In winter we had the company of many Indians in our woods. Four or five Norwegian families were here when we came, we were the first Swedes in this place. In the spring of 1856 the Chilgren brothers, from Rickanum in Skåne arrived, with Mons Hokanson and wife, my sister Bengta — all had stopped a while in Princeton before coming here. Swen Larsson and family from Färlöf, Skåne, and some others came later that summer direct from Sweden, but did not stay here long. My brother Nils and family came from Princeton. In 1857 Anders Westerberg and family from Småland, and Carl Hamberg and family from the same area, came here after spending a short time in Geneva, Illinois. The same year brought Nils Nilsson and family, Christian Anderson and family, and others from Färlöf.

"1858 arrivals were Martin Peterson, John Nilsson, Carl

Nilsson and family, Erik Johnsson and Pehr Carlsson and families all from Skåne, and Ekelund and family and others from Småland."

"Religious and Churchly Matters

"In 1856 my family and I began to be concerned about spiritual matters. We were not satisfied with our situation. We began to feel the need of the privilege of a congregation. Now and then I spoke about this to the small group of Swedes and Norwegians living here. We had visits by Methodist preachers toward the end of 1856. We were happy for this. We had no notion of their doctrines. Most of the meetings were in our home. In 1857 we had regular visits every month, and after six months we were on trial as to whether a congregation should be formed. One time I asked the Methodist minister what was the difference between the Methodist and the Lutheran doctrines. He answered, "Dear brother, there is no difference. We Methodist accept Luther as long as he reaches, and then John Wesley who completed the Reformation". In my ignorance I could not contradict him. Indeed I was glad that such was his answer. On the occasion when the Methodist congregation was to be organized, I was the first to be asked to sign my name. After a pause, I said, "Not now, I will wait." All the others were silent; no congregation was formed. The minister was astonished. His name was Tidlund.

"A few days later Pastor Hasselquist visited Minnesota, and came to our place and my house. Now a new day dawned for us. We received instruction and fatherly advice. Later we were visited by Pastor Cederstam, and then by Pastor P. Carlson from Carver. The Methodist preacher made a final visit. His farewell sermon was everything but evangelical.

"The first Swedish Lutheran congregation in Scandian Grove was organized May 30, 1858, by Pastor Cederstam who then was active among us. This took place in my home. The first members were:

A. Thorson and family

Nils Andersson and family

Anders Westerberg and family

Nils Thorson and family

Carl Hamberg and family

Martin Peterson and family

John Abramsson and family

Peter Benson and family

A. Nilsson and family

N.P. Chilgren and family

M.P. Chilgren and family

N. Youngdahl and family

O. Monsson and family

Swen Larsson and family

Nils Nilsson and family

C. Andersson and family

E. Larsson

A.R. Andersen

Anna Andersen and family

"All but four families were from the Kristianstad area. Two were from Småland — Westerberg and Hamberg. Two were from Norway. The form of constitution recommended by the United Conference was adopted with insignificant change. This congregation together with the one in St. Peter called Pastor Cederstam. He resided in Scandian Grove.

"On June 13th after the adoption of the constitution the following were elected deacons: A. Thorson, A. Anderson. A. Westerberg, Nils Anderson. Incorporation took place June 23 and P. Benson, John Nilsson and Nils Liljequist were elected as trustees.

"At a meeting of the parish on November 4, 1859 it was decided to build a log structure for our meetings, but on November 16th this was changed to a frame church, 30 ft. long, 24 ft. wide, 13 ft. high. Built in 1860 the church cost around $600.

"The congregation was small but unified in spirit. Contentment prevailed and the members were attentive at services; the prospects were bright. There have been no stirring awakenings, but on the whole the members have wanted to be known as a good congregation and have striven to keep it so. One might wonder if they have been more concerned about the witness of men rather than of God. Still there were those who manifested the beginning of God's work in their hearts. Cederstam was a good and faithful steward, and I miss him and his successor." So far A. Thorson.

Cederstam served the congregation until 1862 when he left because of the Indian ravages. He was succeeded by Pastor John Pehrson who led the congregation for many years.

Among the men in this congregation who have had marked success and always shown interest in the local church and the community is Andrew Nilsson, a brother-in-law of A. Thorson. By hard work, compassion, good management, and most of all by the blessing of God, he has become one of the wealthiest farmers in Minnesota. He has represented his country in the state legislature. All the while he has been a strong supporter of Gustavus Adolphus College in St. Peter.

Chapter 18

Vista. Waseca County, Minn.

Waseca is one of the smaller counties in southern Minnesota. The LeSueur River flows through it. The land is somewhat hilly, with the ordinary type of leafy woods especially in the northern part, but mostly it is natural prairie. Where the ground now is more level it used to be lowland, but now dry. The soil is good, easily cultivated, and among the most fertile in the state. Waseca is the principal town, located by a pretty lake, and growing rapidly in recent years. Wilton was an older town, with considerable promise, but when it was by-passed by railroads on either side, it withered and was left to its fate.

The First Swedes in This Place

Early in the spring of 1857 some families and single persons came to Minnesota from West Point, Attica, and the area around LaFayette, Indiana, and remained a short while in Cannon Falls. But they stayed only until late summer and early fall, until they had time to explore the land for themselves and friends. They found what they wanted in Waseca County. Though they had around 50 miles to Cannon Falls, and about 70 to Red Wing and Hastings, as their nearest market places, they did not hesitate to venture out into the wilderness. They were not altogether empty handed, some had oxen and conveyances, but no one had more than bare necessities. They needed great courage and ability to sacrifice if they were to survive the first years. Their homes were caves or a combination of log, fencing material, and earth. When they made their trips on ox-carts to Hastings or Red Wing, it took a whole week. It could happen when they got to the point of selling grain that all they gained on the sale was consumed on the journey before they got home. But little by little, year after year, they went ahead. They ploughed the land, got good harvest of excellent wheat, which brought high prices when the war began. They built better homes, bred horses, cows and pigs, etc. improving their condition in every way. In time railroads were built in their neighborhood, giving better communication. Now the land looks splendid, well cultivated and built up. Some Norwegians began to settle here about the same time as the Swedes, and the two have always lived together peaceably.

A Swedish Evangelical Lutheran Congregation 1858

I visited the place in August 1858, among these countrymen who had formerly belonged to my church in Indiana. A Lutheran congregation was then organized which has maintained itself ever since. From the *Minutes* of the meeting August 8, 1858, we get some information on this event as well as on the people and congregation here: "Following the service in the afternoon the settlers went out to decide on a place for church and cemetery. They found a spot and while assembled they adopted this resolution: 1. that we unite in a congregation on the basis of the unaltered Augsburg Confession, and that we adopt the form of congregational constitution proposed by the United Chicago and Mississippi Conference on the Constitution of this congregation; 2. that the name be The Swedish Ev. Lutheran congregation in the Vista settlement, Waseca County, Minnesota; 3. that we accept the plan and place of church and cemetery, which John Nilsson is donating on his land, one acre now viewed by the congregation, said site being on the western 40 acre lot of the north half of the northeast quarter of section 28, Town. 106, Range 22; 4. that we now dedicate the cemetery; 5. that at the first opportunity we fence in the church property; 6. that we proceed to the election of deacons, Johan Peterson being elected for 3 years, Lars Fredrik Peterson for 2 years, and John Larson for one year; 7. that the members of the congregation be listed thus:

Carl Johanson with wife and 1 child
Johan Andersson with wife and 1 child
Anders in Hultamålen, a widower
Lars Fredrik Peterson with wife and 1 child
Lars Hokanson with wife and 4 children
Johan Larson with wife and 2 children
Johan Nilson with wife and 2 children
Carl Johanson
Nils Kant
Swen Swenson
Magnus Johnson
Gottfred Bjorklund
Johan Peterson
Johannes Peterson, a widow with 3 children
Johan Peterson
Greta Anderson
sum 36 persons.

"That these resolutions have been unanimously adopted is witnessed by E. Norelius, presiding, L.F. Peterson, John Peterson, Lars Hokanson, Gottfred Bjorklund.

"After these decisions had been made the cemetery was solemnly dedicated, making a deep impression on all of us."

The list above includes all the Swedes then living in the place. Most of them we have already met in the story of the congregation in Indiana.

A Short Sketch of the First 25 years of the Settlement and Congregation.

I will repeat for this purpose an address I made in Vista on Sept. 5, 1883, when the congregation celebrated its 25th anniversary. Introduction and theme were based on Psalm 68:10, "In Thy goodness, O God, Thou didst provide for the needy". "As we now are assembled here to celebrate the organization of this congregation 25 years ago we have occasion to consider, "How God provides for the needy by His goodness."

"We are instructed and urged to give thanks to God by stopping at certain points and looking back on the days that are gone, for one can then compare them with the present and noting the difference especially those who most deeply experienced the need of the pioneer period but also the wonderful help of the Lord, can exclaim with David, "God, Thou dost provide for the needy in Thy goodness."

"You older folk who were here on August 8, 1858 at the organization of the congregation, could you then have imagined that 25 years would bring such changes and experiences? The first few families and individuals who settled here were from the parishes of Småland on the southeast shore of Lake Vettern, and had spent a few years in Indiana, and most of these had been members of my first pastorate. Some of you cannot now recall without emotion the towns of West Point, LaFayette, Attica, Milford, and Yorktown and the many happy and edifying times we had there together when in the simplicity of our hearts we read and considered the Word of God and approached Him in song and prayer. Strangers from another land, scattered as we were, it felt good to come together, exchange thoughts, and encourage each other on the way to the eternal home. Division and discord had not yet at that time given birth to that unruly spirit which did its destructive work in this circle of friends—

"It was in the summer of 1857 when the first Swedes settled here. The difficulties and sacrifices they had to contend with can be better imagined than I can describe if we remember that they were all in straitened circumstances, and had from 60 to 75 miles to the closest market places where they could obtain necessities. Those years were among the hardest in the history of this country. In each new and remote place it required courage of the strong men when he saw wife and child crying for bread. Yet even greater than the temporal were the spiritual and eternal needs. It could not be otherwise among a people who before had been impressed by the Word that alone quickens the soul. Early in the summer of 1858 I had repeated invitations to come here and break the bread of life among my countrymen who had made their home here. But I could not make the trip until early in August. Forgive me if I describe my journey and what I experienced here, but it can cast light on those times and prove that in more than one way since that time the Lord in His goodness has provided for the needy. The whole summer had been rainy. Brooks and streams were overflowing, bridges were washed away, lowlands were almost impassable. I walked from Red Wing to the Norwegian settlement in the southwestern part of Goodhue County. From there I rode the post carriage to Owatonna, a dangerous and tiring ride. On the prairies the water reached up to the hub of the wheels. As we entered the forest at the Strait River it was night and pitch dark, so we could see nothing. In a house at the edge of the forest we borrowed a lantern with a tallow candle, but in the woods a mass of mosquitos got into it so we blew out the light, and then got stuck on a stump. To get the wagon free we had to get down into the mud, which reached half way up our legs, and lift it off the stump. We had to swim across the river at Clinton Falls, also at Owatonna, for the bridges had floated away. We finally reached Owatonna at 2 a.m. in thick darkness and not a dry thread on our bodies. The next day I went with the post carriage toward Wilton, 18 miles away. When we came to the bridge over the LeSueur River, I got off and started through the wilderness in the direction where I thought the settlement lay. In those days there were many bogs in this region, some of them quite extensive. In order not to lose time and my way, I put my bag on my head and waded over the swamp in the direction I wanted to go. I finally arrived, but then there were no such manor houses as you now have. Some lived in caves, some in log huts. Most had plenty of dripping through the roof — outside the rain was at least clean. It rained hard the first night, but I preferred to lie under open sky on new cut hay in a wagon to be in a cave without floor and with a soaked roof which offered no refuge from the rain. I was tired and slept well. I mention this not to discredit the pioneers, on the contrary, we wonder at their ability to endure such privation—

"14 had then claimed land — the whole Swedish population consisted of 36 persons, young and old. They were content and happy and faced the future with those singular feelings and anticipations which almost everywhere inspired our pioneers and enabled them to maintain their courage. 'If we could only have a congregation, a pastor and a church, everything will be alright here', so they said to each other. With few exceptions they were young people, with both desire and habit to work and feed themselves in the sweat of their brow. A service was announced for Saturday afternoon, August 7th, when I spoke on Lamentations 3:22-26 'The steadfast love of the Lord never ceases, his mercies never come to an end; they are new every morning, great is Thy faithfulness. 'The Lord is my portion' says my soul 'therefore I will hope in Him'. The Lord is good to those who wait for him, to the soul that seeks him. It is good that one should wait quietly for the salvation of the Lord.'

"The 18th of August was the 10 Sunday after Trinity, and I had as theme: 'Jesus weeps over Jerusalem, yet an exhortation to repentance'. In the afternoon we gathered out on a hill on the prairie for a devotional period and then the Swedish Ev. Lutheran congregation in Vista was organized, and the cemetery dedicated. The name Vista came from the Vista district in Jönköping County, and was chosen because so many came from this area in Småland. Later the site intended for the church was changed because the community developed in a direction not then foreseen. The beginning was small. A few poor strangers in a wilderness, some needy souls who realized the necessity of God's Word and sacraments. In their innocence they drew together and founded a Christian congregation, hoping that the Lord would provide. Their hopes were not put to shame.

"Later that year the Minnesota Conference was organized, greatly aiding the poor scattered congregations and uniting them. From its first meeting we have this resolution: 'Since the Swedish Lutheran congregation in Vista is in need of care, Pastor Cederstam, who lives closest to the settlement is asked to visit there as often as he can. Though Pastor Cederstam, then living in Scandian Grove, was not able often or even any time that year to make a visit, for he was almost 50 miles away without a road between the places, and because of other duties, it will show that the Conference was concerned. At the winter meeting 1859 the Conference urged Pastor Beckman and Cederstam to visit the congregation, which they did until the winter of 1861. There were now between 30 and 40 members. At its meeting in February 1861 the Conference was informed that the Norwegian pastor Nils Olsen had accepted a call from the Norwegian congregation in the northern part of Waseca County, and arrangements were made to have him also serve the Swedish congregation. Olsen was a member of the same Conference and Synod to which the congregation belonged. I was commissioned to introduce him and to help him order the affairs of the church. He remained as its pastor until 1869, but from 1866 he shared the care of the congregation with Beckman and J. Pehrson. The two latter continued to visit here from 1868 to 1871, when Pastor L.A. Hokanson accepted a call and remained here until 1877. Prof. J.P. Nyquist served a part of 1877 and 1878 and since the summer of that year Pastor S. Anderson has been in charge.

"The plain but pleasing church was erected in 1868, and after Hokanson's arrival a parsonage was added — witnesses of love and sacrifice for the sake of the Lord."

"It is not possible to give an account of the growth of the congregation in the early years by reference to the statistical tables of the Synod, because there are no reports there for the first 6 years, unless one can suppose that LeSueur River is identical with Vista, which is not certain. In 1865 Vista appears in the tables as having 118 communicants. This year (1883) there were only 113. The decrease since 1876 was caused partly by removal of members to other places, partly by separation of members influenced by the Waldenstrom movement which started in Sweden. In general, however, the growth has been normal considering how small the group was in the beginning—"

My going beyond the limits of this treatise is due to the celebration of the 25th anniversary.

Chapter 19

Other Swedish Settlements Prior to 1860 in which Lutheran
Congregations had not yet been Organized.

Wisconsin

Before 1860 there were few Swedish settlers in Wisconsin. Since
then the number has indeed increased, especially on the western edge
bordering Minnesota. But on the whole Wisconsin has not proved
very attactive to our Swedish immigrants.

Swedes were in Milwaukee even in the early 1840's, but never in
great enough numbers to identify them as such. There is still no
Swedish Lutheran congregation.

The same is true of Sheboygan where there were a few Swedes
in early years.

A Swedish settlement was found in Waupaca and Portage
Counties before 1860.[1] Andrew Jackson, later a pastor in the
Augustana Synod, wrote about this place in April 1859: "The
Swedish settlement in Waupaca and Portage Counties, Wisconsin
has considerably decreased in size lately and the prospect is that it
will become even smaller. At the beginning of last year there were 22
families. But during the year 9 of these sold their farms and moved to
Minnesota, intending to settle in the lovely and fertile area west of
Forest City and Green Lake, about 100 miles west of St. Paul. Most
of those remaining expect to leave as soon as they can. It is about 8
years since the Swedes first began to come here. With few exceptions
they have not had great success in accumulating this world's goods,
principally because of the inferior quality of the soil. Their spiritual
condition is much better than one might reasonably assume when
one considers that they have lived so long in a wilderness without
much care. I have been happy to learn to know some of them who
seem to me true disciples of Jesus, and others who are anxious about
entering the narrow gate. In general there seems to be a certain inner
conviction about the necessity of having the means of grace among
them even in those who have not come to a true concern about the
salvation of their souls. They have had no pastor of their own, but
for about 2 years have been visited by a Norwegian Lutheran pastor
from a near-by Norwegian settlement once every 7 or 8 weeks.
Otherwise they have been without religious care. Yet they have met

[1]Cf. Part I, Chapter 2(1)

occasionally for public devotional purposes, when one of the group read from an approved Postil. This has, I believe, served both to awaken, instruct and to inspire the members. Myself I have had many fine, enlivening hours at such meetings and can therefore, from my own experience recommend them when there is no opportunity to hear the Word of the Lord from the mouth of a servant sent by the chief Shepherd himself.[1]"

The majority of these Swedes are now to be found in the New London area, Kandiyohi County, Minnesota.

Superior City on Lake Superior had some Swedes in 1850's. A country man who paid a call to the editor of *Hemlandet* in Galesburg in December 1857 gave the following information: "Not less than 100 Swedes live in Superior City and the surrounding area. Most of them are single men, there are only 5 families. The reason for their being there seems to be that American speculators came to Chisago Lake and induced them to come to Lake Superior and take up claims, not for themselves, but for the Americans. For this they were usually paid $100. Five persons accepted the offer and followed. In time the American speculators occupied the land. The Swedes received their pay and the deal was supposedly closed. Town lots were laid out on some of the land, on other mining was begun. But when the owners sought deeds on the land from the government they discovered only the original claimant could secure it. Now the Swedes demanded high prices for their names. Some of them saw their mistake and took advantage of their position. Four demanded and received the sum of $14,000 to transfer the claim. One had even higher notions of the value of his name and would not permit the use of his name for less than $20,000. This may seem exorbitant, but it was but a fraction of what the Americans had gained and still expected to gain." A description of the land appeared in a letter written in English but by a Swede, Mr. Chaseur, alleged to be from Gotland, who had been in America 18 years. The letter was included in a comprehensive report on Wisconsin and the Lake Superior region. It was written March 24, 1857. The description is quite colored, especially in what it says of soil and vegetation, and one suspects that it was propaganda to attract settlers.[2]

After the first flames of speculation had burned down, there

[1]*Hemlandet* 1859, No. 16
[2]*Hemlandet* 1857, No. 25

followed a long period of darkness and hopelessness, and for many, many years nothing was heard of Swedes near Lake Superior, though one or another family may have lived there the whole time. Only recently the area has blossomed again and many Swedes have begun to come there.

Minnesota

There were Swedes before 1860 in various places in Minnesota where as yet no Lutheran congregations had been formed.

Among them was *Stillwater*, one of the oldest towns in Minnesota, on the St. Croix River, 18 miles from St. Paul, and a center for the lumber industry. Many Swedes early sought work at the saw mills and in the floating of logs. But for a long time no large number of families made their homes here. A widow Smith and her son-in-law Borén were among the first. Not a few Swedish girls were employed by American families in the city. For many years it was a preaching place, as our pastors made their visits up the St. Croix River.

In *Afton*, 9 miles south of Stillwater, Washington County, there were some farmers before 1860. Most were from Skåne. Fahlstrom, the first Swede in Minnesota, lived here. Of those who came later I recall Bengt Monson, now a very wealthy man, Jons Isberg, an old sailor, now in Vasa, Rosenquist, Piculell, Ostrom, Peterson, etc. Our pastors visited this place, too, but very irregularly, so that no congregation came into being. The Methodists worked here also and gathered a small congregation, but had no great success.

The situation in Hastings was similar, where a few Swedes were located. The oldest and best known in the place was the wagon-maker, John Ostergren, from Stockholm, who carried on an extensive business.

Minneapolis had very few Swedes before 1860.

In Meeker and Kandiyohi Counties Swedes began before 1860 to settle west of Big Wood. They came on the two main roads here from the East, the one via Carver, Glenco, Hutchinson, Lake Ripley, etc., the other via St. Cloud to the northern part of Kandiyohi County. They located at Swede Grove or Grove City, Lake Ripley, Nest Lake, Eagle Lake and beyond — the "world's end" they called it at that time, indicating the extreme edge of the settlement.

We have some notices from these places that tell us of the conditions of our fellow countrymen there at that time. E.A. Lind had been travelling around in the area wrote from St. Peter to *Hemlandet* in February 1859, and said that 20 Swedish families, and about the same number of Norwegians were already established in the so-called Green Lake settlement. The distance from St. Paul was about 100 miles, from Carver, 80 miles. Another letter, of March 2, 1859, from Acton (the area around Grove City) reads thus: "Since we are urged to tell of the situation of our countrymen every where, both in spiritual and temporal matters, I want to account for how we have it here. At present we are 10 families and many single folk, have claimed land, and Swedes are ranged over a stretch of 30 miles from East to West forming several communities. Our settlement has not yet a name, another one is called Eagle Lake and still another Kandiyohi. There is said to be unclaimed land twelve miles beyond Eagle Lake but I don't know of what kind. Where we are prairies abound and of good quality. Southwest and northwest of us are large amounts of prairie and forests.

"As to the spiritual situation in our place, we have no church and no leader. On holidays we have indeed gathered to consider the Word of God, but since some are Baptist inclined there is, as known, no unity. I want to mention that most of us are still loyal to the Lutheran Church. The Baptist preacher Nilson from Clear Water Lake made us a visit once, or rather an attempt, and left some copies of Viberg's book on baptism and other doctrinal literature.

"We have here 5 unbaptized children. No one has been here to baptize them — some of the children are 1 1/2 years old.

"I want now to tell briefly about our temporal conditions. Myself I left Sweden 1857 and settled here 15 miles west of Forest City. Opportunities and income are small, but some others have it better than I. In time, if the Lord will, things will improve — beginning and end are not the same. Here we have good land and woods beyond our needs, so if necessary we could sell some.

"After I had written a few friends came to me and asked that if you could you would send us a minister of the Word who could proclaim God's Word to us. We are in a wilderness here and like straying sheep who have no shepherd. Some of us have not received the Lord's Supper for two years. If it is His will who has called us He will doubtless provide someone. We are too few, and poor, to be able to support a pastor, but we always expect more who would increase the congregation.

Ola Monson, from Kristianstad
Nils Welander, P.J. Lund."

From this time the Swedish immigration grew greatly in volume to this region. The economic development was seriously hampered by lack of communication with the more thickly settled parts of the state and by distance from markets. Living conditions were the most primitive. Money was absent. Muskrat skins had to serve as means of exchange, valued at about 10 cents a piece.

The Andrew Jackson who had moved here from Waupaca, Wisconsin wrote in 1859 and gave an account of both the economic and political situation in the region. From his description we give the following: "Marine Lund, Meeker County, Minnesota, September 28, 1859.[1] Our farmers out here have been very troubled for some time because of the anticipated sale of lands. Those who had cattle were prepared to sell their last cow in order not to become homeless. Those who had none — yes, they were probably the luckiest, at least they were least worried, for they comforted themselves that 60 to 100 miles farther west there still was land not yet in the market. They might go there and begin again, by hunting, fishing, and digging. Meanwhile we might get a generous government who would give a poor man 160 acres without payment. So they were prepared with their naive dream.[2] There have been all kinds of proposals circulating these days, proving that the Swedes hold to the ancient proverb, 'better breadless than planless.' — Now since the land is no longer on the market there is calm again for a while, and the Democrats begin to emphasize how grateful the people should be.—"[3]

The Minnesota Conference early turned its attention to these regions and listened to their pleas for help. At its second meeting, held in East Union February 10-12, 1859, Forest City and the surrounding area were discussed. It was resolved that "since there are already around 50 families in this place the Conference considered it of utmost importance not to leave these countrymen without spiritual care, and urged Brother P. Carlson to undertake a missionary visit there as soon as possible."

At the next meeting June 15-18, 1859, held in Scandian Grove, Pastor Carlson reported that he undertook the visit at the end of May in his own carriage, "but because of the poor roads and the deep water he had to turn back after driving 40 miles, and leaving horse

---

[1]Ola Monson's letter of 1857 came from this place.
[2]The Homestead Act was not yet enacted.
[3]*Hemlandet* 1859 No. 41.

and buggy had to return home on foot." This was not the end of the project. At the August meeting in Spring Garden Carlson was able to announce that during the summer he had visited the Forest City region and there organized 3 small congregations. He had found some 70 families there. Our source does not identify the three, but they were most likely Lake Ripley, Marine Lund or Swede Grove, and Eagle Lake and Nest Lake. This, however, is uncertain. The three congregations were not included in the Synod records and cannot be considered as fully organized before 1860. The real founder of the congregation in this region was Pastor A. Jackson, but this was at a later period.

At a few other places in Minnesota there were some Swedish families, as in Cambridge, Isanti County, where six families resided in 1859; at Fish Lake there was a family or more at this date; in Geneva, Freeborn County, etc. As yet these places were not significant.

Iowa

In northeast Iowa, near the Mississippi River, there were two small settlements long before 1860, one near Lansing, the other by McGregor. It took a long time before any orderly church life was created, and even since conditions have been less than promising.

The first Swede to locate near Lansing was Erik Sannman from Hudiksvall. He emigrated to America in 1849 and came here in 1850. In his company from Sweden were G.A. Swedberg from Hudiksvall, and Erik Sund from Tuna, born in Hassela. They followed Sannman after a short stay in Illinois. Others from northern Sweden joined them, such as Anders Brostrom from Hudiksvall, Anders Erson from Gnarp, etc. G. Palmquist visited them around 1852 and they became Baptists. Later some Lutheran families settled near them, but never in large numbers. The leader was Anders Danielson, from Östergötland if I remember right. Before 1860 Pastor P. Beckman visited them and occasionally the writer did. Among the Baptists Swedberg was minister. Not until many years later did the Lutheran congregation enjoy regular pastor care for any length of time.

As to McGregor I include here first an article from *Hemlandet*, October 1858, which gives some information about the place at this time. I quote: "The settlement is not large and is not thought to increase greatly because all uncultivated land has been purchased by speculators who are holding it for prices of $6 to $10 an acre. The land is much like that in New Sweden, Iowa, wooded areas mixed with land covered with brush, the soil is good. This year the winter wheat crop looks fair. — Eight of the Swedish families and two of the Norwegian have each from 80 to 120 acres. There are some who own no land. Altogether there are between 60 and 70 souls, a third are Norwegians. The settlement lies 4 1/2 miles south of McGregor, half way between McGregor and Clayton on the Mississippi. The Norwegian pastor Elling Eielsen has made several visits and Pastor Esbjörn has been here once. This fall two Swedish Lutheran pastors have visited these places and the people could hear the Word of God proclaimed in spirit and in truth in their own language. The writer of this letter rejoices over the festive occasion they then experienced and expresses the hope that the Lutheran pastors would not pass by but visit these places."

Professor S.M. Hill has written a fine, brief history of their settlement in *Augustana*, December 1889, from which I quote: "One of the oldest Swedish settlements in America is situated at Sny McGill brook in northeastern Iowa. It was founded in the Spring of 1851 by Staffan Petersson, Staffan Staffanson, and Jon Larsson, all from Norrland. Staffan Petersson had a brother-in-law Ola Jonsson, a fervent friend and follower of the sadly notorious Erik Jansson. Ola Jonsson was along in the exodus to America and wrote back to his brother-in-law Staffan to come here. He lived then in Långeby, Hede parish, in Herjeådalen. A friend of his youth Staffan Staffansson from the village of Viken came with him." They did not like it in Illinois, so they started out in the company of Jon Larsson from Gestrikland, who had come to Illinois earlier. They landed at McGregor where a Scotchman with that name had located and given his name to the place. They liked the land and settled nearby, "The plentiful fish in the river and the extensive forest provided for their support. They cut down trees and floated the logs to Dubuque. There they reduced them to firewood and sold it for $3 per cord. With this money they bought a pair of oxen, with which they could the more easily bring the wood to the river."

Staffan P. wrote home for his brother Erik and a youthful companion, Anders Ersson from Ransjö. "When they left Sweden in the winter of 1853 two Norwegians joined them, Andreas Lange and Thron Pedersen from Röräs. The journey from Trondheim to Racine, Wisconsin took 18 weeks. There they bought a pair of oxen and travelled by oxcart to their new home, covering the distance in 2 weeks. Thus a total of 20 weeks for their American trip."

In the early years the place was visited by Elling Eielsen and other Norwegian ministers. Toward the end of the 1850's Pastor P. Beckman began to come to McGregor and Lansing. Occasionally some one of our other Swedish pastors would make a visit, but under the circumstances regular pastoral care was not possible. According to Hill Pastor Beckman encountered some opposition, and this is not unlikely in view of the religious tenets Eielsen sought to impress on some of these Swedes and Norwegians.

Much later the settlement received its first resident pastor, Brink, and after him J.P. Mattson. There was then no church building — services were held in a school house. "Now for a long time no pastor has been stationed there. Pastor Pihlgren from Clinton, Iowa, occasionally visits there."

In Lansing a congregation was organized in 1860, with the name Åby. A frame building was erected in 1873. In 1889 there were 12 communicant members. The McGregor congregation was organized in 1865. Here a frame church was built in 1887. In 1889 there were 80 communicants.

Michigan

Quite early some Swedes began to settle in eastern Michigan or the Lower Peninsula. As far as is known the first settlement was in the town of Sparta, Kent County, near Grand Rapids. Pastor Erl. Carlsson visited there in September 1859 and thus described the place: "The train left Grand Haven at 8 o'clock in the evening and at 10 o'clock we were in Grand Rapids, 30 miles from the lake. There was a not inconsiderable amount of business. It is an attractive and lively town, much larger than I had supposed. I was up early the following morning looking for Swedish people, and fortunately I found a man who knew where they lived. He told me that Sparta was 16 miles from Grand Rapids. He promised to drive me there, but he also knew how to get well paid. Around Grand Rapids the land is sandy and full of gravel. Farther on the soil becomes more fertile, and the landscape varies with forest, cultivated clearings, pleasant hills and valleys. The Swedes live in quite an attractive area, with rich soil, abundant woods, and good water.

"It is in Kent County and Sparta township that our countrymen here have found themselves a home. They have lived here about 5 or

6 years, though it is somewhat longer since they came from Sweden. They number 9 or 10 families, or about 50 persons altogether. Most are from Löfby and Svenljunga parishes in Jönköping County. They have had to encounter the same hardships and sacrifices which the newcomers in other places have had to experience. Most of them have overcome the first obstacles in that they have not only bought but in most cases have paid for their land, built their homes, cut down trees and cleared from 5 to 10 or 20 acres. All the land has been bought up and now costs from 5 to 10 and 15 dollars an acre. Houses are rather close, roads laid out and already in good shape. School houses have been built and the prospects for advancement and comfort are very bright and hope-inspiring. Our countrymen here have an advantage above those in many other places in that they can easily market both their cattle and their crops. Beside Grand Rapids they have a market in Berlin, 8 or 10 miles from where they live. There are both a railway station and a trading place. The railroad will carry their products either to Grand Haven or Detroit. Thus they are closer to the centers of world trade than are our farmers either in Illinois or in the other states of the West and Northwest.

"Their greatest lack is that they have no church or pastor. On Sunday, September 17th, the 13th Sunday after Trinity, they had the first opportunity of holding a service and celebrating the Lord's Supper since they came to this country. This was truly a festive day, one that will long be cherished in memory. It was to me, too, an occasion of special joy in experiencing how these people through the many years had not forsaken the Word of God, but with sincere love were loyal to their church and its teachings, and evidenced a deep spiritual need. There were children to baptize, not less than three in each of two families, and some so grown that I could converse with them about their Saviour.

"I had to leave these friends after several days of visiting. I felt deeply for them and pray that in His great mercy the Lord will send a pastor to them. They are yet few, but expected a family from Plymouth, Michigan in the Fall, and hope to grow gradually in number."[1]

It is certain that there were more families here and there in Michigan, but I am not acquainted with the origins of any settlement before 1860.

[1]*Hemlandet*, 1859, No. 43.

Illinois

There were Swedes in several places in Illinois before 1860 where no Lutheran congregation existed, as in Victoria and its neighborhood. It was in Victoria where the Methodist preacher J. Hedstrom lived and worked. There and in Stark County were the many who early left Bishop Hill out of dissatisfaction with Erik Jansonism, and influenced by Hedstrom to leave most of them went over into Methodism.

Galva, 5 miles from Bishop Hill, began as a daughter-colony, in 1853-1854. It was on the railroad nearest to Bishop Hill and served as a junction point for the colony. The name reminds one of Gevle; most of the Swedes were Jansonists. The Swedes soon became a minority but long remained dominant in the business community.

It was here in 1856 that the Bishop Hill people started the journal *Svenska Republiukanaren*, with S. Crousioe as editor. The response, however, was not as good as anticipated.

The first Swedes in Kewanee also came from Bishop Hill. Erik Eriksson from Nora in Westmanland moved there in 1855. Others came from there and elsewhere in 1856 and 1857, most of whom were from Gestrikland.

A few Swedish families were also to be found in Wyanet, New Boston, Peoria, etc.

Indiana

A few families were scattered here and there, but there were no colonies beyond those already mentioned.

Buena Vista, Hamilton County, was the home of some Swedes before 1857, among them Magnus Hake from Grenna and C.G. Thil from Kronoberg County. They enjoyed a good reputation until a young man from Gothenburg proved guilty of fraud in business matters and disappeared. This cast a pall of suspicion on all the Swedes in the place who suffered though innocent, and became anxious to leave.

Kansas

The oldest Swedish settlement in Kansas arose in Mariadahl at the Big Blue River in Pottawatomie County around 1855-1856. Kansas was then a veritable battleground where bloody battles were fought between the Free State party and the defenders of slavery for domination in that state. Kansas lay at that time far from the developed regions and lacked the means of communication and blessings of civilization enjoyed there. Removal and establishment there meant great difficulties and was no child's play or excursion. To move out to this insecure wilderness required courage on the part of J.A. Johnson and his relatives from Horns parish in Östergötland. Some of them came over to America in 1852 and in 1856 followed Johnson in the stream of Free State people moving to Kansas. Then came his brothers, sisters and Mary, the mother. They were delighted in the landscape of the Big Blue Valley and its resources and made their home there. St. Joseph in Missouri was the nearest place where they could procure provisions. Beside the usual obstacles which they had to overcome the first year in their struggle with Nature they had to endure constant fear of the slave people and expect to be driven away or murdered by them. They had no choice but to be involved in the feuds which raged all over this territory.

The Big Blue River empties into the Kansas at Manhattan. Its fertile valley is from 2 to 3 miles wide and consists of rich bottomland. Considerable woods of various leaf trees line the river. For about 30 miles north the bluffs flatten and the valley widens. The river runs in many curves and in clear weather its water appears strangely blue, wherefore its name. About 20 miles north of Manhattan the present Swedish settlement begins and stretches up the river more than 10 miles. The prairie on both sides is as high as the bluffs by the river. Springs abound in the bluffs and numerous ravines run from the river into the prairies. At first the Swedes kept to the river, while the bluffs and prairies bordering the valley on both sides were unclaimed and used for common pasture. Gradually these were occupied and the settlement spread on both sides of the valley. Thus in time the Swedish settlement Wahlsburg developed on the west side of the river in Riley County, and Olsburg on the east side.

A correspondent to *Hemlandet*, Lars Person from Hjersås and Warestorp, wrote from Randolph P.O., Riley County, on February 7, 1859: "At present we are 8 Swedish and 2 Danish families living here. This place is 110 miles from the Missouri River, situated on both sides of the Big Blue River. The land is so-called 'bottom land', both low and high along the river, mixed with sand. Away from the rim the soil is firm clay loam. The land is laced with many brooks of crystal clear water, guaranteeing a supply of water. Along the shore

of the river and the brooks is plenty of woods for building and fencing. Where there is less of woods on the higher places there is fine
stone for buildings and fences and enough limestone for processing of
lime. —Three good markets are less than 30 miles away, namely
Manhattan, Fort Riley and Marysville, and we can buy everything
we need in Leavenworth City." Note that to the last named place it
was only 110 miles!

Before the Civil War, however, the Swedish settlement in Kansas
was minor. The first Swedish Lutheran congregation in Kansas, that
in Mariadahl, dates from October 14, 1863. It was organized when
Pastor John Johnson from Illinois was the first Swedish pastor to visit
Kansas. The members of the congregation were doubtless among the
first Swedes in the Big Blue Valley and in Kansas. They were J.A.
Johnson, C.A. Dahlberg, Peter Johnson, David Johnson, N.P. Axelson,
J. Sanderson, N. Kristenson, Melker Falleen, and their families.

New York

From early times there were Swedes in New York, but their
number was undoubtedly small before 1840 and the Swedish immigration that began soon thereafter. As we have seen, it was through
the Methodist Scandinavian seamen's mission which Pastor O.G.
Hedstrom started that the presence of Swedes in New York received
public attention; this gave them a place to meet and learn of each
other on the Bethel ship. The work of the Lutheran Church began
much later. We have noted that when Pastor Agrelius landed in New
York an attempt was made to organize a Lutheran congregation. He
failed and then joined the Methodists. A man by the name of G.P.
Pehrsson from the Kristianstad area tried around 1854 to gather the
Lutherans for devotional meetings but had no success in forming a
congregation. He intended well, had some spiritual experience, was
zealous in his loyalty to the Lutheran Church, but lacked the education and personality necessary for the project. In a letter to Pastor
Cederstam, August 2, 1854, he gave an account of his religious life
and his doctrinal position, and describes his activities: "My task is to
serve, as God gives grace, as a missionary colporteur among Swedes,
Norwegians and Danes, and to gather on Sundays for a service in a
Lutheran church." Eventually he received license to preach and was
later ordained, presumably by the New York and New Jersey Synod
[German]. He continued in his work for many years, in New York

and also in Boston. But though he had friends and followers he seems never to have won recognition by the Swedish residents. A number of our pastors visited in New York, as L.P. Esbjörn in 1851, and T.N. Hasselquist, 1854; S.G. Larson, a student, spent the summer of 1859 there, learned of the spiritual needs and described them in a letter to *Hemlandet*. But it was not until 1865 that a Lutheran congregation was formed — the Gustavus Adolphus church — through the efforts of Pastors Erland Carlsson and A. Andrén.

Boston

Boston too had Swedish persons in early years. By 1860 there were probably several hundred. But we know of no organization among them, in societies or congregations, until much later.

Brocton, Massachusetts

Campello and North Bridgewater, about 23 miles from Boston, were originally separate places but in time came under the common name of Brocton. Here was the first Swedish colony in New England. In Part I we have seen that Daniel Larson from Haurida made his home here in 1844 and through him a large number of Swedes settled in this place.

I have the following information on the Swedes in Brocton before 1860 from Johan Swanstrom from Grenna, now in Red Wing, Minnesota. Swanstrom came to America 1849, lived in Brooklyn and Williamsburg, New York, until 1853, when he moved to Campello with his family. There were then three families there, headed by Daniel Larson, his brother-in-law Andrew Johnson, and the aged Bengtsson from Västergötland, together with a large number of single men. Swanstrom lived there 8 years, or to 1861. He remembers the names of some who were there for various lengths of time; Gustaf Nyman, Andrew Johnson, P. Blomstrand, Gustaf Swensson, Daniel Larson, the brothers Johan and Wilhelm Larsson, Peter Johnson; Johan Lagergren and his father Swen Lagergren from Grenna, Carl Fr. Swanstrom; Gustaf Magn. Englund, Frans Joh. Swenson, Pet. G. Veber, Henric Grönberg, Johan Björkman from Jersnäs; B. Danell from Jönköping. The foregoing were from Jönköping, Grenna, and nearby parishes. Further: Andrew Olson, who died in the War, Jacob Johansson, Peter Larson and Samuel Johnson from Västergötland;

L. Lindstedt, Arvidson, Oppgren, Andrew Strommert from Stockholm. Further: a Wrangel, a son of Lieut. Col. Wrangel, Lindquist, a widower, and Swen Ljungquist, both from Bottnaryd; Sv. Kullberg, Andrew and Swen Bengtsson. There were very few young women. When Swanstrom came only two had their own homes, namely, Daniel Larson and Andrew Johnson. Most of these are no longer in Brocton. Some have died, others have moved to other places, especially to Minnesota. They worked as shoemakers, earning from one to two dollars a day — shoes were soled for 10 cents a pair. Payment was always in cash. The living costs were not high — flour, beef and pork cost most. Before the war groceries were very cheap. Many served in the army and died there.

In those days there was no church activity. The Swedes lived pretty free. If they wanted to attend a church service there were no others than the English speaking Methodist and Congregational churches. In the Fall of 1853 Pastor O.G. Hedstrom of New York visited the place and preached, but organized no congregation.

The notorious Holmgren came to Campello a couple times in 1855-1856, after he had effected some kind of organization in Boston. He was well paid for his services, but as soon as he revealed his true character no one cared for his help. No Evangelical Lutheran congregation came into existence before 1867.

INDEX

Norelius provided only a scant index for his two volumes. From the great number of names in these chapters I have tried to identify the leaders of the immigration groups, the religious leaders, the settlements, the first members of church councils, and the sources of information. Also included are references to the land, and economic conditions, to church practices, schools, and immigrant ships.

INDEX

Acton (Grove City) Minn. 402
Agrelius, C.P. Pastor, Swedish 274, 277, 298, 303
Ahlberg, P., Pastor, Swedish 136
Ahlmark, Louisville, Ky. 91
Ahlstrom, A.M., Chisago Lake 286
Ahlstrom, P.J., St. Peter 384, 385
Akerman, soldier (or Okerman) 45
Altona, congregation organized 1859, 128
Ambrosius (Ship) 31
American Bible Society 371
American Home Missionary Society 18, 73, 74, 86-8, 124, 304
American Tract Society 371
Americanization 43
Andersen, Paul, Norwegian Lutheran pastor 14, 32, 75, 147, 176
Anderson, A., Bishop Hill 13
Anderson, A. Jamestown 244
Anderson, A., Scandian Grove 392
Anderson, Abram, Moline 129, 132
Anderson, Adolf, soldier 187
Anderson, Anders, St. Charles 35, 174, 299
Anderson, Andrew, Taylor's Falls 35
Anderson, C.J., Chicago 155
Anderson, J.P., New Sweden 57
Anderson, Johannes, Rockford 190
Anderson, John, Andover 19, 68, 84
Anderson, Jonas, St. Charles, 173, 201
Anderson, Jons, Bishop Hill 13
Anderson, Lars, Princeton 202
Anderson, Nils, Scandian Grove 392
Anderson, P.M., St. Paul 304
Anderson, Per, Chisago Lake 129, 256, 258, 261-64, 280, 285
Andersson, Erik, Stockholm, Wis. 354
Andersson, Olof, Gotaholm 377
Andover, 19, 27, 65-6
    First settlers 15
    Unonius visit 69-71
    Esbjörn, L.P., ministry 71
    Congregation organized 1850, 83
    Charter members 84-5

Temperance Society 85
    Correspondence Am. Home Miss. Society 73-84, 86-8
    Church building 104-105
    Bergenlund problem 108
Andrèn, A., Lutheran pastor 190, 191, 193, 195-8, 210, 222
Andrèn, O.C.T., Lutheran pastor 136, 138, 141, 145, 293
Anfinson, O., Norwegian Lutheran lay pastor 61
Ansgar, St. Chicago 147
Attica, Ind. — West Point 34, 209, 214, 217, 219
    Congregation organized 1855, reorganized 1858, 211, 222
    Church building 223
    Norelius pastor 1859, 60
    Methodist congregation 225
Augustana 405
Augustana College and Seminary 168, 251
Aurora 173, 182
Badger, Milton, Galesburg 74
Baileytown, Ind. 226
    Congregation organized 1857, 226
    Old and new church buildings 233
Beckman, P., Lutheran pastor 298, 353, 361-2, 365, 406
Batavia 173, 182
Bengtson, Olaus, Moline 10, 129, 132
Benson, P. Scandian Grove 390, 392
Berg, John, Rusheby, Mn. 300
Berg, P., Chisago Lake 30, 129, 132, 257, 276
Bergenlund, B.G.P., Lutheran pastor 106-14, 151, 180, 236, 298-9
Bergholm, Ia. 54, 63-64
    Congregation organized 1856, 64
    Hokanson, pastor 54
Berglund, Anders, Bishop Hill 12
Bergner, Peter, New York 4, 8
Berlin (Swedona), Ill. 103
Bethel, Ship, N.Y. 4, 5, 6, 7, 8
Bishop Hill 11, 13, 19, 408

Bjork, John, Bishop Hill 13
Bjorkholm, John, Chicago 155
Blanchard, J., Galesburg 75-6
Bodelson, Per, Moline 142
Bolin, C.P., Chisago Lake 288
Boren, J.P.C., Lutheran pastor 290, 298, 341, 343, 354
Boston 122, 411
Bowman, soldier, 175
Bredberg, J., Episcopal pastor 239-40
Bremer, Fredrika, author 249
Brocton, Mass. 10, 411-12
Brown, Daniel, adventurer 368
Brydolph, soldier 58
Buena Vista, Ind. 408
Buffalo, N.Y. 14, 23
Burlington, Ia. 51, 58-9, 259, 381
 Congregation organized 1859, 60
California 19, 66, 67, 68, 388
Cambridge, Mn. 37, 404
Campello, Mass. See Brocton
Cannon River 362
 Congregation organized 1857, 364
 P. Beckman, pastor, 365
Capital University 91
Carlson, C.J., Rockford 190
Carlson, Peter, Lutheran pastor 38, 181, 290, 298, 368, 371, 380, 403
Carlson, Sven, E. Union 373
Carlsson, Anders, Red Wing 346
Carlsson, Carl, Vasa 333
Carlsson, Erland, Lutheran pastor 35, 128, 174, 176, 178, 180, 181, 189, 196, 210, 231, 257, 274, 283, 309, 406
Carver Co. 59, 253, 367, 377
Cederstam, P.A., Lutheran pastor 202, 203, 257, 282, 283, 287, 298, 301, 372, 385, 410
Cervin, A.R., Lutheran pastor 123
Cervin, Eva (Mrs. Hasselquist) 32
Charleston, S.C. 389
Chellberg, Albert, New York 7
Chicago, St. Ansgar congregation, Unonius, pastor, 147
 Norwegian Congregation, Paul Andersen, pastor 147
 Immanuel congregation, organized 1853, 149
 Erland Carlsson, pastor, 35, 152
 First members 153-55
 Church building 155-6
 Confirmation 151, 165
 Salem congregation 157
 School building 167
 Publication Society 156
 Augustana College & Seminary 168
 Liturgy 163
 Discipline 169
 Tract Society 170

Chisago Lake 253, 255, 304
 Description 253
 Early settlers 22, 31, 34, 37, 122, 160, 256, 268-273
 Congregation organized 1854, 276
 Church site, 284 building 285
 School 286, 292 Sunday School 286
 Cedarstam, pastor 282-3
 Hedengren, pastor 292, 293
 Cemeteries 293
Cholera 14, 32, 34, 37, 120, 160-61. 174, 209
Cobb, George T. N.Y. 4
Cobden (Ship) 18
Collini, Louis, Louisville, Ky. 91
Colonization 43
Condor (Ship) 13
Congregational Church, Ill. 73
Constitution, Congregation 131, 141, 155, 158, 204, 211-13, 331-33
Crousioe, S. editor 408
Dahlberg, New Sweden 45
Dahlhjelm, A.M., Chisago Lake 274, 276
Dalander family, Swede Point 60-61
Danielson New Sweden 45, 48
DeKalb 173, 183
 Congregation organized 1859, 183
Discipline 125, 141, 142-3, 169, 285-6, 353
Doing, Presbyterian pastor 442
Dolk, Charles, LaPorte, Ind. 229
Dunkirk, N.Y. 39
Economic conditions 13-14, 55-6, 68-9, 124-5, 127, 140-41, 162, 186, 229, 258, 263, 301, 313, 317, 335, 361, 393, 407
Ekman, A.J., St. Paul 302
Elgin 151, 173, 176, 183
Emigration Causes, 1
Erie Canal 14
Engberg, J. 2, 165, 211, 220, 334
Erikson, A., Methodist preacher 50, 62
Erikson, N.J. Moline 142
Erlander, John Rockford 187, 188
Erson, Matts, Andover 19, 68, 84
Esbjörn, L.P. Lutheran pastor, 17, 18, 19, 20, 24, 28, 31, 32, 49, 50, 52, 59, 68, 71-74, 86-88, 89-94, 97, 101-103, 108, 127, 168, 180, 202-3, 223-25, 231, 327, 368, 411
Esmeralda (Ship) 38
Evansville, Ind. 34
Fagercrantz, P., Princeton 202
Fahlstrom, Jacob, Minn. 252, 303
Farnham, Eli, Galesburg 76
Fjellstedt, Peter, Sweden 35, 136, 149, 152, 281, 306
Flack, Gustaf, Chicago 11, 13
Flink, C., Jamestown 244
Flodin, Peter, E. Union 373
Frankean Synod 81

Friberg, Anders, Moline 130
Frid, S., Princeton 202
Galesburg 31, 79, 80, 82, 86, 96, 99, 117-8, 381
    Congregation organized 1851, 118
    Hasselquist's ministry 119
    Condition of immigrants 124-5
    Religious dissension 125
    Second Lutheran Congregation 126
Galva 408
Geneseo, Ill. Congregation organized 1859, 145-6, 359
Geneva 38, 173, 360
    Congregation organized 1853, 176
    Church building 176
Goodhue, Minn. 313
Gotaholm (Watertown) 377, 381
    Congregation 1858, 380
Green Lake 399, 402
Gustafsson, J.P., Spring Garden 362
Gustavus Adolphus College 349, 383
Gustus, John, Geneseo 146
Hammarback, Bishop Hill 13
Hammerén, Methodist preacher 239
Harkey, S.W., Lutheran pastor 180, 196, 224
Hasselquist, T.N., Lutheran pastor 31-3, 50-2, 54, 57, 103, 106-08, 119, 122, 127, 149, 180, 202-3, 222, 226, 231, 280, 385, 411
Hattstrom, Carl, Stockholm 357
Hedbergians, Sweden 22
Hedengran, C.A., Lutheran pastor 292, 298, 301, 304, 371
Hedstrom, Jonas, Methodist preacher 3, 8-10, 12, 15, 18, 19, 47, 69, 72-3, 77, 97, 150
Hedstrom, Olof, Methodist preacher 1-8, 12, 31, 240.
Hellstom, Jonas, East Union 373
Hemlandet — newspaper 21, 55-6, 112, 122, 133, 145, 168, 171, 176, 179, 182, 193, 196, 204, 222, 223, 226, 227, 231, 238, 241, 243, 246, 257, 266, 297, 314, 346, 378, 381, 387, 400, 401, 403, 404, 409, 411
Hessle Valley (Sugar Grove), Pa. 235
    First settlers 15
    Description 235, 246
    Bergenlund, B.G.P., pastor 151, 237
    Congregation organized 1854, 237
    Swensson, Jonas, pastor 240
    Pehrson, John, pastor 248
Hill, S.M., letter 405
Hilliard, Martin, soldier, Rockford 187
Hinderson, Olof 132
Hokanson, F.M., Lutheran pastor 46, 54, 62, 64 (also Hocanson)
Hokanson, John, Chisago Lake 276
Hokanson, Nils, West Point 213, 221
Hokanson, Nils, Consul 33
Hokanson, soldier 213

Holm, Per, soldier 360
Holm, P.W. Andover 237
Holmgren Adventurer, preacher 371, 412
Holmquist, John, Rock Island, 142
Hoof, 169, 175
Hult, Johannes, E. Union 38-9, 368
Indian Missions, Minn. 250
Jackson, And., Lutheran pastor 399, 403, 404
Jacobson, John Moline 142
Jacobsson, Swen, Vasa 129, 321, 333
Jacoby, Dr., St. Louis 91
Jamestown, N.Y., 235, 243
    Bergenlund ministry 106-08
    Congregation organized 1857, 244
    Pehrson ministry 248
    Methodist congregation 236, 243, 247
Jansen, Julius, St. Paul 305
Janson, Erik, Bishop Hill 11, 24, 72, 75
Janson, Samuel, Andover 104
Jocknick, soldier, 48
Johanson, Anders, Andover, 15, 66-7
Johansson, J.M., St. Peter 385
Johansson, Johan St. Paul 310
Johnson, Alfred, Baptist preacher 382
Johnson, C.A., St. Peter 385
Johnson, Carl, LaFayette 213
Johnson, Edmond, Capt. LaPorte 228
Johnson, Fredrick, Hessle Valley 236
Johnson, Germund, Buffalo, Sugar Grove 15, 16, 235
Johnson, J.A. Mariadahl 409
Johnson, John, Burlington 31, 51, 54
Johnson, John, Lutheran pastor 31, 128, 410
Johnson, Lewis, Geneseo 146
Johnson, Magnus, Chisago lake 34
Johnson, N.J. Andover 15, 66
Johnson, Nils, St. Charles 173
Johnson, Olof, Bishop Hill 12, 13
Johnson, S.W., St. Peter 385
Johnston, L.A. Lutheran pastor 16
Joint Synod of Ohio 50
Jonsson, Christen, Galesburg 30-31
Jonsson, Germund, St. Peter 385
Jonsson, Sven, E. Union 373
Kaeding, George, *Swedes of Rockford* 184, 188
Kallman, Peter, Methodist preacher 50
Kandiyohi County, 400, 401
Kassel, Peter, New Sweden 11, 45, 62
Kewanee 408
Kilberg, N.M., Swedona 16, 104, 116
King, Lucius, Dr., New York 7
Kirby, William, Galesburg 76
Klang, C., Jamestown 244
Knox College 86, 118-19
Knoxville, Ill. 33, 65, 122, 127
    Congregation organized 1853, 127

church 1855
Knudson, J., St. Peter 385
Korsbaneret, religious annual 118, 119-20, 125-6, 148, 156, 157, 168, 318
LaFayette, Ind. 34, 216, 218
Lansing, Iowa 259, 260, 404
LaPorte, description 226
  Congregation organized 1857, 226
  Church building dedicated 230
Larsen, L. Prof 370
Larson brothers — Anders, Lars, Thim, St. Charles 35, 174
Larson, Daniel, immigrant leader 10, 411
Larson, John A. Andover 66-7
Larson, John Vista 394
Larson, Jonas, Rockford 190
Larson. L.G., Bishop Hill 12
Larson, Per Moline 142
Larson, S.G., Lutheran pastor 411
Larsson, Charles, LaPorte 229
Liljequist, N., Scandian Grove 392
Lincoln, A. 348
Lind, E.A., Minn. 401
Lind, Jenny 50, 89, 148
Lind, Sven, LaPorte 229
Lindeblad, N., Princeton 202
Lindgren, Jos., Rockford 190
Lindman, Carl Moline 136-7, 142
Lindquist, N.P., Princeton 202
Lindstrom, C.J., St. Paul 304
Lindstrom, Nils, E. Union 373
Liturgy 74, 106, 126, 137, 158-9, 164, 262, 285
  Confirmation 165-6
  Lord's Supper 81, 166
  Vestments 80, 126, 163
Lovendahl, J. organ builder, 57
Lund, P.J., Acton 402
Lundbeck, Johan, Rockford 190
Lundeen, I., St. Peter 385
Lundgren, J.E., Pastor, Sweden 281
Lundholm, L.J., St. Peter 385
Lutheran Confessional Books 102
Lutheran Home Missionary Society 225
Magnuson, P.M. Swedona 116
Manitowac, Wis. 28
Mankie, A.T. 94
Mariadahl, Kansas 408
Marie (Ship) 28
Marine, Congregatioon organized 1854, 295-8, 299
Marine Mills 129, 299
Mattson, Hans, Col. 31, 36, 314, 316
McGregor, Ia. 95, 404
Meeker County 401, 403
Melodion, 144, 164
Methodism, Swedish 9, 56, 57, 124, 129, 391
Miller, J.P. Gotaholm 378

Milwaukee 13, 399
Minnesota 240
Minnesota Synod 350
Minnesota Posten, 204, 343
Minona (Ship) 38, 242
Mission Point Fox River 13
Mobeck, Frank, St. Paul 304
Moberg, Carl P., Indiana 33
Moline, description 138-39
  Congregation organized 1850 131
  Early settlers 37, 89, 93, 129-140
  Church building 133, 139
  Parsonage 140
  Valentin ministry 103
  Andrén, O.C.T., ministry 138
Monmouth 122, 128
  Congregation organized 1853
Montmorency, Ind. 216
Mormons 53
Munson, Ola, Acton 402
Munter, Magnus, teacher 165, 182, 194, 227
Music, Church 57, 164-5, 168, 286, 352
Neill, E.D. *History of Minn.* 252
Nelson, John, Rockford 185, 190
New London, 29, 400
Newman, S.B., Methodist preacher 210
New Orleans, 34
New Sweden 45, 55, 56
  Kassel company 45
  Hokanson's ministry 46
  Congregation organized 1853, 50
  H. Olson's ministry, 56-7, 58
Newton (Ship) 22-3
New York City 122, 410
Nilson, Daniel, Marine, 28, 129, 132, 295, 297
Nilson, F.O., Baptist preacher 50, 51, 56, 59, 103, 278, 370, 402
Nilson, Jacob, Swede Point 61
Nilson, John, Chicago 155
Nilson, Nils Andover 65
Nilson, Ola Andover 31
Nilson, Ola, E. Union 373
Nilson, Sven Andover 65
Nilson, Sven New Sweden 54
Nilsson John, Scandian Grove 392
Nilsson, Per, Vasa 327
Nordberg, E. U., Chisago Lake, 253, 256, 257, 258
Nordin, Olof, Andover 19, 68, 84
Norelius, A., Baptist preacher 50
Norelius, Erik, Lutheran pastor 8, 22, 88-89, 89-94, 96, 134, 180, 182, 213, 217, 221, 223, 247, 264, 277, 306, 311, 325, 326, 338, 395
Norin, Jamestown 244
Northern Illinois Synod 107, 108, 134, 155, 179, 201, 237, 309, 350
Northwestern Gazeteer, 73

Norwegian Lutheran Church, Chicago 147-8, 156, 171-2
Norwegian Lutheran Synod, 307
Nyberg, P., Methodist preacher 50, 56, 63
Nylund, Bishop Hill 13
Nyman, Jacob, Princeton 202
Nyman, Per 205
Ocean voyage 12, 22-3, 185-6
Oden (Ship) 21
Ofelt, Johan, soldier 334
Ofelt, N.P. St. Paul 302
Ogden, B.W., Chicago 13
Ohlsson, Ola Sr., Vasa 333
Okerman, soldier 45
Olsen, Nils, Lutheran pastor, Vista 398
Olsen, Sten, E. Union 373
Olson, H. Methodist preacher 2
Olson, Hokan, Lutheran pastor 54, 56-58
Olson, Jonas, Bishop Hill 12, 14
Olsson, Hokan, Red Wing 319, 346
Olsson, Jon (Stenbo), Moline 29, 30
Olsson, Lars, Stockholm 355
Olsson, Ola, Vasa 321
Olsson, Olof, Bishop Hill 12, 29
Ophiem 17, 68, 103
Oqwaka, Ill 122,
Organ, 165
Orion 103
Ottumwa, Ia. 63
Owen, music teacher, LaPorte 231
Palm, Swante, Texas 21
Palmquist, Gustaf, Baptist preacher 22, 50, 59, 94, 260-61
Parker, L.H., Galesburg 76
Passavant, Wm., Lutheran pastor 225, 329
Passavant Orphans Home 141, 165
Paulsen, Hans, E. Union 373
Paulsen, Ole, E. Union 367, 373
Pecatonica 195
    Congregation organized 1857, 196
    Church building 196
    Andrén, A., pastor 196
    Segerstrom controversy 197
Pehrson, G.P. Swedish pastor 410
Pehrson, John, Lutheran pastor 38, 182, 248
Peterson, Anders, Ind. 213
Peterson, Carl, Chisago Lake 276
Peterson, Daniel, Chisago Lake 285
Peterson, Erik, Stockholm 37, 353, 357
Peterson, Isac, Chicago 155, 187, 190
Peterson, Jacob, Stockholm 357
Peterson, Johan Vista 394
Peterson, John, Rockford 190
Peterson, Lars, F., Vista 394
Peterson, Magnus, E. Union 373
Peterson, M.P., Moline 132
Peterson, O.P., Methodist preacher, 5

Peterson, Ola, E. Union 373
Peterson, Olof, Vasa 333
Peterson, P., West Point 210
Petterson, A.G., St. Peter 385
Phebous, Dr., N.Y. 2
Pickney, Caroline 2
Pietisten Swed. Journal 151
Pillsbury, Galesburg 65, 199
Princeton 26, 39, 89, 95, 122, 136, 199, 390
    Congregation organized 1854, 201
    Esbjörn, L.P., pastor 203
    Valentin, pastor 201
    Church building 203
    Vossner failure 205
Psalmodikon 311, 337
Publication Society 141, 156
Rainsler, van, Minn. 266
Ramsay, Gov. Minn 249
Randau, Nils Chicago 32
Red Wing 221, 309, 313, 344, 359
    Description 314-15, 317
    Congregation organized 1855, 320, 345
    Charter members 345-6
    Norelius' ministry 343, 346
    Church building 347
    Boren ministry 349
    School, G.A. College 349, 351-2
Religion unifying force 43-4
Rockford 37, 185
    Conditions 184, 186
    Cholera 188
    First Christmas 189
    Congregation organized 1854, 190
    Church building 190
    Andren's ministry 190-94
Rock Island 37, 87, 88, 95, 130, 160
    With Moline congregation 103
    First Baptist Congregation 94, 98, 100
Roggs, William C. N.Y. 4
Roos, Carl, soldier, 325
Rosenberg, John, Stockholm, 356
Rusheby 295-6, 300-1
    Congregation organzied 1860
Rydberg, C., Jamestown 244
Saint Ansgar Academy 377
St. Charles 38, 150-51, 173
    (with Geneva until 1882)
    Congregation organized 1853, 176
    First building 178-79
St. Louis 39, 57, 257
St. Paul 122, 249, 202, 302
    Congregation organized 1854, 305, 309
    Synodical membership 309
    Church site 307
Saint Peter 383
    Congregation organized 1857, 384
    Charter members 385

Cederstam's ministry, with Scandian Grove, 386
Samuelson, Carl Rockford 190
Samuelson, Carl J., Ophiem 17, 68, 85
Samuelson, Johannes, Ophiem 17, 68, 84
Samuelson, Karl, Geneva 175, 181
Sandberg, C.J., St. Peter 385
Sandblad, itinerant preacher 368
Sannman, (also Sandman) Erik, McGregor 21, 99, 260, 404
Scandia (Clear Water Lake), Baptist congregation 59, 381
Scandian Grove 39, 386, 387
    Congregation organized 1858, 388
    Charter members 391
    Cederstam's ministry 386
Scandinavian Fire Ins. 125, 144
Scandinavian professorship 141, 203, 205, 294
Schaeffer, Lutheran pastor 64
Schneidau, Capt. B. von 11, 13, 147
Schools 167-69, 182, 193, 220, 334, 366, 376
Scott, George, England 17
Second Lutheran Church, Galesburg 126
Segerstrom, L., Pecatonica 195, 196-7
Sheboygan, Wis. 10, 396
Shogren, Eric Methodist preacher 189
Sjogren, Peter, Red Wing 346
Skone, John, E. Union 373
Smith Prot. Methodist preacher 50, 62
Smith, A., Chicago 13
Smith, Gustaf, Chicago 147
Smith, Hans, Moline 139, 260
Soderberg, Karin 132
Soderberg, Karolina 132
Soderstrom, P. 94, 102, 130
Sofie (Ship) 28, 295
Sonberger family 9
Sorensen, P., St. Paul 305
Sparta, Mich. 400
Spring Garden 328, 359, 361
    Congregation organized 1858, 361
    Beckman, pastor 364
Steamships 39
Steel, Daniel (Boston), Meth. Prof 3-4
Stenberg, Olof, Olsson, Bishop Hill 12, 13, 29
Stillwater 401
Stockholm, Wis. (Lake Pepin) 37, 353-57
    Congregation organized 1856, 355
    Beckman, pastor 356
    Boren, pastor 357
Stomberg, Anders E. Union 39, 367, 373
Strid, S.P. soldier 68
Sultana (Ship) 23
Superb (Ship) 11
Superior City 400
Superior (Ship) 10
Svanstrom, Johan Campello 17, 411

Svenska Republikanen, newspaper 356, 408
Svenskarni i Illinois History, 8-9, 12, 19, 65-6, 68-9, 94, 117, 129, 173, 174, 183, 195, 199, 200, 201, 204
Svithiod (Goodhue) 357-8
Swedberg, A.G. 21, 404
Swedberg, Hokan L., Chisago Lake, 276, 280-1
Swede Bend 61-3
    Methodists, Baptists 62-3
    Lutheran congregation organized 1859, 63
Swede Point 60-61
    Dalander family 60-61
    Congregation organized 1859, 61
Swedish Missionary Society 72
Swedona (Berlin) 103, 116
    Congregation organized 1859, 116
Swenson, Goran, Chicago 155, 183
Swenson, Nils, Moline 142
Swenson, S.M., Texas 20
Swensson, Anders, Chisago Lake 276
Swensson, Carl A., Lutheran pastor 243
Swensson, Jonas, Lutheran pastor 114, 115, 240, 244
Sycamore 183
Tanaro (Ship) 34
Taylor's Falls 160, 257, 287, 299-300
    Congregation organized 1860
Telleen, J., Lutheran pastor 160
Temperance Society, Andover 85
Terry, Dr. Methodist, N.Y. 4
Texas, 20
Theorin, Lars, Soldier 389
Third Angel's Messengers 230
Thompson, Peter New London, 29
Thorson, A. Scandian Grove 39, 388, 391
Tidlund, Methodist preacher, 303, 370, 391
Torkjorsen, Halvor, E. Union 373
Tottie Chas. (Ship) 16, 67
Trimper, A., Lutheran pastor 203
Trulson, Gisell, Chicago 155
Union, East 39, 367
    Congregation organized 1858, 368, 372
    Charter members 374-5
    P. Carlson, pastor 372
    St. Ansgar Acad. 377
Union, West 376
    Congregaton organized 1858, 377
Unonius, Gustaf 10, 14, 24, 46, 69-71, 147-8, 189, 261-2, 303
Valentin C.J., Lutheran pastor 50, 103, 134-5, 136 (soldier), 201
Vasa 36, 221, 313
    Early settlers 321-325
    Description 315-16
    Congregation organized 1855, 320, 331
    Norelius, pastor 320, 338
    Church building 347

Viberg, A. Baptist preacher 22, 95, 279
Victoria, Ill. 9, 19, 21, 408
Virginia (Ship) 14, 66
Virstrom, Capt. 17, 19, 66
Vista 222, 393, 400
  Congregation organized 1858, 394
  Charter members 394
Wais, Charles, LaPorte 229
Wais, Gustaf, LaPorte 229
Warren, Prof. Boston, 6
Wataga, Ill. 28, 122, 128
  Congregation organized 1856
Watertown, 377
Waupaca, Wis. 28, 29, 399
Webster County, Ia. 61
Welander 402

Wesley, John (Ship) 4
West Point, Ind. 34, 209, 213, 219, 363, 393
  Congregation organized 1855, 211
Wester, Eric, Princeton 26, 199, 206
Westerberg, A., Scandian Grove 392
Westergren, Methodist preacher 189
Westman, G. Rusheby 300
Westerlund, A., Princeton 26-27
Westerlund, Erik, Andover 104, 259
Wicklund, P. 257, 299
Wigren, John, Attica, Methodist preacher 210, 218
Willard, S.J. Vasa 316, 321, 333
Williamson, Per Olson Wataga 28
Williamson, Thos., Minn. 251
Yorktown, Ind. 33, 215